Optimal Routing Design

Russ White, CCIE No. 2635

Don Slice, CCIE No. 1929

Alvaro Retana, CCIE No. 1609

Cisco Press

800 East 96th Street
Indianapolis, IN 46240 USA

Optimal Routing Design

Russ White, Don Slice, Alvaro Retana

Copyright© 2005 Cisco Systems, Inc.

Cisco Press logo is a trademark of Cisco Systems, Inc.

Published by:
Cisco Press
800 East 96th Street
Indianapolis, IN 46240 USA

Printed in the United States of America   8 9

Eighth Printing: January 2014

Library of Congress Cataloging-in-Publication Number: 2003116562

ISBN: 1-58714-244-9

Warning and Disclaimer

This book is designed to provide information about scalable IP network design. Every effort has been made to make this book as complete and as accurate as possible, but no warranty or fitness is implied.

The information is provided on an "as is" basis. The authors, Cisco Press, and Cisco Systems, Inc. shall have neither liability nor responsibility to any person or entity with respect to any loss or damages arising from the information contained in this book or from the use of the discs or programs that may accompany it.

The opinions expressed in this book belong to the author and are not necessarily those of Cisco Systems, Inc.

Trademark Acknowledgments

All terms mentioned in this book that are known to be trademarks or service marks have been appropriately capitalized. Cisco Press or Cisco Systems, Inc. cannot attest to the accuracy of this information. Use of a term in this book should not be regarded as affecting the validity of any trademark or service mark.

Corporate and Government Sales

Cisco Press offers excellent discounts on this book when ordered in quantity for bulk purchases or special sales.

For more information, please contact U.S. Corporate and Government Sales at 1-800-382-3419 or at corpsales@pearsontechgroup.com.

For sales outside the U.S., please contact International Sales at international@pearsoned.com.

Feedback Information

At Cisco Press, our goal is to create in-depth technical books of the highest quality and value. Each book is crafted with care and precision, undergoing rigorous development that involves the unique expertise of members from the professional technical community.

Readers' feedback is a natural continuation of this process. If you have any comments regarding how we could improve the quality of this book or otherwise alter it to better suit your needs, you can contact us through e-mail at feedback@ciscopress.com. Please make sure to include the book title and ISBN in your message.

We greatly appreciate your assistance.

Publisher	John Wait
Editor-in-Chief	John Kane
Cisco Representative	Anthony Wolfenden
Cisco Press Program Manager	Jeff Brady
Executive Editor	Brett Bartow
Production Manager	Patrick Kanouse
Senior Development Editor	Christopher Cleveland
Senior Project Editor	Marc Fowler
Copy Editor	Karen A. Gill
Technical Editor(s)	Neil Lovering, Danny McPherson, Steven Moore
Team Coordinator	Tammi Barnett
Book and Cover Designer	Louisa Adair
Composition	Mark Shirar
Indexer	Tim Wright

CISCO SYSTEMS

Corporate Headquarters
Cisco Systems, Inc.
170 West Tasman Drive
San Jose, CA 95134-1706
USA
www.cisco.com
Tel: 408 526-4000
    800 553-NETS (6387)
Fax: 408 526-4100

European Headquarters
Cisco Systems International BV
Haarlerbergpark
Haarlerbergweg 13-19
1101 CH Amsterdam
The Netherlands
www-europe.cisco.com
Tel: 31 0 20 357 1000
Fax: 31 0 20 357 1100

Americas Headquarters
Cisco Systems, Inc.
170 West Tasman Drive
San Jose, CA 95134-1706
USA
www.cisco.com
Tel: 408 526-7660
Fax: 408 527-0883

Asia Pacific Headquarters
Cisco Systems, Inc.
Capital Tower
168 Robinson Road
#22-01 to #29-01
Singapore 068912
www.cisco.com
Tel: +65 6317 7777
Fax: +65 6317 7799

Cisco Systems has more than 200 offices in the following countries and regions. Addresses, phone numbers, and fax numbers are listed on the
Cisco.com Web site at www.cisco.com/go/offices.

Argentina • Australia • Austria • Belgium • Brazil • Bulgaria • Canada • Chile • China PRC • Colombia • Costa Rica • Croatia • Czech Republic
Denmark • Dubai, UAE • Finland • France • Germany • Greece • Hong Kong SAR • Hungary • India • Indonesia • Ireland • Israel • Italy
Japan • Korea • Luxembourg • Malaysia • Mexico • The Netherlands • New Zealand • Norway • Peru • Philippines • Poland • Portugal
Puerto Rico • Romania • Russia • Saudi Arabia • Scotland • Singapore • Slovakia • Slovenia • South Africa • Spain • Sweden
Switzerland • Taiwan • Thailand • Turkey • Ukraine • United Kingdom • United States • Venezuela • Vietnam • Zimbabwe

About the Authors

Russ White, CCIE No. 2635, is a member of the Routing Deployment and Architecture team at Cisco Systems in RTP, North Carolina. He works in all areas of routing protocol design, routed network design, and routed network deployment. He is a regular speaker at Networkers, has coauthored several books on routing protocols and several IETF RFCs, and periodically contributes to network journals.

Don Slice, CCIE No. 1929, is a development engineer on the Distance Vector Routing Protocol Team, responsible for creating new features and resolving software defects with EIGRP and RIP. Previously, Don worked on the Routing Deployment and Architecture Team and Routing Protocol Escalation Team designing, implementing, and troubleshooting networks running all of the IP routing protocols.

Alvaro Retana, CCIE No. 1609, is a technical leader in the IP Routing Deployment and Architecture Team at Cisco, where he works first hand on advanced features in routing protocols. His current work includes topics such as BGP Security and Ad Hoc Networking.

About the Technical Reviewers

Neil Lovering, CCIE No. 1772, is a design consultant with Cisco Systems. He has been a network consultant for more than 10 years, and has worked on various routing, switching, dialup, security, and network design projects for many customers all over North America. Neil currently works with large systems integrators in the Washington DC area. When not at the keyboard or at a customer site, Neil enjoys spending time with his wife and two children in Virginia.

Danny McPherson is currently the director of architecture and development at Arbor Networks, Inc., and has extensive technical leadership in the telecommunications industry. He has more than 12 years of experience as a network architect for global Internet service providers such as Qwest and MCI, in addition to network equipment vendors such as Amber Networks.

Danny is a common contributor within the routing, operations, and Internet areas of the IETF and global network operations community. He has authored several Internet protocol standards, books, and other documents related to Internet routing protocols, network security, Internet addressing, and network operations. His most recent work, *Practical BGP*, was published in mid-2004. You can reach Danny at danny@tcb.net.

Steve Moore, CCIE No. 4927, is an engineer with the Cisco IP Routing Deployment and Scalability team, which is a part of the IOS Technologies division of Cisco Engineering. He is responsible for discovering, testing, validating, and assisting in the customer deployment of new ideas relating to the scalability of routing protocols. He works closely with customers and with development, support, testing, and consulting groups within Cisco. A part of Steve's job is to educate; he does so by working with customers directly, writing whitepapers, and speaking at various Networkers conferences. Within the nine years that Steve has worked at Cisco, he has become known for his experience with routing protocols, WAN technologies, and optical networking.

Dedications

Russ White: I would like to thank my wife, Lori, for putting up with a little more computer time than usual when I'm writing. For Bekah and Hannah—we can build those monkey bars now! I also thank God for my family and their support, including my mother and stepfather, and my wife's family, for their support through the years.

Don Slice : I would like to thank my wife, Pam, and my daughters Jessica, Amy, and Heather, for being understanding when I've been distracted by the work required to write this book. I also praise God for sustaining me in this effort and providing me with the time and ability to put these thoughts down on paper.

Acknowledgments

We'd like to thank our technical editors, Steve Moore, John Cavanaugh, Danny McPherson, and Neil Lovering, for their perseverance; your help improved this book immeasurably. Thanks to Brett Bartow, who puts up with our missed deadlines, and with Chris Cleveland, who actually tries to make sense out of our various ramblings and make them fit for printing.

Thanks to all the managing and marketing people at Cisco Press, who make these books possible.

This Book Is Safari Enabled

The Safari® Enabled icon on the cover of your favorite technology book means the book is available through Safari Bookshelf. When you buy this book, you get free access to the online edition for 45 days.

Safari Bookshelf is an electronic reference library that lets you easily search thousands of technical books, find code samples, download chapters, and access technical information whenever and wherever you need it.

To gain 45-day Safari Enabled access to this book:

- Go to http://www.ciscopress.com/safarienabled

- Complete the brief registration form

- Enter the coupon code ALE8-1LRF-4OIY-F4F5-Z4UG

If you have difficulty registering on Safari Bookshelf or accessing the online edition, please e-mail customer-service@safaribooksonline.com.

Contents at a Glance

Contents

Icons Used in This Book

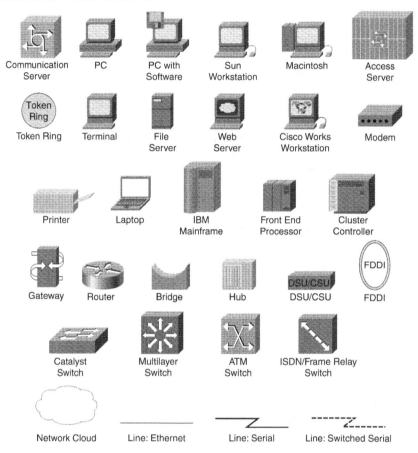

Command Syntax Conventions

The conventions used to present command syntax in this book are the same conventions used in the IOS Command Reference. The Command Reference describes these conventions as follows:

- **Boldface** indicates commands and keywords that are entered literally as shown. In actual configuration examples and output (not general command syntax), boldface indicates commands that are input manually by the user (such as a **show** command).

- *Italics* indicate arguments for which you supply actual values.

- Vertical bars (|) separate alternative, mutually exclusive elements.

- Square brackets [ ] indicate optional elements.

- Braces { } indicate a required choice.

- Braces within brackets [{ }] indicate a required choice within an optional element.

Foreword

I first logged into the predecessor of the Internet—the Arpanet—in 1980. My task as a teaching assistant was to download two compilers for our new Computer Science Department VAX from a colleague at MIT. In the process I also learned about email and two games—Adventure and Zork. In line with today's environment, this led to a significant amount of time spent online.

The mechanics of how my session on a VAX in Halifax could move to another computer at MIT was hidden from me as a user, but fascinating to think about. As I began my working career as a systems programmer, I specialized in computer communications and have looked back.

The emergence of TCP/IP and routing protocols later in the 1980's permitted the growth of what we now know as the Internet. Today it has evolved from its simple origins in those early years to a collection of interconnected networks involving myriads of service providers, government agencies and private companies. The architecture and design of networks have become a science unto itself.

At Cisco Systems, Russ White, Alvaro Retana, and Don Slice have played an integral part in the support and design of customer networks. Their efforts have been recognized by numerous internal awards, IETF RFCs, drafts and publications. Indeed, they have progressed from using routing protocols for network design to completing the feedback loop and working with the routing community within Cisco and the IETF to improve the routing protocols themselves. One needs only to perform a search on the Google search engine with their names and IETF to get a sense of their involvement in the industry.

The complexity associated with overlaying voice and video onto an IP network involves thinking through latency, jitter, availability and recovery issues. *Optimal Routing Design* offers keen insights into the fundamentals of network architecture for these converged environments. As such, I recommend this book to any professional or student working in network architecture or design.

John Cavanaugh, CCIE No. 1066

Distinguished Services Engineer - Advanced Services, Cisco Systems, Inc.

Introduction

In 1998, when we first started writing *Advanced IP Network Design*, we had no idea that the future would bring us more and more deeply into the realms of routed network design or that we would work together in the same place in closely related teams for all of these years. We originally wrote *Advanced IP Network Design* to help answer some of the questions we heard on a regular basis as engineers working in the Cisco Technical Support Center Routing Protocol and Escalation teams.

In many ways, we wrote this book for the same reason: to help customers we meet on a daily basis with the answers to the questions we always hear. What is the best way to build addressing for my network? How do I redistribute between two protocols without blowing up my network? When and why should I use BGP?

In other ways, however, this book is completely different. Of course, the most obvious difference is that the authors have worked on thousands more networks and interacted with thousands of different customers since that book was written. Each time a network engineer approaches us with a new problem to be solved or we see a good solution for a problem, we learn more about network design.

Less obvious, though, are the lessons that failed networks and bad designs have given us. Each time we propose something that does not work, we learn new things about routing design that we did not know before, and we learn to watch for new problems that we might not have expected before. Our goal in this book was to amalgamate these experiences, both good and bad, into a readable, understandable whole so that network engineers at all skill levels can draw on them. We are in a position to see new networks, new problems, and new solutions every day; this book is an attempt to share that experience with other network engineers.

Who Should Read This Book?

Network engineers who want to understand the concepts and theory of designing and deploying a large-scale network, network engineers who are currently managing large-scale networks, and engineers who are studying for their CCIE or Cisco network design certifications will find this book useful. Readers should be familiar with basic routing protocols concepts, including the mechanics of how each protocol works, basic Cisco router configuration, and physical layer interconnectivity. Some review of routing protocol operation is provided in the appendixes, but these are by no means comprehensive reviews.

How This Book Is Organized

This book is broken into four distinct parts. Part I begins with a consideration of network design issues on a broad scale:

- Chapter 1, "Network Design Goals and Techniques," discusses the goals that a network designer needs to keep in mind, including tradeoffs among goals. You will find a good bit of discussion on the tradeoffs among network scaling, convergence speed, and resiliency.

- Chapter 2, "Applying the Fundamentals," discusses the basic techniques that are applicable to any network design, regardless of the routing protocol. Here we talk about hierarchy, addressing, summarization, and information hiding, all critical aspects of a good network design.

Part II of *Optimal Routing Design* covers each interior gateway protocol in depth, generally starting with a discussion on deploying the protocol on a three-layer hierarchy and then on a two-layer hierarchy. Each chapter then discusses deploying the protocol over specific topologies, such as full mesh and hub-and-spoke topologies. Each chapter ends with case studies that are specific to the protocol.

- Chapter 3, "EIGRP Network Design," covers the deployment and operation of EIGRP on large-scale networks. The operation of EIGRP on a number of specific topologies and specific techniques for deploying EIGRP are included.

- Chapter 4, "OSPF Network Design," covers the deployment and operation of OSPF on large-scale networks. The operation of OSPF on a number of specific topologies and specific techniques for deploying OSPF are included.

- Chapter 5, "IS-IS Network Design," covers the deployment and operation of IS-IS on large-scale networks. The operation of IS-IS on several specific topologies and specific techniques for deploying IS-IS are included.

Part III of the book leaves the IGP-specific realm and looks toward more advanced topics in network design.

- Chapter 6, "BGP Cores and Network Scalability," discusses when and how to use a BGP core in a large scale network and then moves into connections to outside networks, such as an Internet service provider or extranet.

- Chapter 7, "High Availability and Fast Convergence," goes into detail on the techniques and tradeoffs for reaching the magical five-9s of network uptime.

- Chapter 8, "Routing Protocol Security," covers some of the concepts surrounding securing a routing system, some baseline best practices, and some future work that is underway in this area.

- Chapter 9, "Virtual Private Networks," covers the concepts of virtual private networks and the various mechanisms used for creating them. This chapter includes various techniques for carrying routing information through a VPN.

Part IV of the book provides short appendixes dealing with the fundamentals of how each routing protocol that is discussed in the book works. These are not intended to be complete references, but rather just an introduction and a place to go when the corresponding chapter discusses some aspect of the protocol operation that you are not familiar with.

- Appendix A, "EIGRP for IP Basics of Operation," discusses the basic operation of EIGRP, including how neighbors are formed, the metrics used, the DUAL algorithm, and the processing of changed or withdrawn routing information.

- Appendix B, "OSPF Basics of Operation," covers the basic operation of OSPF, including how neighbors are formed, how information is flooded throughout the network, and how you can use the SPF algorithm to find loop-free paths through the network.

- Appendix C, "Integrated IS-IS Basics of Operation," discusses the basic operation of IS-IS, including how neighbors are formed, how information is flooded throughout the network, and how the SPF algorithm helps you find loop-free paths through the network.

- Appendix D, "Border Gateway Protocol 4 Basics of Operation," covers how BGP works, including how neighbors are built and how BGP ensures loop-free routing in an internetwork.

- Appendix E, "IP Network Design Checklist," provides a checklist that network designers can use to determine where they need to look in a network for problems and possible hidden issues and where to gain an understanding of the overall network design. This is useful mostly for engineers who are approaching a network for the first time.

- Appendix F, "Answers to Review Questions," provides the answers to the review question exercises found at the end of Chapters 1 through 9.

- Appendix G, "Which Routing Protocol?" provides an overview of the routing protocols, comparing their strengths and weaknesses. This is designed primarily for engineers who have a knowledge of one protocol and are trying to gain an understanding of the other protocols, or engineers who are considering which routing protocol to run on a specific new network design or if they should switch from one protocol to another.

Final Words

Overall, we have developed *Optimal Routing Design* to be read, not just used as a reference. We strongly believe that understanding network design with all the available protocols makes you a better network engineer. Learning how to deploy multiple protocols, even if you will never use them, helps you to understand and apply the underlying principles and find techniques to work around problems that you might encounter.

We hope that you find the time spent reading our little missive to be well spent—and we expect to welcome you on the list of excellent network designers! So, kick back, put your feet on your desk, and read through from the front to the back. You can tell your boss you are learning how to design your network to scale.

Network Design Overview

CHAPTER 1

Network Design Goals and Techniques

When you first consider adding to, designing, or redesigning a network, whether large or small, what are the first things you think about? Do you begin by thinking about the types of links you would use, the types of routers you would like to use, or even the routing protocol you would use? You shouldn't! Instead, you should think about what you would like the network to do. What should the characteristics of the network be? What are the goals of this network design? How can the network carry traffic so that it best serves the business needs?

Goals for Network Design

Network users see the network as a bundle of applications, rather than as a bundle of wires, fiber connections, protocols, routers, and switches. What capabilities will a network need if it is going to carry traffic to support applications? What are some of the goals common to most network designs?

- The network should stay up all the time, in spite of what the world throws at it in terms of failed or dirty links, failing equipment, and overload conditions.

- The network should reliably deliver packets within reasonable delay and jitter characteristics from any host to any host.

- Troubleshooting should be fairly easy, because failures occasionally occur. Finding and fixing a problem should not take many hours, no matter how esoteric, or in what corner of the network the problem is found.

- The network should be secure. It should provide few places and opportunities for an attacker to disrupt it, consequently disrupting the traffic flow and applications that rely on it.

- The network should have some sort of monitoring facility to determine what is going on at any given time with devices, protocols, links, and traffic levels.

- The network should be easily modifiable to account for network growth or just changes in general. You do not want to deal with "flag days," or days when the network must be turned down to make a major infrastructure change.

If you look at each of these ideas carefully, you can find three underlying, fundamental goals:

- **The network must be reliable and resilient**—Packets must be reliably delivered with fairly consistent travel times, and major changes in the topology, intentional or unintentional, should impact network performance as little as possible.

- **The network must be manageable**—You need to be able to find and correct problems quickly within the network.

- **The network must be scalable**—The network should be able to grow and change without requiring a forklift upgrade.

The following sections provide more detail for each of these three concepts. After providing an overview of reliability, manageability, and scaling, this chapter covers some common elements of network design, including redundancy and layering.

Reliability

Reliability and resiliency often go hand in hand; a resilient network tends to provide a more reliable and stable platform for applications, and a close examination of a reliable network tends to uncover a good amount of resiliency. Do not mistake resiliency for redundancy, however. Although redundancy is one good way to provide resiliency in some situations, simply adding redundancy to a network does not always increase resiliency.

The place to start is defining what a *reliable network* is. A reliable network provides a platform on which applications a business can rely on for day-to-day operations. What do applications rely on a network for? Applications rely on a network for reliable and timely data transmission. In other words, a reliable network delivers virtually every packet accepted by the network, to the right destination, within a reasonable amount of time. This definition has four important points:

- Not every packet that is transmitted by devices attached to the network will be accepted for delivery.

- Not every packet that is accepted by the network is going to be delivered.

- Accepted packets need to be delivered quickly.

- Accepted packets need to be delivered consistently.

Although diving deep into issues such as quality of service (QoS) is beyond the scope of this book, considering and keeping in mind packet delivery issues from a high level is important when designing a network.

Packet Delivery Reliability

If the job of a network is to reliably deliver data in the form of packets transmitted by devices that are attached to the network, why should a network reject traffic? It is because the aggregate traffic that is offered by the devices attached to the network will most likely always be higher than the total amount of traffic that the network can handle. For instance, the street in front of your house might generally have light traffic on it. If all your neighbors went out of their house at the same time one day, got into their cars, and tried to leave, all of them using the street simultaneously, however, there would be little chance that the road could handle the aggregate traffic. Some people would end up waiting a long time to traverse the road, whereas other people would give up and go home or simply stay home. The size of the road can be said to limit the amount of traffic offered from your area into the highway system.

Almost all networks limit the amount of traffic accepted into the network at some point, generally at or close to the edge of the network. For instance, a moderate speed serial link between a remote office and the distribution router in a network imposes a traffic acceptance policy near the edge of the network. The remote site cannot send more data than will fit onto the moderate size serial link that connects it to the main site.

QoS techniques, such as weighted fair queuing (WFQ), low latency queuing (LLQ), and others, are not technically packet admission policies. They can, however, determine which traffic is allowed into the network after the limiting impact of link bandwidth, for example, comes into play.

Generally, network engineers can determine how much legitimate traffic is offered to the network, at specific times and under specific conditions, and plan network capacities and policies accordingly. Tradeoffs always exist between the ability to carry more traffic and the cost of carrying extra offered traffic. The correct balance between cost and carrying capacity is going to depend on business factors primarily, rather than network design factors. You can take some steps to curb illegitimate use of the network, such as blocking certain protocols or blocking access to specific servers, but limiting traffic based on these sorts of techniques alone is rare.

After the network has accepted data, it must be able to deliver the accepted data reliably. Of course, "reliable delivery" can mean something different for every application. For instance, it is usually better to drop voice and video packets than to deliver them out of order or late. On the other hand, delivering a packet slowly in an File Transit Protocol (FTP) stream is better than dropping it.

This is because dropped packets in a Voice over IP (VoIP) stream, if the loss rate is low enough, are undetectable. Small numbers of dropped packets in an FTP stream can, however, make the transfer speed so slow as to make the network unusable. FTP runs over Transmission Control Protocol (TCP), and TCP regulates the speed of data transfer based on the number of dropped packets, among other things.

Therefore, one issue you need to consider when building a network is the types of applications that are using the network and the sorts of traffic those applications will offer to the network. You need to decide what sorts of edge admittance policies you are going to enforce for various types of traffic and other QoS issues. This book does not consider many of these sorts of questions. Instead, it focuses mostly on routing design. A network is a system, however, and considering all aspects of the network design, even while considering each component of the network design separately, is a good practice to follow.

Packet Delivery Times

Generally, the first thing that comes to mind when discussing timely delivery of packets is the total delay through the network—the amount of time it takes for a packet that is transmitted by one device to be received by a second device. This is not the only, or sometimes even the primary, issue when dealing with packet delivery times, however. In many cases, the delay through the network (the *propagation delay)* is not the only important thing; consistency of the delay (the *jitter*) also matters. Figure 1-1 illustrates the difference between delay and jitter through a network.

Figure 1-1   *Increasing Jitter as a String of Packets Moves Through a Network*

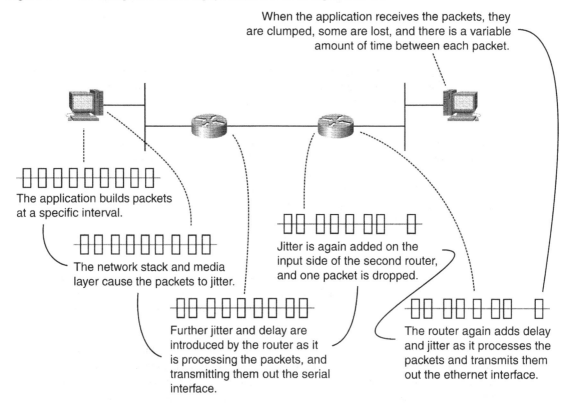

Of course, some applications are more sensitive to propagation delay than others:

- It is impossible for a user to know when a packet in a streaming audio connection is transmitted; therefore, propagation delay is not necessarily important. Jitter between streaming audio packets, however, can ruin the quality of the audio.

- Interaction with a remote host through a terminal program does not generally expose jitter between packets in the traffic stream, but long propagation delays can make the session feel sluggish or even unusable.

- VoIP generally works best in environments that have small to moderate amounts of propagation delay in the network, but jitter must be kept low enough to allow receiving devices to buffer and play back received packets at a constant pace.

Delay and Jitter Budgets

To determine how much propagation delay and jitter the network can be allowed to exhibit and still meet the requirements imposed by each of the applications running on it, you need to examine each type of traffic and determine delay and jitter budgets for each application's traffic. Because QoS is not the focus of this book, you will see little coverage on how to build these budgets. However, spending the time to build them is still important.

The Impact of Network Design on Delay and Jitter Budgets

Because this book focuses primarily on Layer 3 network design, including routing protocols, the question you need to look at when considering QoS issues is this:

What impact can network design, specifically in the area of routing protocol deployment, have on the QoS within a network?

More specifically, consider this:

- In several places, the routing and the design of the routing system can impact the QoS within a network.

- The topology and design of the network determines how long the path is between any two points in the network, impacting the jitter and the propagation delay.

- Routing protocols direct traffic through the network. Directing traffic along the right link at any point in the network (traffic engineering, or TE) can be an important part of tuning a network to perform well.

- The reliability of the network impacts its capability to provide the level of service expected by applications that are running on the network. If a network is not reliable, it cannot reliably deliver packets or reliably deliver packets within the allowed propagation delay and jitter budgets.

For instance, comparing the delay and jitter budgets along each path that traffic takes across the network and the maximum delay and jitter across each of those paths is a useful exercise, as illustrated in Figure 1-2.

In this network, the path from Host A to Host B through Router C and Router D is a lightly loaded moderate speed link. In contrast, the path through Router E and Router F is a high speed but heavily loaded trunk. Packets that are delivered along the path through Router E and Router F tend to have a lower delay; however, because the link is so heavily loaded, they also tend to have higher jitter or more variable delivery times. The path through Router C and Router D tends to have higher delay, but the link is lightly loaded, so the jitter that is introduced between packets tends to be lower.

Figure 1-2   *Understanding the Jitter and Delay Characteristics of Different Paths Through a Network*

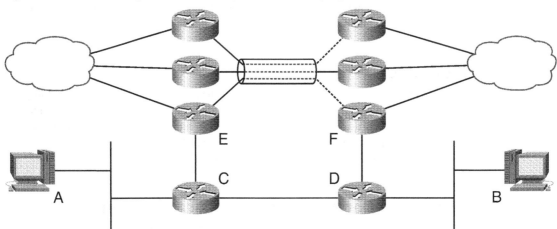

After you understand these sorts of factors in the physical and topological design of the network, you can compare them to the application requirements for each application that is running on your network and build an effective plan for making the network deliver what the applications require, including various QoS techniques (outside the scope of this book) to ensure that those class of service (CoS) requirements are met.

NOTE   The Cisco Press books *End-to-End QoS Network Design*, by Tim Szigeti and Christina Hattingh, and *Cisco QOS Exam Certification Guide*, by Wendell Odom and Michael Cavanaugh, are excellent resources on the topic of QoS.

Reliability and Resiliency

Applications cannot run if the network is not forwarding data between the attached devices. If the network is down, applications that are running across the network do not work. A network must be *reliable* if you are going to build applications that require connectivity to be available between attached devices. This might seem like an obvious statement, but as you investigate this concept a little further, you will find that it is more complicated than it appears on the surface.

Given the importance of reliability, how do you build a reliable network? The most obvious answer is to reduce the rate of change within the network. The less change that a network has, the more stable and reliable it is.

Changes in networks are a fact of life. The larger that a network becomes, the more likely at least some component of the network is changing or has failed on any given day. For instance, if any given device in your network fails or changes once in every five years (if every change or failure is one hour, this is an uptime rate of 99.99997 percent), and you have only five devices in your network, you are likely to have only one component change or failure every year. If you have 500 devices in your network, however, you are going to have 100 component changes or failures per year, at least one every three days. Figure 1-3 shows the compounding effect of multiple changes on multiple devices.

Figure 1-3   *Network Changes Versus Device Changes*

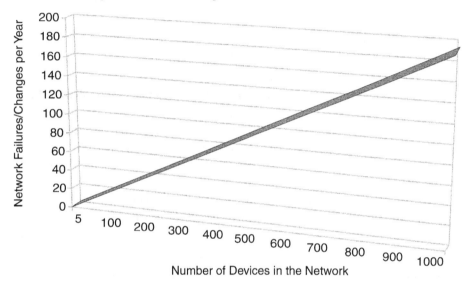

Obviously, even with high rates of reliability, a network of any large size is going to be in a state of almost constant change, either because of component failures or modifications to the network.

Therefore, although you can gain some measure of reliability by reducing the rate of changes and failures in the network, you are not going to be able to prevent changes from occurring. Along with deploying higher reliability devices and employing methods to limit the amount of change occurring in the network within any given time window, you need to design the network around the changes you know are going to occur. This is what *resiliency* refers to.

Network resiliency is the capability of a network to adapt to changes (because of configuration changes or failure) without the network failing. You build reliable networks by determining how much change you want the network to be able to handle within specific timeframes and then building enough resiliency into the network design to prevent the network from failing with the level of change you have decided the network must handle.

Defining Network Failure

The chart in Figure 1-3 looks scary. As a network grows, no matter how reliable the devices in the network are, more component changes will occur because of changes in network equipment or failure of network equipment. However, does a change or failure in a network component equate to a network failure?

Go back to the original goal of building a reliable network. A network is working as long as it is delivering most of the packets offered at the edge in a timely manner. If a single link fails, can a network continue to deliver packets in a timely manner?

Even if a single link fails, the network will still be operational from the perspective of an application if the following points are true:

- The network can continue to deliver packets in a timely manner if an alternate way exists to carry the packets, such as a second path that is parallel to the failed path.

- The network could still be said to be delivering most of the packets offered at the edge in a timely manner if the application or set of users impacted by the change or failure is not important to the primary goals of the network. For instance, the inability to reach a specific game server might not be important in a network that is designed to provide banking services.

The definition of a network failure, then, depends on the applications that are deployed on the network and their function within the larger picture as much as it is on network design. For each application that is running over the network, network designers need to consider the following:

- What is the cost of this service being unavailable?

- Are specific sections of the network more important than others for this application?

- Does this application require a specific set of links to be operational before it can work correctly?

For instance, e-mail might be the primary means of communication among the company's employees. In this case, a five-minute e-mail outage might be an inconvenience, but a five-hour e-mail outage might translate into the company losing a large sum of money. Defining the specific level of service that each application requires, in terms of maximum downtime before impacting the bottom line, is an important exercise in network design.

Each application might also have specific servers or hosts requiring reliable connectivity. Again, using the e-mail example, every user who loses his connection to the network at the same time will have the same impact as the e-mail server becoming disconnected from the network: loss of e-mail service.

Some time-critical applications might actually fail on a wide scale even though the network does not fail in the traditional sense—even though no packets or just a few packets are actually dropped. For instance, a single link failure could cause widespread voice call resets if the network does not adjust to the change in topology quickly enough, causing just a small number of dropped or heavily delayed packets.

Other types of applications can be time sensitive, such as financial transactions that depend on quickly changing rates or prices. This could be especially true in high volume, high speed transactional models, such as large stock and financial instrument trading operations.

Beyond network failures in the traditional sense, you need to consider what impact a network failure is going to have on the timeliness of packet delivery for some applications. It is important to analyze each application and host (or host type) that is connected to your network and build a definition of what a network failure means for each one. Without this definition of failure, the concept of *five 9s reliability* (explained in more detail in the later section, "The Mean Time Between Failures") will have no meaning, because you won't be able to define which failures are "network failures," and you won't be able to accurately measure the uptime or downtime of your network (or the availability of the applications that are running over the network).

Network Recovery Time

Although the analysis of which applications require what types of network availability is outside the scope of this book, network recovery time after a component within the network is changed or fails is the primary topic of the remainder of this book. If a network fails once a year, but it takes three weeks to recover from the failure, the network is not going to have good uptime rates.

Network recovery has several levels, each with its own time:

- The time it takes for the network to recover from a failure. For instance, when a link fails, and the routing protocol routes around the link failure, the time it takes for the routing protocol to adjust the paths through the network to the failed link is the network recovery time. The remainder of this book deals with this issue in more depth.

- The time it takes to troubleshoot and correct a problem caused by a component failure or change when the network cannot automatically adjust to it. If a device or link fails, how long does it take to track down the problem and correct it? This time factors in the manageability of the network and several other issues.

Manageability

Network geeks generally do not like to manage things—that is why they are network geeks, and not managers, right? Network designers still need to consider the manageability of the network when they are considering various design options, however. An intricate way of configuring something so that it works "just right" might have a large "cool factor," but it is not going to be so cool when it fails or makes the network hard to troubleshoot or modify as requirements change. An easily managed network always scales as the network grows and is easier to modify to adjust to changing business requirements.

This book will not berate you with the importance of network management, trying to convince you that network management is the best thing since sliced bread. You can use plenty of other books to discover the many intricacies of network management. Network management is not as hard as it looks, most of the time, and some basic network management can increase the resiliency of a network.

NOTE	You could compare a network without some sort of management to driving blindfolded. Although it can be done, it is not a good idea—you will eventually end up in an accident. Network management is a critical part of network design and scaling.

The following sections examine two specific areas where network manageability is important:

- Day-to-day operational maintenance
- Emergency management

Day-to-Day Operational Maintenance

On small networks, it hardly seems worth the effort to monitor the day-to-day operation of the network, and on large networks, no one attempts to actually monitor the network, because it appears to be such an overwhelming challenge. In fact, day-to-day monitoring of networks is probably the least favorite job of every network engineer, right next to going to the company picnic and hobnobbing with the folks in accounting.

However, it is important to perform these types of maintenance to find and correct growing problems or required design and deployment problems before they result in a network failure. In addition, this type of monitoring and maintenance provides a base to work from when network failures do occur. What sorts of maintenance do you consider absolutely required, regardless of the network size? You should always do two essential tasks:

- Take a periodic network baseline.
- Document the network.

The following sections follow cover these activities in greater detail.

Taking a Network Baseline

Network baselines consist of normal traffic flow levels and device utilization taken periodically. Figure 1-4 illustrates a simple network baseline, taken four days of normal network operations.

Figure 1-4   *Sample Network Baseline*

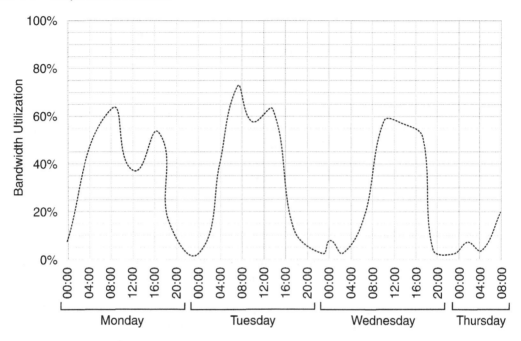

Figure 1-4 illustrates the utilization of a specific link in the network across four days, at different times of the day. This sort of baseline can be invaluable when you are determining network capacities and troubleshooting slow traffic flows and hard-to-find problems. It is also useful from a network design perspective to be able to determine when traffic shifts are occurring within the network, and to be able to see traffic shifts when a topology change occurs. This sort of information can help the network designer design routing for appropriate responses to equipment failures and changes.

For instance, network designers often plan backup paths for critical paths through a network, assuming that the backup path will be capable of meeting the bandwidth and delay requirements of the traffic offered. A baseline might expose areas in the network where the expected backup path simply will not work. In those cases, other backup paths must be chosen, or the backup path needs to be corrected to support the traffic it is expected to carry.

Numerous network management books discuss the tools and techniques you can use to monitor network parameters. Following are some of the things you should be monitoring to aid in network design:

- Link utilization across primary and backup paths for those applications whose loss would severely cripple the business.

- Delay through primary and backup paths for those applications whose loss would severely cripple the business.

- Router and switch processor utilization, making certain to differentiate between processor utilization because of processes, and utilization because of packet switching.

- Router and switch memory utilization.

- Routing and switching table sizes.

- Routing table stability. An easy way to estimate routing table stability is by examining the timers in the routing table, but they do not really indicate what you might think they indicate, so you should be careful with them. Other good ways to determine the stability of the routing table might be to put a monitor router (or other device) on the network and log routing table changes, or monitor protocol event logs to determine how often routes change.

NOTE   Some are confused about what the timers in the routing table of a router that is running Cisco IOS Software really mean. When you first look at them, you might think they simply indicate when the route was installed or modified in some way, such as a change in the next hop, metric, or other parameter. In fact, however, this timer is changed every time the route is touched in any way—even if the route does not actually change when it is touched. For instance, if Enhanced Interior Gateway Routing Protocol (EIGRP) receives an update for a specific route, it recalculates the best path to the destination indicated and reinstalls the route in the routing table. Even if the route does not change, the timer is reset, and it looks like the route has changed.

Network Documentation

Everyone documents his network, right? Wrong. In fact, finding a well-documented network in the real world is rare. The network is too large to document properly because it is managed by numerous people and is difficult to document, or it is "too small to document." None of these are good excuses for not documenting a network, though.

What sorts of documentation do you need to manage and plan changes in a network? The primary documentation you keep should at least contain the following:

- A physical layer topology of the network
- A logical layer topology of the network
- An addressing and summarization plan

Device configurations, change logs, and other sorts of documentation can be useful, but these three pieces of documentation are critical to troubleshooting a network when it is failing and planning future network changes. Figure 1-5 illustrates a network that is documented at the physical and logical layers to show the difference between the two types of documentation.

Figure 1-5   *Layer 2 Versus Layer 3 Network Diagrams*

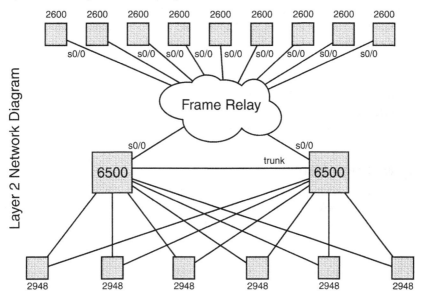

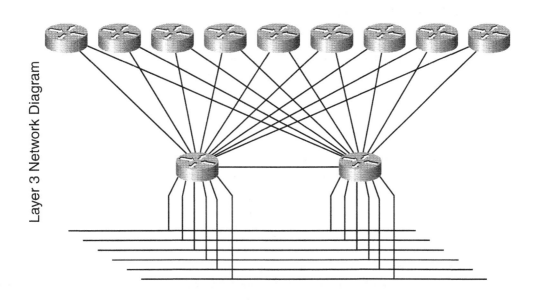

The addressing and summarization plan can be a spreadsheet or database indicating which addresses are allocated to each area of the network, preferably referring to topological areas illustrated on the Layer 3 network diagram and what summaries are advertised from each area of the network.

NOTE   See the section "Addressing and Summarization," in Chapter 2, "Applying the Fundamentals," for more information.

Emergency Management

It is 2:00 a.m. and the network operations center has called you because the backups are failing—and it looks like a network problem. You crank up your laptop, open a Virtual Private Network (VPN) to the firewall, and log into the router to which the backup server is connected. You examine the configuration and notice that it does not look the same as the last time you looked at it. Why was it changed? Does the new configuration make sense? How does that prefix list interoperate with the route map it is being used in, and why are routing updates being tagged?

This is what is what is referred to in the industry as the "two in the morning test." Any time you configure a router or design a new solution to the problem, take the two in the morning test. Will you understand the configuration and be able to relate all the parts together correctly when you are half asleep at two in the morning?

Following are some basic rules for designing a network for manageability:

- If you can configure a specific capability or solve a certain problem in two different ways, and one way is simpler than the other but otherwise they are about equal, choose the simpler configuration.

- Apply controls at the point closest to where the control is being used, if possible. For instance, if you can configure packet filtering at the interface or globally, and the actual packets filtered are the same, configure the filtering at the interface level. Balance this rule with the first rule, because bringing the control to the point closest to where the control actually applies can complicate the configuration needlessly.

- If the configuration documentation is longer than a small book, the configuration is too complex. Most likely, the configuration should not require more than a few lines of documentation to be understood quickly by everyone on the engineering team or by technical support when a problem occurs that you need help with.

When considering how to handle a specific area of the network design and the configuration of actual devices within the network, always consider the maintainability of the design. Example 1-1 demonstrates two configurations accomplishing the same thing, but one is more complex than the other.

Example 1-1 *Two Equivalent Configurations*

```
! first configuration
!
hostname router-a
!
interface serial 0/0
 ip address 10.1.1.2 255.255.255.254
!
interface serial 0/1
 ip address 10.1.1.4 255.255.255.254
!
interface serial 0/2
 ip address 10.1.1.6 255.255.255.254
!
interface serial 0/3
 ip address 10.1.1.8 255.255.255.254
!
interface fastethernet 1/0
 ip address 10.1.2.1 255.255.255.0
!
router ospf 100
 network 10.1.2.0 0.0.0.255 area 0
 redistribute connected route-map someserials subnets metric 10
!
access-list 10 permit 10.1.2.2 0.0.0.1
access-list 10 permit 10.1.2.4 0.0.0.1
!
route-map someserials permit 10
 match ip address 10
! second configuration
!
hostname router-a
!
 interface serial 0/0
 ip address 10.1.1.2 255.255.255.254
!
interface serial 0/1
 ip address 10.1.1.4 255.255.255.254
!
interface serial 0/2
 ip address 10.1.1.6 255.255.255.254
!
interface serial 0/3
 ip address 10.1.1.8 255.255.255.254
!
interface fastethernet 1/0
 ip address 10.1.2.1 255.255.255.0
!
router ospf 100
 network 0.0.0.0 0.0.0.0 area 0
 passive-interface default
 no passive-default fastethernet 1/0
```

The goal is to include the serial 0/2 and 0/3 interfaces in Open Shortest Path First (OSPF), but not serial interfaces 0/0 and 0/1. To include these addresses in OSPF in the first configuration, use the **redistribute static** command combined with the route map someserials. This route map relies on **access-list 10** to list the networks that should or should not be redistributed into OSPF. Thus, to understand the configuration, you need to examine **access-list 10.** Then examine the route map **someserials** and consider which interfaces on the router will be redistributed as externals into OSPF and which will not.

The second configuration configures **network** statements under the OSPF configuration directly, including serial interfaces 0/2 and 0/3. The configuration then marks the default interface state as passive, which means that OSPF will advertise the connected networks as OSPF internal routes, but it will not form neighbor adjacencies on those interfaces. The configuration marks FastEthernet 1/0 as active (by configuring **no passive-interface fastethernet 1/0**), allowing OSPF to form neighbor adjacencies on them. This configuration is simpler, because all the control over which networks are included as OSPF routes is entirely within the OSPF router configuration. Further, you have fewer lines of configuration to digest.

Scalability

How many routers does a scalable network have? Perhaps when your network has 100 routers, it has become a large-scale network and you have proven your skills as a network designer. Or is it 1000 routers? Or does size really have anything to do with network scalability? Consider the following situations when you think about what a large-scale network means:

- Some networks are large, with thousands of routers, and are unstable, require major changes to add to or modify the network topology, and cannot be adapted to new applications without major work being done.

- Some networks are large, with thousands of routers, and are stable and can be adapted to changing conditions with minimal effort.

- Some networks are small, with tens of routers, and are unstable and difficult to change, fail with small modifications, and take a long time to troubleshoot when they fail.

These three observations imply that scalability has little to do with network size. Instead, a scalable network can adapt to its environment, can be resized as needed, and is manageable no matter what size it is. In short, a scalable network is built around a flexible design and easy management.

If a network technically can scale, but managing it would be incredibly difficult or even impossible to manage, it cannot scale in the real world.

It is important, then, to disconnect the idea of the size of a network from its scaling properties. Regardless of the size of the network you work on, making it scalable should be your goal. Set foundations and make changes so that the network can be more easily adapted to future needs.

This decreases network downtime by reducing the time required to troubleshoot and fix those inevitable component failures.

At this point, it should be clear to you what the fundamental network design goals are. The network should be reliable, manageable, and scalable. The rest of this chapter covers some of the techniques you can use to achieve these goals, beginning with redundancy.

Redundancy

Most network engineers, when they think of network resiliency, automatically think of adding redundancy. Redundancy does not just impact the resilience of a network, however; it also impacts manageability and scalability.

The following sections contain ways of evaluating redundancy in relation to network resilience. You will find that a tradeoff exists, a point of diminishing returns where adding more redundancy does not improve but can actually harm network resilience, manageability, and scaling.

How Redundancy Increases Resiliency

In many cases, adding redundant hardware or redundant links to a section of the network can increase the resiliency of the network as a whole. For instance, in the network illustrated in Figure 1-6, adding some redundancy could increase the uptime of the network.

Figure 1-6   *Increasing Redundancy to Increase Network Resilience*

In the network illustrated in Figure 1-6, two hosts are connected through one pair of routers, Router A and Router B. These routers are connected via a single link. In the first change, an alternate link is added between Router A and Router B (shown with a dashed line in the illustration), so a single link failure will not result in the loss of connectivity between the two hosts. Although this prevents the single link failure from causing a network disruption, it leaves Router A and Router B as single points of failure. If either one of them fails, the entire network fails. To resolve this, you can add another pair of routers, Router C and Router D, as shown in Figure 1-7.

Figure 1-7   *Adding a Second Pair of Routers for Redundancy*

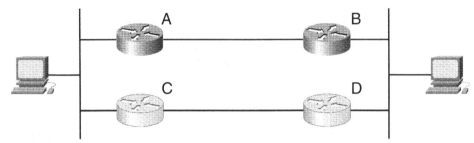

The additional routers increase network resiliency by providing a backup for Router A and Router B. In this network, a single link can fail with no impact, a single router can fail with no network impact, or a pair of routers, as long as they are both attached to the same link, can fail. However, if one router fails on each link, such as Router B and Router C, the network still fails. Therefore, although this network has no single points of failure, it has some double points of failure. Resolving all of the double points of failure would involve adding a third router at both sites, but you can resolve some of the failure points by adding another pair of links into the network, as illustrated in Figure 1-8.

Figure 1-8   *Removing Some Double Points of Failure by Adding Redundancy*

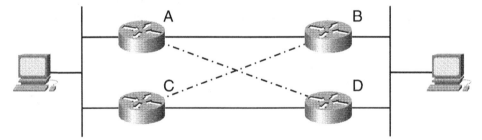

After the links between Routers A and D and Routers B and C are added (illustrated as dashed lines), any pair of links between the routers can fail, or any one router and any one link or some pairs of routers can fail, and the network will still be capable of passing traffic.

How then, do you determine how much redundancy to build into a network to provide a given amount of resiliency? The method described thus far—analyzing the points of failure in the network and comparing this to the number of failures that the network should be able to resist at any point—is a common way of determining the amount of redundancy required at each point.

For instance, if you determine that a single equipment or link failure should not cause the network to fail, you need to eliminate all single points of failure in the network. If you decide that any two failures should not cause the network to fail, you need to examine the network for points where double points of failure exist and determine how to avoid them.

Statistical Analysis

Is there any other way you can analyze redundancy in the network and compare it to the resiliency to determine how much redundancy should be installed at any point? Yes. For many years, the managers of road, power, and telephone networks have used statistical methods of determining network resiliency. These methods use the mean time between failures (MTBF) for each component of the network to determine the mean time between failures for the network as a whole. Combining the MTBF for the network to the amount of time required to bring the network back up after a failure, the mean time to repair (MTTR), you can predict the amount of downtime the network will experience each year.

The Mean Time Between Failures

First, you need to consider the MTBF for each component within a system. Generally, this is expressed as the amount of time, in hours, that a particular component will run before it fails. This number is a bit trickier than it first appears. For instance, if you have ten identical components with a MTBF of 5 years, 43,800 hours, and you ran them for five years, how many would you expect to still be running after 2.5 years? To find out, you need to calculate the failure rate from the MTBF, which is done as follows:

$$R = e^{-T/MTBF}$$

e is approximately 2.718, a number used commonly when calculating natural logarithms. To find the percentage of devices with an MTBF of 43,800 hours that will fail in 21,900 hours, you would take the following:

$$2.718^{-21900/43800} = .60656$$

This means that each device has a 60.66 percent chance of operating for 2.5 years without failing. Thus, you would expect about six of the ten devices to be functioning at the end of 2.5 years. The reason that most components have MTBF in the millions of hours is to increase this ratio of operational devices within the average time for which the component will be used. For instance, if the devices each had an MTBF of 1,000,000 hours, each one would have a 97 percent chance of being operational at the 2.5 year mark. Most likely, all ten devices would still be operational at the 2.5 year mark.

Calculating the MTBF of a System

Suppose that you have a system built out of several components, each with its own MTBF. How can you calculate the MTBF of the system? You can use the following formula to compute the MTBF for a system using the MTBF of each component of the system.

$$\frac{1}{\dfrac{1}{MTBF_1} + \dfrac{1}{MTBF_2} + \dfrac{1}{MTBF_3} \cdots}$$

Therefore, calculating the MTBF of a system containing three components, one with an MTBF of 20,000 hours, a second with an MTBF of 25,000 hours, and a third with an MTBF of 35,000 hours, would result in the following:

$$\frac{1}{\dfrac{1}{20000} + \dfrac{1}{25000} + \dfrac{1}{35000}} = 8433$$

Again, you can see the importance of the long MTBF that manufacturers place on their products. The MTBF of a system is much lower than the MTBF of any of its components.

MTTR

The MTBF, however, provides only one part of the equation that you need to determine regarding the percentage of time that a network will be available to users over a given time period. The second number you need is the MTTR, which is the average amount of time required to bring a system into an operational state after it has failed.

Suppose, for instance, that you have a device with the following requirements:

- Four hours to replace a card, and every fourth outage involves replacing a card
- One hour to load a new version of software, and every fourth outage involves replacing the software
- 15 minutes to reload, and every other outage requires a simple reload to return to an operational state

From these simple numbers, you can calculate an average outage for this device to be as follows:

$$\frac{4 + 1 + (2 * 15)}{4} = 1.375$$

Each time this device fails, it requires an average of 1.375 hours to restore it to service. If you combine this with the MTBF for the device, you can determine how much time the device should be unavailable in a given year. Assume that this device will fail an average of once every 3 years; this means that it will be unavailable:

$$\frac{1.375}{3} = .459$$

.459 hours is about 30 minutes a year. To compute the uptime rate, take the number of minutes in a year and divide this into the 30 minutes of estimated downtime per year:

$$\frac{30}{365 * 24 * 60} = .00005$$

You know that the device will be down .00005 percent of the time, so it should be up for 99.99995 percent of the time. This would be considered six 9s of reliability, in common parlance. The same sort of reasoning applies to systems, but it is almost impossible to know the MTTR for a system, other than by working with the system and gaining experience with it. Again, that is why it is important to keep good records about your network, in this case the frequency and length of outages. These records allow you to build a good picture of the reliability of your network and project changes in reliability resulting from changes in the network design.

How Redundancy Can Increase Management Complexity

So far, you have learned how redundancy can improve the resilience of a network and several ways of evaluating the resilience provided through redundancy. Does redundancy have any downsides, though? Yes. For instance, increasing redundancy also increases management complexity.

Management complexity generally consists of three elements:

- The ability to configure the network, otherwise known as the "two o'clock in the morning" test. If someone who is unfamiliar with your network works on it at two o'clock in the morning, will that person be able to understand the configurations and why they are there?

- The ability to monitor the network.

- The ability to troubleshoot the network when a failure occurs.

As redundancy is increased, the difficulty of each of these management functions increases. For instance, when you are attempting to configure the network, a set of five or ten possible parallel paths through multiple intermediate devices can make it difficult to understand what the traffic flow should look like and to configure the devices to achieve the desired traffic flow.

Troubleshooting a highly complex redundancy scheme can also be difficult. Which direction should traffic be flowing? Is a transient loop across ten paths normal, or is it a symptom of the network failure you are working on?

One of the most useful tactics that an engineer has when beginning to work on a network failing to converge is to remove redundancy until the network converges. After the network stabilizes, perform a post mortem to determine what happened and how to prevent it from happening again.

Although management complexity is difficult to measure, experience indicates that two parallel paths is the optimum balance between management complexity and good resilience. This balance might vary from situation to situation—sometimes one path will be all the situation calls for, and sometimes three paths can be useful—but two parallel paths tends to be a good rule of thumb.

How Redundancy Can Reduce Scalability

Another tradeoff that the network engineer makes when increasing redundancy in a network is between resilience and scaling. Each additional path added to a network can decrease the speed of convergence in the network. If you consider the job of a routing protocol and how routing protocols operate, this makes sense. The more paths that a routing protocol must examine before determining the best path to a destination, the longer it is going to take to determine the best path. Again, this is often difficult to quantify, but Figure 1-9 offers some guidance.

Figure 1-9   *Redundancy Versus Convergence Time*

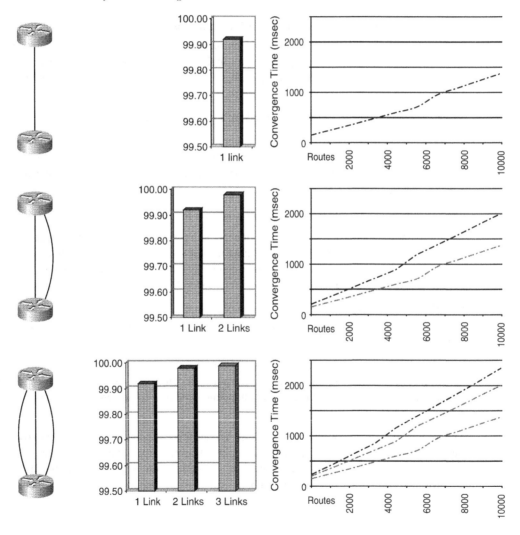

This figure is based on a small network, illustrated on the left side, running EIGRP. Several routes are injected at one router using a router emulator. The amount of time required to switch from one path to another path, when a single link is flapped, is measured, with the results shown on the far right graph.

From this illustration, you can see that the convergence times increase as the number of routes increases, as you would expect in all routing protocols. As the number of paths available increases, the convergence time also increases. The question is this: Will the network experience more total downtime because of increased convergence time with more parallel links, or will it experience less downtime because of the decreased downtimes involved with having more links?

The answer depends on the frequency of link failure, the amount of time required to restore a failed link, the number of routes in the network, the number of times the network converges on a given route, and other factors, so the answer is not straightforward. In most situations, however, adding a third parallel link tips the scales against higher resilience because of increased convergence times, with few gains in link uptime. To know for certain, you would need to calculate the uptime rates and the convergence time, and then compute total uptimes based on the number of convergence events versus the number of link failures.

NOTE   Another point to consider when adding a third link is the additional memory and processing requirements added with more links. With distance vector protocols, such as EIGRP and BGP, each link represents another entire copy of the information learned from a specific neighbor (or peer), which implies additional memory and processing requirements. For link-state protocols, the additional information exchanged is not greater, but the total size of the database and the time and processing required to calculate the best paths through the network both increase with each path that is added.

Layering

Layering is a classic mechanism used in engineering and life in general to reduce the complexity of a problem. Layering allows you to work with one level of complexity at a time. For instance, when you drive a car, you are concentrating on driving, rather than how the engine works or any other system within the car. The car is a layered system, with one layer focused on operations, another focused on pushing the car forward, another on stopping the car, and so on.

A key characteristic of an elegant solution is the ability to examine the system in several abstract pieces, with minimal reference to other pieces of the system, for troubleshooting and design purposes. Networks are layered, too, using the familiar seven-layer Open System Interconnection (OSI) reference model (although Internet Protocol (IP) was designed around a less familiar four-layer model). When you are dealing with physical layer problems, you rarely consider IP addresses or TCP parameters; you focus on electrical or optical signaling, and so on. At the same time, a key characteristic of an inelegant design (commonly known as a hack) is the inability to divide the problem, or breaking layering boundaries. Most difficult problems in networking, if examined closely, involve some interlayer interaction or carrying information across layers.

These same concepts apply to network design and network technologies. A layered network allows different problems to be isolated from one another and resolved within a smaller set of parameters. This section discusses some of the concepts of layering within network design, including how layering hides information and separates functionality.

Hiding Information

Hiding information is critical to the success of any network design, because large, complex networks contain far too much information for any commonly available system to process and react to on a real-time basis. Two types of information can be hidden in a network:

- Topology information
- Reachability information

Hiding Topology Information

The topology of the network is its physical layout, or the interconnection graph. It is the set of connections and devices that provide physical paths across which traffic travels, or the paths available for traffic to travel along, if you want to examine the topology from the packet level.

Each of the three types of routing protocols (link-state, distance vector, and path vector) treat topology information differently:

- Link-state protocols calculate the best path to each reachable destination by examining the topology information directly. Each device advertises the state of each of its links; this information is used to build a directed graph to each destination. The directed graph is a subset of the physical topology, containing only those paths used to reach at least some destination.

- Routers that are running distance vector protocols advertise only reachability information to their peers, not topology information. The best path to any reachable destination is determined by comparing the cost of reaching a destination as advertised by each neighbor. The topology of the network is not considered when determining the best path.

- Path vector protocols advertise a set of "hops" through the network that the update has passed through. This does not represent a path to the destination necessarily, but rather a set of systems through which the path might pass; this path proves that the path advertised is loop free. Path vector protocols do not rely on cost to determine a loop-free path to the destination; thus, they can choose a *suboptimal* route in terms of cost to support or implement a policy.

Figure 1-10 illustrates the way that topology information is handled in each type of routing protocol.

Figure 1-10   *Routing Protocol Types and Distribution of Topology Information*

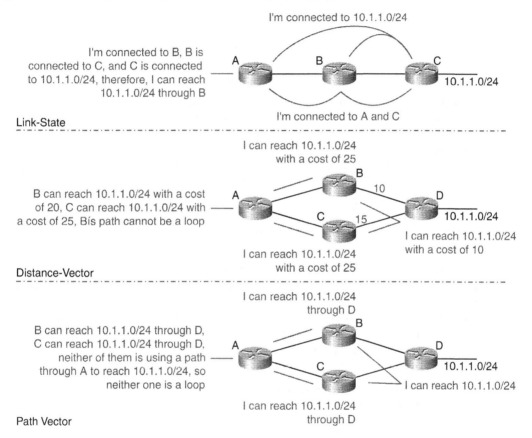

In the link-state illustration, Router C floods the information about its connected links to Router B, which retransmits this information to Router A. Router B also floods information about its connected links to Router A and Router C. From this information, Router A can build a directed graph representing the topology of the network and choose the best loop-free path through the network. Router A knows that it is connected to Router B, and Router B likewise claims connectivity to Router A. Because both routers claim connectivity to each other, the link is entered into the tree. In the same way, the link between Router B and Router C is entered into the tree. Router C claims to be connected to a stub network, 10.1.1.0/24, which is also entered into the directed graph, and Router A finds that it has a path to 10.1.1.0/24, with a next hop of Router B.

Every pair of routers receiving each other's flooded link states is said to be in the same *flooding domain;* every router in the same flooding domain must share the same view of the network topology for it to provide consistent, loop-free routing. Link-state networks almost never consist of a single flooding domain, however, but are broken into *areas* (OSPF) or *domains* (IS-IS). The router at the edge of a flooding domain adds the total cost to each reachable destination within the domain and advertises these destinations as though they were directly connected to the border router, with the cost computed. The border domain router, then, *summarizes* the information from the flooding domain by hiding information about the topology of the network within the flooding domain.

In the distance vector illustration, Router D advertises that it can reach 10.1.1.0/24 with a cost of 10. No topology information is supplied with this advertisement. Router B and Router C know only that Router D can reach this destination, not what path Router D uses to reach it. Router B and Router C add their cost to reach Router D and advertise reachability to 10.1.1.0/24 to Router A. Again, no topology information is included. For all Router A knows, Router B and Router C could be directly connected to 10.1.1.0/24 with varying cost interfaces. Distance vector protocols rely on geometric proofs that the path with the lowest metric cannot be a loop (as long as every router along the way has added its cost to reach the next hop). Each hop hides information about the topology of the network behind it, so each router only advertises given destinations that are reachable at a given cost.

In the path vector illustration, each node that the update passes through attaches a marker indicating the node to the update. If a node in the network receives an update with its own marker attached, it rejects the update, because the update would represent a looped path. The path in a distance vector protocol appears to provide information about the topology of the network, but it really does not; it simply guarantees that a given path is loop free. When routes are filtered or aggregated, topology information is lost, so the entire topology of the network is not known from the paths that are contained in updates.

As you can see from examining the three types of routing protocols currently in use, all three hide topology information at some point:

- Link-state protocols hide topology information at the edge of a flooding domain.
- Distance vector protocols hide topology information at every hop.
- Path vector protocols hide topology through filtering and aggregation.

You will return to these concepts in the discussion of hierarchical network design in Chapter 2 and in the discussion of the deployment of link-state and path vector protocols in later chapters.

Hiding Reachability Information

Reachability information is not really hidden in a network; rather, it is *summarized* or *aggregated.* Figure 1-11 illustrates.

Figure 1-11   *Aggregating Reachability Information*

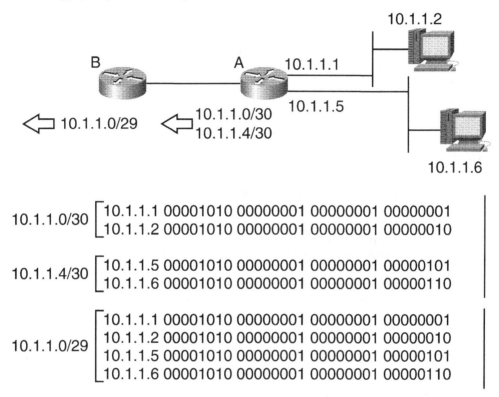

10.1.1.0/30 [10.1.1.1 00001010 00000001 00000001 00000001
             10.1.1.2 00001010 00000001 00000001 00000010]

10.1.1.4/30 [10.1.1.5 00001010 00000001 00000001 00000101
             10.1.1.6 00001010 00000001 00000001 00000110]

10.1.1.0/29 [10.1.1.1 00001010 00000001 00000001 00000001
             10.1.1.2 00001010 00000001 00000001 00000010
             10.1.1.5 00001010 00000001 00000001 00000101
             10.1.1.6 00001010 00000001 00000001 00000110]

In this illustration, Router A is attached to hosts 10.1.1.2 and 10.1.1.6, and it is using IP addresses 10.1.1.1 and 10.1.1.5. When Router A advertises 10.1.1.0/30 to Router B, it is, in effect, stating the following:

"Any IP address between 10.1.1.0 and 10.1.1.3 is reachable through me."

Thus, Router A is summarizing the information about which IP addresses are connected to it. Router A also advertises 10.1.4.0/30, effectively stating this:

"Any IP address between 10.1.1.4 and 10.1.1.7 is reachable through me."

When Router B receives these two advertisements, it now has reachability information for IP addresses 10.1.1.0 through 10.1.1.7. Rather than building two routing updates to advertise reachability to these eight IP addresses, it can simply advertise 10.1.1.0/29, effectively stating the following:

"Any IP address between 10.1.1.0 and 10.1.1.7 is reachable through me."

Thus, Router B has *aggregated*, or *summarized*, the routing information that it received from Router A. This is how routing protocols hide reachability information.

Technically, this is not hiding reachability information; it is simply summarizing it. However, when you summarize, you are "hiding" more specific reachability information inside less specific reachability information. In other words, you are hiding the specific nature of the reachability information.

Chapter 2 discusses route summarization in more detail.

Separate Functionality

One of the two primary purposes behind a layered network design is to separate functionality. Networks typically need to do the following:

- Provide a place for users and services to attach.
- Implement policy, including marking packets for quality of service, perform admission control, implement security measures, implement routing policy, and others.
- Aggregate traffic and network topology information.
- Forward traffic between major topological areas or sites within the network.
- Connect to outside networks, or internetworks.

If you attempted to solve all these problems in one place, the network would likely be hard to troubleshoot and manage. Instead, you can break up these goals and place each one in a different layer.

Chapter 2 discusses network hierarchy and which layers perform which functions in greater detail.

Summary

You have covered a lot of basic material up to this point, including the following:

- The basic goals of network design and the network as a tool providing functionality within the larger picture of the business
- The difference between reliability and resilience and how they relate to each other
- How network design, network management, and network manageability are intertwined
- The interaction between redundancy, manageability, and scalability
- Layering as a tool to reduce complexity by hiding topological information and reachability information

The next chapter puts these theoretical concepts into practice, showing you how to apply them to real-world situations. The important point to remember from this chapter is this:

> Good network design is not about the number of routers you can connect; it is about a flexible, resilient, manageable network. An optimal network is easy to manage and troubleshoot and easy to change when business needs alter the underlying requirements.

Review Questions

1 What is the first thing you should think about when designing a new network?

2 What are the primary goals in any network design?

3 How do you define a reliable network?

4 What elements in Layer 3 network design impact the delay and jitter budgets through the network?

5 What are the two primary considerations when determining when a network has failed?

6 What elements are important in determining the time required to restore a network to service (or an application running on a network to service) after it has failed?

7 What are important day-to-day management tasks in administering a network?

8 What types of documentation are important for network management and troubleshooting?

9 What two methods can you apply to determine where redundancy is needed in a network to increase resiliency?

10 What are the MTBF and MTTR?

11 What two types of information are typically hidden in networks?

Applying the Fundamentals

Chapter 1, "Network Design Goals and Techniques," discussed the primary goals of network design:

- Reliability
- Scalability
- Manageability

In the process of considering these goals, you also saw some statistical and network design analysis and learned about information hiding. All of this theory is useful, but how do you apply these goals and techniques to real networks? How can you actually build a network to meet these goals?

This chapter narrows its focus on information hiding, covering the two intertwined techniques for hiding information in a network: hierarchy and summarization. The first section of the chapter begins with a discussion of abstraction and how its use through layering helps to hide information in a network.

From there, you learn hierarchical design, beginning with the types of functions specific components of the network need to fulfill, and continuing with the two most common hierarchical designs.

Next, the chapter covers addressing and how it interrelates with summarization. The final section of the chapter discusses using summarization in less than ideal conditions.

Hierarchical Design

In a larger sense, hierarchy is just a special case of abstraction through layering, which is used in all computer systems. Abstraction through layering is one of the most important concepts in computers, warranting some further discussion before considering how it is applied in networks.

Abstraction Through Layering

Engineers are accustomed to dividing a system into abstract components and treating these subsystems as if they were single components in and of themselves. This ability to abstract several individual parts into a single subsystem and treat them in the abstract as a single component is a large part of being able to build large-scale systems.

For instance, when you use a computer, you treat the monitor as a single device, working with interactions between the monitor and the processor. If you find that the computer is defective, you stop thinking about its interaction with the monitor and consider the computer as a system, examining each system within the computer (video driver, main processor board, human interaction devices, software, memory, storage, and other components) to determine which one has failed.

You might find the hardware is fine but a problem exists with the software. In this case, you would begin to treat the software, previously treated as a single unit, as a series of components, examining the operating system, the video drivers, and other components. Figure 2-1 illustrates this concept of layers of systems and subsystems.

Figure 2-1   *Layering Systems and Subsystems*

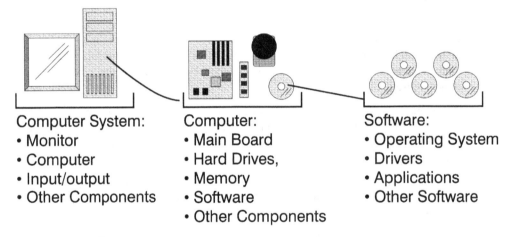

Computer System:
• Monitor
• Computer
• Input/output
• Other Components

Computer:
• Main Board
• Hard Drives,
• Memory
• Software
• Other Components

Software:
• Operating System
• Drivers
• Applications
• Other Software

Networks are no different; you probably think of a network divided into layers based on the Open Systems Interconnection (OSI) reference model, which divides the network software and hardware into seven vertical layers, from the physical layer (Layer 1) to the application layer (Layer 7). Packets are passed down the OSI layers as they leave a device; they are passed back up the OSI layers as they are received by a device.

Horizontal Layers in a Network

You can also treat the entire network at Layer 3 in the OSI model (the network layer) as a single system, breaking the network into subsystems horizontally—along the network layer. In other words, rather than breaking up the network based on the function of each piece in processing data, you can break up the network into layers based on the purpose of each device and its location within the network.

Dividing the network into subsystems enables you to provide the same abstraction levels and to treat a collection of parts as one. That way, you can focus only on the interaction of those parts instead of the components.

In fact, not only does this hierarchy enable network designers and administrators to treat entire parts of the network as a complete subsystem, but it also enables actual devices within the network to treat the network in the same way. You can hide information behind these layering points to control the amount of data that any one device needs to manage. This in turn provides all the benefits of information hiding that were discussed in Chapter 1 — the goals you are trying to reach in your network design.

Networks can be divided into both horizontal and vertical pieces based on operation objectives and topological location, as Figure 2-2 illustrates.

Figure 2-2   *Logical Divisions Within a Network*

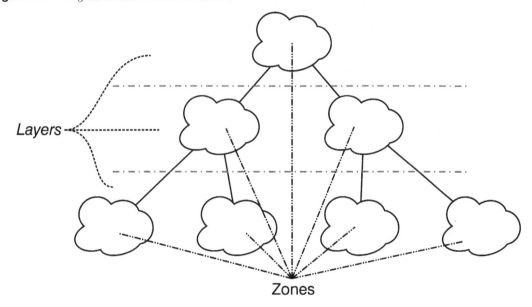

Vertical logical divisions create *hierarchy* within the network. A hierarchical network is divided into two or more layers, depending on its purpose and size, with each layer having specific purposes and interconnection points with other layers.

For ease of reference, we'll call these groups of components, with the components being routers in the case of a network, *zones*.

NOTE	The term *zone* designates a logical set of routers within a layer. This term prevents confusion with the term *area*, used in OSPF, and *routing domain*, used in Intermediate System-to-Intermediate System (IS-IS). In the network illustrated in Figure 2-2, the lowest layer has four zones, the middle layer has two, and the top layer has one.
	This book refers to layers within a network as routed layers, rather than as switched, or bridged, layers. The focus is on routing design and routing protocols deployment. A layer is logically divided through Layer 3, or routing, mechanisms from the layers above and below it.

Layer Functions

Each layer within a hierarchical network design fulfills specific functions. The functions of a zone are determined by the layer of the zone. Separating these functions into layers allows you to hide information, a requirement for building hierarchy.

A layer can provide the following functions in a network:

- Forwarding traffic
- Aggregation of routing information
- Definition and implementation of routing policy
- Providing places for users to attach
- Controlling traffic admittance into the network

The following sections cover each of these in greater detail.

Forwarding Traffic

It almost sounds like a cliché to say that one of the primary objectives of a network layer is to forward traffic. Networks are supposed to do this automatically. However, it is not so simple to just say, "forward traffic." You need to consider four types of traffic:

- Interlayer
- Intralayer
- Interzone
- Intrazone

Interlayer traffic is traffic that is forwarded *within* the network layer, whereas intralayer traffic is traffic that is forwarded *between* network layers. In the same way, interzone traffic is traffic that is forwarded within a network area, whereas intrazone traffic is traffic that is forwarded between network areas.

The number of points at which intralayer and interzone traffic is allowed determines the meshiness of the network. In general terms, meshier networks are more complex from a design standpoint, as Figure 2-3 illustrates.

Figure 2-3   *Increasing Network Complexity with Increasing Points of Interlayer Traffic Exchange*

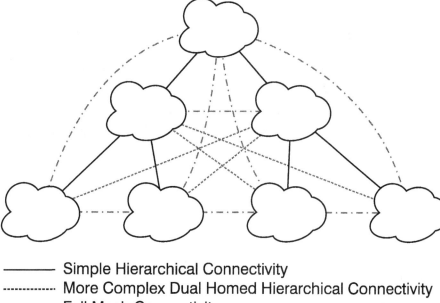

——— Simple Hierarchical Connectivity
------------ More Complex Dual Homed Hierarchical Connectivity
– · – · – · – Full Mesh Connectivity

As you can see from this simple network, as the amount of interconnectivity between the network components increases, the complexity of the network also increases. Not only does the number of links increase, but the number of possible paths through the network also increases, which makes it harder to understand and plan network traffic patterns and troubleshoot the network when something goes wrong. This is similar to the issues faced with increasing redundancy in Chapter 1.

It is important, then, to plan interlayer and interzone communications carefully in a network.

Aggregation of Routing Information

Aggregation is another apparently simple concept with underlying complexity. The two types of aggregation that you need to consider when designing a network are aggregation of traffic and routes. The later section titled "Addressing and Summarization" discusses route aggregation in more detail. The focus of the discussion here is on traffic aggregation.

Traditionally, communication systems have been built on the 80/20 rule: 80 percent of the traffic originated by any given device is going to be destined to another device within the same local area, while the remaining 20 percent is going to be destined to someplace outside the local area. The 80/20 rule uses the concept of geographically local and remote devices to define remote and local, as Figure 2-4 illustrates.

Figure 2-4   *80/20 Rule*

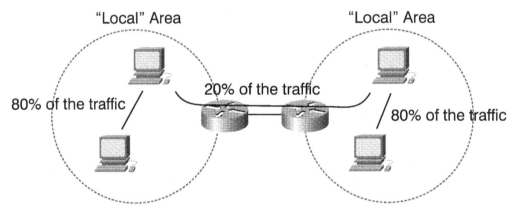

NOTE With the growing ubiquity of networks, however, you can no longer assume that this rule applies. In a typical environment, this rule works because people tend to gather in communities based on their proximity. For instance, if you live in Atlanta, you are more likely to work with, buy from, and sell to other people who live in Atlanta. With the advent of fast, cheap logistical systems to move large quantities of atoms from place to place and networks to move large quantities of information from place to place quickly, this concept of locality is losing some of its strength.

People are increasingly working with global teams, working from their own homes, and buying things from various places without considering how long it will take to receive them because the range of available products is much wider in a larger marketplace. Although human interaction prefers locality and data traffic with it, the ratio varies. It is not always 80 percent local and 20 percent remote.

Traffic aggregation takes advantage of the locality of traffic in two ways:

- Aggregating local traffic at a local point of exchange so that local traffic does not cross wide-area links
- Providing a limited number of points through which traffic can leave a specific region or area

Traffic aggregation points are effectively the edges of the topological zones within a network. Considered in the terms of systems and subsystems, traffic aggregation points are the edges where subsystems within the network interact.

Definition and Implementation of Routing Policies

Routing policies are generally implemented at the edge of two layers in a network, including summarization and filtering. As noted in Chapter 1, you need to hide two types of information to make a network scalable: topology and reachability. Both of these types of information are generally hidden along the core/aggregation edge, as Figure 2-5 illustrates.

Figure 2-5   *Hiding Information on the Core/Aggregation Edge*

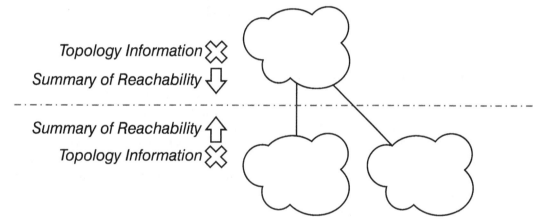

Routing policies can hide the topology of zones within a layer from zones within another layer (and, by extension, the topologies of zones within a layer from each other). Address summarization, discussed in more detail in the "Addressing and Summarization" section of this chapter, is also deployed along the layer edge to reduce the amount of information that is passed between layers in a network.

Beyond information hiding, however, a routing policy can implement traffic flow engineering— directing traffic across specific links (or topologies) at different points in the network so that better use is made of network resources. For instance, two paths might be available within the network between a given set of hosts and a given server. It is better to use both paths where possible, rather than using only the optimal path. At least three traffic engineering technologies are available for this type of network optimization:

- Multiprotocol Label Switching Traffic Engineering (MPLS/TE). See *Traffic Engineering with MPLS* by Eric Osbourne and Ajay Simha (Cisco Press) for further information.
- Multitopology Routing (MTR). Search Cisco.com for more information.
- Policy-Based Routing (PBR). Search Cisco.com for more information.

In the same way, two exit points might exist from a given area within the network to reach a server or device that is used on a regular basis by numerous users. A separate technology, Optimized Edge Routing (OER), can optimize the path chosen to the destination. OER is outside the scope of this book. Search Cisco.com for more information.

User Attachment

If your users did not have a place to attach to the network, your phone would probably ring less—and you would probably not have a network, either. Of course, the point of a network is to carry user traffic, allowing users to reach servers and services that they want to access (entertainment, news, and shopping) or need to access (databases, project information, and so on). In general, user access also is tied to traffic admittance policies, at least at the edge of the network. User access points should be kept within well-defined areas of the network for policy and security reasons.

Controlling Traffic Admittance into the Network

In most situations, making a network large enough to accept a full rate of traffic from every attached device is not practical or necessary. Under most circumstances, any given device transmits only a percentage of the amount of traffic that it could be transmitting. People sleep, go to lunch, go home and spend time with their families, work on local copies of project files, and do other things that do not require the network. During these times, the computer is not transmitting anything on the network (although the computer might be working at times the people are not, such as with grid computing systems).

Planning network capacity becomes a matter of the following:

- **Statistical analysis**—Determining the times during which the network is most heavily loaded and discovering what the load is.

- **Load shifting**—Determining how the load can be shifted from busy network times to times when the network is less busy and shifting traffic from busier links to less used links.

- **Controlling traffic admittance**—Controlling the amount of traffic allowed into the network by controlling the rate at which packets are admitted into the network at any given entry point.

While it might be nice to design your network so it will always be able to handle any traffic offered, it's not always possible. Generally, your budget will stand in the way of this dream. Instead, you must also provide controls on the amount of traffic permitted into the network at the network edge and possibly between the layers or areas within the network.

NOTE   The types of traffic admittance controls available are beyond the scope of this book. If you want to find out more about traffic control mechanisms, see *IP Quality of Service* by Srinivas Vegesna (Cisco Press).

Network Hierarchies

You now know how the work that a network does can be divided and why you would want to divide a network into layers. Two- and three-layer hierarchies are the two dominant layering systems used in networks, each of which is covered in the sections that follow.

Two-Layer Hierarchy

In many networks, you need only two layers to fulfill all of the layer functions discussed in the previous section—core and aggregation, as Figure 2-6 illustrates.

Figure 2-6   *Two-Layer Hierarchy*

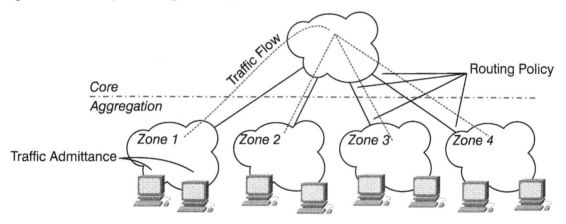

Only one zone exists within the core, and many zones are in the aggregation layer. Examine each of the layer functions to see where it occurs in a two-layer design:

- **Traffic forwarding**—Ideally, all interzone traffic forwarding occurs in the core. Traffic flows from each zone within the aggregation layer up the hierarchy into the network core and then back down the hierarchy into other aggregation zones.

- **Aggregation**—Aggregation occurs along the core/aggregation layer border, allowing only interzone traffic to pass between the aggregation and core layers. This also provides an edge for traffic engineering services to be deployed along.

- **Routing policy**—Routing policy is deployed along the edge of the core and the aggregation layers, generally as routes are advertised from the aggregation layer into the core.

- **User attachment**—User devices and servers are attached to zones within the aggregation layer. This separation of end devices into the aggregation permits the separation of traffic between traffic through a link and traffic to a link, or device. Typically, it is best not to mix transit and destination traffic in the same area of the network.

- **Controlling traffic admittance**—Traffic admittance control always occurs where user and server devices are attached to the network, which is in the aggregation layer. You can also place traffic admittance controls at the aggregation points exiting from the aggregation layer into the core of the network, but this is not common.

You can see, then, how dividing the network into layers enables you to make each layer specialized and to hide information between the layers. For instance, the traffic admittance policy implemented along the edge of the aggregation layer is entirely hidden from the network core.

You also use the core/aggregation layer edge to hide information about the topology of routing zones from each other, through summarization. Each zone within the aggregation layer should have minimal routing information, possibly just how to make it to the network core through a default route, and no information about the topology of the network core. At the same time, the zones within the aggregation layer should summarize their reachability information into as few routing advertisements as possible at their edge with the core and hide their topology information from the network core.

Three-Layer Hierarchy

A three-layer hierarchy divides these same responsibilities through zones in three vertical network layers, as Figure 2-7 shows.

Figure 2-7   *Three-Layer Hierarchy*

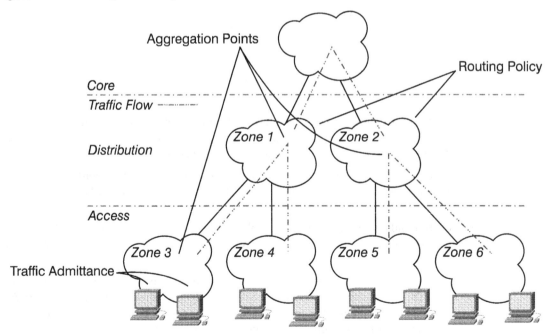

Examine each of the layer functions in a three-layer hierarchy and see where they are implemented.

- **Traffic Forwarding**—As with a two-layer hierarchy, all interzone traffic within a three-layer hierarchy should flow up the hierarchy, through the layers, and back down the hierarchy.

- **Aggregation**—A three-layer hierarchy has two aggregation points:
  - At the edge of the access layer going into the distribution layer
  - At the edge of the distribution layer going into the core

  At the edge of the access layer, you aggregate traffic in two places: within each access zone and flowing into the distribution layer. In the same way, you aggregate interzone traffic at the distribution layer and traffic leaving the distribution layer toward the network core. The distribution layer and core are ideal places to deploy traffic engineering within a network.

- **Routing policy**—The routing policy is deployed within the distribution layer in a three-layer design and along the distribution/core edge. You can also deploy routing policies along the access/distribution edge, particularly route and topology summarization, to hide information from other zones that are attached to the same distribution layer zone.

- **User attachment**—User devices and servers are attached to zones within the access layer. This separation of end devices into the access layer permits the separation of traffic between traffic through a link and traffic to a link, or device. Typically, you do not want to mix transit and destination traffic in the same area of the network.

- **Controlling traffic admittance**—Traffic admittance control always occurs where user and server devices are attached to the network, which is in the access layer. You can also place traffic admittance controls at the aggregation points along the aggregation/core edge.

As you can see, the concepts that are applied to two- and three-layer designs are similar, but you have more application points in a three-layer design.

Determining How Many Layers to Use in Network Design

Which network design is better: two layers or three layers? As with almost all things in network design, it all depends. Examine some of the factors involved in deciding whether to build a two- or three-layer network:

- **Network geography**—Networks that cover a smaller geographic space, such as a single campus or a small number of interconnected campuses, tend to work well as two-layer designs. Networks spanning large geographic areas, such as a country, continent, or even the entire globe, often work better as three layer designs.

- **Network topology depth**—Networks with a compressed, or flattened, topology tend to work better as two-layer hierarchies. For instance, service provider networks cover large geographic areas, but reducing number of hops through the network is critical in providing the services they sell; therefore, they are often built on a two-layer design. Networks with substantial depth in their topologies, however, tend to work better as three-layer designs.

- **Network topology design**—Highly meshed networks, with many requirements for interzone traffic flows, tend to work better as two-layer designs. Simplifying the hierarchy to two levels tends to focus the design elements into meshier zones. Networks that focus traffic flows on well-placed distributed resources, or centralized resources, such as a network with a large number of remote sites connecting to a number of centralized Data Centers, tend to work better as three-layer designs.

- **Policy implementation**—If policies of a network tend to focus on traffic engineering, two-layer designs tend to work better. Networks that attempt to limit access to resources attached to the network and other types of policies tend to work better as three-layer designs.

Again, however, these are simple rules of thumb. No definitive way exists to decide whether a network should have two or three layers. Likewise, you cannot point to a single factor and say, "Because of this, the network we are working on should have three layers instead of two."

Hiding Layers Within Layers

To make the layer issue even more confusing, some networks actually hide several network layers within a single layer of the network. Figure 2-8 illustrates a backbone network controlled by a single group within a large international corporation and the smaller networks hiding within each of the aggregation layer zones.

The corporate backbone network has two layers: a core and an aggregation layer. Each aggregation layer zone connects to several corporate sites, which might then be individual two- or three-layer networks in and of themselves. In the illustrated network, a three-layer network is connected as a single "user" behind one of the aggregation layer zones, managed by a local (geographic or division level) team. Large corporations commonly build their networks this way, with the network backbone acting as a service provider to their individual networks. Hidden behind the aggregation layer of the backbone network might be a series of two- and three-layer networks, each with its own layers and information hiding. Chapter 6, "BGP Cores and Network Scalability," discusses BGP cores used in this way.

Service provider networks are often built this way, hiding the entire customer network behind the aggregation layer of their own network. Service providers sometimes use Multiprotocol Label Switching (MPLS) to extend the customer network into their network, creating virtual topologies within their network to accommodate the customer routing information and traffic. (Chapter 9, "Virtual Private Networks," covers this topic in some detail).

Figure 2-8   *Hiding Layers Within Layers*

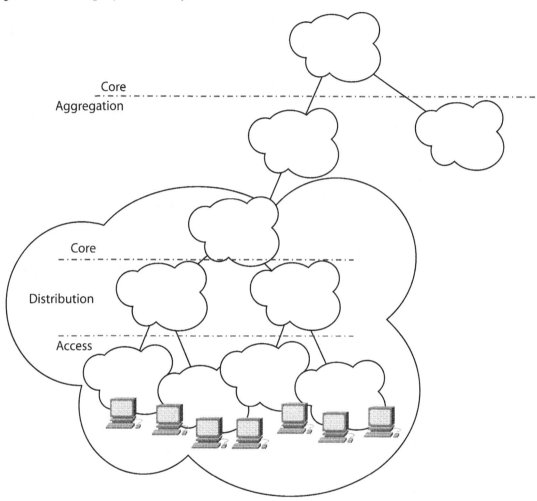

Creating Layers

In general, you should have the physical network design follow the topological network design as much as possible; this allows the topological boundaries to be clean, allowing summarization and functional separation. Network design largely consists of determining how to lay out the physical topology so that logical boundaries make sense. You need to consider two primary factors when laying out the physical topology of a network for hierarchical design:

- Creating choke points on which to place logical boundary points.
- Separation of complexity from complexity. Separate each complex topology design from other complex topologies by placing them in different zones or layers of the network.

Creating Choke Points

Just as the vertical layers in a network have separation points, called *application programming interfaces* or *sockets*, between them, zones within networks also need separation points between them. These separation points mark where the layers and zones meet, providing edges along which policy and aggregation occur. Although it is often tempting from a design perspective to create connections where it is cheap, close, or convenient, the stability of the network is more important in the long run. A failed network can cost you more than several years' worth of circuit costs. Figure 2-9 illustrates a network in which moving some links creates a choke point where none existed before.

Figure 2-9   *Moving Physical Layout to Create Choke Points*

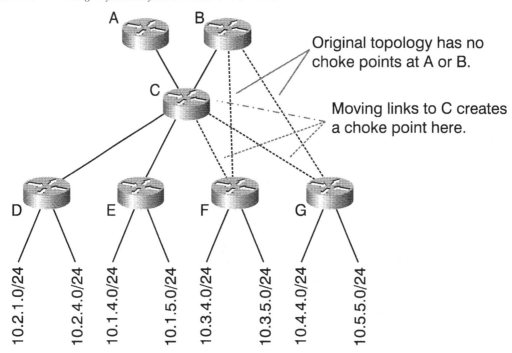

In this network, Routers F and G are connected to Router B, which does not allow a logical boundary at Routers A, B or C. Moving the links between Routers F and G to Router C allows a logical boundary to be created at Router C. When you move links to create choke points for logical boundaries, you need to balance network resiliency with good boundaries for clean separation.

Separating Complexity from Complexity

A general rule of thumb when designing the physical topology of a network is to separate complexity from complexity where possible. Figure 2-10 shows a complex Data Center design coupled with a large-scale hub-and-spoke network.

Figure 2-10   *Separating Complexity from Complexity*

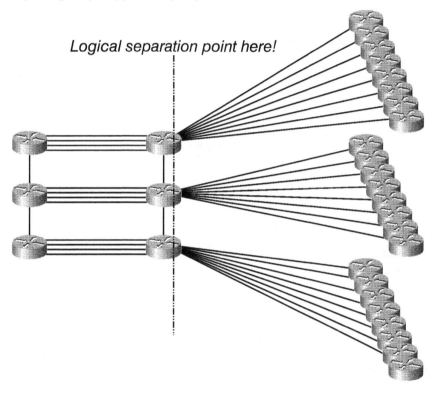

The Data Center has few routers with many parallel links between them, an environment where the primary servers in the company are attached. At one end of the Data Center are three routers acting as hub routers for a large-scale hub-and-spoke network. In this type of design, logically separating the Data Center from the large hub-and-spoke network is important. In fact, this design should be much better with another layer of routers between the Data Center and the hub-and-spoke routers to provide some cushion for policy implementation and logical separation.

Addressing and Summarization

To hide information effectively within a hierarchical network, you need the network IP addressing scheme to work with the edges where you would like to hide information, rather than against them. This seems simple when you look at addressing within a hierarchical design, but it is not so simple when you look at the real world of network deployment.

Assigning Addresses in a Network

Most networks are not addressed with summarization, or network hierarchy, in mind. In fact, many networks assign their IP address space based on other factors than the network design, as Figure 2-11 illustrates.

Figure 2-11   *Various Methods for Assigning IP Addresses in a Network*

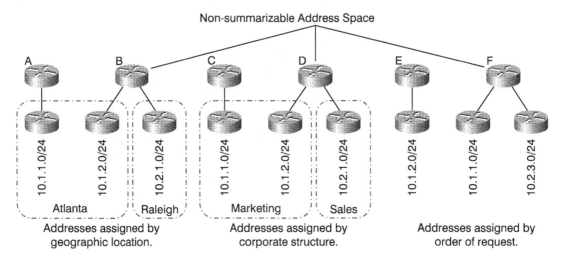

The different mechanisms illustrated include these:

- Assigning addresses based on the physical location of a host within the network might be used as the basis for assigning IP addresses. In the network illustrated, this leads to an unsummarizable range of addresses at Router B.

- Assigning addresses based on the divisions of the network. In the network illustrated, this leads to an unsummarizable range of addresses at Router D.

- Assigning addresses in the order that requests are received. In the network illustrated, this leads to an unsummarizable range of addresses at Router F.

The best way to assign IP addresses in a hierarchical network is to follow the topology of the network. Following are the main problems with assigning addresses based on the network topology:

- Hosts and servers need to be readdressed when they are moved from one topological area of the network to another. Topological moves can occur when a remote site attachment point is moved from one point of connection to another, for instance.

- IP addresses do not provide meaningful information other than the topological attachment point of the device in the network. You can resolve this by "stealing" bits out of a large IP address space and maintaining topologically based IP addressing.

An Example of Inserting Physical Location Data in Topological Addressing

This case study works through an example of how you could set aside bits to indicate the political or physical location of a device, while still maintaining the topological assignment of addresses. Figure 2-12 illustrates the concept.

Figure 2-12   *Stealing Bits for Geographic Information*

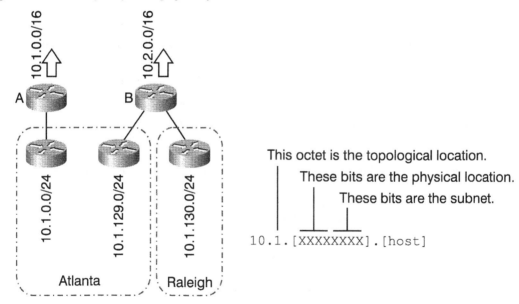

This octet is the topological location.
These bits are the physical location.
These bits are the subnet.

10.1.[XXXXXXXX].[host]

In this network, the second octet of the IP address indicates the topological location of the subnet, and the third octet is split between indicating the physical location and the subnet. You know that any address with the highest-order bit cleared in the third octet (10.x.0.x through 10.x.15.x) is in the Atlanta office, and anything with the highest-order bit set in the third octet (10.x.128.x through 10.x.143.x) is in the Raleigh office. As long as you make certain that the topological information is toward the left of the IP address (toward the higher-order bits, or the most significant digit), you can treat the location, physical or political, as if it were a sort of secondary subnet. This allows you to code this information into the IP address and still maintain summarization within the network.

A Quick Way of Working with IP Addresses: Addresses by the Octet

Working with IP addresses split at odd places is notoriously hard. Almost everyone who works with odd splits in IP addresses uses a chart of some type, usually in binary, to work out the addresses. Generally, network designers try to maintain a consistent IP address prefix length throughout a network, simply to make it easier to design, troubleshoot, and maintain. However, what if you work with many different networks regularly or you work in a network in which the prefix lengths vary considerably? You can calculate prefixes and prefix lengths in several ways; Figure 2-13 shows an effective and easy method using a simple chart.

Figure 2-13 *Simple Chart for Working with IP Addresses*

0	1	2	3	4	5	6	7	8
256	128	64	32	16	8	4	2	1

Following are three problems you probably solve regularly with IP addresses:

- Find the network address (prefix), host address, and broadcast address for a specific IP address.
- Find a set of subnet addresses for several sets of hosts given an address range.
- Find a summary that covers or includes several subnets.

Work through each of these problems using an example, starting with finding the network, host, and broadcast addresses for a specific IP address, 10.98.142.87/22. The first thing to do when using this technique is to figure out which octet you are working in. Although most people tend to think of an IP address as one large number, any given prefix length (or subnet mask) is actually going to impact just one of the four octets in the number. All the octets above the "working octet" will be part of the network address, and all the octets below the "working octet" will be part of the host address. To find the working octet, divide the prefix length by 8 and add 1, ignoring the remainder.

In this example, 22 / 8 is 2, so the first two octets of the IP address, 10.98, are part of the network address; the working octet is the third octet, 142; and the last octet, 87, is part of the host address. Now you are down to working with one number, 142. How many bits in this octet are part of the network, and how many are part of the host? Again, divide the prefix length by 8; the remainder is the number of bits within this octet that are part of the network. 22 / 8 is 2, with a remainder of 6, so 6 bits of the third octet are in the network, and 2 are in the host. Examining the chart, you find the number 64 below 2, so you take the number in the third octet and divide it by 64. The result, multiplied by the divisor (ignoring the remainder, or the decimal part of the division), is the network number: 142 / 64 = 2 * 64 = 128 is the network number. To find the host, subtract the number in the third octet from the network number, 142 − 128 = 14. To find the broadcast address, take the number found in the chart, subtract 1, and add it back to the network address. So, 64 − 1 = 63 + 128 = 191. Now you have the network address, host address, and broadcast address as a result of some simple long division (no decimal work at all) and multiplication.

Now consider the second problem: Given a number of hosts on some different subnets and a range of addresses, find a set of subnets that will provide each network with enough addresses for the hosts that are attached to it. This problem does appear often in the real world, but rumors have been circulating about a test with this sort of problem on it, so …

Assume that you have subnets with 13, 9, 18, and 5 hosts, and you have an address block, 10.1.0.0/24. How can you go about dividing the address space so that each subnet has enough host addresses? First, you sort the list of hosts, placing the largest subnet first in the list, so that you have 18, 13, 9, and 5. Then examine the chart in Figure 2-13 and find the smallest number that is at least 2 larger than the largest subnet. The largest number of hosts is 18, so you need to find the smallest number larger than 20 in the chart, which is 32. 32 is opposite the 3 in the upper row. Add the number in the upper row to the prefix length of the block you started with, and make this the first subnet. Therefore, the first subnet is 10.1.0.0/27. The starting address is 10.1.0.0, and the next subnet starts at 10.1.1.0 + 32, which is 10.1.0.32.

The next subnet has 13 hosts, so you need to find the smallest number larger than 15, which is 16. 16 is opposite 4 on the chart. Add 4 to the prefix length of the block you were given to find the prefix length for this subnet, and use the starting address found when calculating the previous block. The next block is 10.1.0.32/28, which covers the next 16 addresses, up to the broadcast address of 10.1.0.47. The next subnet will start at 10.1.0.48. The next subnet has 9 hosts, and again you find the smallest number larger than 11, which is 16. The next subnet is 10.1.0.48/28, with a broadcast of 10.1.0.63. The final subnet has 5 hosts; the largest number in the chart larger than 7 is 8, which is opposite the 5 in the upper row of the chart. The last subnet is 10.1.0.64/29.

The final problem is to find a summary address covering or containing several subnet addresses. This is the most complex problem to solve. Suppose that you have the subnet addresses 10.1.57.0/24, 10.1.59.0/24, and 10.1.61.0/24. What is the longest prefix length summary that you can use to contain all three of these addresses? Start by making certain the addresses are sorted from the lowest address (closest to 0.0.0.0) to the highest address. Then examine the addresses to determine what octet is changing. It is the third octet in this case. You need to find the bottom of the summary range and the prefix length of the summary, based on the changing octet.

Take the lowest number from the changing octet—here, it is 57—and either use the number directly or subtract one (if it is odd). Subtract 1 to start with 56 in this example. Next, subtract the highest number from the lowest; here, you have 61 − 56 = 5. Now, on the chart, find the lowest number higher than the result; in this case, you find 8. Divide the number from the chart into the lowest number, discard the remainder, and then multiply it back. 56 / 8 = 7 * 8 = 56, so you stick with 56. The third octet of the summary address needs to be 56.

Now subtract the remainder from the origin division, 56 / 8 = 7 with a remainder of 3, so 24 − 3 = 21. This is the prefix length of the summary. Combining the lowest network address with the third octet of the summary address calculated previously and the prefix length just calculated, you find that a summary address of 10.1.56.0/21 is the longest prefix summary containing all three of the networks given.

Working Around Addressing

While the IP addresses in every network in the world should be assigned based on good, sound, network design principles, you have probably seen enough real networks to know this isn't always true. This section covers techniques you can use to work around problems in your network address structure, summarizing as much as possible.

NOTE   The first two techniques, leaking more specifics and using smaller summary blocks, rely on the longest prefix always matching a packet as it is being forwarded by a router. As an example, assume that a router has three routes in its routing table:

10.1.1.0/24 via serial 0/0

10.1.0.0/22 via serial 0/1

10.1.0.0/16 via serial 0/2

If the router receives a packet that is destined to 10.1.1.1, it forwards the packet along the route to 10.1.1.0/24 because it is the longest matching prefix in its routing table. Although the other routes also contain the destination, they have a shorter prefix than the 10.1.1.0/24 route.

Leaking More Specifics

Examining the IP addresses assigned to the networks in Figure 2-14, it does not appear that you can do much to summarize anything from Routers B or C toward Router A.

Figure 2-14   *Example of Leaking More Specific Routes*

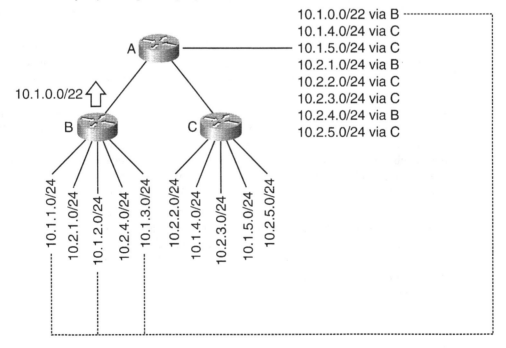

However, if you examine the table more closely at Router A, you will find that you can configure a summary for 10.1.0.0/22 on Router B, and Router A will learn 10.1.0.0/22 through Router B in addition to two routes within the summary range, 10.1.4.0/24 and 10.1.5.0/24, through Router C. Because Router A will always choose the most specific prefix within its local routing table to forward traffic, any packets that have destinations within 10.1.4.0/24 and 10.1.5.0/24 will be routed correctly toward Router C. The remainder of the packets that have addresses within 10.1.0.0/22 will be routed toward Router B. Allowing Router C to advertise longer prefixes within the summary that Router B is advertising maintains correct routing in all cases, so you can configure this summary on Router B and reduce the amount of information that Router A is receiving.

Can you do the same thing on Router C, configuring a summary overlapping with some of the addresses that Router B has configured but allowing Router B to advertise the more specific prefix so that packets are still routed to the right destination? Examine Figure 2-15 for the answer.

Figure 2-15   *Another Example of Leaking More Specific Routes*

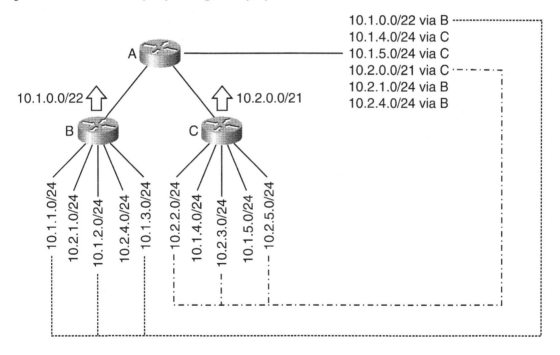

After you have configured this summary on Router C, all the packets that are destined to 10.2.1.0/24 and 10.2.4.0/24 are forwarded to Router B, and packets that are destined to any other address within 10.2.0.0/21 are forwarded to Router C. Because Router A always chooses the longest prefix match for the packet's destination, routing always forwards the packet to the correct destination.

Leaking more specifics past a point of summarization or summarizing and then allowing the exceptions to the summary to leak through is an effective way to summarize even when the address spaces that are assigned are not perfect for summarization.

Smaller Summary Blocks

Take this concept of leaking more specific routes beyond a summary point one step further and use summaries of different prefix lengths to maintain correct routing, while continuing to reduce the amount of routing information in the routing table. Look at Figure 2-16 for an example of how this works using smaller summary blocks.

Figure 2-16   *Using Mixed Prefix Length (Smaller) Summaries*

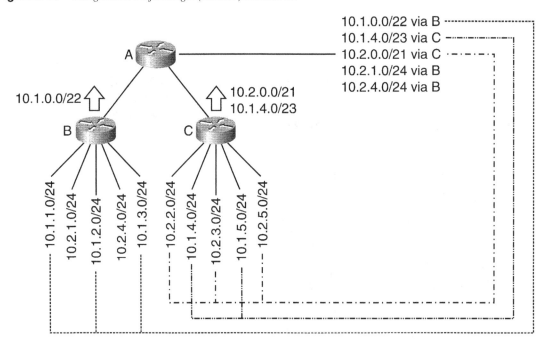

If you examine the Router A's routing table closely, you will find one more pair of summarizable routes. You can configure Router C to advertise 10.1.4.0/23, which contains 10.1.4.0/24 and 10.1.5.0/24. All the packets that are received at Router A are still forwarded to the correct destination at Routers B and C.

Although this technique of relying on longer prefix matches in the routing table, configuring varying length summaries, and leaking more specifics through summary points can be difficult to configure and manage, it is often worth the effort in terms of network convergence speed and stability. These types of techniques should be considered in large networks with some small address misalignments or where you have no other option for summarizing addresses.

Change the Logical Layout

It is sometimes possible to change the logical layout of the network by shifting the routing zone boundaries from a point where summarization cannot be used to a point where summarization is possible. Figure 2-17 illustrates a network in which shifting the logical boundary from one point to another allows summarization to be used.

Figure 2-17   *Shifting Logical Boundaries for Summarization*

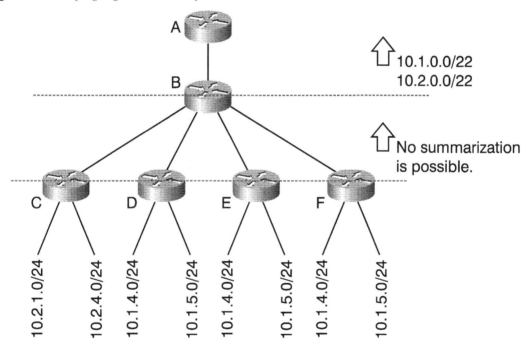

If you place the logical boundary at Routers C, D, E, and F, no summarization is possible in the network. On the other hand, shifting the logical boundary to Router B allows you to create two summaries covering all the address space.

Summary Issues

Network designers face three primary issues when summarizing routes:

- Summary black holes
- Suboptimal routing
- Managing summary metrics

The sections that follow address each of these problems in more detail.

Summarization Black Holes

Summarization black holes occur because of a bad combination of summarization and network design. Figure 2-18 illustrates a summarization black hole.

Figure 2-18   *Summarization Black Hole*

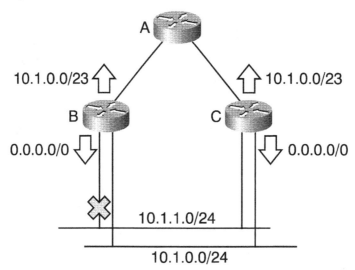

Both Routers B and C are connected to two segments: one with the address 10.1.0.0/24, and the other with the address 10.1.1.0/24. The routers are advertising just along these segments, and both of them are a summary, 10.1.0.0/23, toward Router A.

Assume Router A chooses the path through Router B as the best path to 10.1.1.0/24, and installs this route in its routing table. After the network has converged, the link connecting Router B to 10.1.1.0/24 fails. Although Router B has lost one component of the 10.1.0.0/23 summary it is advertising, it still has another component, 10.1.0.0/24, so Router B will continue advertising the summary route. Even though the link from Router B to 10.1.1.0/24 has failed, Router A still believes Router B can reach anything within 10.1.0.0/23, including 10.1.1.0/24.

Router A, then, continues forwarding packets destined to hosts in 10.1.1.0/24 via Router B. Because Router B no longer has a route to this destination, it drops the packets. Although a valid route is still available to 10.1.1.0/24, packets that are destined to hosts on the 10.1.1.0/24 segment are being dropped.

How can you resolve this? From the network design point of view, you have only one option: making certain that a link of some type exists between Routers B and C carrying full routing information between them. In other words, Routers B and C should exchange full routing information with at least one of the links that connects them (or through a tunnel connecting them, keeping in mind the various scaling problems associated with tunnels). It is probably a good idea for the routers to carry full routing information across more than one link, because a single link failure can still cause a routing black hole in this situation.

NOTE   At press time, efforts are underway to resolve this problem at the protocol level in EIGRP, OSPF, and BGP.

Summary Suboptimal Routing

Another common issue with summaries is suboptimal routing caused by the information hidden in the summary. Figure 2-19 shows a network where this happens.

Figure 2-19   *Summary Suboptimal Routing*

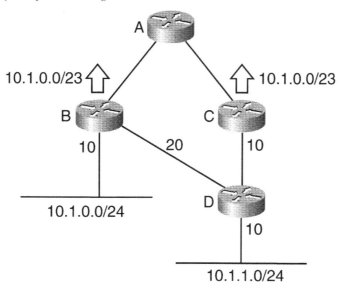

Router B has two components of the 10.1.0.0/23 summary in its local routing table:

- 10.1.0.0/24 with a cost of 10
- 10.1.1.0/24 with a cost of 30

Router C also has two components of the 10.1.0.0/23 summary in its local routing table:

- 10.1.0.0/24 with a cost of 40
- 10.1.1.0/24 with a cost of 20

Suppose that you choose to use the metric from the lowest cost component when building the summary metrics at Routers B and C. What will the impact be? Router B advertises the 10.1.0.0/23 summary with a metric of 10, whereas Router C advertises the summary with a metric of 20. Router A chooses the path through Router B, which is optimal for the 10.1.0.0/24 network but suboptimal for the 10.1.1.0/24 network.

You can reverse the result by having the routing protocol choose the metric of the highest component as the summary metric; now both Routers B and C advertise the summary with a cost of 30. Router A load shares between the two summary routes it is learning. If Router A chooses to send packets destined to 10.1.1.1 to Router B, the traffic follows the suboptimal path. Likewise, if Router A chooses to send traffic destined to 10.1.0.1 via Router C, the traffic follows a suboptimal path.

What can you do to resolve this situation? You can elect *not* to summarize, but not summarizing is bad for the overall health of the network. One option is to put a high-speed link between Routers B and C and pass full routing information across this link. Rather than routing suboptimally within the zone, then, Routers B and C pass traffic that is entering the zone suboptimally between them, routing the traffic optimally within the zone.

Finally, you can simply design the network behind Routers B and C with this problem in mind, attempting to provide relatively equal access to both of the routers that are summarizing toward the core of the network.

Summary Metrics

One of the primary reasons to summarize routing information at logical boundary points in the network is to hide information, particularly information about changes in topology, as shown in Figure 2-20.

Figure 2-20   *Impact of Metrics on Information Hiding Through Summaries*

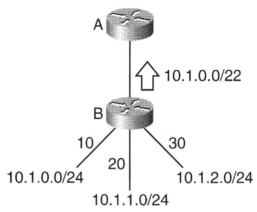

At Router B, three components of the summary route are advertised to Router A in the local routing table:

- 10.1.0.0/24 with a cost of 10
- 10.1.1.0/24 with a cost of 20
- 10.1.2.0/24 with a cost of 30

Assume that the routing protocol is designed so it always pulls the metric of the lowest cost component within the summary to use as the summary metric. In this case, Router B advertises 10.1.0.0/22 toward Router A with a cost of 10. Suppose that the link from Router B to 10.1.0.0/24 fails; the only remaining components within the summary are 10.1.1.0/24 and 10.1.2.0/24, with the lowest cost being 20. Router B replaces its previous route to 10.1.0.0/22, metric 10, with a new route to 10.1.0.0/22, metric 20. In reality, you have hidden the individual networks from Router A, but a network failure behind Router B still causes Router A to rebuild its routing information. The summary is less than effective at hiding information.

To resolve this, you need to make the summary metric constant, regardless of what the metrics of the component routes within the summary are. You can accomplish this in at least two ways:

- Create a component to control, or set, the summary metric regardless of what other components are available. For instance, creating a loopback interface on Router B, with a metric fixed so that it is always the lowest-cost component within the 10.1.0.0/22 summary, forces the summary metric to remain the same despite what happened behind Router B.

- Manually set the summary metric through configuration commands. For instance, many routing protocols allow the summary metric to be set when the summary is configured or through a route map or other policy-based mechanism as the summary is advertised by Router B.

Of the two solutions available, creating a component to control the summary metric tends to be the easiest to configure and manage. You should be careful with a loopback address on the summarizing router, however, because the router might lose all other connectivity to the networks behind it and still advertise the summary. That is because a local interface exists with an address within the summary range.

Redistribution

The following are reasons for redistributing routing data into an interior gateway protocol:

- Connecting to outside resources, such as an extranet or the Internet.

- Merging two corporate networks after a corporate merger.

- Connecting through a network running a different routing protocol than the internal network uses. This might happen when an outside service that is providing only one routing protocol option is used to provide interconnections between sites — and the routing protocol option provided is different from the routing protocol that is used internally.

IGP-to-IGP redistribution is probably one of the most difficult areas of a network to plan and execute correctly in a network design. In fact, redistribution is not normally planned; rather, it is something imposed on the network through a corporate merger, outsourcing, or another unplanned event into the original network design. This section first covers alternatives to redistribution between routing protocols. Then it covers single and multiple points of redistribution.

Alternatives to IGP to IGP Redistribution

In many situations, you can avoid redistribution between two IGPs by using static routes at the edge of your network. Generally, when you connect to an outside resource, such as a corporate partner or a customer for access to specific resources, it is better either to use BGP to carry the external routes required or to use a static route redistributed into your IGP than to redistribute from IGP to IGP. Figure 2-21 illustrates both of these options.

Figure 2-21   *Using BGP or Static Routes Rather Than IGP Redistribution*

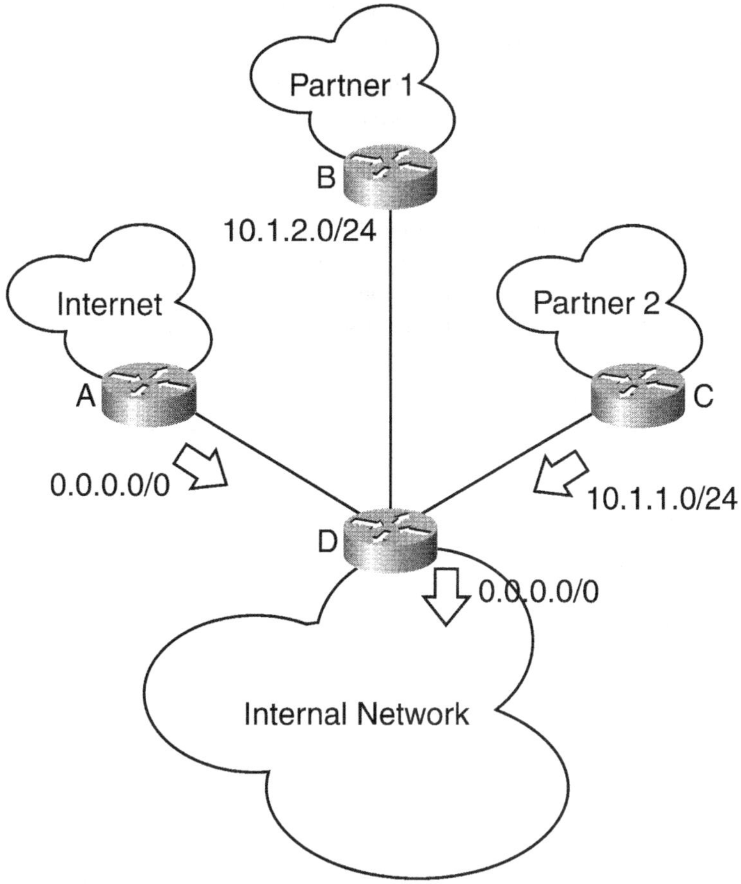

Three external networks are connected to one peering router in this network.

NOTE   It is probable that not all the external connection points in a network are connected to one router. However, other than connections to the Internet, the connection points should be contained within a small number of well-defined connection points, if possible. Reducing external connection points promotes routing control and policy execution, which are important when considering the security of the network routing system. Chapter 8, "Routing Protocols Security," covers this in more detail.

Assume that the Internet service provider (ISP) is sending a default route (0.0.0.0/0), Partner 1 is sending no routes, and Partner 2 is sending a route to 10.1.1.0/24. How would you configure Router D to avoid IGP-to-IGP redistribution?

Make certain that Partner 2 is not sending its routing information through an IGP; instead, set up a pair of private BGP autonomous systems and exchange the route over this BGP session.

For Partner 1, you can configure a local static route. If this is the only exit point from the network, you do not need to redistribute this route into the interior gateway protocol. Instead, you can rely on the default route getting all the external traffic into this external peering router, and then use locally configured routing information to direct the traffic along the correct external link. If you need this external routing information to be injected into the internal network, redistribute a locally configured static into the internal protocol. Example 2-1 illustrates what the Router D configuration can look like.

Example 2-1   *Router D Configuration*

```
!
hostname router-d
!
ip route 10.1.1.0 255.255.255.0 <router-b>
!
router eigrp 100
 ....
 ! only put in this redistribution if we need the routes to router-b
 ! in the local routing table
 redistribute static
 default-metric 10000 1 255 1 1500
!
router bgp 65000
 neighbor x.x.x.x <router-a>
 neighbor y.y.y.y <router-c>
```

NOTE   Chapter 8 spends some time on the filters you should configure.

Single Point of Redistribution

A single point of redistribution is easy to control and manage. It is unlikely that a routing loop will occur between two routing domains when only one point of redistribution is configured. Figure 2-22 illustrates a single point of redistribution, and Example 2-2 presents a sample configuration.

Figure 2-22   *Single Point of Redistribution*

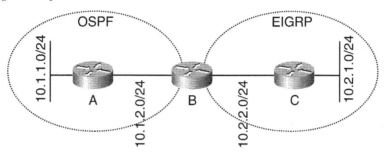

Example 2-2   *Possible Configuration for Network in Figure 2-22*

```
!
hostname router-a
!
router ospf 100
 network 10.1.0.0 0.0.255.255 area 0
```
```
!
hostname router-b
!
router ospf 100
 network 10.1.0.0 0.0.255.255 area 0
 redistribute eigrp 100 metric 10 subnets
!
router eigrp 100
 network 10.2.0.0 0.0.255.255
 redistribute ospf 100 metric 10000 1 255 1 1500
```
```
!
hostname router-c
!
router eigrp 100
 network 10.2.0.0 0.0.255.255
```

Redistribution and Connected Routes

If you have an interface configured to run one routing protocol, and then configure a second
routing protocol, redistributing the first protocol into the second, will the second protocol
advertise the interface's network? Consider the following sample configuration to understand
the question.

```
!
interface serial 0/0
 ip address 10.1.1.1 255.255.255.0
!
router eigrp 100
 network 10.1.1.0 0.0.0.255
!
router ospf 100
 redistribute eigrp 100 metric 10 subnets
```

Will Open Shortest Path First (OSPF) redistribute 10.1.1.0/24 and other routes learned through Enhanced Interior Gateway Routing Protocol (EIGRP) process 100? It depends on the source and destination protocol. The chart in Table 2-1 shows which combinations will redistribute the connected route covered by a **network** statement in the source protocol and which ones will not.

Table 2-1   *Redistribution Possibilities*

		Destination		
		EIGRP	IS-IS	OSPF
Source	**EIGRP**		Yes	Yes
	IS-IS	No		No
	OSPF	Yes	Yes	

Essentially, any protocol will redistribute locally connected routes from EIGRP or OSPF, but no protocols will redistribute locally connected routes from IS-IS.

Multiple Points of Redistribution

Configuring a single point of redistribution is simple and straightforward, but it does create a single point of failure within the network. To resolve this, many network operators create two points of redistribution between the two areas of the network running different routing protocols (the two different routing domains); however, multiple points of redistribution bring their own set of problems to the network. Multiple points of redistribution are probably one of the most common causes of routing loops and network meltdowns, so you must configure them carefully. Figure 2-23 illustrates a network with multiple points of redistribution, showing how a permanent routing loop can occur if no precautions are taken.

Figure 2-23   *Permanent Routing Loop Using Multiple Points of Redistribution*

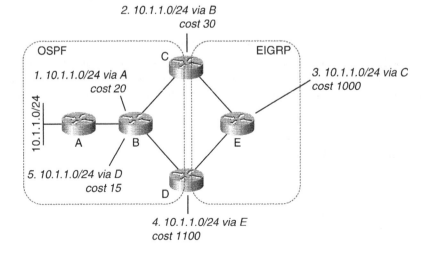

Following the steps outlined in the figure, the following occurs:

1 Router A advertises 10.1.1.0/24 through OSPF.

2 Router B receives this advertisement and chooses the route through Router A with a cost of 20.

3 Router C receives the route to 10.1.1.0/24 and prefers the route through Router B. Router C redistributes the route into EIGRP with a metric of 900.

4 Router D receives 10.1.1.0/24 as an EIGRP external and readvertises it to Router E.

5 Router E receives the route to 10.1.1.0/24 and prefers this external. Router E redistributes this route into OSPF with a cost of 5.

6 Router C receives the route from Router E and prefers the route with a cost of 5 over the route with a cost of 20 through Router A.

At this point, you have a permanent routing loop in this network. To solve this problem, you need to ensure that any routes redistributed from OSPF into EIGRP are not redistributed back into OSPF at some other point in the network, and any routes redistributed into OSPF from EIGRP are not redistributed back into EIGRP. Two techniques are normally recommended for preventing routes that are redistributed at one of two mutual redistribution points from being redistributed back into the originating protocol at the other redistribution point:

• Filters

• Route tags

Filters

Filters are the traditional mechanism that blocks redistributed routes from being redistributed back into the originating protocol. Figure 2-24 shows the same network, with filters applied at Routers C and E to prevent the routing loop.

Figure 2-24 *Filtering Routes to Prevent a Routing Loop*

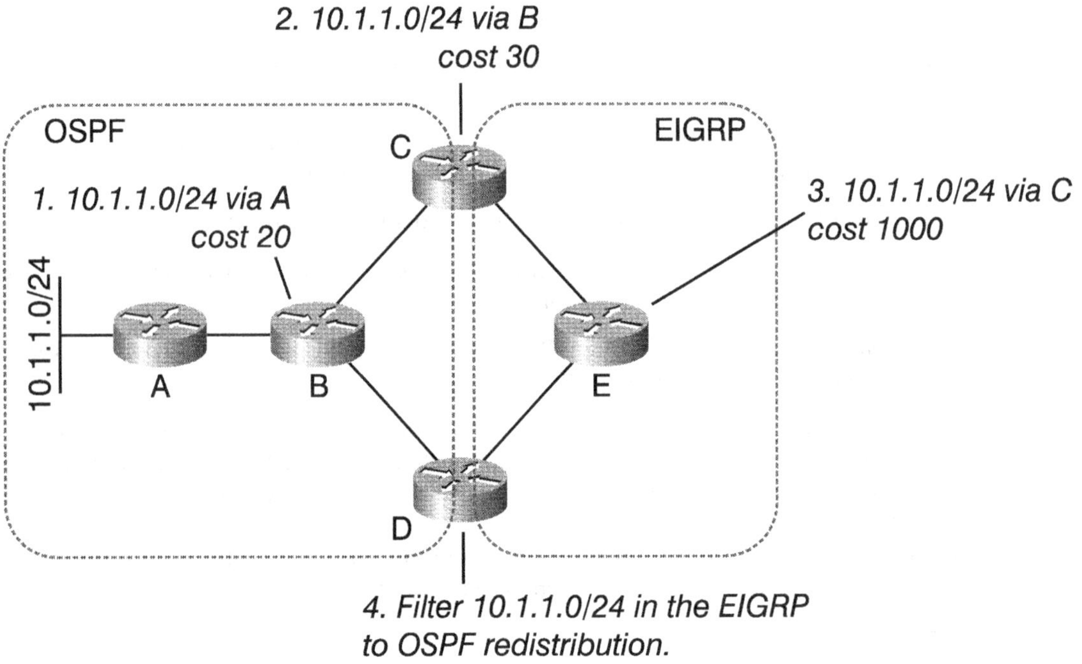

2. *10.1.1.0/24 via B*
cost 30

OSPF

EIGRP

C

1. *10.1.1.0/24 via A*
cost 20

3. *10.1.1.0/24 via C*
cost 1000

10.1.1.0/24

A   B   E

D

4. *Filter 10.1.1.0/24 in the EIGRP*
to OSPF redistribution.

Again, following the steps shown in the figure, the process works as detailed next:

1   Router A advertises 10.1.1.0/24.

2   Router B prefers the route through Router A to reach 10.1.1.0/24.

3   Router C prefers the route through Router B to reach 10.1.1.0/24 and redistributes this route into EIGRP.

4   Router D receives this route and prefers the route through Router C to 10.1.1.0/24.

5   Router E receives the Router D advertisement. It still prefers the route through Router D, but a filter has been placed on the redistribution between EIGRP and OSPF to prevent the route from being redistributed back into OSPF.

This final step inhibits the routing loop from forming, by preventing Router B from receiving the 10.1.1.0/24 advertisement from Router E. What types of filters can you use on Router E to block the readvertisement of 10.1.1.0/24 toward Router B? An access list that you apply as a route map or a distribution list between the routing processes is the most common option, as demonstrated in Example 2-3.

Example 2-3   *Using an Access List to Block the Readvertisement of 10.1.1.0/24 Toward Router B*

```
!
hostname router-e
!
access-list 10 deny 10.1.1.0 0.0.0.255
access-list 10 permit any
!
route-map block-loop permit 10
 match ip address 10
!
router ospf 100
 ....
 redistribute eigrp 100 route-map block-loop
```

You can also use a prefix list to filter a list of routes that should not be redistributed for some protocols.

The primary problem with using any type of hand-built list to block routing loops is that the list also has to be hand maintained. It is better to use some automatic mechanism to block this sort of routing loop, if possible.

Tags

The easiest and simplest automatic mechanism to block routing loops with advanced interior gateway protocols is to tag the routes as they are redistributed into the routing protocol. Figure 2-25 illustrates the use of tags in a more complex redistribution scenario.

Figure 2-25   *Using Tags to Block Routing Loops*

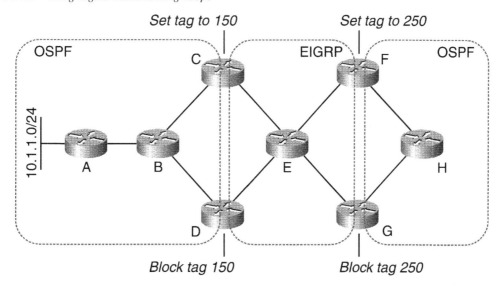

Follow the single route, 10.1.1.0/24, through the network in one direction. Sample configurations follow:

- Router A advertises 10.1.1.0/24.

- Router C receives the advertisement for 10.1.1.0/24 and redistributes it into EIGRP. As it redistributes the route, it marks the route with a tag of 150.

- Router D receives the redistributed advertisement for 10.1.1.0/24, tagged with 150. Router D is configured not to redistribute routes with a tag of 150, so it does not redistribute the route back into OSPF, preventing the potential routing loop.

- Router F receives the routing advertisement for 10.1.1.0/24, tagged 150. Router F has no filters for this tag, so it redistributes the route into OSPF and tags the route with 250.

- Router G receives the redistributed route from Router F, tagged 250. Router G has a filter to block routes that are tagged 250, so it blocks this update, preventing the second possible routing loop.

You can use routing tags in creative ways to prevent routing loops in almost any redistribution scenario. You still need to be careful with tags, however; if someone redistributes a route without its being tagged, a permanent routing loop could form in the network.

Example 2-4 shows the configuration on Routers C and D.

Example 2-4   *Using Routing Tags: Router C and Router D Configuration*

```
!
route-map filter-tags deny 10
 match tag 150
route-map filter-tag permit 10
 Set tag 150
!
router ospf 100
 ....
 Redistribute eigrp 100 route-map filter-tags metric 10 subnets
!
router eigrp 100
 ....
 Redistribute ospf 100 route-map filter-tags metric 10000 1 255 1 1500
```

Example 2-5 shows the configuration on Routers F and G.

Example 2-5   *Using Routing Tags: Router F and Router G Configuration*

```
!
route-map filter-tags deny 10
 match tag 250
route-map filter-tag permit 10
 Set tag 250
!
router ospf 100
 ....
 Redistribute eigrp 100 route-map filter-tags metric 10 subnets
!
```

Example 2-5   *Using Routing Tags: Router F and Router G Configuration (Continued)*

```
router eigrp 100
 ....
 Redistribute ospf 100 route-map filter-tags metric 10000 1 255 1 1500
```

NOTE   When you are using tags, matching the route map names and tag numbers with the area numbers, process numbers, or other indicators of topological areas in the network is useful and more intuitive to work with than not matching the names and numbers. For instance, in the network illustrated in Figure 2-25, it might be helpful to have the route map named **filter-tags-100** and set the tags to 100, rather than 150. If the network is as small as the network illustrated in Figure 2-25, it might not matter too much, but if fairly complex redistribution schemes are in use in your network, naming things consistently and in reference to each other can make determining what the configuration is supposed to do at some future point much easier.

Review Questions

 1 What is one of the key concepts required to build a large-scale network?

 2 What four types of traffic are you concerned with when considering hierarchical network layers? Why is it important to plan interzone and interlayer connectivity carefully in a network?

 3 What is the general rule of thumb in communications networks for traffic that is destined to local and remote destinations? Is this rule always true?

 4 What is the point of traffic aggregation in a network design?

 5 What is meant by routing policy? What types of policy are included in this concept?

 6 What are the primary functions of each layer in a two-layer hierarchy?

 7 What are the primary functions of each layer in a three-layer hierarchy?

 8 What are the primary considerations when deciding how many layers a network should have?

 9 Explain the concept of hiding layers within layers.

 10 What is the best method for assigning IP addresses within a hierarchical network?

 11 What are some techniques you can use to work around poor addressing schemes or misplaced addresses?

 12 Why does a summarization black hole occur, and how can you solve it?

 13 What are the alternatives to IGP-to-IGP redistribution?

 14 What two techniques can help you overcome possible permanent routing loops when using multiple points of redistribution?

PART II

Interior Gateway Protocols

CHAPTER 3

EIGRP Network Design

The previous two chapters described many of the important network design techniques used to meet the design goals of high resiliency, manageability, and scalability. Now it is time to put these techniques into practice using the Cisco advanced distance vector routing protocol, Enhanced Interior Gateway Routing Protocol (EIGRP). These techniques will be applied to the networks shown in Figure 3-1.

For more information on how EIGRP functions, refer to Appendix A, "EIGRP for IP Basics of Operation." EIGRP has numerous advantages over its link-state routing protocol counterparts, but it also has limitations and behaviors that a network designer must understand to successfully implement a scalable EIGRP network. This chapter describes some of these behaviors and provides techniques that network designers can use to improve the performance and scalability of EIGRP networks.

This chapter helps you to do the following for both two-layer and three-layer hierarchical networks:

- Analyze summarization at each layer of the EIGRP network.

- Analyze the use of the stub feature for access routers.

- Analyze the best way to deal with external connections, common services, and dial-in clients.

- Explore case studies on summarization methods, query propagation, excessive redundancy, troubleshooting common problems, and redistribution issues.

Deploying EIGRP on a Large-Scale Three-Layer Hierarchical Network

Many networks have been built around the core, distribution, and access layer model, because it provides a well-defined separation of functions into the various portions of the network. It also provides an excellent topology to apply scalability improvement techniques such as summarization.

Using the network described in Figure 3-1, this section describes how you can implement the information hiding technique of summarization at each of the three layers: core, distribution, and access.

Figure 3-1 *Large-Scale Three-Layer Hierarchical Network*

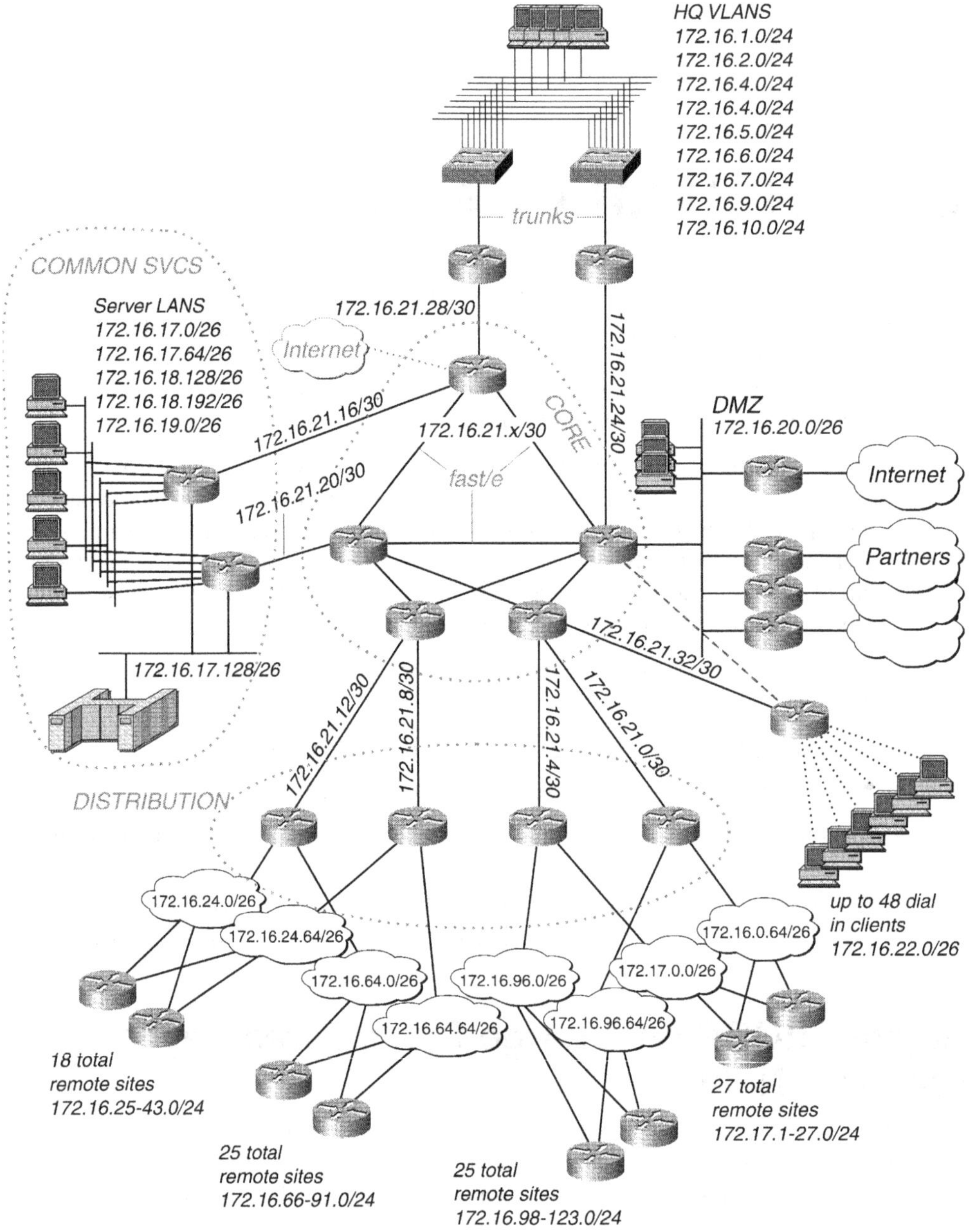

HQ VLANS
172.16.1.0/24
172.16.2.0/24
172.16.4.0/24
172.16.4.0/24
172.16.5.0/24
172.16.6.0/24
172.16.7.0/24
172.16.9.0/24
172.16.10.0/24

trunks

172.16.21.24/30

COMMON SVCS

Server LANS
172.16.17.0/26
172.16.17.64/26
172.16.18.128/26
172.16.18.192/26
172.16.19.0/26

172.16.21.28/30

Internet

172.16.21.16/30

172.16.21.x/30

CORE

DMZ
172.16.20.0/26

Internet

172.16.21.20/30

fast/e

Partners

172.16.17.128/26

172.16.21.32/30

172.16.21.12/30

172.16.21.8/30

172.16.21.4/30

172.16.21.0/30

DISTRIBUTION

up to 48 dial in clients
172.16.22.0/26

172.16.24.0/26

172.16.24.64/26

172.16.0.64/26

172.16.64.0/26

172.16.96.0/26

172.17.0.0/26

172.16.64.64/26

172.16.96.64/26

18 total
remote sites
172.16.25-43.0/24

27 total
remote sites
172.17.1-27.0/24

25 total
remote sites
172.16.66-91.0/24

25 total
remote sites
172.16.98-123.0/24

Analyzing the Network Core for Summarization

The network core in EIGRP has the same requirements as those presented in Chapter 2, "Applying the Fundamentals." Adequate redundancy and bandwidth must be provided in the core to ensure rapid, reliable delivery of packets presented to it from the distribution layer and destined to common resources or other distribution layer routers. The core should present as little impediment to the delivery of packets as geographic distances and budgets allow. Network designs are much more scalable if it does not matter where a packet enters the core from the distribution layer. The core should appear to be a high-bandwidth service that the distribution layer uses to reach common resources and other distribution layer routers.

If the network has been designed well, including addressing, the edge of the network core will be an ideal place to summarize. The sections that follow discuss the best ways to summarize at the network core to provide maximum stability and resiliency. These methods include the following:

- Summarizing from the network core to the distribution layer
- Summarizing into the core at its edge

Summarizing from the Core to the Distribution Layer

The "Addressing and Summarization" section in Chapter 2 explained how stability and scalability are best when a network is implemented with good summarization. If your network core topology is robust enough to present a minimum of delay to transit packets and your IP addressing is well designed, you are free to summarize to the fullest from the core to the distribution layer.

In the example network shown in Figure 3-1, you can perform maximum summarization because the network core has adequate bandwidth and redundancy. You can put summarization statements on the serial links that connect the core to the distribution layer, either presenting only the two major network routes (172.16.0.0/16 and 172.17.0.0/16) or just the default route (0.0.0.0/0) to the distribution layer, as shown in Figure 3-2. Refer to the "Summarization Methods" case study later in this chapter for an examination of the various summarization techniques available in an EIGRP network.

Figure 3-2   *Summarizing Outbound from the Core*

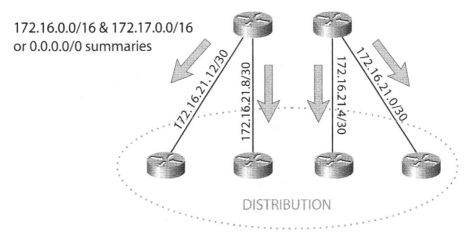

172.16.0.0/16 & 172.17.0.0/16
or 0.0.0.0/0 summaries

172.16.21.12/30

172.16.21.8/30

172.16.21.4/30

172.16.21.0/30

DISTRIBUTION

Minimizing the updates sent to the distribution layer routers from the core greatly reduces the query range and simplifies the process of bringing up neighbors across these critical links in the network. Refer to the later case study, "Controlling Query Propagation," for details on how important it is to limit the reach of queries in an EIGRP network.

If the destination subnet is closer in the topology to one core router than another, the shortest path from the distribution layer router to the target network might not be the one taken. (The traffic might take a suboptimal route.) If the network core presents minimal delay to traffic, the addition of an extra hop will not be significant when compared to increased stability.

Summarizing into the Core at Its Edge

Summarizing into the core at its edge is only useful if the distribution layer routers along the edge of the core are not also summarizing towards the core. As Figure 3-3 illustrates, the core routers could summarize toward the other core routers so that each core router has full component knowledge of the subnets inside of the regions to which it is connected but only summary knowledge of the other regions.

Figure 3-3   *Summarization into the Core from Its Edge*

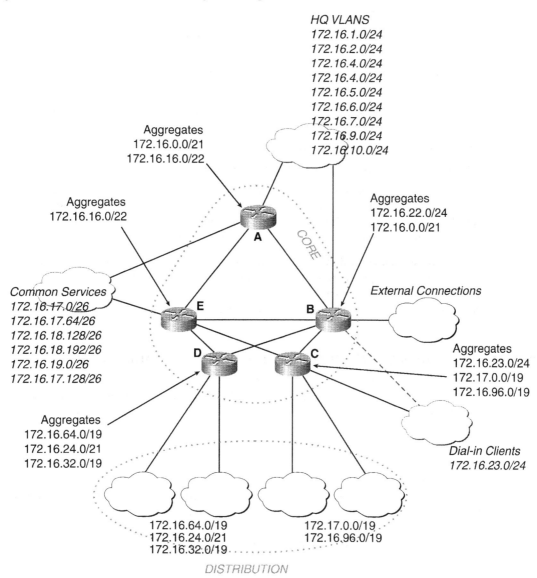

HQ VLANS
172.16.1.0/24
172.16.2.0/24
172.16.4.0/24
172.16.4.0/24
172.16.5.0/24
172.16.6.0/24
172.16.7.0/24
172.16.9.0/24
172.16.10.0/24

Aggregates
172.16.0.0/21
172.16.16.0/22

Aggregates
172.16.16.0/22

Aggregates
172.16.22.0/24
172.16.0.0/21

Common Services
172.16.17.0/26
172.16.17.64/26
172.16.18.128/26
172.16.18.192/26
172.16.19.0/26
172.16.17.128/26

External Connections

Aggregates
172.16.23.0/24
172.17.0.0/19
172.16.96.0/19

Aggregates
172.16.64.0/19
172.16.24.0/21
172.16.32.0/19

Dial-in Clients
172.16.23.0/24

172.16.64.0/19
172.16.24.0/21
172.16.32.0/19

172.17.0.0/19
172.16.96.0/19

DISTRIBUTION

The following list describes the routing advertisements resulting from the topology and configurations in Figure 3-3:

- Router A advertises 172.16.0.0/21 for the HQ VLANs and 172.16.16.0/22 for the common services out toward the other core routers.

- Router B advertises 172.16.22.0/24 for the external connections and 172.16.0.0/21 for the HQ VLANs toward the other core routers.

- Router C advertises 172.16.23.0/24 for the dial-in users, 172.17.0.0/19 for remote sites, and 172.16.96.0/19 for remote sites.

- Router D advertises 172.16.64.0/19, 172.16.24.0/21, and 172.16.32.0/19 for remote sites.

- Router E advertises 172.16.16.0/22 for the common services.

The advantage of this approach is that the core routers have full knowledge about all remote locations in their region and can choose the optimum route from the core router to the remote site. The disadvantage of this approach is that the core routers for each region are directly involved in the query path for any link failure inside of their region.

Should you summarize within the core of the network? Because this makes the configuration of the core more complicated and moves work from the distribution layer into the network core, you probably should not adopt this solution. In any case, you need to hold off on making a final decision until you have dealt with summarization in the distribution layer.

Analyzing the Network Distribution Layer for Summarization

The distribution layer goals in hierarchical networking are to summarize and aggregate traffic. The following sections on summarizing toward the network core and summarizing toward the remote sites give you a better idea of what you can do with summarization in the distribution layer.

Summarizing Toward the Network Core

You can apply summarization to the inbound links toward the core to limit their advertisements to one or more summary routes representing all the subnets that are reachable through a given distribution router. For example, in Figure 3-4, summarization is configured outbound on Router A and Router B on the serial links toward the core router.

Figure 3-4   *Summarization Between the Distribution Layer and Core*

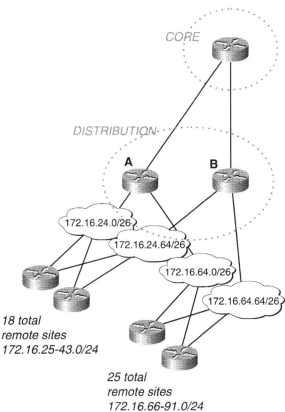

In this network, Routers A and B can advertise the following routes to the core:

* 172.16.64.0/19
* 172.16.24.0/21
* 172.16.32.0/19

However, one problem can occur with this summarization method unless proper steps are taken. If both Router A and Router B advertise summaries representing the same sets of remote networks into the core, you can create a *routing black hole* if one of the distribution routers loses access to one of the remotes. For example, even if Router A loses its connection to the remote site advertising 172.16.64.0/24, it will continue advertising the 172.16.64.0/19 summary route. In this case, all packets destined to hosts within 172.16.64.0/24 forwarded to Router A will be dropped.

This problem has two solutions. The first solution is to summarize at the edge of the core into the core rather than between the distribution and core routers, as covered in the previous section, "Summarizing into the Core at Its Edge." This solution defeats the goals of the distribution layer, however, and causes queries for networks in the branches to be propagated into the core.

A second solution is to have another reliable link connecting the distribution layer routers within a region. Routes that are advertised over this link will not be summarized, but both distribution layer routers will contain all of the components from each other. The link between the distribution layer routers should be robust enough to support both any remote-to-remote traffic and traffic passed between the two routers advertising summaries in the case of multiple remote site link failures. On most corporate networks, remote site to remote site traffic is negligible, but there are some situations where the traffic levels can be a major consideration, for instance, when voice over is running between the remote sites.

Another, similar solution is to configure a tunnel between the distribution layer routers and use this link as an alternative path in the event of a distribution-access link failure. This technique is often used if the cost or availability of robust links from distribution router to distribution router precludes the use of a physical link.

Obviously, the preferred solution to the summarization toward the network core problem is to have a relatively high-speed and reliable link connecting the distribution layer routers within a region, given that little remote-to-remote traffic will exist. Figure 3-5 illustrates the new design.

Figure 3-5   *Links Between Distribution Layer Routers*

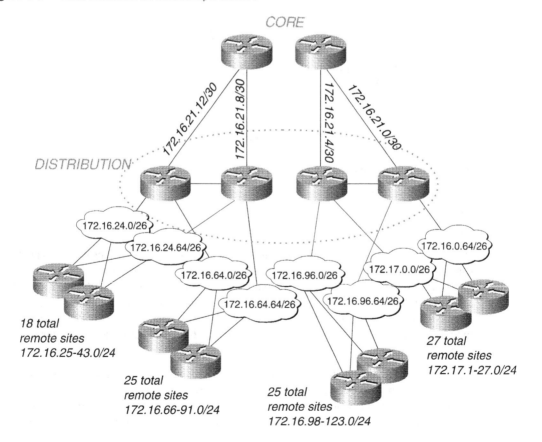

The first thing to note in Figure 3-5 is that no link exists between the two center distribution layer routers. A link here would cause too much route leakage between the distribution sublayers.

Summarizing Toward the Remote Sites

You should perform summarization on the interfaces outbound to the remote sites and toward the core. The purpose of this summarization is to limit the routing updates to the remote routers so that they contain only a default route or major net routes. Without the summarization, all the components in the region are sent to the remote sites. As explained later in this chapter in the case study "Troubleshooting Stuck-in-Active Routes," unnecessarily sending intraregion component routes to remotes causes the remote sites to be included in the query process, which is not good. The easiest way to create convergence problems in a large-scale EIGRP network is to do nothing about restricting the range of queries initiated when a route is marked active by a router. Each hop a query must take to resolve the reachability status of a specific destination increases the chances of a major convergence failure in your network.

In addition, if the routes are not summarized from the distribution routers to the remote routers, significantly more work and traffic are required to start up the distribution-to-remote neighbor relationship. Because smaller bandwidth links tend to be used between remote sites and the distribution layer, decreasing the EIGRP bandwidth requirements at startup is wise. You can use either a **summary-address** or a **distribute-list** statement to summarize routing information toward remote sites.

NOTE   For more information on how to implement the **summary-address** and **distribute-list** statements, refer to the "Summarization Methods" case study later in this chapter.

In the section "Summarizing into the Core at Its Edge," you discovered that summarization within the network core has some advantages, but it also adds undesirable complexity. Summarizing from the distribution layer into the core decreases the EIGRP query range while reducing complexity within the network. Therefore, it is better to summarize into the core instead of within the core.

After you have decided to summarize from the distribution layer into the core, summarization within the core is unnecessary. Because each distribution layer router is sending only summary information to the core, you should not have much to summarize at the core edge into the core.

Analyzing Routing in the Network Access Layer

Normally, you can classify access layer routers as single-homed or dual-homed. The sections that follow present each type along with alternative methods of supporting them.

Single-Homed Sites

Single-homed sites are those that have only a single path into the rest of the network; single-homed remote sites typically have few routes to advertise upstream. True single-homed sites do not have dial backup or any other additional path into the distribution layer. As such, true single-homed remote sites tend to be less common.

Generally, you can handle singled-homed remote sites in two obvious ways:

*   Running EIGRP out to them (allowing them to advertise their locally connected networks)
*   Not running EIGRP out to them

If EIGRP is running out to the remote router of the single-homed remote site, the remote router can advertise any reachable destinations using EIGRP. In this case, the question becomes this: What should the distribution layer router to which the single-homed remote is connected advertise to the remote site?

By definition, a single-homed remote site really does not have routing decisions to make. That is, if the address is not local, it must be reachable through the link to the distribution layer. For this reason, limiting the routes that are sent from the distribution layer to the remote to the minimum number possible is particularly appropriate. Believe it or not, the minimum can be one or even none.

You can either send a single default route from the distribution layer router to the single-homed remote site, or you can filter out all updates from the distribution layer router to the remote site and define a static default route in the remote site pointing back to the distribution layer router. The latter is more efficient. In this way, the routes from the remote site are learned dynamically for delivery of traffic to the remote site, but a static route is used for the traffic that is inbound from the remote site.

If you do not want to run EIGRP between single-homed remote routers and the distribution layer router, you can use static routes at both routers. Because EIGRP is not running between the remote and the distribution layer routers, the distribution layer router cannot learn dynamically about destinations that are reachable at the remote site.

To provide the rest of the network with information about destinations that are available at each single-homed remote site, you can configure static routes at the distribution layer router pointing to the appropriate access router for each remote network. This is ideal when links to the remote sites are not robust. Because EIGRP is not running over the link, it is not affected a great deal if the link often fails. Therefore, it cannot create problems for the remainder of the network because of Stuck-in-Actives (SIAs).

The disadvantages of this approach are the administrative overhead of defining a multitude of static routes and then maintaining them when the network topology changes. Typically, you should only use this approach if you are trying to eliminate problem links from the query and update path for EIGRP.

Dual-Homed Remotes

The second category of access layer routers, dual-homed remotes, is much more common than single-homed remotes. Some are permanent dual-homed remotes, like the remotes illustrated in Figure 3-1, with two or more low-speed connections to two different distribution routers from each remote site. Although the purpose of the two connections from the remote could be for load balancing, they are usually for redundancy. These important remote sites are connected in such a way that a Frame Relay permanent virtual circuit (PVC) failure or distribution layer router failure does not cause them to lose access to the core of the network.

Sites with a single permanent link combined with an on-demand backup link, such as a dial-up, ISDN dial-up, or on-demand switched virtual circuit, also need to be treated as if they are dual homed remotes. Even though such sites don't have two permanent connections into the network distribution or core layers, when the permanent link and the backup link are both in operation (which normally happens after a primarily link failure has been corrected, and the backup link has not yet been disconnected) the remote site will present all the same challenges as a dual homed remote.

Distribution layer routers that are attached to these dual-homed remotes see each of the remotes as an alternative path to reach elsewhere in the network. They appear to be transit paths or alternate paths through the network. For an example, look at Figure 3-6.

Figure 3-6   *Dual-Homed Remote as a Transit Path*

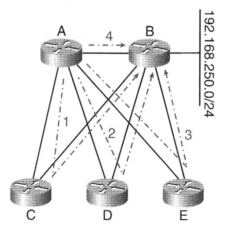

With a default EIGRP configuration that is running on all the routers shown in Figure 3-6, Router A sees four paths to the 192.168.250.0/24 network:

- Router C to Router B
- Router D to Router B
- Router E to Router B
- Through Router B

Router A would normally choose the route directly through Router B to reach 192.168.25.0/24, but if that route fails, Router A chooses between the remaining three routes or, possibly, load shares between them. This might be fine from a traffic standpoint; you can size the links to handle the load, and so forth.

From a network scaling perspective, however, this is more problematic. Router A sees each of these paths as a path through which it must query if the 198.162.250.0/24 network fails, and it holds each of these paths in its topology table, consequently wasting memory.

Summarizing outbound from the distribution layer, as discussed in the section "Summarizing Toward the Remote Sites," effectively limits the number of paths Router A sees to reach the 192.168.250.0/24 network. Because the remote routers will not have routes to this specific network through Router B, they cannot advertise it back to Router A.

This fact is important in the EIGRP network and most common EIGRP network designs because so many remotes are dual-homed. Summarizing to the greatest possible extent from the distribution layer into these remote site routers is important. Configure the distribution layer routers with distribution lists or summary address statements so that the access layer routers receive only a default route whenever possible.

Dual-Homed Remotes and Best Next Hop

Some remote sites might have links into geographically diverse locations with distinct sets of services available at each hub site. For instance, a single remote site might have links to New York City, where a mainframe with all the financial applications resides, and to San Jose, where all the human resources applications reside. In this situation, it may be better to direct traffic towards the hub location closest to the server (and application) the source host is trying to reach, rather than just routing to one of the two hubs based on a load sharing algorithm, or routing to the closest hub.

If a dual-homed remote site needs to select the best next hop to reach certain destinations (typically Data Centers or common services areas), specific routes to those destinations must be propagated to the remote routers so that path selection can take place. Of course, allowing these additional routes increases the work required to bring up the adjacency between the distribution router and the remote router and possibly allow the feedback of routes from distribution router to remote router to distribution router as described previously. How do you deal with this situation?

If a limited number of routes is being allowed from the distribution layer router to the remote router, the additional overhead of bringing up the link should not be severe. Limit the number of routes advertised to the remotes to a bare minimum.

What about those additional paths that the remote routers will be advertising back into the distribution layer? You need to eliminate the possibility of the distribution layer routers seeing the remote routers as transit paths back to other distribution layer routers.

You can prevent those routes from being readvertised from the remote routers back into the distribution layer by configuring distribution lists (filtering the routes advertised by the remote routers toward the distribution layer routers), allowing only the routes at that remote site in routing updates. In other words, the filters permit routes that originate at the remote site, and not routes that are learned via the links to the distribution layer.

Configuring route filters at the remote site's routers can prevent information learned through one hub from being forwarded to the other hub, and can also act as an insurance policy against remote site router misconfiguration disasters. A missing summary address statement or distribution list on a distribution router causes the remote site to learn more routes than it should, possibly causing havoc.

In some situations, a route that inadvertently leaks from the distribution layer toward a remote router might be the best route at the other distribution layer router, causing all the traffic to be routed through the remote site. This could be a disaster because it is not likely that the links to the remotes are provisioned to support the traffic that is transmitted through the site if this occurs. It could cause failed neighbors and network instability.

In the sample network shown in Figure 3-6, the distribution lists in the remotes are not necessary because every distribution router has the same level of summarization. To be safe, however, you should configure distribution lists.

Analyzing Use of the Stub Feature in Access Routers

Configuring a remote router as a stub, when used in conjunction with the summarization techniques described in the previous sections, can dramatically improve scaling in dual-homed remote routers. Because many networks are composed of large numbers of small access routers, which are either single- or dual-homed to the distribution layer, the stub feature is extremely valuable in many EIGRP networks. What does configuring a router as a stub actually do? Stubs limit the query scope and simplify the network topology, improving EIGRP network convergence.

NOTE   Throughout this section, you will see discussion of controlling query propagation as an important part of configuring a remote router as a stub. Discussion of the importance of controlling query propagation occurs in the "Controlling Query Propagation" case study later in this chapter. In summary, queries are always propagated one hop past a summarization point. If you configure summarization on the distribution routers toward the remote routers (as recommended in the previous sections), queries are propagated one hop beyond the distribution layer routers, to the remote site routers in the access layer, even though the answer to the query is never found there. This is not much more work on the remote site routers, but it causes a great deal more work on the distribution layer routers, because they need to generate and track one query per remote router. Therefore, summarization succeeds at limiting updates to the remotes, but it still allows queries to reach the remote routers.

The active process is designed to find unknown loop free paths through the network. Why not take a short cut in the active process, and simply not search in places where you know an alternate path could not exist? You could cut down on the query range, and improve network convergence time, dramatically. In fact, there are routers a network designer knows, just by examining the network design itself, will never be used as an alternate path, or a transit path, no matter how many links in the network fail. In EIGRP terms, these are stub routers.

A stub router is a router on the edge of the network, or, in other words, a router with no routers farther from the core attached to it. If you view the network topology as a tree (the same way a link-state protocol would build a tree of the topology within a flooding domain), edge routers are always nodes at the farthest point possible from the center of the tree, and through which no traffic should (or would) ever pass. EIGRP allows the network designer to explicitly mark stub routers as stub routers. EIGRP will never search for an alternate path through a router marked as a stub.

How does configuring a router as a stub stop the router from receiving queries? When a router is configured as a stub, it flags itself as a stub by setting bits in its hello packet. Each neighbor of a stub router notes these flags and sets corresponding flags in the neighbor's data structure.

When the EIGRP process on a router loses all the successors and feasible successors for a route, it begins a diffusing update by marking the route active and sending queries to each of its neighbors (except, possibly, those attached to the same interface as the old successor). Before sending these queries, however, it looks at the peer information to determine if a peer is a stub router. If a peer is a stub router, it is removed from the list of neighbors to send queries to. Figure 3-7 illustrates the impact of declaring the remote routers as stubs. As illustrated in Figure 3-7, declaring your remote routers as stubs dramatically reduces the number of queries on the network. In that diagram, only one query is sent instead of many.

Figure 3-7   *Queries and Stub Routers*

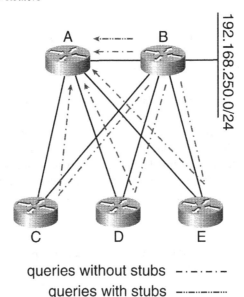

queries without stubs — · — · — · —
queries with stubs —··—··—···—

Another important aspect of the stub feature is how it decreases the apparent complexity of the topology by limiting the types of routes that a router advertises. In Figure 3-8, Router A finds four alternate paths to 192.168.250.0/24, one through each remote router, and one directly to Router B.

Figure 3-8   *Paths Through Remotes and Stub Routers*

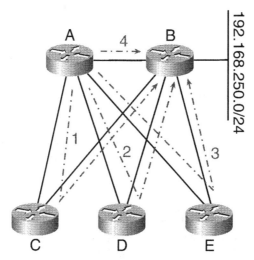

The stub feature significantly alters this behavior, simplifying the convergence process. When a router is defined as a stub, it must be configured with the types of routes that the stub router will advertise. By definition, an EIGRP stub router does not advertise dynamically derived routes (routes learned from other EIGRP neighbors). In Figure 3-8, this means that Routers C, D, and E will not advertise any route they learned from Router B. If Routers C, D, and E are configured as stub routers, Router A is left with one path to 192.168.250.0/24, through Router B.

The command syntax for configuring the stub feature is as follows:

```
rtrA(config)#router  eigrp 1
rtrA(config-router)#eigrp  stub ?
  connected     Do advertise connected routes
  receive-only  Set IP-EIGRP as receive only neighbor
  redistributed Do advertise redistributed routes
  static        Do advertise static routes
  summary       Do advertise summary routes
```

Most of the options are relatively obvious:

- **connected** tells EIGRP to advertise connected routes only.

- **receive-only** tells EIGRP not to advertise routes, just to accept routes it receives from neighbors.

- **redistributed** was added a couple of years after the stub feature was created because of requirements given by customers in the Customer Proof of Concept labs at Cisco. This option allows a stub router to re-advertise routes learned through redistribution.

- **static** permits the router to advertise locally redistributed static routes. Although this option is no longer necessary (because the **redistributed** option was added), it has not been removed. That way, it will not surprise customers who have it defined in their configurations.

- **eigrp stub static** does not cause the redistribution of static routes, but allows only the advertisement of redistributed static routes. You still need to configure static route redistribution, using **redistribute static**, to redistribute static routes on the stub router.

- **summary** tells EIGRP to advertise locally created summary routes. Because these are a special category of local routes, they need to have their own operand.

You can define more than one operand on the **eigrp stub** command. For example, you can define the following command:

```
eigrp stub connected summary redistributed
```

This command causes EIGRP to advertise all connected, summary, and redistributed routes. If you do not define operands (you configure just **eigrp stub**), both connected and summary routes are advertised.

Analyzing Routes to External Connections

Another area to be concerned with is injecting information learned from other routing protocols into EIGRP. Typically, you would inject this information along the edge of the network, or from networks not originally planned to be a part of the EIGRP routing domain, such as the network of an aquired or partnering company. You can classify these external sites in two ways:

- Those that have a limited scope of addresses, such as connections from the routing domain into another company's network or other divisions of the company that fall under other administrative control.

- Those that do not have a limited scope of addresses, such as an Internet connection.

This section describes several methods to propagate information about these external destinations. First, if the external routing domain has a limited number of IP networks, you can redistribute the routes into EIGRP from the other routing domain.

NOTE   Carefully consider the security of the routing system when redistributing routes from an external routing domain. See Chapter 8, "Routing Protocols Security," for more information on this topic.

Redistributing routes into EIGRP can be a reasonable choice if done correctly. If done poorly, however, redistribution can create a disaster. Refer to the "Redistribution" case study later in this chapter for techniques on preventing problems when redistributing routes from EIGRP into and from other routing protocols. The "Case Study: Redistribution" section focuses more exclusively on redistribution between Interior Gateway Routing Protocol (IGRP) and EIGRP for combining networks and for transitioning from IGRP to EIGRP.

NOTE   If you have not already transitioned from IGRP to EIGRP in your network, you should. IGRP is being removed from Cisco IOS Software Release 12.3, so now is the perfect time to make the switch.

If the external connection is to the Internet, redistributing the routes into EIGRP is probably not a good idea, unless you enjoy cleaning up after complete network failures. The Internet has entirely too many routes; you would overpopulate the routing tables. Generally, from within a routing domain, you should use a default route to reach the nearest border with the Internet, and then use the more specific routing information on the border router to route correctly toward the Internet.

You can propagate information about the default route into EIGRP in two ways. First, you could define a static route to 0.0.0.0/0 and redistribute this route into EIGRP from a border router. One problem with this approach is routers configured with **ip summary-address eigrp** *AS* **0.0.0.0 0.0.0.0** will not forward traffic to a default route (0.0.0.0/0) learned from a neighboring router. Why not?

A local summary route has a default administrative distance of 5, whereas the external default route has an administrative distance of 170. Therefore, a redistributed static route will never be installed if a competing locally generated summary default route exists. Either the local router must have a static route with a better administrative distance than the summary, or the summary must be configured with an administrative distance higher than 170.

The second way to propagate information about the default route into EIGRP is to mark a route as a candidate default using the command **ip default-network**. However, this is not the preferred method of providing a default route into an EIGRP network.

NOTE   The capability to distribute a default route through the command **default-information originate** is planned for a future release of Cisco IOS Software.

NOTE   Cisco is planning to remove support for the command **ip default-network** in a future Cisco IOS release.

Analyzing Routes to the Common Services Area

In the network illustrated in Figure 3-9, common services are connected to the core through two distribution routers and via multiple, parallel Fast Ethernet links. Whether these are truly separate physical links or VLANs that are connected through switches, to EIGRP they present the appearance of multiple parallel paths interconnecting the two distribution routers. One of the more typical errors that network designers make is to include all of these parallel paths as alternative paths for routes to reach much of the rest of the network.

Ideally, the servers on these segments point their default gateway to a Hot Standby Router Protocol (HSRP) address shared by the two distribution routers. This design allows the servers on these segments to adapt to a router or link failure almost immediately.

Figure 3-9   *Common Service Connections*

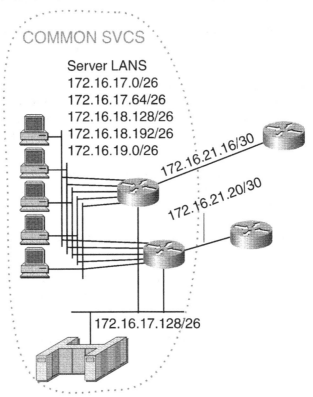

The networks that connect the servers to the routers are not designed for transit traffic; traffic is not expected to enter the common services distribution router from the core, go through one of the Fast Ethernet links used by the common services, and then exit through the other distribution router back to the core. EIGRP, however, does not know this, because every link between the two distribution routers appears as a possible path to every destination in the network. EIGRP treats each of these links as an alternate path, stores information about them in the topology table, and propagates queries through them. These alternate paths complicate the EIGRP convergence.

To eliminate the possibility of these networks being used for transit traffic, the network manager should run EIGRP on as few of these links as possible. Configuring **passive-interface** *interface* for an interface or subinterface removes EIGRP from these interfaces. Although EIGRP will continue to advertise the IP addresses for the interfaces that are declared passive, EIGRP Hellos will not be sent and neighbors will not be formed on them. This eliminates their use as transit paths for traffic.

To prevent the rest of the routers in the network from going active on individual segments that support these servers, you should use the same strategy that is used everywhere else in the network. Summarize the subnets that reside on the common service Ethernet connections in both distribution layer routers so that they send only a single summary route to the core. If a single Ethernet connection goes down in the common services area, the remainder of the network does not start the query process to find an alternative path. The query stops at the first router that does not have knowledge of the specific subnet that has failed, which is a core router.

This strategy has one problem, though: It can create routing black holes in the same way that dual-homed remotes can. To understand why, examine Figure 3-10, which has all but two of the common services networks removed.

Router A and Router B both advertise a summary of 172.16.16.0/22, which covers the entire address range but does not overlap with other addresses in the network. If the Router A interface on the 172.16.18.192/26 network fails, Router A continues advertising the 172.16.16.0/22 summary toward the core. If, however, one of the core routers forwards a packet that is destined to the 172.16.18.192/26 network toward Router A, Router A drops it because it has no route for this destination. Even worse, it might send the packet back toward the core along its default route.

To resolve this situation, Router A must know that 172.16.18.192/26 is reachable through Router B. This is why you should run EIGRP over at least one of these parallel Ethernet links. To do this, do *not* put a **passive-interface** statement into the configuration for at least one Ethernet link. A better solution is to have one or two links between these routers for dedicated redundancy (with no servers or other devices on them) to account for just this situation.

Figure 3-10   *Simplified Common Services*

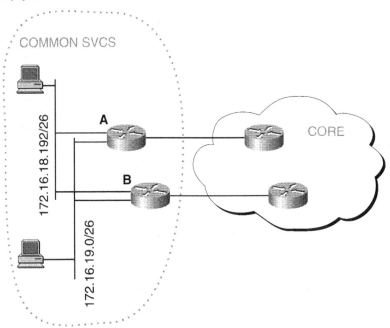

Analyzing Routes to Dial-In Clients

Dial-in access creates several issues and complications. This section discusses host routes created by the dial process and EIGRP bandwidth concerns.

Host Routes

Typically, dial in is handled through PPP. When a PPP session is initiated, a host route (/32) is created on the access server for the remote site, and the host route is removed when the call is dropped. If the number of dial-in clients is large, this can create a significant amount of network activity because the network reacts to these host routes appearing and disappearing.

You can eliminate this influx of network activity in EIGRP in two ways. First, you can define the command **no ip peer host-route** on the interface(s) of the access server, which stops the host route from being created in the first place.

Second, you can summarize the host routes learned via the dial interfaces, allowing only this summary route to be advertised toward the core. You can do this summarization either by configuring **ip summary-address** *autonomous system* **eigrp** on the links toward the core, or by configuring a **distribute-list out** on the links toward the core, as discussed in the "Summarization Methods" case study later in this chapter.

If the routes advertised by a router dialing into the network are normally summarized someplace other than the router accepting the dial-in connection, you can wind up with some major problems in your network. There are several problems with routers advertising routes towards the core of the network beyond the point where those routes are normally summarized.

As long as the dial-up link is up, the path through the dial-up link will be preferred towards the remote site. Once the primary link is fixed, it's common for the dial-up link to remain up for some time. In this situation, it's not desirable for the traffic to the remote site to continue to be routed over the dial-up link.

To make matters worse, once the primary link is repaired, the dialing router may actually leak more specific routes into the core of the network through the dial-up link, drawing all the traffic for every possible destination behind the summary onto the dial-up link. If you configure your dial-up links so a remote router will dial in to a destination between the summarization point for the routes advertised by that remote router and the core of the network, you need to make certain you take these possible problems into consideration in the network design.

Figure 3-11 illustrates the technique of making certain the dial-up links are terminated behind the summarization point, in relation to the network core.

Figure 3-11 *Addressing Dial-In Clients*

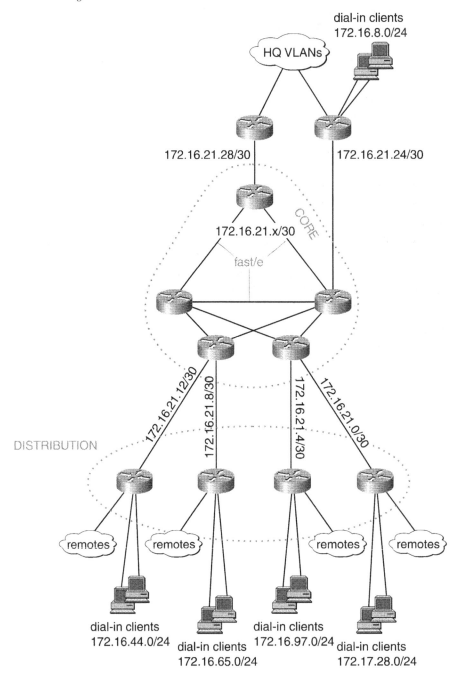

Bandwidth Issues

Bandwidth can be an issue when routers, rather than individual hosts, are dialing into an access server. EIGRP uses the bandwidth that is configured on the interface (using the **bandwidth** command) to determine the rate to pace EIGRP packets. EIGRP paces its packets so that it will not overwhelm the link by using 50 percent of the defined bandwidth by default. Because EIGRP relies on the bandwidth that is configured on the interface for packet pacing, it is important for the interface to be configured correctly. The interface should reflect the real bandwidth that is available on the link.

If EIGRP believes that the interface has more bandwidth than what is actually available, it can dominate the link, not allowing other traffic to flow. If EIGRP believes the interface has much less bandwidth than it actually does, it might not be able to successfully send all the updates, queries, or replies across the link because of the extended pacing interval.

To make things more complicated, the bandwidth that is used to determine the pacing interval is divided by the total number of remote peers on Integrated Services Digital Network (ISDN) PRI and dialer interfaces in an attempt to fairly distribute the available bandwidth between the neighbors that are reachable through that interface.

With Frame Relay multipoint interfaces, this works fine. With ISDN or dialer interfaces, however, you never know how many neighbors will be dialed in. If only one Basic Rate Interface (BRI) is dialed in, the bandwidth should be defined as 64 kbps. If 23 BRIs are dialed in, the bandwidth should be 1.544 Mbps. Because the defined bandwidth does not change with the number of neighbors dialed in, you should set the bandwidth to make it work for both extremes by doing the following:

- Define the dial-in interfaces as dialer profiles instead of dialer groups or dialer interfaces. This allows you to set the bandwidth per dialed-in peer. However, it is an intense administrative approach.

- Summarize the EIGRP updates out of the dial link to make the amount of traffic so insignificant that it can fit across the link regardless of how much actual bandwidth is available. Refer to the earlier section titled "Summarizing Toward the Remote Sites" for more detail on this approach.

Deploying EIGRP on a Two-Layer Hierarchical Network

Now that you have had an opportunity to consider many of the techniques that are available to improve EIGRP stability and scalability in a three-layer hierarchical network design, you can explore another common design choice. Many companies that have smaller networks either geographically or topologically, or networks that have stricter latency requirements, use a two-layer network design instead of the traditional three-layer design. This section discusses how to use some of the techniques described in the previous sections on the three-layer hierarchy in the simpler, two-layer environment.

NOTE   Some networks that have three layers from a switching or bridging perspective are actually two-layer networks from a routing perspective. A switched access layer combined with a routed distribution layer actually appears as one logical routing domain from the perspective of the routing protocol. They combine to form an aggregation layer.

As described in Chapter 2, a two-layer hierarchy consists of the core and aggregation layers. The sections that follow describe the scalability and design techniques that are appropriate for each of these two layers. The design principles that are outlined in the discussion of a three-layer hierarchy also apply in a two-layer hierarchy.

Summarization in the Core

The core in a two-layer hierarchy performs the same functions as the core in the three-layer hierarchy, moving traffic as quickly as possible. The biggest, fastest routers in the network reside at the network core. They are configured with minimal performance-degrading features to minimize latency and maximize performance. Typically, route policy, filtering, and summarization are avoided in the heart of the core.

Even though summarization in the center of the core is normally not encouraged, summarization from the core to the aggregation layer is often an excellent design choice. If the core is robust enough (and it should be), summarizing from the core to the aggregation layer can minimize the information known in the aggregation zones and minimize the number of queries sent into the aggregation zones. The design principles, problems, and solutions that are common in core-to-distribution and distribution-to-access layer summarization are also applicable in core-to-aggregation layer summarization.

Summarization in the Aggregation Layer

The aggregation layer within a two-layer hierarchy takes on the same attributes as the access and distribution layers, compressed into a smaller topological space within the network. Summarization toward the core of the network is the primary concern, with the same problems and solutions discussed in relation to summarization from the distribution layer in a three-layer hierarchy into the core.

Summary of EIGRP Network Design

The previous sections explored how you can apply the best summarization techniques to an EIGRP network to improve its scalability. Several techniques were discussed and numerous recommendations were made to summarize routes at various points in the network. These points include the following:

- Summarizing from the network core to the distribution layer
- Summarizing from the distribution layer to the network core
- Summarizing from the distribution layer to the remote sites
- Placing distribution lists on the remote routers to limit their advertisements to contain only those routes that originate at the remote site
- Summarizing from the common services area to the network core
- Implementing passive interfaces on all but one or two common services Ethernet/Fast Ethernet links
- Summarizing from the dial access servers into the network core

By taking these steps, the network will be robust and scalable. Adding more sites requires only that the same techniques are applied to the new routers. You can add new regions by using the same summarization/distribution list techniques to minimize the scope of queries and updates in the EIGRP network and providing the most robust, stable networking environment that is possible.

New Features in EIGRP

The sections that follow present several new features that you can use to solve tricky situations you might encounter in EIGRP networks. By using these new features, you can create the most effective design for a particular network.

Third-Party Next Hop

Numerous problems are addressed by the EIGRP Third Party Next Hop feature. Generally, the Third Party Next Hop feature addresses the situation in which the best next hop to reach a destination is not known via an EIGRP neighbor. Prior to the creation of this feature, packets often took an extra hop to reach their destination. Two types of networks that are particularly susceptible to the extra hop problem are hub-and-spoke networks using nonbroadcast multiaccess (NBMA) networks such as Frame Relay or ATM multipoint technologies.

NBMA Hub-and-Spoke Network

The network shown in Figure 3-12 illustrates an NBMA hub-and-spoke topology to connect the distribution layer router (hub) to the access layer routers (spokes). Because most of the traffic typically flows from the access routers to the distribution routers and on to the core, the network designer often chooses not to define PVCs between the access routers. This works fine, but it can lead to the extra hop problem for any traffic that goes from one access router to another.

Figure 3-12 *Hub and Spoke with Extra Hop Problem*

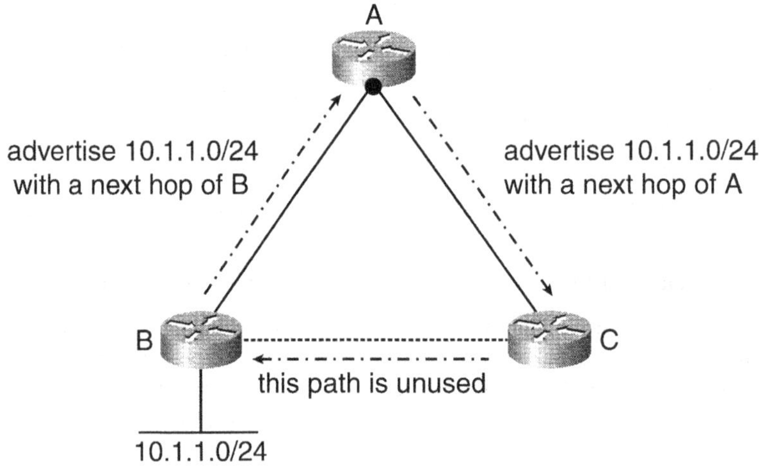

In Figure 3-12, Router B sends an update containing 10.1.1.0/24 to Router A, which then propagates the route to Router C. This causes the network traffic originating on a host behind Router C and destined to a host behind Router B to go from Router C to Router A, where it is routed back out to Router B.

Some providers allow the network designer to provision switched virtual circuits (SVCs) to connect the access routers or to define the spoke-to-spoke PVCs without the broadcast option to minimize the routing complexity. In either case, a data plane connection exists between access routers, but an EIGRP neighbor relationship is nonexistent.

With the addition of the Third Party Next Hop feature, you can avoid this extra hop problem, without enabling the neighbor relationship between the access routers. By defining the command **no ip next-hop-self eigrp** *autonomous-system* on the NBMA interface of the hub router, the behavior changes significantly, as Figure 3-13 illustrates.

NOTE   Strangely enough, prior to the coding of the next-hop feature, a **next-hop** field already existed in the update packet. Until the Third Party Next Hop feature, however, the field always contained **0.0.0.0**, which meant the receiver of the update was to use the sender's IP address as the next hop. This is what caused the extra-hop behavior illustrated in Figure 3-12.

With the new feature, things have changed. When the NBMA interface on the hub in Figure 3-13 is configured with **no ip next-hop-self eigrp** *autonomous-system*, EIGRP fills in the next-hop field in the updates and sends out the NBMA interface if the source and destination of the update are also reachable through the same NBMA interface. By definition, this means that the router advertising the route and the router receiving the route must be on the same NBMA network.

Figure 3-13   *Hub and Spoke with Third Party Next Hop*

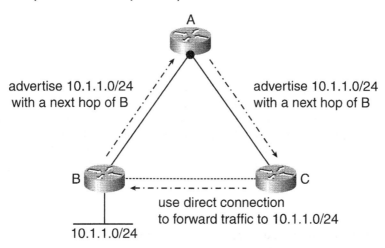

For example, in the network shown in Figure 3-13, the hub router (Router A) is connected via an NBMA multipoint network with Routers A, B, and C. The hub receives an update from Router B for network 10.1.1.0/24 with a source IP address of 10.1.2.2 (the NBMA interface on Router B). When Router A advertises 10.1.1.0/24 to Router C, it leaves the source, 10.1.2.2, in the next-hop field of the update.

When Router C receives the update, it has information about the correct next hop to use when reaching destinations on 10.1.1.0/24, so it can use the direct link between Router C and Router B to send the traffic, rather than the path through Router A.

In Example 3-1, the output of **show ip eigrp topology 10.1.1.0/24** on Router C shows a path to reach 10.1.1.0/24 with a next hop of 10.1.2.2, even though the associated **show ip eigrp neighbor** shows no neighbor relationship between Router A and 10.1.2.2. This could easily confuse support personnel if they do not understand this new feature.

Example 3-1   *EIGRP Topology Table Using* **no ip next-hop-self eigrp**

```
router-c#show ip eigrp topology 10.1.1.0 255.255.255.0
IP-EIGRP topology entry for 10.1.1.0/24
  State is Passive, Query origin flag is 1, 1 Successor(s), FD is 281600
  Routing Descriptor Blocks:
  10.1.2.2 (Serial0/1), from 10.1.2.1, Send flag is 0x0
      Composite metric is (3840000/0), Route is Internal
      Vector metric:
        Minimum bandwidth is 1000 Kbit
        Total delay is 5000 microseconds
        Reliability is 255/255
        Load is 1/255
```

Example 3-1 *EIGRP Topology Table Using* **no ip next-hop-self eigrp** *(Continued)*

```
        Minimum MTU is 1500
        Hop count is 1
router-c#show ip eigrp neighbor
IP-EIGRP neighbors for process 100
H   Address                  Interface      Hold Uptime  SRTT   RTO  Q   Seq Type
                                            (sec)        (ms)        Cnt Num
0   10.1.2.1                 Se3/0          14   1w2d        4   200  0   4
```

One extremely important requirement must be met for the next-hop feature to be implemented successfully. The link between Router B and Router C must be resilient at Layer 2, or traffic can be lost. In other words, EIGRP on Router A is trusting that it is appropriate to advertise a next hop of Router B to Router C even though it is unable to directly determine that such a path exists and is usable. Before you plan to use the next-hop feature, verify that the Layer 2 delivery mechanisms will heal Layer 2 connectivity if a link failure between the remote sites fails.

Redistributed Next Hop

Sometimes as a network designer, you encounter a situation in which the redistributing router experiences significant overhead when it shares a network with both EIGRP routers and routers that are running the redistributed protocol. To resolve this, you can configure only one of the two routers to redistribute from the external protocol into EIGRP, as Figure 3-14 illustrates.

Figure 3-14 *Redistributed Next Hop*

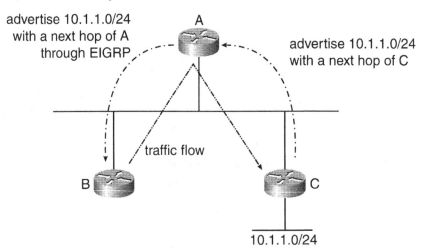

In this network, Router A redistributes between EIGRP and RIP and shares that same Ethernet segment with other EIGRP speakers, including Router B. Router A receives RIP routes from Router C, redistributes them into EIGRP, and then sends them back out the same interface to Router B through an EIGRP update. Example 3-2 shows the topology table for the redistributed route for this network.

Example 3-2   *Topology Table for Redistributed Route*

```
router-b#show ip eigrp topology 10.1.1.0
IP-EIGRP (AS 100): Topology entry for 10.1.1.0/24
  State is Passive, Query origin flag is 1, 1 Successor(s), FD is 2172416
  Routing Descriptor Blocks:
  10.1.3.1 (Ethernet3/0), from 10.1.3.1, Send flag is 0x0
      Composite metric is (2172416/258560), Route is External
      Vector metric:
        Minimum bandwidth is 1544 Kbit
        Total delay is 20100 microseconds
        Reliability is 255/255
        Load is 1/255
        Minimum MTU is 1500
        Hop count is 1
      External data:
        Originating router is 10.1.3.1
        AS number of route is 0
        External protocol is RIP, external metric is 2
        Administrator tag is 0 (0x00000000)
```

Examining the EIGRP topology table on Router B, you can see the route to 10.1.1.0/24 with a next hop of Router A. Although Routers B and C connect to the same network segment, traffic between them must go through Router A, consuming more bandwidth on the network segment.

You can use the same solution that was used for the NBMA hub-and-spoke network in the previous section to solve the redistributed next-hop problem. As shown in Figure 3-15, the network administrator can configure a **no ip next-hop-self eigrp** *autonomous-system* command on the Ethernet interface that Router A shares with Routers B and C.

Figure 3-15   *Redistribution Next Hop with Third-Party Next Hop*

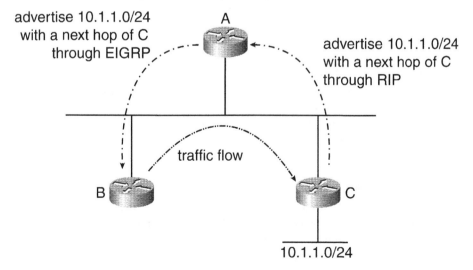

When Router A sends an EIGRP update to Router B, Router A looks for locally redistributed routes with next hops that are reachable via the same interface where the update is destined. If Router A finds a route matching this criterion, then Router A can determine the next-hop IP address from the routing table and insert this address in the next-hop field of the update.

When Router B receives this update, it installs the IP address from the next-hop field into the routing table as the next hop for this destination. Note that the output of **show ip route 10.1.1.0** in Example 3-3 looks similar to Example 3-1 for the NBMA hub-and-spoke topology.

Example 3-3   *Topology Table with* **no ip next-hop-self** *and Redistributed Routes*

```
router-b#show ip eigrp topology 10.1.1.0 255.255.255.0
IP-EIGRP (AS 100): Topology entry for 10.1.1.0/24
  State is Passive, Query origin flag is 1, 1 Successor(s), FD is 2172416
  Routing Descriptor Blocks:
  10.1.3.3 (Ethernet3/0), from 10.1.3.1, Send flag is 0x0
      Composite metric is (2172416/258560), Route is External
      Vector metric:
        Minimum bandwidth is 1544 Kbit
        Total delay is 20100 microseconds
        Reliability is 255/255
        Load is 1/255
        Minimum MTU is 1500
        Hop count is 1
      External data:
        Originating router is 10.1.3.1
        AS number of route is 0
        External protocol is RIP, external metric is 2
        Administrator tag is 0 (0x00000000)
```

Note in Example 3-3 that the next hop is set to the interface address of Router C. As a result, traffic that is destined to addresses on 10.1.1.0/24 flows directly from Router B to Router C instead of through Router A.

Enhanced Route Map Support

Although EIGRP has supported route maps in a limited fashion from the beginning, recent enhancements to EIGRP now allow much more robust and flexible use of route maps. First, you will learn what has always worked. Then you will move on to the new facilities that are available through the enhanced route map feature.

Before Enhanced Route Map Support

Before the route map enhancements were created, EIGRP supported the **route-map** command, but EIGRP had little route map capability. Some of the supported route map commands included **set tag**, **match tag**, and **set metric**. Unfortunately, the only time you could apply these **set** and **match** clauses was on a redistributing router. That is because EIGRP redistributed the routes out of the routing table and into EIGRP. Therefore, not only could you set or match fewer things, but you could only do it on a minimal number of routers in your network.

Many network designers use the **route-map** command to filter routes based on setting and matching tags, but route maps only support filtering based on tags during redistribution, as Figure 3-16 illustrates.

Figure 3-16 *Using Enhanced Route Map Support*

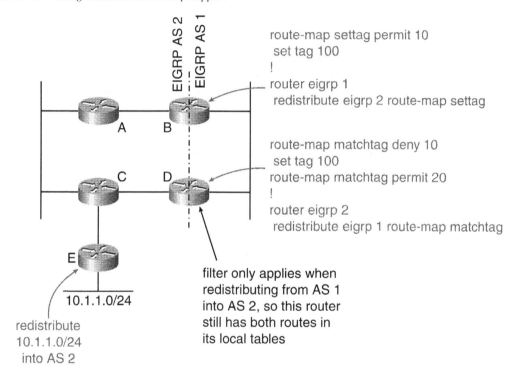

NOTE   The topology in Figure 3-16 is not recommended. This topology simply demonstrates the limitations of the route map support prior to the recent enhancements.

One of the dangers of this type of topology is the likelihood of creating routing loops or suboptimal routing because of information lost in the redistribution process. Normally, you should not connect multiple EIGRP autonomous systems at multiple points and redistribute at all of them. Occasionally, this sort of topology might be required. When it is required, you as the network designer should do everything you can to protect the network from routing loops.

In the network in Figure 3-16, routes that are leaving AS 1 are tagged with a value of 100 when they are redistributed into AS 2, and routes that are redistributed into AS 1 from AS 2 are tagged with a value of 200. When Router D redistributes routes from AS 2 to AS 1, it first tests the tag to make sure it is not a route that originated in AS 2. It seems like this approach will work fine.

Prior to the route map enhancements, however, you could apply the **route-map** command only on the **redistribution** statement. To see the limitation that this causes, follow an external AS 2 prefix that is being redistributed into AS 1. Prefix 10.1.1.0/24 exists in AS 2 as an external route (redistributed static or connected, possibly) and is propagated throughout AS 2. When prefix 10.1.1.0/24 reaches Router B, it is redistributed into AS 1 and a tag of 100 is applied.

10.1.1.0/24 is then propagated throughout AS 1 and eventually arrives at Router D. When Router D attempts to redistribute the route back into AS 2, redistribution is blocked by the route map's **match tag** filter. Unfortunately, the tag can be tested only as the route is being redistributed out of the routing table after being installed there in AS 1. This means that the routing loop will be blocked (the AS 2 route cannot be relearned in AS 2), but Router D can populate its local routing table with incorrect information. The route is filtered only after it is accepted in AS 1. What you really want to do is block routes that have a tag of 2 from being learned on Router D via AS 1.

Route Map Enhancements

One of the most significant enhancements to the route map support is the ability to filter routes as they are being received or sent, not just as they are being redistributed. This is accomplished via the following command:

```
router eigrp 1
  distribute-list route-map {route-map name} ?
     in
     out
     <cr>

  distribute-list route-map {route-map name} in ?
     serial
     ethernet
     ...
     <cr>
```

This permits the network designer to do the inbound filtering, which was impossible prior to the enhancements. By configuring **distribute-list route-map foo in Serial0**, for example, routes can have their tags tested prior to installing them in the topology table. This allows you to filter them prior to putting them in the routing table, which is quite an improvement over the old support.

In addition, more **match** and **set** clauses are supported by EIGRP than before the enhancements. As mentioned earlier, the only **match** clause that was supported was **match tag**, and the only set clauses were **set tag** and **set metric**. Again, you could apply these **set** and **match** clauses to external routes only as they were redistributed into EIGRP. After the enhancements, more set and match clauses are available. You can apply them anywhere that you need:

- **match ip address**—Matches routes from the prefix list or access list.

  Routes can be filtered (denied) or have their attributes modified (via **set** clauses) based on whether a prefix matches the lists. Note that the direction of the distribution list defines what happens with this match clause. If it is applied on a **distribute-list in**, routes are accepted or rejected based on matching the supplied prefix or access list. If this **match** clause is applied via **distribute-list out**, routes are included or excluded from routing updates before sending the updates to neighbors.

- **match ip route-source**—Matches routes based on the source or neighbor list.

  The **route-source** that is supplied in this **match** clause is compared to the source of a received route, which allows you to make filtering choices or change route attributes based on the source of the route.

- **match ip route-source redistribution-source**—Matches external routes based on the originating router ID.

  Although this **match** clause seems similar to the **match ip route-source** clause, it is actually quite different. External routes include information about the router that performed the redistribution from the other protocol into EIGRP. This **match** clause allows you to take actions based on the router redistributing an external prefix into EIGRP. This **match** clause has no effect on internal routes, because no originating router is propagated in internal routes.

- **match interface**—Matches routes based on the interface that is used for the next hop.

  When this clause is used on **distribute-list in**, it limits the filter to routes that are received across the defined interface. On **distribute-list out**, the clause filters only routes that have a next-hop interface that matches the interface on the **match** clause.

- **match tag**—Matches internal or external routes based on the tag.

  This tag must have been set at some other point in the network via a **set tag** clause. As stated in the previous section, EIGRP has been able to set and match tags for years. A new capability included with the route map enhancements is the capability to set and match tags on internal routes. In the past, only external routes could be tagged, and only at the redistribution point. Now internal routes can also be tagged and filtered based on tags.

  One limitation with tags on internal routes, however, is that the number space is significantly smaller than with tags on external routes. External routes in EIGRP have always contained a 32-bit field to hold the tag value, which means that they can have values from 1 to 2^{32}. When you add the tag capability to internal routes, however, the luxury of using a 32-bit field did not exist. Because one of EIGRP's requirements was that it always remain backward compatible, it was necessary to limit the tag on internal routes to a reserved field that was already available. This reserved field is only 8 bits wide, so the value of an internal tag can only be from 1 to 255. Although this is a significant limitation, it should certainly serve most, if not all, tagging requirements for internal routes.

- **match ip next-hop**—Matches routes based on the next hop.

  If you set the next hop for a route using the third-party next-hop feature, the next-hop and route-source fields of a route might be different. If the two fields are different, this **match** clause matches the next-hop field and filter or changes route attributes based on that next hop.

- **match metric [+−]**—Matches routes based on metric with deviation (+−).

  Filter or change route attributes based on the composite metric of a route. The deviation (+/−) allows you to match a metric within a certain range of values. It does not have to be an exact match.

- **match metric external {+−}**—Matches routes based on the external protocol metric.

  This is similar to the **match metric** [+−] command, except that the metric value it is testing is the metric of the external route at the point it is redistributed into EIGRP. If you display the topology table entry for an external route using **show ip eigrp topology** *network mask*, you see that external routes contain information on the metric from the original routing protocol. This **match** clause looks at that metric value, rather than the one inside EIGRP.

  The capability of looking at the metric from the other routing protocol before redistributing into EIGRP allows you to make filtering decisions or change route attributes based on the metric value of the external protocol. You can then favor a route taking you to the exit point of the EIGRP network that is closest to the destination in the external routing protocol.

- **match route-type external**—Matches external route based on external protocol and AS.

  This clause allows you to filter based on the external protocol (including AS number) that an external route is redistributed from. You can then deny or change route attributes if a route originally came into EIGRP from RIP, for example.

- **set metric**—Sets metric components (cannot decrease metric).

- **set tag**—Sets tag on internal or external routes.

Examples 3-4 through 3-8 provide some practical samples of how to use these **match** and **set** clauses to solve real problems.

With the configuration in Example 3-4, EIGRP filters (denies) routes matching **access-list 1** that are received from any neighbors on Serial 0/0. All other prefixes are permitted from neighbors on that interface or any other interface.

Example 3-4   *Using a Route Map to Select Which Routes to Advertise*

```
router eigrp 1
 distribute-list route-map stoproutes in Serial0/0

route-map stoproutes deny 10
 match ip address 1
route-map stoproutes permit 20
 match ip address 2

access-list 1 10.1.0.0 0.0.255.255
access-list 2 0.0.0.0 255.255.255.255
```

What if you want to deny different routes from different neighbors on multiple interfaces?

Using the commands in Example 3-5, EIGRP is instructed to filter (deny) routes matching **access-list 1** if they are received via interface Serial 0/0, and filter routes matching **access-list 2** if they are received on interface Serial 1/0. This gives much more flexibility in deciding which routes to accept.

Example 3-5   *Selective Filtering Based on Interface*

```
router eigrp 1
 distribute-list route-map stoproutes in

route-map stoproutes deny 10
 match interface Serial 0/0
 match ip address 1
route-map stoproutes deny 20
 match interface Serial 1/0
 match ip address 2

access-list 1 10.1.0.0 0.0.255.255
access-list 2 20.10.0.0 0.0.255.255
```

What if you want to accept specific routes from one neighbor on an interface, but not from another neighbor on the same interface?

The configuration in Example 3-6 tells EIGRP to filter (deny) routes matching **access-list 1**, but only if they are received from 10.1.1.1. This provides more granularity in filtering.

Example 3-6   *Selective Filtering Based on Neighbor*

```
router eigrp 1
 distribute-list route-map stoproutes in

route-map stoproutes deny 10
```

Example 3-6   *Selective Filtering Based on Neighbor (Continued)*

```
 match ip route-source 10.1.1.1
 match ip address 1
route-map stoproutes permit 20
 match ip address 2

access-list 1 10.1.0.0 0.0.255.255
access-list 2 0.0.0.0 255.255.255.255
```

What if you do not actually know which prefixes you want to filter, but you do know what part of the network they come from?

On the router that is injecting the prefixes into the network, enter the configuration in Example 3-7.

Example 3-7   *Setting Tags on Redistributed Routes*

```
router eigrp 1
 distribute-list route-map settag out Serial 0/0

route-map settag permit 10
 set tag 20
```

On the router where you want to do the filtering, enter the configuration in Example 3-8.

Example 3-8   *Filtering Routes Based on Tag*

```
router eigrp 1
 distribute-list route-map matchtag in
route-map matchtag deny 10
 match tag 20
```

Using the commands in Example 3-7 and 3-8, EIGRP tags every route being advertised into the network through Serial 0/0 from the first router and then filters the routes if they match the tag on the second router. This removes the need for knowing all the specific prefixes that are being injected at the first spot so that the filter can reflect those prefixes in the second router. This is much easier to manage than dealing with specific lists of prefixes.

By using the enhanced route map capabilities, you can define a much more specific filtering policy.

Enhanced EIGRP Active Process

If you ask the network administrators of several large-scale EIGRP networks what their least favorite message to see in a log is, you would probably get a single, common answer—EIGRP SIAs. The active process in EIGRP is used to discover whether alternate paths to a specific destination exist, or whether existing alternate paths are loop free. If the query process fails, which generally happens only because a router does not reply to a query within a fixed time, the EIGRP process on the originating router is outside the Diffusing Update Algorithm (DUAL) state machine. The only way out is to reset the relationship with the neighbor that has not replied to a query.

NOTE   The EIGRP active process is covered in detail in Appendix A.

Begin by reviewing the active process before it was enhanced, using Figure 3-17.

Figure 3-17   *EIGRP Active Process*

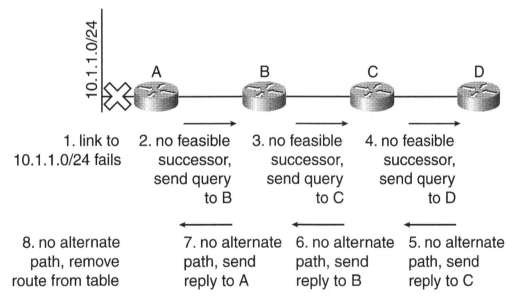

The list that follows describes the labeled sequence of transactions as depicted in Figure 3-17.

1 The Router A link to 10.1.1.0/24 fails.

2 Router A examines its local topology table and finds it has no feasible successors for 10.1.1.0/24. (It has no alternate paths that are known to be loop free.) Router A marks the route as active, builds a query about 10.1.1.0/24, and sends it to Router B.

3 Router B receives this query, examines its local topology table, and determines that it has no feasible successor for 10.1.1.0/24. Router B marks the route as active, builds a query, and sends it to Router C.

4 Router C receives this query, examines its local topology table, and determines that it has no feasible successor for 10.1.1.0/24. Router C marks the route as active, builds a query, and sends it to Router D.

5 Router D receives the Router C query, examines its local topology table, and determines that it has no feasible successor for 10.1.1.0/24. Router D has no other neighbors, so it marks 10.1.1.0/24 as unreachable and sends a reply to Router C.

6 Router C receives this reply and finds that it has no other paths through which it could reach 10.1.1.0/24. (Router C received the original query from Router B, and it just received a reply from Router D.) Router C marks 10.1.1.0/24 as unreachable and sends a reply to Router B.

7 Router B receives this reply and finds that it has no other paths through which it can reach 10.1.1.0/24. (Router B received the original query from Router A, and it just received a reply from Router C.) Router B marks 10.1.1.0/24 as unreachable and sends a reply to Router A.

8 Router A receives this reply and finds that it has no other possible paths to 10.1.1.0/24. Therefore, it marks the destination as unreachable, eventually removing 10.1.1.0/24 from its local routing and topology tables.

When Router A originally marks the route to 10.1.1.0/24 as active, it sets a 3-minute timer, called the *active timer*. If this timer expires before the Router B response is received, Router A resets its neighbor relationship with B. When this timer expires, the Router A EIGRP process has gone outside the DUAL finite state machine. Furthermore, no other alternative exists besides resetting the neighbor relationship to correct the problem.

What could go wrong with the active process? Suppose that Routers C and D have a problem communicating. Router D could be low on memory, or the link between them could be dropping a large percentage of the packets that are transmitted. While Router C is waiting on a reply from D, the active timer in Router A is still running. In fact, if it takes more than 3 minutes for the query to reach C in the first place and for D to respond to C, the active timer in Router A is guaranteed to expire before Router C receives the reply from Router D. This causes Router A to reset its neighbor relationship with Router B. There is obviously a problem here, because a glitch between Router C and Router D causes a neighbor relationship to be reset between Router A and Router B.

The EIGRP enhanced Active process (also known as the *SIA rewrite*) fixes this problem by adding a state so that the neighbor relationship reset happens where the actual network problem is. Figure 3-18 illustrates.

Figure 3-18   *The Enhanced EIGRP Active Process*

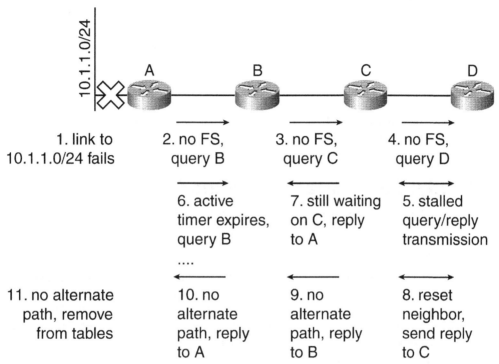

The list that follows describes the labeled sequence of transactions as depicted in Figure 3-18.

1 The Router A link to 10.1.1.0/24 fails.

2 Router A examines its local topology table and finds that it has no feasible successor to 10.1.1.0/24. It marks the route active, sets a 1-minute active timer, and sends a query about 10.1.1.0/24 to B.

3 Router B examines its local topology table and finds that it has no feasible successors for 10.1.1.0/24. It marks the route active, sets a 1-minute active timer, and sends a query about 10.1.1.0/24 to C.

4 Router C examines its local topology table and finds that it has no feasible successors for 10.1.1.0/24. It marks the route active, sets a 1-minute active timer, and sends a query about 10.1.1.0/24 to D.

5 The query/reply mechanism fails between Routers C and D. Both routers continue retransmitting.

6 The active timer in Router A expires. Router A builds an SIA query and transmits it to B.

7 Router B receives this SIA query and examines the state of its local topology table. Router B finds that it is still waiting on a reply from Router C, so it sends this information to Router A. This preserves the neighbor relationship between Routers A and B.

8 Routers C and D fail in their retransmission attempts and reset their neighbor relationship.

9 Router C now has no alternate path to 10.1.1.0/24, so it sends a reply to Router B.

10 Router B has no alternate path to 10.1.1.0/24, so it sends a reply to Router A.

11 Router A has no path to 10.1.1.0/24. It marks the route as unreachable and eventually removes 10.1.1.0/24 from its local topology and routing tables.

Case Study: Summarization Methods

You can use two basic tools to summarize routes in EIGRP:

- IP summary addresses
- Distribute lists

These two methods, which are uniquely useful, provide significantly different approaches to limiting the routing updates to a summary of the information. The best solution to a summarization problem is often a mixture of both approaches. One or both of these basic tools is applied in all three layers—core, distribution, and access—to provide the maximum in summarization, stability, and scalability. The next sections look at each tool so that you can understand the pros and cons of each.

IP Summary Addresses

The first summarization tool is an IP summary address, configured using the command **ip summary-address eigrp AS network mask** *distance*, applied to an interface. An IP summary address provides two related functions:

- An IP summary address creates a summary route in the routing table (identified as a summary route with a next-hop address of null0). It then propagates to any neighbors out of the interface with the summary address statement defined. This is called the *discard route*, which is created to prevent forwarding loops.

- An IP summary address filters out the components of the summary that would normally have been sent out of the interface with the **summary address** statement. In this way, an IP summary address sends *only* the summary information.

Although IP summary addresses are extremely flexible and powerful, they can be administratively wearisome and possibly error-prone. As mentioned previously, you need to apply the **summary-address** statement to each interface that you want to advertise the summary. On routers that contain dozens or even hundreds of interfaces and subinterfaces, you can have numerous **summary-address** statements to correctly define.

A summary route is created and sent only if EIGRP has an internal component of the summary. This means that if all components that make up the summary disappear, or only external (redistributed) components exist, the summary route is not installed and advertised.

One unfortunate side effect of the discard route is created when a IP summary address is configured. If the router that is generating the summary receives a route matching the summary (with the same network and mask) from another source, the router does not accept it. This is because the discard route that is generated by the **summary-address** command has an administrative distance of five by default, which is always better than the administrative distance of a dynamically learned route.

To illustrate, suppose that you have a router that is learning its default route through an external source (see Example 3-9) .

Example 3-9   *A Router Learning Its Default Route via an External Source*

```
router#show ip route
....
Gateway of last resort is 172.19.1.1 to network 0.0.0.0
....
D*EX 0.0.0.0/0 [170/2195456] via 172.19.1.1, 00:00:09, Serial0
```

You want to configure a **summary-address** statement that advertises the least number of routes possible out of interface serial 1 as follows:

```
router(config)#int serial 1
router(config-if)#ip summary-address eigrp 100 0.0.0.0 0.0.0.0
```

Example 3-10 shows the resulting routing table after this configuration.

Example 3-10   *Routing Table with Summary Default Route*

```
router#show ip route
....
Gateway of last resort is 0.0.0.0 to network 0.0.0.0
....
D*   0.0.0.0/0 is a summary, 00:00:49, Null0
```

This is a problem. Any packets that should follow the default route directed toward 172.19.1.1 are sent to **null0**, the bit bucket.

To resolve this, you can use a new addition on the **ip summary-address** command:

```
router(config-if)#ip summary-address eigrp 100 0.0.0.0 0.0.0.0 200
```

The final **200** sets the administrative distance of this summary route to 200, effectively preventing the use of the discard route. Although the downstream router still receives only the 0.0.0.0/0 route, the summary is not installed in the routing table of this router because the administrative distance is higher than the external EIGRP route that you currently have. This feature is not available in all releases of Cisco IOS Software prior to Release 12.0(5)T, when the feature was integrated.

NOTE	The discard route is created to prevent routing loops when a summary is configured. Using the administrative distance to prevent a discard route from being installed in the local routing table removes this protection. Use this feature carefully, generally only when summarizing toward a nontransit section of the network, such as a dual-homed remote site.

Distribute Lists

The second method that filters and summarizes routes in EIGRP involves defining a distribute list under the EIGRP configuration. This method uses a different approach than the **summary-address** statements, but it provides similar functionality. With the distribute list approach, you explicitly tell EIGRP which routes are allowed to be advertised out any or all interfaces. You enter the following command for this approach in EIGRP configuration mode:

```
distribute-list {access-list-number | prefix prefix-list-name} out [interface-name
    | routing-process | as-number]
```

The access list that is associated with the distribute list describes the route, or routes, that you can send out the interface defined under the **distribute-list** command. You can supply a wildcard mask in the access list so that more than one route is permitted under the same access list.

Alternatively, you can supply a prefix list instead of an access list. A prefix list is similar to an access list, but it is referenced by name instead of number and has a few additional options.

A key difference between distribute lists and summary addresses is that distribute lists do not automatically create the summary route you need to advertise. If the route that is permitted by the access list does not exist, the route is not sent. Typically, the network manager defines a static route to match the access list so that the route is always there to advertise. This static route can be floating (that is, with a high administrative distance) so that if the same route is learned from elsewhere, it is accepted and used. The static route is used only if the dynamically derived route disappears.

Case Study: Controlling Query Propagation

Not only do summarization statements and distribute lists limit the size and content of the updates that are sent to neighbors from a router, but they also control the scope of EIGRP query propagation. (See Appendix A for further details on the query process.) Consider a query propagating through the network as illustrated in Figure 3-19.

Figure 3-19   *Controlling Query Propagation*

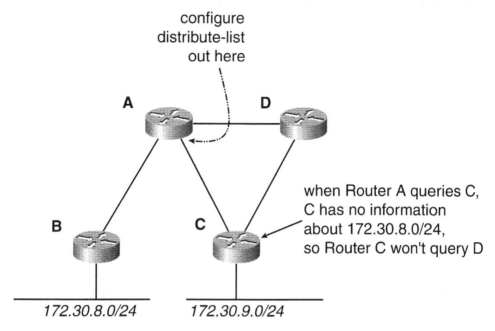

If Router B loses its route to 172.30.8.0/24, which is directly attached, it queries each of its neighbors in search of a different path to reach this destination. Because Router B has only one neighbor, Router A is the only router that Router B queries. Router A then queries each of its neighbors, Router C and Router D, looking for an alternative path to 172.30.8.0/24. Router C queries Router D. Therefore, Router D receives two queries:

* One from Router A
* One from Router C

You know from looking at the network topology that Router D does not have a route to 172.30.8.0/24 unless Router A does. Why should you bother Router D with two queries about this network? Well, you can configure Router A so that Router D does not receive two queries.

A query stops propagating when it reaches a router that has no knowledge of the active route. Therefore, if you remove the knowledge that Router C has of 172.30.8.0/24, Router C does not propagate a query that it receives from Router A to Router D. This is where summarization and distribution lists come into play; they keep Router C from learning about 172.30.8.0/24.

On Router A, you can advertise a summary of all the routes available in the remainder of the network, 172.30.0.0/16, to Router C. When Router C receives a query for 172.30.8.0/24, it examines its local topology table and finds that it does not have a topology table entry for this particular destination network. When Router C discovers that it does not have alternate paths to 172.30.8.0/24, it replies to Router A noting that the active route is not reachable.

Case Study: A Plethora of Topology Table Entries

One of the common problems in an EIGRP network is the sheer number of alternate paths through which a given destination can be reached. Each alternate path in the topology table represents a query that must be generated if the path currently being used fails. These alternate paths, however, are not always obvious when you look at the topology table, as demonstrated in Example 3-11.

Example 3-11   *Alternate Paths to a Destination Are Not Always Displayed in a Topology Table*

```
router#show ip eigrp topology
IP-EIGRP Topology Table for process 100

Codes: P - Passive, A - Active, U - Update, Q - Query, R - Reply,
       r - Reply status

P 172.19.2.128/25, 1 successors, FD is 2297856
        via 172.28.1.2 (2297856/128256), Serial0.1
P 172.19.10.0/24, 1 successors, FD is 2297856
        via 172.28.1.2 (2297856/128256), Serial0.1
```

The topology table in Example 3-11 shows what appear to be two destinations, each with a single path to reach it. However, the paths shown here are only a subset of what is known by EIGRP. This output does not show all the available paths. It shows only the ones that DUAL has calculated to be loop free.

To get a more accurate picture of which paths are available, you can execute **show ip eigrp topology all** or **show ip eigrp topology** for a particular destination, as demonstrated in Example 3-12.

Example 3-12   *Displaying All Paths to a Destination*

```
router#show ip eigrp topology all
IP-EIGRP Topology Table for process 100
 Codes: P - Passive, A - Active, U - Update, Q - Query, R - Reply, r - Reply status

P 172.19.2.128/25, 1 successors, FD is 2297856
        via 172.28.1.2 (2297856/128256), Serial0.1
        via 172.28.2.2 (3879455/2389454), Serial0.2
        via 172.28.3.2 (4893467/2389454), Serial0.3
        via 172.28.4.2 (4893467/2389454), Serial0.4
        via 172.28.5.2 (4893467/2389454), Serial0.5
        via 172.28.6.2 (4893467/2389454), Serial0.6
        via 172.28.7.2 (4893467/2389454), Serial0.7
        via 172.28.8.2 (4893467/2389454), Serial0.8
        via 172.28.9.2 (4893467/2389454), Serial0.9
        via 172.28.10.2 (4893467/2389454), Serial0.10
P 172.19.10.0/24, 1 successors, FD is 2297856
        via 172.28.1.2 (2297856/128256), Serial0.1
        via 172.28.2.2 (3879455/2389454), Serial0.2
        via 172.28.3.2 (4893467/2389454), Serial0.3
        via 172.28.4.2 (4893467/2389454), Serial0.4
```

Example 3-12 *Displaying All Paths to a Destination (Continued)*

```
                 via 172.28.5.2 (4893467/2389454), Serial0.5
                 via 172.28.6.2 (4893467/2389454), Serial0.6
                 via 172.28.7.2 (4893467/2389454), Serial0.7
                 via 172.28.8.2 (4893467/2389454), Serial0.8
                 via 172.28.9.2 (4893467/2389454), Serial0.9
                 via 172.28.10.2 (4893467/2389454), Serial0.10
router#show ip eigrp topology 172.19.10.0 255.255.255.0
IP-EIGRP topology entry for 172.19.10.0/24
  State is Passive, Query origin flag is 1, 1 Successor(s), FD is 2297856
  Routing Descriptor Blocks:
  172.28.1.2 (Serial0.1), from 172.28.1.2, Send flag is 0x0
      Composite metric is (2297856/128256), Route is Internal
  ....
  172.28.2.2 (Serial0.2), from 172.28.2.2, Send flag is 0x0
      Composite metric is (3879455/2389454), Route is Internal
  ....
  172.28.3.2 (Serial0.3), from 172.28.3.2, Send flag is 0x0
      Composite metric is (3879455/2389454), Route is Internal
  ....
  172.28.4.2 (Serial0.4), from 172.28.4.2, Send flag is 0x0
      Composite metric is (3879455/2389454), Route is Internal
  ....
  172.28.5.2 (Serial0.5), from 172.28.5.2, Send flag is 0x0
      Composite metric is (3879455/2389454), Route is Internal
  ....
  172.28.6.2 (Serial0.6), from 172.28.6.2, Send flag is 0x0
      Composite metric is (3879455/2389454), Route is Internal
  ....
  172.28.7.2 (Serial0.7), from 172.28.7.2, Send flag is 0x0
      Composite metric is (3879455/2389454), Route is Internal
  ....
  172.28.8.2 (Serial0.8), from 172.28.8.2, Send flag is 0x0
      Composite metric is (3879455/2389454), Route is Internal
  ....
  172.28.9.2 (Serial0.9), from 172.28.9.2, Send flag is 0x0
      Composite metric is (3879455/2389454), Route is Internal
  ....
  172.28.10.2 (Serial0.10), from 172.28.10.2, Send flag is 0x0
      Composite metric is (3879455/2389454), Route is Internal
```

Although this particular destination has only one successor, the number of different paths is numerous. This almost always indicates a topology that has too much redundancy; this router has at least ten neighbors, and each of them has a path to this destination. Unfortunately, no definite rules spell out how many paths are too many in the topology table. The number of alternative paths, however, indicates the total query paths in the network and, therefore, how much work the routers in the network need to do when converging on a topology change.

In general, avoid running EIGRP over multiple parallel links between two routers unless you intend transit traffic to be passed over all of them.

Case Study: Troubleshooting EIGRP Neighbor Relationships

EIGRP might experience problems establishing neighbor relationships for various reasons. To determine the source of the problem, the first thing to do is to add the command **eigrp log-neighbor-changes** under the router process in the configuration of every router. Doing so provides much more information about the cause of neighbor problems.

This case study describes two common problems that prevent EIGRP from establishing neighbors successfully:

- The first problem occurs when the primary addresses that are used by the routers trying to be neighbors do not belong to the same subnet.

- The second common problem occurs when the underlying media is failing to deliver either unicast or multicast traffic in one direction or both.

EIGRP Neighbor Relationships: Common Problem 1

Because Cisco routers permit the definition of both primary and secondary IP subnets on the same interface, many network implementers treat the primary and secondary addresses as equal. As Figure 3-20 reveals, this is not necessarily the case.

Figure 3-20   *EIGRP Neighbors with Different Primary Addresses*

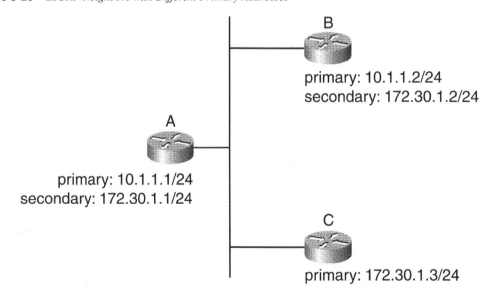

In this network, Router C has its primary (and only) IP address in the same subnet as the secondary addresses of Routers A and B. You can see this easily by executing **show ip eigrp neighbors** on all three routers, as demonstrated in Example 3-13.

Example 3-13 **show ip eigrp neighbors** *with Primary/Secondary Address Mismatch*

```
router-a#show ip eigrp neighbors
IP-EIGRP neighbors for process 1
H   Address                Interface    Hold Uptime    SRTT   RTO  Q   Seq
                                        (sec)          (ms)        Cnt Num
1   172.30.1.3             Et0          13  00:00:15   0      5000 1   0
0   10.1.1.2               Et0          13  00:09:56   26     200  0   323
router-b#show ip eigrp neighbors
IP-EIGRP neighbors for process 1
H   Address                Interface    Hold Uptime    SRTT   RTO  Q   Seq
                                        (sec)          (ms)        Cnt Num
0   172.30.1.3             Et1          11  00:00:03   0      3000 1   0
1   10.1.1.1               Et1          11  00:11:09   23     200  0   3042
router-c#show ip eigrp neighbors
IP-EIGRP neighbors for process 1
```

As the output in Example 3-13 indicates, Router A and Router B see Router C as a neighbor (a neighbor with a problem, however—note the Q count and lack of Smoothed Round Trip Time [SRTT]). Router C does not see Routers A or B as neighbors. This is because Routers A and B match the IP address of the source of the hello packet with any of its addresses on that interface. Because Router C falls in one of the subnets, Router A and Router B accept Router C as a neighbor.

NOTE

The Q count, shown in **show ip eigrp neighbor**, indicates the number of items from the topology table that need to be sent to this neighbor. Some (or all) of these items might never be sent because of split-horizon, distribution lists, summaries, or other things. Therefore, the Q count does not indicate the number of packets that need to be sent or the number of routes that are being sent.

The SRTT, shown in **show ip eigrp neighbor**, indicates the average amount of time it takes for a neighbor to respond to packets that require an acknowledgement. It is a smoothed (or weighted) average over multiple transmit/acknowledgement cycles.

On the other hand, when Router C compares the source address of the received hellos, it does not match any of the addresses on that interface, so Router C rejects them. In some versions of IOS, the message **neighbor not on common subnet** printed on the console indicates this problem.

Because the source address of Router C is on a different subnet than Router A and Router B, a proper neighbor relationship is not established between Router C and the other two routers on this subnet. To resolve this problem, Router C needs to be re-addressed so that its primary address is on the 10.1.1.0/24 subnet.

EIGRP Neighbor Relationships: Common Problem 2

Another problem often experienced with EIGRP neighbor establishment occurs when the underlying media fails to deliver unicast or multicast traffic in one direction or both. The remainder of this case study describes how it looks when you are missing multicast traffic in one direction using the network diagramed in Figure 3-21.

Figure 3-21 *EIGRP Neighbors with Multicast Delivery Problems*

Example 3-14 shows the **show ip eigrp neighbors** output for Router A.

Example 3-14 *Displaying the Router A Neighbors*

```
router-a#show ip eigrp neighbors
IP-EIGRP neighbors for process 1
H   Address              Interface    Hold Uptime    SRTT   RTO  Q  Seq
                                      (sec)          (ms)        Cnt Num
0   192.168.10.2         Se1          13 00:00:10       0   5000  1  0
```

Notice that Router B is seen in the neighbor table of Router A, but the Q count is not zero and the SRTT is not set to a value. If you have **eigrp log-neighbor-changes** configured (as you should), you also get messages on the console, or syslog, reporting that this neighbor is being restarted because the retransmit limit is exceeded. These symptoms indicate that you cannot get updates delivered and acknowledged to this neighbor, but you can see the neighbor hellos.

Now look at the **show ip eigrp neighbors** output for Router B in Example 3-15.

Example 3-15 *Displaying the Router B Neighbors*

```
router-b#show ip eigrp neighbors
IP-EIGRP neighbors for process 1
```

Here, notice that Router B does not have Router A in its neighbor table. This indicates that the multicast packets that are sent by EIGRP as hellos are not being delivered to this neighbor. Common reasons for this include a missing broadcast keyword on a dialer map or **frame-relay map** statement, misconfiguration of Switched Multimegabit Data Service (SMDS) multicast groups, or other problem with the delivery mechanism.

Example 3-16 demonstrates a correct configuration for a multipoint Frame Relay interface.

Example 3-16 *Multipoint Frame Relay Configuration*

```
!
interface Serial 0
 encapsulation frame-relay
 ip address 172.30.14.1 255.255.255.0
 frame-relay map ip 172.30.14.2 100 broadcast
 frame-relay map ip 172.30.14.3 104 broadcast
 frame-relay map ip 172.30.14.4 210 broadcast
```

Note the **broadcast** keyword inserted at the end of each **frame-relay map** configuration command.

This symptom could also indicate that traffic from Router A is not being delivered to Router B. You can determine whether this is the case by pinging Router B from Router A. If the unicast ping works, but EIGRP is unable to see Router A from Router B, you should ping 224.0.0.10 (the multicast address of EIGRP) from Router A and see if Router B responds.

The router should forward a multicast ping to 224.0.0.10 onto every interface, and every adjacent EIGRP neighbor should respond to it. Example 3-17 demonstrates a neighbor having a packet delivery problem, and the use of the **ping** command to determine the scope of the problem. As you can see, the neighbor with a problem, 192.168.10.2, successfully responds to unicast pings but does not answer pings sent to the multicast address 224.0.0.10.

Example 3-17 *Troubleshooting Neighbor Problems*

```
router#show ip eigrp neighbors
IP-EIGRP neighbors for process 1
H   Address                 Interface    Hold Uptime   SRTT   RTO  Q  Seq
                                         (sec)         (ms)       Cnt Num
4   192.168.10.2            Se1          14 00:00:05     0   3000  8  0
3   10.31.1.2               Se0.1        12 00:00:11   132    792  0  1668
2   10.31.2.2               Se0.2        12 00:00:12   131    786  0  1670
1   10.31.3.2               Se0.3        11 00:00:12   166    996  0  1669
0   10.1.2.1                Et0          10 1w4d        13    200  0  60131
router#ping 182.168.10.2
Type escape sequence to abort.
Sending 5, 100-byte ICMP Echos to 192.168.10.2, timeout is 2 seconds:
!!!!!
Success rate is 100 percent (5/5), round-trip min/avg/max = 16/16/20 ms
router#ping 224.0.0.10

Type escape sequence to abort.
Sending 1, 100-byte ICMP Echos to 224.0.0.10, timeout is 2 seconds:

Reply to request 0 from 10.1.2.1, 12 ms
Reply to request 0 from 10.31.3.2, 112 ms
Reply to request 0 from 10.31.2.2, 104 ms
Reply to request 0 from 10.31.1.2, 100 ms
```

Example 3-17 *Troubleshooting Neighbor Problems (Continued)*

```
Reply to request 0 from 10.250.1.1, 12 ms
Reply to request 0 from 10.200.1.1, 12 ms
Reply to request 0 from 10.1.3.2, 12 ms
```

Case Study: Troubleshooting SIA Routes

SIA routes can be some of the most challenging problems to resolve in an EIGRP network. For more detail on the EIGRP active process, refer to Appendix A. In summary, a route becomes active when it goes down or its metric worsens, and no feasible successors exist. When a route goes active on a router, that router sends queries to all of its neighbors (except through the interface where the route was lost) and awaits the replies. A 3-minute timer starts when the router marks the route as active. If the timer expires without getting all the replies, the route that was active is considered stuck in active processing (thus the label "stuck in active" routes) and requires drastic actions.

Three minutes is an incredibly long time to a router. You need to understand why the replies could take longer than 3 minutes. Figure 3-22 shows a simple network that is reacting to a lost route so that you can understand how to troubleshoot it.

Figure 3-22 *Troubleshooting EIGRP SIA Routes*

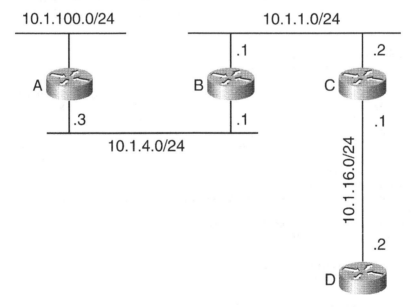

Router A loses network 10.1.100.0/24 when its interface on that interface is shut down. Router A then goes active on the route and sends a query to Router B, which looks in its topology table for another successor, or feasible successor, for 10.1.100.0/24. In this case, Router B does not have other successors or feasible successors. Therefore, it goes active on the route and sends a query to Router C. Router C goes through the same decision process, and the query continues on to Router D (and farther if possible).

During this entire process, the 3-minute timer of Router A has been running because a reply is not returned from Router B until it receives an answer from Router C, which is waiting on Router D. If something happens somewhere downstream (as it does in this case study), the timer on Router A might expire, and Router A considers the path through Router B unreliable. When that happens, Router A resets its neighbor relationship with Router B and tosses all routes previously learned through Router B. (Relearning these routes requires rebuilding the neighbor relationship.) This can be brutal if the link between Router A and Router B is a core link in your network.

You can see how to troubleshoot SIA routes on the example network in Figure 3-22. How do you know you are getting SIA routes? You know because you see messages in your log similar to this:

```
Jan  19 14:26:00: %DUAL-3-SIA: Route 10.1.100.0 255.255.255.0 stuck-in-active
   state in IP-EIGRP 1. Cleaning up
Jan  19 14:26:00: %DUAL-5-NBRCHANGE: IP-EIGRP 1: Neighbor 10.1.4.1 (Ethernet1) is
   up: new adjacency
```

The DUAL-3-SIA message identifies which route is getting stuck—10.1.100.0/24 in this case—but it does not reveal which neighbor did not answer. You need to have **log-neighbor-changes** configured (as recommended earlier) to get the message immediately after the DUAL-3-SIA message, stating new adjacency for the neighbor (or neighbors) that was reset because of the SIA. You can also tell which neighbors have been recently reset by looking for a short uptime in the **show ip eigrp neighbors** output. However, you cannot be sure that their reset condition was because of the SIA. Again, ensure that **log-neighbor-changes** is configured on every router. Also, send the log entries to the buffer via **logging buffered** or to a syslog server.

Because the log captured SIA messages, you need to try to determine where the source of the problem is. Ask the following two questions about SIA routes:

* Why are the routes going active?
* Why are they getting stuck?

You should work on both aspects of the problem, but the second is the most important by far and probably the most difficult to resolve. If you determine why a route is going active and resolve this part of the problem without determining why it became stuck, the next time a route goes active, it could become stuck again. Therefore, finding the cause of the stuck route is more important than finding the cause of the route going active.

Even though it is more important to find the cause of routes becoming stuck than why they went active, do not ignore why routes are going active. Using the **DUAL-3-SIA** messages printed to the router console, you can determine whether the routes that are going active are consistent. That is, are all of them /32 routes from dial-in clients coming and going, or are all of them the result of poor-quality lines at the fringes of the network? If all of them are host routes caused by dial-in users, you should try to minimize these active routes through summarization or other methods. If the active routes are because of unstable links, you need to get these Layer 2 problems resolved.

How do you troubleshoot the stuck part of the SIA? If the SIA routes are happening regularly, and you are monitoring the routers during the time of the problem, this is a fairly straightforward job. If the problem happens infrequently, and you were not monitoring the routers when the problem happened, it is almost impossible to find the cause. For this case study, assume that the problem is happening regularly enough for you to catch the routes that are having problems.

Referring back to Figure 3-22, on Router A (where you are receiving the DUAL-3-SIA messages for 10.1.100.0/24), you look for active routes using the **show ip eigrp topology active** command, as demonstrated in Example 3-18. As you can see, the output reveals information about the state of the active route.

Example 3-18 **show ip eigrp topology active** *Output*

```
routerA#show ip eigrp topology active
IP-EIGRP Topology Table for process 1
 Codes: P - Passive, A - Active, U - Update, Q - Query, R - Reply,
         r - Reply status

A 10.1.100.0/24, 1 successors, FD is Inaccessible
     1 replies, active 00:01:23, query-origin: Local origin
         via Connected (Infinity/Infinity), Loopback0
     Remaining replies:
```

The **A** on the left side of the address shows that this is an active route. **active 00:01:23** reveals the duration of the wait on a reply to this query. It is normal in a large network to see routes go active, but if the amount of time that the routes stay active is more than a minute, something is certainly wrong, and SIAs might occur soon.

Notice the field Remaining replies; any neighbors that are listed under this field have not yet replied to this query. Depending on the timing of when the command is issued, you often see neighbors who have not replied with a lowercase r beside the address, but not under Remaining replies. For example (but not directly related to this case study), consider the output in Example 3-19.

Example 3-19 *Nonresponsive Neighbor Not Under Remaining replies*

```
router#show ip eigrp topology active
IP-EIGRP Topology Table for process 1 Codes:
P - Passive, A - Active, U - Update, Q - Query, R - Reply,
r - Reply status A 10.1.8.0 255.255.255.0, 1 successors, FD is 2733056
     1 replies, active 0:00:11, query-origin: Multiple Origins
         via 10.1.1.2 (Infinity/Infinity), r, Ethernet0
         via 10.1.5.2 (Infinity/Infinity), Serial1, serno 159
         via 10.1.2.2 (Infinity/Infinity), Serial0, serno 151
Remaining replies:
         via 10.1.1.1, r, Ethernet0
```

The first entry in the output identifies a neighbor that you are waiting on but that is not under the Remaining replies section. Keep your eye out for both forms.

Now the discussion gets back to troubleshooting. Because the **show ip eigrp topology active** on Router A revealed that you were waiting on neighbor 10.1.4.1 for 1 minute and 23 seconds, you know which neighbor to look at next: Router B. Log into Router B and execute the **show ip eigrp topology active** command again to see why Router A has not received an answer from Router B. Example 3-20 shows the resulting output.

Example 3-20   **show ip eigrp topology active** *Output for Router B*

```
router-b#show ip eigrp topology active
IP-EIGRP Topology Table for process 1 Codes:
P - Passive, A - Active, U - Update, Q - Query, R - Reply,
r - Reply status
A 10.1.100.0/24, 1 successors, FD is Inaccessible
    1 replies, active 00:01:36, query-origin: Successor Origin
        via 10.1.4.3 ((Infinity/Infinity), Ethernet
    Remaining replies:
        via 10.1.1.1, r, Ethernet0
```

Router B is still waiting on a reply from 10.1.1.1, which is Router C. Therefore, the next logical step is to log into Router C and see why it is not answering Router B. After you are on Router C, you issue the command **show ip eigrp topology active** again and get the results in Example 3-21.

Example 3-21   **show ip eigrp topology active** *Output from Router C*

```
router-c#show ip eigrp topology active
IP-EIGRP Topology Table for process 1 Codes:
P - Passive, A - Active, U - Update, Q - Query, R - Reply,
r - Reply status A 10.1.100.0/24, 1 successors, FD is Inaccessible, Q
    1 replies, active 00:01:49, query-origin: Successor Origin
        via 10.1.1.2 (Infinity/Infinity), Ethernet1
    Remaining replies:
        via 10.1.16.1, r, Serial0
```

Router C is in the same condition as Router A and Router B. Router C has not answered Router B because it is still waiting on an answer. Now log into 10.1.16.1, which is Router D, to see if this router is having the same problem. As Example 3-22 indicates, the output of **show ip eigrp topology active** on Router D provides different results.

Example 3-22   **show ip eigrp topology active** *Output from Router D*

```
router-d#show ip eigrp topology active
IP-EIGRP Topology Table for process 1
```

Router D is not waiting on anyone. Router C is waiting on Router D, but Router D is not waiting on replies from any other router. This indicates that the link between Router C and Router D is unreliable, and you need to start exploring why the communications between Routers C and D are not working correctly. The first thing you need to establish is whether the neighbor relationship is up by issuing the **show ip eigrp neighbor** command, as demonstrated in Example 3-23.

Example 3-23 **show ip eigrp neighbor** *Output from Router D*

```
router-d#show ip eigrp neighbor
IP-EIGRP neighbors for process 1
H   Address                 Interface    Hold Uptime    SRTT   RTO   Q  Seq
                                         (sec)          (ms)      Cnt Num
0   10.1.16.2               Se0            14 00:10:27 1197   5000  1  741
router-d#
%DUAL-5-NBRCHANGE: IP-EIGRP 1: Neighbor 10.1.16.2 (Serial0) is down:
  retry limit exceeded
%DUAL-5-NBRCHANGE: IP-EIGRP 1: Neighbor 10.1.16.2 (Serial0) is up: new adjacency
```

The Q count of 1 is not a promising sign. Then you get the error message **retry limit exceeded** on the console because you configured **eigrp log-neighbor-changes** on this router. The **retry limit exceeded** message indicates that acknowledgements are not being received for reliable packets. You need to determine why this is. By going back to Router C and checking the state of the neighbor relationship with Router D, you find the information in Example 3-24.

Example 3-24 **show ip eigrp neighbor** Output *from Router C*

```
router-c#show ip eigrp neighbor
IP-EIGRP neighbors for process 1
H   Address                 Interface    Hold Uptime    SRTT   RTO   Q  Seq
                                         (sec)          (ms)      Cnt Num
0   10.1.16.1               Se0            14 00:10:33  479   5000  1  1388
1   10.1.1.2                Et1            11 00:11:46   28    300  0  5318
RouterC#
%DUAL-5-NBRCHANGE: IP-EIGRP 1: Neighbor 10.1.16.1 (Serial0) is down:
  retry limit exceeded
%DUAL-5-NBRCHANGE: IP-EIGRP 1: Neighbor 10.1.16.1 (Serial0) is up: new adjacency
```

Router C also complains about the inability to exchange reliable traffic with Router D. You need to use your normal troubleshooting skills to resolve this packet delivery problem. You need to issue pings, look at interfaces, and take the other normal steps to find the true cause of the problem.

Other common problems that can cause a router not to answer queries include the following:

- Low memory.

- Congestion on the link, possibly caused by too many routes for the pipe to handle or by queue drops that are too small.

- MTU problems, possibly caused when small packets are delivered over the link, but not large packets.

Without taking the steps following the chain of waiting routers with the **show ip eigrp topology active** command, you never would have been able to find the failing link and start troubleshooting it.

Case Study: Redistribution

You often want to redistribute routes from EIGRP into other protocols and routes from other protocols into EIGRP. The main problem with redistribution between protocols is that it is easy to create redistribution routing loops. Look at Figure 3-23 to see why.

Figure 3-23   *Redistribution Routing Loop*

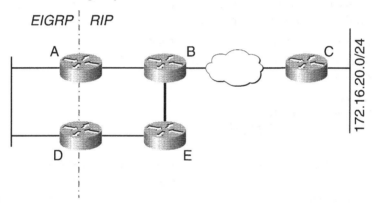

The list that follows describes the sequence of transactions depicted in Figure 3-23.

1 Router C advertises the 172.16.20.0/24 network to Router B. Assume that it has a metric of 3 hops when it reaches Router B.

2 Router B advertises this route with a metric of 4 hops to Router A.

3 Router A redistributes the route into EIGRP with some metric and advertises it to Router D.

4 Router D redistributes it back into Routing Information Protocol (RIP) with a default metric of 1 hop, for example, and advertises it to Router E.

5 Router E advertises this route to Router B with a metric of 2 hops, which is better than the route through Router C (which is, in fact, the correct route).

With the EIGRP use of an administrative distance of 170 for external sites, the preceding problem should not happen, should it? The example is simplified to make it clear. In reality, when Router D gets the route from Router A, Router D should prefer the route it had already received from RIP because it has an administrative distance of 120. What is the problem?

The problem occurs if Router E temporarily loses the route to 172.16.20.0/24 and withdraws it from Router D. If this happens, Router D advertises to Router E the route to 172.16.20.0/24 because of the redistribution from EIGRP. This means that the alternative path is working fine. Unfortunately, because the hop count on the redistribution is set to 1 because of the default metric, when Router E receives the real route back from Router B, it does not use it because the one it received from Router D is better. This is not what you want to happen.

This is a classic redistribution routing loop. How do you solve it? The easiest thing to do is to filter the destinations that are redistributed from RIP into EIGRP and from EIGRP into RIP.

Using Distribute Lists to Prevent Redistribution Routing Loops

The first, and simplest, way to handle this problem is to set up a distribute list specifically blocking the routes that you do not want to redistribute. For example, on Router D, you could build the distribute list in Example 3-25.

Example 3-25 *Using a Distribution List to Block Redistribution Routing Loops*

```
access-list 10 deny 172.16.20.0 0.0.0.255
access-list 10 permit any
!
router rip
 redistribute eigrp 100
 distribute-list 10 out serial 0
```

Assuming that Serial 0 is the link between Router D and Router E, this resolves the problem. RIP does not advertise the 172.16.20.0/24 route from Router D to Router E. If you have more than one connection back into the RIP side of the network, it can be difficult to manage the distribution lists that must be maintained.

Using Route Maps to Prevent Redistribution Routing Loops

An alternative to using a distribute list is to configure a route map on Router D, as demonstrated in Example 3-26.

Example 3-26 *Using a Route Map to Stop a Redistribution Routing Loop*

```
access-list 10 deny 172.16.20.0 0.0.0.255
access-list 10 permit any
!
route-map kill-loops permit 10
 match ip address 10
!
router rip
 redistribute eigrp 100 route-map kill-loops
```

This configuration allows only those networks that are permitted by access list 10 to be redistributed into RIP. This has the same effect as the distribute list used in the preceding solution, but it applies the filter in the redistribution rather than in the advertisement to Router D.

Another alternative is to match all external EIGRP routes in the route map, as demonstrated in Example 3-27.

Example 3-27   *Using a Route Map to Filter External Routes*

```
route-map kill-loops deny 10
 match route-type external
route-map kill-loops permit 20
```

However, this approach also destroys any external EIGRP routes that are learned from a protocol other than RIP. In other words, it prevents external destinations elsewhere in the EIGRP network from being reached by the hosts that are attached on the RIP side of the network.

Using Prefix Lists to Prevent Redistribution Routing Loops

In addition to using distribute lists and route maps to troubleshoot redistribution routing loops, you can use prefix lists. For example, you can configure Router D with the prefix lists in Example 3-28.

Example 3-28   *Using Prefix Lists to Prevent Redistribution Routing Loops*

```
ip prefix-list loop-list 10 deny 172.16.20.0/24
ip prefix-list loop-list 20 permit 0.0.0.0/0 le 32
!
route-map kill-loops permit 10
 match prefix-list loop-list
!
router rip
 redistribute eigrp 100 route-map kill-loops
```

Prefix lists allow you to match based on prefix length (the subnet mask) and the actual prefix (destination network). Many possibilities for filtering exist when this application is considered, but they are not covered here.

Setting the Administrative Distance to Troubleshoot Redistribution Routing Loops

Whereas all the previous mechanisms rely on the configuration (and maintenance) of an access list to prevent a redistribution routing loop, setting the administrative distance of all external routes learned by Router D from Router A does not rely on access lists. You can configure this technique using the **distance** command. On Router D, you would configure the following:

```
router eigrp 100
  distance 255 172.16.21.1 0.0.0.0
```

If the Router A address is 172.16.21.1, Router D assigns an administrative distance of 255 to any routes that it receives from Router A. A route that has an administrative distance of 255 is never inserted into the routing table; therefore, it is not redistributed into RIP from EIGRP. (Redistribution always occurs from the routing table rather than any private databases that the various routing protocols use.)

The only problem with this approach is that Router D refuses all routes learned from Router A, including legitimate ones. You can remedy this by adding the access list back into the equation, as demonstrated in Example 3-29.

Example 3-29   *Using the* **distance** *Command with an Access List to Block Redistribution Loops*

```
access-list 10 permit 172.16.20.0 0.0.0.255
!
router eigrp 100
 distance 255 172.16.21.1 0.0.0.0 10
```

By providing an access list that identifies a particular range of addresses and blocks all others from this neighbor, you can accomplish slightly more selective filtering.

One additional limitation of this approach is that the **distance** command is applied to both internal and external routes. Therefore, if you are trying to limit the filtering to stop the receipt of external routes, you cannot use the **distance** command to accomplish it.

Using External Flags to Prevent Redistribution Routing Loops

All of the previously mentioned troubleshooting methods work, but they require either configuring a list of networks or removing the alternative route through the other protocol as a possible backdoor route in the case of failure. Tagging EIGRP externals to block routing loops resolves these two problems and is fairly straightforward to configure.

Connecting Router A to Router B and Router C to Router D has recently merged the two networks in Figure 3-24. At some point in the future, the network administrators intend to replace RIP with EIGRP; for now, they are redistributing between RIP and EIGRP on Routers A and C.

Figure 3-24   *Complex Redistribution Routing Loop*

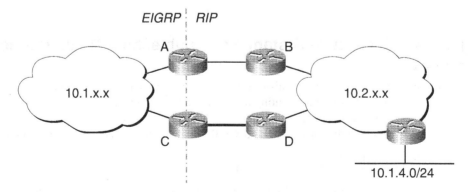

This setup produces a classic redistribution routing loop:

1   Router B learns about some destination, such as 10.1.4.0/24, through RIP. Then it advertises this route to Router A.

2   Router A redistributes this route into EIGRP and advertises it to Router C.

3   Router C redistributes this route back into RIP and advertises it to Router D.

4   Router D advertises the route back to Router B (possibly with a better metric than Router B learned in the original advertisement).

Almost all of the EIGRP network in this figure uses addresses from the 10.1.0.0/16 address space, and almost all of the RIP network uses addresses from the 10.2.0.0/16 address space. However, some exceptions exist, such as the 10.1.4.0/24 network.

If it were not for the exceptions, this redistribution routing loop would be easy to resolve. You would simply prevent Router A and Router C from advertising routes in the 10.2.0.0/16 address range to Router B and Router D and prevent Router B and Router D from advertising routes in the 10.1.0.0/16 address range to Router A and Router C. Distribution lists combined with summarization would make this configuration easy.

Because of the exceptions, though, preventing this redistribution routing loop is more difficult. You could build distribution lists around the subnets present on each side and apply them on Router A, Router B, Router C, and Router D, but this adds some serious administrative overhead if many exceptions exist. Specific distribution lists would also require modification for each new exception added.

It is easier to use an automatic method to flag the routes learned through RIP on Router A and Router C. Then you can prevent any route that is flagged from being redistributed back into RIP. For example, Router A still learns about the 10.1.100.0/24 network through EIGRP and advertises this destination to Router B through RIP.

Router B still advertises 10.1.4.0/24 to Router A, which redistributes it into EIGRP and advertises it to Router C. However, Router A flags this route as coming from the RIP domain so that Router C does not advertise it back into RIP. Using some sort of tag like this means that adding a new network in the RIP AS should not require reconfiguration on the routers that are doing the redistribution. This type of routing loop is a good use for EIGRP administrator tags.

Administrator tags are applied and matched using route maps. On Router A and Router C, you create the route maps and then apply them to the redistribution between EIGRP and RIP by issuing the commands in Example 3-30.

Example 3-30   *Setting Administrative Tags on Redistribution*

```
route-map setflag permit 10
  set tag 1
route-map denyflag deny 10
  match tag 1
route-map denyflag permit 20
```

The **setflag** route map sets the administrator tag on any route to 1, whereas the **denyflag** route map denies routes with a flag of 1 and permits all others. On Router A and Router C, you apply these route maps to the redistribution between EIGRP and RIP by issuing the commands in Example 3-31.

Example 3-31 *Applying Tag Filtering on Redistribution*

```
router eigrp 4000
  redistribute rip route-map setflag
router rip
  redistribute eigrp 4000 route-map denyflag
```

As routes are redistributed from RIP to EIGRP, the **setflag** route map is applied, setting the EIGRP administrative tag to 1. As the routes are redistributed from EIGRP to RIP, the administrative tag is checked; if it is 1, the route is denied so that it is not redistributed.

Case Study: Retransmissions and SIA

Two timers that can interact in EIGRP to cause an SIA route in EIGRP are the SIA timer and the hold timer between two peers. How do these two relate? This section examines the two timers independently and then looks at how they interact.

The Hold Timer

The obvious use for the hold timer is to determine how long to hold up a neighbor relationship without hearing EIGRP hellos. Each time a router receives a hello packet from a neighbor, it resets the hold timer to the hold time contained in the hello packet and decrements it once for each second that passes.

After the hold timer reaches zero, the neighbor is assumed dead. All paths through that neighbor are marked unusable (DUAL is run over these destinations to determine if the route needs to go active), and the neighbor is marked down.

However, the hold timer is also used by the EIGRP reliable transport mechanism as an outer bound on how long to wait for a neighbor to acknowledge the receipt of a packet. As mentioned in Appendix A, EIGRP attempts to retransmit 16 times or until retransmission has been occurring for as long as the hold timer, whichever is longer.

In the network depicted in Figure 3-25, assume that the Router D hold timer is 240 seconds. (Ignore the Hello timer because these are separate timers.)

Figure 3-25 *Interactions Between Hold Timers and SIA Timers*

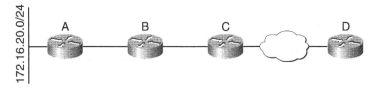

If Router C sends a packet to Router D, and Router D does not acknowledge the packet, Router C continues retransmitting until it has retransmitted 16 times. Then Router C checks to see if it has been retransmitting for 240 seconds. If it has not, Router C continues sending the packet until it has been retransmitting for 240 seconds. After Router C has attempted retransmission for 240 seconds, it assumes that Router D is never going to answer and clear its neighbor relationship.

SIA Timer

The other timer that you need to concern yourself with is the SIA timer because it determines how long a query can be outstanding before the route is declared SIA and the neighbor relationship with the router that has not answered is torn down and restarted.

Prior to the SIA enhancements explained in the section "Enhanced EIGRP Active Process," the active timer is, by default, 3 minutes (although there has been talk of changing it). This means that a router waits 3 minutes after it has declared a route active until it decides that any neighbor that has not replied for this active route has a problem and restarts the neighbor.

Going back to Figure 3-25, this means that if Router A loses its connection to 172.16.20.0/24, it sends a query to Router B. If it does not receive a reply to that query within 3 minutes, it restarts its neighbor relationship with Router B. Note that two completely different things are being discussed here:

- How long to wait before getting an acknowledgement for a packet
- How long to wait for a reply to a query

Interaction Between the Hold Timer and the SIA Timer

You can work through an example of how these two timers interact. Assume that Router A in Figure 3-25 loses its connection to 172.16.20.0/24. Because it has no other paths to this destination, it marks the route as active and sends Router B a query.

Router B acknowledges the query and sends a query to Router C; Router C, in turn, acknowledges the query and sends a query to Router D. Router D, for some reason, never acknowledges the query. Router C begins retransmitting the query to Router D. It attempts to do so until it has retransmitted for the length of the hold timer.

For the entire time that Router C is trying to get an acknowledgement from Router D, the Router A SIA timer is running. Because the SIA timer is 3 minutes, and the Router D hold timer is 4 minutes, it is safe to assume that the Router A SIA timer will go off before Router C gives up retransmitting the query to Router D and clears the neighbor relationship.

Therefore, Router A registers an SIA and clears its neighbor relationship with Router B. It is important to remember when designing your network that the hold timer for any given link should never be more than or equal to the SIA timer for the entire network.

In this case, two solutions are possible:

- Reduce the Router D hold time to something less than the SIA timer (90 seconds, for example) by using the interface level command **ip eigrp hold-time**.

- Increase the SIA timer to something greater than the hold timer (five minutes, for example) by using the command **timers active** under the router EIGRP configuration.

Knowing which option to choose without more information is difficult. If the link between Router C and Router D is congested often enough that an acknowledgement takes 4 minutes to get through, it is probably going to be necessary to increase the SIA timer.

On the other hand, if it seems unreasonable to wait 4 minutes for a simple acknowledgement across a single link, it is better to decrease the hold timer on Router D. Remember to decrease the Hello timer, too, or you will have problems maintaining neighbor relationships. If a router is still sending hellos every 60 seconds, but the hold time is reduced to 90 seconds, the neighbor can be torn down if only two hellos are lost instead of three. The best practice is to always set the hold timer as a multiple of three hellos. If you reduce the hold time, you need to reduce the hello interval accordingly.

The two tradeoffs are as follows:

- The hold timer should be a reasonable amount of time, given the nature of the link and the likelihood of an EIGRP packet being delayed for a given period of time.

- The SIA timer bounds the time that the network is allowed to remain unconverged.

You need to balance these two tradeoffs for your network. There are no magic numbers (although there are defaults) .

Case Study: Multiple EIGRP Autonomous Systems

One design that is used commonly in EIGRP to limit query range and improve stability is multiple autonomous systems, but is this really effective? Look at Figure 3-26 for some answers.

Begin by assuming that Router D is redistributing all the routes from AS 100 into AS 200 and all the routes from AS 200 into AS 100. If Router C loses its direct connection to 172.30.9.0/24, it notes that it has no feasible successor, places the destination in active state, and queries each of its neighbors.

When Router D receives this query, it looks through its topology table and, seeing no other routes to this destination within this AS, immediately sends a reply to Router C that this route is no longer reachable. Router C acknowledges the reply and removes the route from its topology table (so far, so good).

Figure 3-26   *Multiple EIGRP Autonomous Systems*

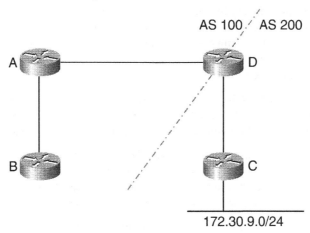

Return to Router D once more. Router D was redistributing this route into AS 100. When Router D loses the route, it goes active on the AS 100 topology table entry and queries its neighbors (in this case, Router A). Router A, in turn, queries Router B; the entire query process runs in AS 100 for this route.

In short, AS boundaries do not really stop queries. The query itself might stop, but a new query is generated at the AS border and propagated through the neighboring AS.

Therefore, AS boundaries do not help with query range issues, but can they really harm anything? Look at Figure 3-27 for a moment.

Figure 3-27   *Autosummarization Across an AS Boundary*

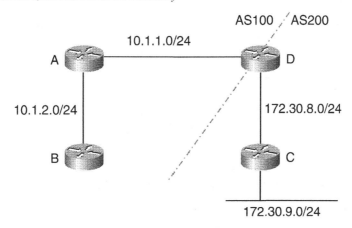

In the network that is illustrated, not only does Router D redistribute between AS 100 and AS 200, but an autosummary for the 10.0.0.0/8 network on Router D is also being advertised toward Router C, and an autosummary for 172.30.0.0/16 is being advertised toward Router A. Because of these autosummaries, the query range is bound at Router A for 172.30.9.0/24. In other words, Router B never receives a query about this network because Router A should not have information about it in its topology database.

The problem is that EIGRP does not autosummarize externals unless an internal component exists in the topology table. Router D does not build summaries for the 10.0.0.0/8 and 172.30.0.0/16 networks automatically; it advertises all the components.

The really confusing part comes in if you decide to add something in the 10.0.0.0 network on Router B. Suppose that you add an Ethernet link to Router B and address it as 10.1.5.0/24. Router B summarizes this to be 10.0.0.0/8 and advertises it toward Router A (remember that this is an internal component), and Router A advertises it to Router D.

When Router D sees an internal component in the 10.0.0.0 network within AS 100, it begins summarizing the external sites toward Router A, advertising only the 10.0.0.0/8 route. This means that Router A has two routes to 10.0.0.0/8—a confusing situation at best.

What if you do not try to put a major net boundary on an AS boundary and rely on manual summarization? Multiple autonomous systems have no other problems, do they? As a matter of fact, they do. Look at Figure 3-28 for a third problem.

Figure 3-28   *Discontiguous Autonomous Systems*

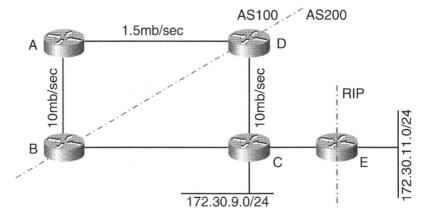

Router B and Router D are redistributing between AS 100 and AS 200. Router E is redistributing from RIP into EIGRP AS 200. Router B receives two routes for 172.30.9.0/24:

- An internal route through Router C
- An external route through Router A

Which route does Router B choose? The route through Router A probably has a better metric, but Router B chooses the path through Router C because the administrative distance of internal routes is better than the administrative distance of external routes.

If all of these routers were in a single AS, Router B would choose the shortest path to 172.30.9.0/ 24; using multiple autonomous systems causes the routers to choose suboptimal routes.

Consider the route to 172.30.11.0/24 next. Which route does Router B choose for this destination? Router B should choose the route through Router A because both routes are externals. The administrative distances are the same for both routes.

However, the behavior in this instance is undefined. In other words, Router B could choose either route, regardless of which one has the better metric.

All in all, it is best to stick to one AS unless you have carefully considered all the issues involved in multiple AS designs. With good design, you can limit the query scope within the network through summarization and distribution lists.

If an EIGRP network grows large enough to need splitting, it is better to use a protocol other than EIGRP to do so (preferably BGP) .

Review Questions

1 What are the two basic tools you can use to summarize routes (or hide destination details) in EIGRP?

2 How can you tell that a route is a summary when you look at the routing table?

3 What is the default administrative distance for a summary route? What is the problem with this?

4 What bounds a query?

5 How far beyond one of the possible query bounds does a query travel?

6 What is the primary advantage to summarizing between core routers rather than between the distribution layer and core?

7 How is it possible to "black hole" packets when summarizing destinations behind dual-homed remotes into the core?

8 Why should summarization be configured outbound from the distribution layer routers toward access layer routers at remote sites?

9 What is the most common problem with dual-homed remotes? What options are available to resolve it?

10 What methods can you use to break a redistribution routing loop?

11 Under what conditions is the administrative distance ignored between EIGRP and IGRP?

12 What options do you have for generating a default route in EIGRP?

13 How can you prevent multiple parallel links within a network from being used as transit paths?

14 What does EIGRP use to pace its packets on a link?

CHAPTER 4

OSPF Network Design

Open Shortest Path First (OSPF) is one of the most widely deployed routing protocols in networks worldwide, stretching across markets from service provider, to Enterprise, to various government organizations. OSPF was standardized by the Internet Engineering Task Force (IETF) as RFC 1131 and then updated through a series of RFCs:

- RFC 1247 in 1991
- RFC 1583 in 1994
- RFC 2178 in 1997
- RFC 2328 in 1998 (most recent)

A series of RFCs describes options and additional capabilities added to the protocols since its original specification, including RFC 3101, "The OSPF Not-So-Stubby Area (NSSA) Option."

NOTE   For more information on OSPF operation, see Appendix B, "OSPF Basics of Operation," and Routing TCP/IP Volume I, by Jeff Doyle, available through Cisco Press.

This chapter begins with coverage of summarization and aggregation in OSPF and then examines OSPF deployment in a three- and two-layer hierarchy. The chapter continues with coverage of some specific topologies, including dial-in links, hub-and-spoke networks, and full mesh networks. The chapter concludes with coverage of redistribution and other issues.

Summarization and Aggregation

A network has two types of summarization:

- **Aggregation of address space**—This hides reachability, so multiple networks are advertised through one routing update.
- **Summarization of topology information**—This hides what the topology looks like, advertising just which destinations are reachable, not how to get there.

Whereas distance vector protocols summarize topology information at every router, link-state protocols do not. When considering the deployment of OSPF, you need to take into account summarization points for both topology information and reachability information. How do you hide topology information in OSPF? You do this by limiting the domain within which topology information is flooded—by controlling the size of the network flooding domains.

Where can you summarize reachability information in an OSPF network? Because you cannot summarize reachability information without blocking topology information, you can only configure reachability summaries at the edge of a flooding domain. This ties the points where aggregation of reachability and topology information can be hidden together. You cannot simply pick the points where aggregating reachability information is optimum or where summarizing topology information is optimum.

| NOTE | This chapter uses the term *aggregation* to discuss the summarization of reachability information; *summarization* refers to the summarization of topology information. |

How do you know the correct balance between aggregation and summarization? In other words, if you are in a position to choose between better aggregation and better summarization, which one is more important to the stability and convergence speed of the network? As a rule of thumb, it is better to focus on better summarization and then make smaller changes to optimize aggregation.

| NOTE | Chapter 5, "IS-IS Network Design," better illustrates this focus through some test results, providing insight on this specific question. |

The rule of thumb when working with an OSPF network design is this:

Separate complexity from complexity where possible.

After you have determined the points of complexity in the network and determined where, within a range of routers, the optimal point to divide the flooding domains is (where the area border routers [ABRs] can be placed), decide which point to use based on optimal aggregation. Refer to Figure 4-1 for the following explanation.

Where is the optimal aggregation and summarization point? Following the rule of thumb, you want to separate the two Data Centers and the hub-and-spoke network from each other (because all three are complex topologies or areas of complexity). Because you can insert only one flooding domain division into the network, you can separate the two full mesh Data Centers into two separate flooding domains, but you need to place the hub-and-spoke network into one of the two flooding domains created.

Figure 4-1   *Balancing Optimal Summarization and Aggregation*

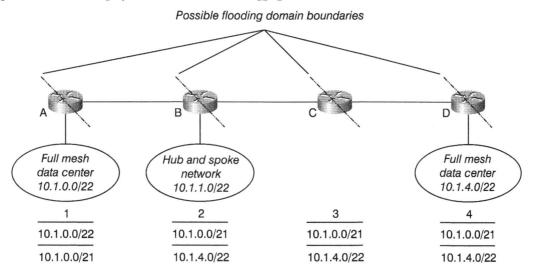

By examining the network addressing and determining where you will get the best aggregation of reachability information, you can determine which flooding domain is the best one to put the hub-and-spoke network into. Any of the following are possible:

1   Router A advertises 10.1.0.0/22 toward Router B and aggregates 10.1.0.0/20 into the Data CenterData Center behind Router A. Routers A, B, C, and D all have three routes, just counting the routes shown in Figure 4-1.

2   Aggregate at Router B, advertising 10.1.0.0/21 toward Router C, and advertise 10.1.4.0/22 toward Router A. Router A has two routes, Router B has three routes, and Routers C and D each has two routes.

3   Aggregate at Router C, advertising 10.1.0.0/21 toward Router D, and advertise 10.1.4.0/22 toward Router B. Routers A, B, and C have three routes, and Router D has two routes.

4   Aggregate at Router D, advertise 10.1.0.0/21 into the area behind Router D, and advertise 10.1.4.0/22 toward Router C. All four routers have three routes.

If you are trying to reduce the number of routes in the network, you should choose summarization and aggregation at Router B.

Deploying OSPF on a Three-Layer Hierarchy

Three-layer hierarchies pose an interesting problem for OSPF. OSPF provides two layers of hierarchy within its flooding domain and summarization models. Where, then, do you put the border between the flooding domains in a three-layer hierarchy? The usual answer applies: It depends. The sections that follow examine some various situations in a three-layer network, and, working with the general rules outlined in the last section, determine the best summarization and aggregation points.

The Core Routers as ABRs

In a three-layer hierarchy, you have two primary choices when deciding where to place the ABRs:

- At the edge of the core
- Within the distribution layer

If you define the ABRs at the edge of the core, the core itself becomes area 0. However, if you place the ABRs within the distribution layer, area 0 is split between the core and the distribution layers of the network. Figure 4-2 illustrates a small network with the ABRs placed at the edge of the core.

Figure 4-2   *Placing the ABRs at the Core Edge*

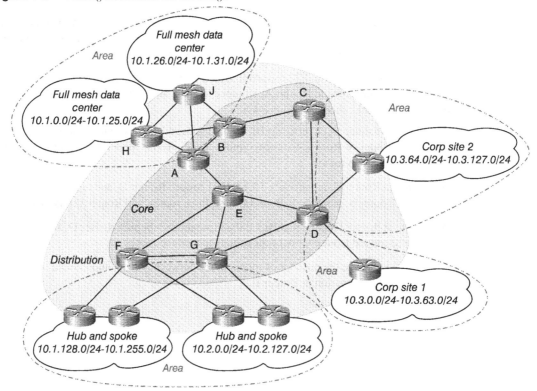

Following are some of the advantages of placing the ABRs at the edge of the core:

- Area 0 is contained. Its size and scope are easy to manage because the core of a network tends to be the area with the least amount of change and growth over longer stretches of time. This can make network planning and the design of new network elements easier.

  In the network in Figure 4-2, limiting area 0 to the core limits it to Routers A through G. New corporate sites could easily be attached to Routers C and D, additional hub-and-spoke topologies could be connected to Routers F and G, and new Data Centers could be connected to Routers A and B. It is difficult to think of a situation in which moderate growth within this network would require the size of the core to be expanded.

- It should be easy to optimize aggregation of routes. The core should have a well-defined set of connections to the distribution layer, providing a good set of aggregation points within the network.

  In the network illustrated in Figure 4-2, Routers A and B can advertise 10.1.0.0/19, Routers C and D can advertise 10.1.3.64/18, Router D can advertise 10.1.3.128/19, and Routers F and G can advertise 10.1.128.0/17 and 10.2.0.0/17. The core would have only a handful of routes.

- Managing redundancy within the distribution layer of the network is generally easier to do. Because the core is naturally divided from the distribution layer redundancy and design, making the distribution layer redundancy invisible to the core routers is easy. Further, dual-homed remotes tend to be dual homed into the distribution layer, and hiding the impact of dual-homed remote sites in hub-and-spoke networks by placing the aggregation and summarization boundary at the edge of the core is easy.

  In the network illustrated in Figure 4-2, the mesh of connectivity among Routers A, B, H, and J would be placed in a flooding domain outside area 0, simplifying the area 0 topology, for instance.

Placing the area borders at the core also has some disadvantages:

- **Added design complexity at the distribution layer**—If you summarize at the edge of the core, you are effectively pushing much of the design complexity within the network into the distribution layer.

  In the network illustrated in Figure 4-2, the flooding domain that contains the two Data Centers and the flooding domain that contains the two hub-and-spoke areas appear to have complex topologies with several routes.

- **The distribution layer can become extraneous**—If you summarize at the core router, you can effectively take the distribution routers out of the network, because all they are providing is a bit of redundancy. By placing the area borders at the core of the network, you might effectively make the network a two-layer hierarchy.

In the network shown in Figure 4-2, all the traffic that passes between the two full mesh Data Centers behind Routers H and J uses the direct link between these two routers, because the link is an intra-area path between them. This might be okay, depending on the link sizing and other design criteria, but it might also cause problems with the link between Routers H and J overloading in some situations.

The Distribution Layer Routers as ABRs

Another option is to place the ABRs in the distribution layer of a three-layer network design. The advantages and disadvantages of placing the ABRs within the distribution layer are almost the opposite of the ones covered when discussing placing the summarization and aggregation points at the edge of the core. Refer to Figure 4-3 to consider the advantages and disadvantages of placing the ABRs at the distribution layer.

Figure 4-3 *Placing ABRs Within the Distribution Layer Only*

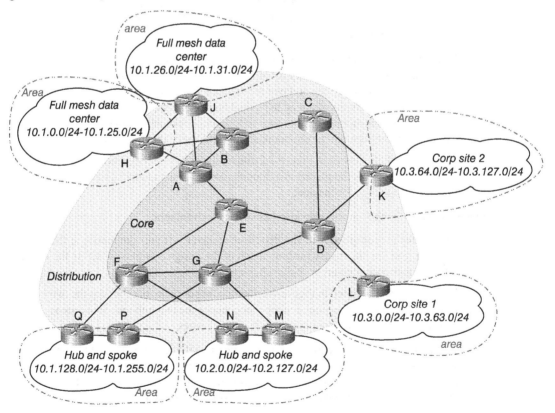

Advantages of the network setup in Figure 4-3 include the following:

- **Limits the complexity of areas that are created within the network**—You might wind up with more areas, because you are generally going to split what was normally one area connected to a core router into multiple areas, each one touching a small number of distribution layer routers.

  In the example shown in Figure 4-3, the two hub and spoke topologies are split apart when you move the ABRs to the distribution layer, and the two full mesh Data Centers are also seperated into two different areas. You have added only a small amount of complexity into area 0, but you have decreased the complexity of each of the outlying areas dramatically. This can be a major factor in network stability and scaling.

- **Allows the distribution layer to work**—Aggregation of routing information and controlling the path traffic takes into the network core are distribution layer tasks. These tasks fall within the distribution layer naturally if the distribution layer routers are configured as ABRs.

  As noted previously when discussing the network illustrated in Figure 4-2, the link between Routers H and J would carry all the traffic between the two full mesh Data Centers. Therefore, the distribution layer would not be in a position to control the traffic flow between these two Data Centers into the network core. In Figure 4-3, summarization is configured on the distribution layer routers, rather than the core routers. Because summarization is one of the normal functions of the distribution layer, it is more natural, in terms of layer functionality, to configure the distribution layer routers as ABRs.

Disadvantages of the network setup in Figure 4-3 include the following:

- The size and complexity of area 0 is harder to control as the network grows and changes to meet business needs. If several groups are working within different parts of area 0, the network shape could change drastically in a short period, impacting services that the network provides without much oversight or capability to control the changes from a routing protocol perspective.

  In the network shown in Figure 4-3, you can see that area 0 grows slightly in size and complexity when you move the ABRs from the core edge to the distribution layer. Each new hub-and-spoke topology, each new corporate site, and each new Data Center could possibly add to the complexity of area 0.

- Aggregation of routing information might not be well defined at the distribution layer. (In a network that has more flexible addressing architectures or a network that is designed to provide maximum summarization at the distribution layer, this should not be an issue.)

When you place the ABRs at the edge of the core in Figure 4-3, the core receives
5 summary routes and contains 9 routes, for a total of 14 routes. When you place
the ABRs in the distribution layer, you have this:

— Router H advertising 10.1.0.0/20, 10.1.16.0/21, and 10.1.24.0/23

— Router J advertising 10.1.26.0/23 and 10.1.28.0/22

— Router K advertising 10.3.64.0/18

— Router L advertising 10.3.0.0/18

— Routers M and N advertising 10.2.0.0/17

— Routers Q and P advertising 10.1.128.0/17

— 21 links within area 0

This provides a total of 30 routes within area 0. This is a major difference in the
number of routes within area 0, given the small size of this network.

- The redundancy between the distribution layer routers and the core of the network is
  exposed within area 0. This could add considerably to the complexity of the area 0
  topology.

  This is specifically the case with Routers A, B, H, and J, connecting the two Data
  Centers. The full mesh "box" between the Data Centers and the core is exposed
  to area 0 when you place the ABRs within the distribution layer.

Mixing ABR Locations

Probably the most successful solution for placing flooding domain boundaries is to consider the
placement for each ABR independently. To provide an example of this type of analysis,
examine Figure 4-4.

Look at the advantages and disadvantages in each case:

- At Routers A, B, H, and J, you trade off the number of routes advertised and the
  complexity added to the core against splitting up the two full mesh Data Centers to reduce
  the complexity within the area. The Data Centers seem to be small (32 routes between the
  two of them), so the weight is toward reducing the complexity of area 0 and reducing the
  routes that are advertised by the ABRs. Here, you place the ABRs at the edge of the
  network core.

- At Routers C, D, and K, you can either include Routers C and D in the area with Corporate
  Site 2, or you can include Routers C and D in area 0. You will not see much difference in
  the outcome as far as the number of routes and the complexity of each area, so leave the
  ABR in the distribution layer of the network. This allows summarization to occur in the
  most natural place within the three-layer hierarchy.

- At Routers D and L, you can either include Router D in the area with Corporate Site 1, or you can place the ABR at Router L so that Router D is entirely in area 0. Again, you will not notice much of a tradeoff in terms of routes advertised into the core or the complexity of either the outlying area or area 0, so you might as well leave the ABR positioned on the distribution layer router.

- At Routers F, G, N, M, P, and Q, you must choose among splitting up the two hub-and-spoke topologies, making the hub routers ABRs, or placing both hub-and-spoke topologies in the same area. The hub-and-spoke topologies seem to be moderately sized, with more than 100 remote sites per topology, so you will split the two hub-and-spoke topologies from one another, placing each in a separate area. This decision is strengthened after examining the results of splitting the two hub-and-spoke topologies into two areas. Two routes are advertised into the network core regardless of how you divide the areas.

Figure 4-4   *Mixing ABR Locations*

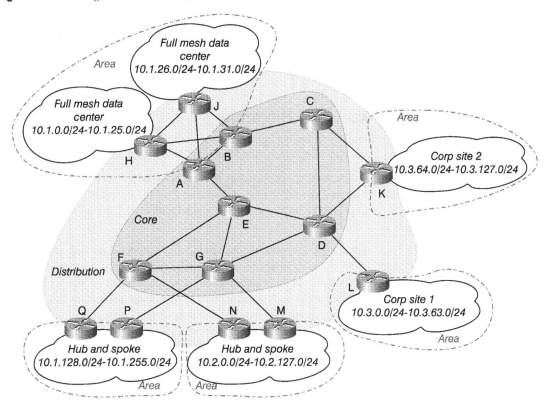

NOTE   In general, you should lean toward placing the ABRs in the distribution layer where possible, making exceptions where needed to control complexity and increase your ability to aggregate routing information.

Examining each of these decisions more closely, you will find that you are attempting to balance a three-cornered triangle:

- **Complexity separation**—It is a good rule of thumb, when designing a link-state network, to place flooding domain boundaries so that complex areas of the network are separated from other complex areas of the network.

- **Flooding domain complexity**—It is best not to have one flooding domain that is complex and the remainder of the flooding domains simple. Balance the complexity level among the flooding domains through boundary selection.

- **Route aggregation**—Flooding domain boundaries should always consider the aggregation that is possible at the boundary edge. Route aggregation is one of the most important keys to building a robust, stable, and scalable network.

Deploying OSPF on a Two-Layer Hierarchy

With the three-layer hierarchy in the background, consider how you would place flooding domain borders in a two-layer hierarchy, using Figure 4-5 as a reference model.

In general, determining where to place the flooding domain boundaries in a two-layer hierarchy is much simpler. The boundary should be placed on the edge of the core, unless specific situations arise that indicate the boundary should be placed within the core or within the aggregation layer.

For instance, in this small sample network, the flooding domains around the hub-and-spoke topologies at Routers M, N, P, and Q might be better divided at the hub routers themselves, rather than at the edge of the core. In this case, you also have more than two levels of route hierarchy. You will always find areas of ambiguity in flooding domain placement that has three levels of routed hierarchy. You can use the same design criteria and concepts outlined previously, when considering three-layer hierarchy placement, to determine where to place the flooding domain boundary in these situations.

Figure 4-5 *Deploying OSPF in a Two-Layer Hierarchy*

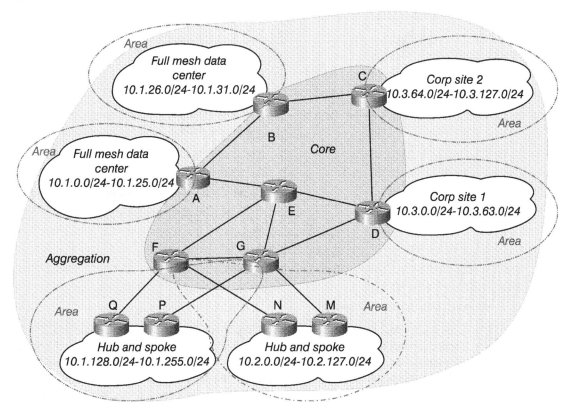

Reducing Flooding Through Stub Areas

Stub areas maximize the concepts of hiding topology and reachability information. The more "stubby" that an area is, the less topology and reachability information that is flooded into the area. Obtaining a better understanding of stub areas warrants a quick review of the information that is flooded within an OSPF area and between OSPF areas. Figure 4-6 illustrates.

Figure 4-6   *Information Flooded Within an Area and Between Areas*

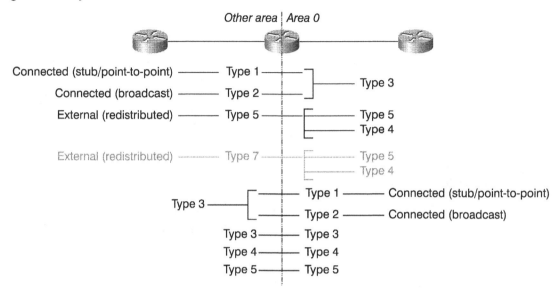

Normally, you have the following:

- Type 1 link-state advertisements (LSAs), representing an adjacent neighbor or a connected stub network with no neighbors on it. This is translated into a Type 3 LSA, a summary, at an ABR. The Type 3 LSA does not, without specific configuration, aggregate addresses learned from Type 1 LSAs. Instead, the Type 3 advertises reachability and cost, without the topology information contained within the Type 1 LSAs, into the receiving area. This LSA is called the *router LSA*. It contains other information about the advertising router beyond reachable neighbors and connected stub networks.

- Type 2 LSAs, representing a designated router (pseudonode) on a broadcast network. These are, again, converted into a Type 3 summary LSA by the ABR.

- Type 3 LSAs, which are just reflooded by the ABR, from one area to another.

- Type 4 LSAs provide reachability to Autonomous System Border Routers (ASBRs), which redistribute external routing information into OSPF. Type 4 LSAs are generated for any router with the border router, or E bit, set in its Type 1 LSA.

- Type 5 LSAs, providing reachability to external networks or reachability information redistributed into OSPF. ABRs reflood these into and out of the areas they are connecting.

- Type 7 LSAs, providing reachability to external networks or reachability information redistributed into OSPF. These are generated only within an NSSA, discussed more in this section and in Appendix B. Type 7 LSAs are translated by the ABR into Type 5 external LSAs.

With this information in mind, consider each stub area type and the information that it prevents the ABR from flooding into the area.

NOTE   Suboptimal routing is always possible when you remove information from a routing system. See the "Summary Suboptimal Routing," section in Chapter 2, "Applying the Fundamentals," for more details and examples of suboptimal routing caused by aggregation of routing information. Stub areas are no exception. They are explicitly designed to remove information from the routing system to improve the scaling and performance characteristics of a network. You will almost always find suboptimal routing when you use stub areas that have more than one exit point.

Stub Areas

ABRs do not flood Type 5 LSAs into or out of stub areas, as outlined in RFC 2328, section 3.6. This means there can be no external sources of routing information within a stub area (no ASBRs), and the path taken to external destinations injected from other areas does not matter. Figure 4-7 illustrates the LSA types flooded into and out of a stub area.

You can see that the bottom two types of LSAs—Type 4s and Type 5s—are not flooded into a stub area. This reduces the complexity of the OSPF database in routers within the area. Externals, Type 5 LSAs, cannot be originated within a stub area.

Each ABR that is connected to a stub area is required to generate a default route into the area. Therefore, destinations that are normally reachable through external routing information can still be reached through the default route.

Figure 4-7   *Flooding in a Stub Area*

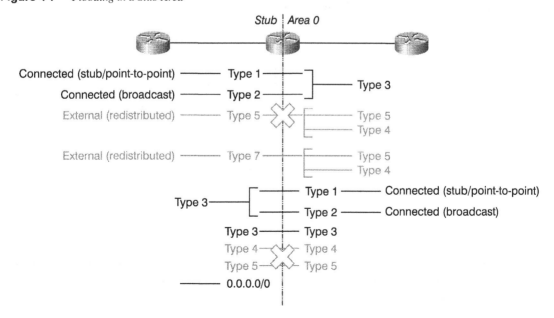

To configure an area as a stub area in Cisco IOS Software, use the **area stub** command:

```
area area-id stub
```

All the routers within an area must be configured with this command, including the ABR, for the OSPF routers to form adjacencies and exchange routing information.

Totally Stubby Areas

Not only are type 5 LSAs not flooded into totally stubby areas, Type 3 LSAs are not flooded into totally stubby areas, either, as Figure 4-8 illustrates. This takes the concept of a stub area one step further, simplifying the network's topology to routers within the totally stubby area to the largest possible degree.

Routers within a totally stubby area choose their exit point by simply calculating the cost to the nearest ABR. This may lead to dramatic suboptimal routing, so only use totally stubby areas when the exit point out of the area isn't important from a traffic flow perspective.

Figure 4-8   *Flooding in a Totally Stubby Area*

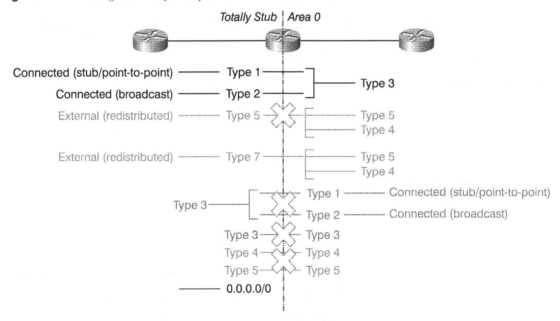

Each ABR that is connected to a totally stubby area must generate a default route into the area. That means destinations normally advertised through Type 3 or Type 5 LSAs will remain reachable.

To configure an area as a totally stubby area in Cisco IOS Software, use the following command:

```
area area-id stub no-summary
```

Type 3 LSAs are known as summary LSAs; the **no-summary** option blocks these summary LSAs. Every router within the totally stubby area, including the ABR, must be configured with this command.

Not-So-Stubby Areas

After stub areas had been designed and deployed for some time, numerous large network designers concluded that it was not always possible to design an area with no ASBRs injecting external information, but it would still improve network stability if they could use some form of stub area. To meet both requirements of having an ASBR redistributing information into OSPF within a stub area, a new type of LSA was created, along with rules on how to treat this LSA. RFC 3101 describes this new type of area, a Not-So-Stubby Area (NSSA). Figure 4-9 illustrates flooding into and out of an NSSA.

Figure 4-9   *Flooding into and out of an NSSA*

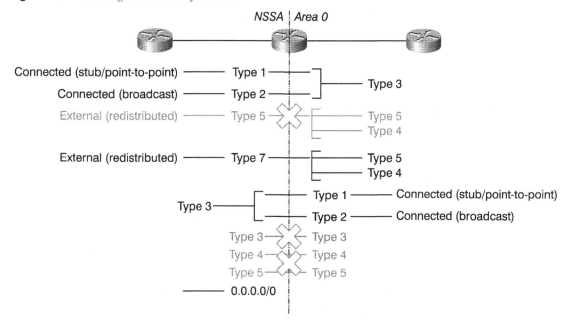

The new type of LSA created is the Type 7, which is formatted identically to a Type 5 LSA. If a router is within an NSSA and is also redistributing reachability information from outside OSPF, the router advertises itself as a border router and generate Type 7 LSAs containing the external information.

When an ABR receives the Type 1 LSA of the redistributing router with the border bit set, it generates a Type 4 LSA into area 0, just like an ABR that is connected to a normal area. Each Type 7 LSA that an ABR receives, however, is translated into a Type 5 LSA and then flooded into area 0. To routers outside an NSSA, the area appears to be a normal area, rather than an NSSA.

Routers inside an NSSA, however, do not receive type 5 external information reflooded from area 0 through their ABR. Instead, they must rely on a default route generated by the ABRs to reach external destinations. Routers inside an NSSA do receive Type 7 LSAs and treat them the same as they would a Type 5 LSA.

NOTE   This translation between Type 7 and Type 5 LSAs can be processor intensive, so most implementations have a timer that batches Type 7-to-Type 5 translations. Timing these translations, however, can have a large negative impact on the performance of your network, especially where external routes are concerned. In some cases, it might be better either to redesign an area so that no external routing information is injected through it or to configure the area as a normal (not stubby) area and filter the routing information injected into the area.

To configure an area as an NSSA in Cisco IOS Software, use the **area nssa** command in the OSPF router configuration mode:

```
area area-id nssa [no-redistribution] [default-information-originate [metric]
    [metric-type]]
```

The **no-redistribution** option prevents routes redistributed on the ABR itself from being imported into the NSSA through Type 7 LSAs. Because routers within the NSSA are receiving a default route from the ABR, there is generally no reason to inject routes redistributed at the ABR into an NSSA, unless you need to optimally route to these external destinations.

You should almost always use the **default-information-originate** option on ABRs along with the **area nssa** command, unless you are certain that some other default is always going to be carried into the NSSA. This way, routers within the NSSA can reach external destinations for which routing information is not injected into the area. As always, every router within an NSSA must be configured for NSSA operation using the **area nssa** command; otherwise, it will not form neighbor adjacencies and exchange routing information.

Totally NSSA

A totally NSSA is related to an NSSA in the same way that a totally stubby area is related to a stub area; no summary or external routing information is flooded into a totally NSSA, as Figure 4-10 illustrates.

In Figure 4-10, you can see that the same mechanism is used for external information redistributed within the totally NSSA; Type 7 LSAs are created and translated into Type 5 LSAs at the ABR. You can also see that Type 3 summary information, Type 4 border router information, and Type 5 external information are not flooded into the NSSA.

An ABR that is connected to an NSSA must generate a default route into the NSSA so that all destinations are still reachable from the devices within the NSSA.

Figure 4-10   *Flooding into and out of a Totally NSSA*

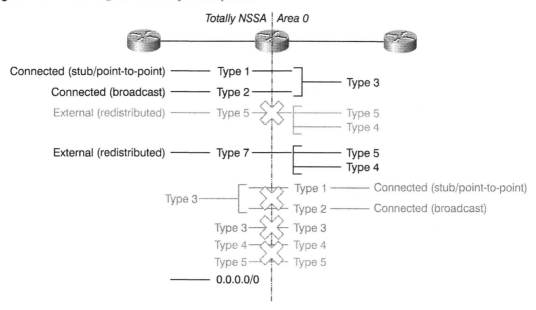

To configure an area as a totally NSSA in Cisco IOS Software, use the **area nssa** command in the OSPF router configuration mode:

```
area area-id nssa [no-redistribution] [default-information-originate [metric]
   [metric-type]] no-summary
```

Note the addition of the **no-summary** keyword, indicating that summary routes (Type 3 LSAs) should not be flooded into this area. The other options are the same as described earlier in the section, "Not-So-Stubby Areas."

Totally Stubby Not Really Full Areas

With the totally stubby not really full area (TSNRFA), you find that the ABR translates Type 5 LSAs from within the area into Type 7 LSAs, as long as no overlapping Type 3 is in its local database. The ABR floods Type 1 and Type 2 LSAs into area 0, unless the network administrator has configured the "really stubby" option.

Actually, this type of area is made up. It does not exist. The authors just thought you might need a break after wading through all the real stub area types.

When to Use Stub Areas

When should you use stub areas? Always.

NOTE   We would have made the preceding sentence flash, but the publisher told us that inserting an LED panel into the book was too expensive. Just read it as if it were blinking.

Well, almost always, anyway. The general rule of thumb is to configure an area as a stub unless you have some specific reason not to, such as the translation time between Type 7 and Type 5 external routing information in NSSAs, or if suboptimal routing is unacceptable. In either of these cases, however, you should consider using filtering or aggregation of routing information at the ABR, as described in the sections, "Aggregating Routes in OSPF," and "Filtering Routes in OSPF," which follow.

Using stub areas within networks is important because experience indicates that stub areas greatly enhance the scaling and convergence properties of an OSPF network. You should always default to configuring an area as a stub area, unless some specific factor convinces you that the area does not need to be a stub area.

Aggregating Routes in OSPF

Routing information can be aggregated at any OSPF, ABR, or ASBR. To aggregate routing information at an ABR, use the **area-range** command:

```
area area-id range ip-address mask [advertise | not-advertise] [cost cost]
```

The area in this command is the area that you want the summary to be announced into, rather than the area that the routes you are summarizing are in. The **advertise** and **not-advertise** options allow you to determine whether the aggregate route that is generated by the ABR will actually be advertised. Configuring an aggregate and specifying **not-advertise** effectively filters the routes within the range of addresses specified from being advertised into the area configured. (The aggregate and the aggregate's components are not advertised.)

To configure route aggregation on an ASBR, use the **summary-address** command:

```
summary-address {{ip-address mask} | {prefix mask}} [not-advertise] [tag tag]
```

The options here are similar to the options with the **area-range** command, including the **not-advertise** option. A **tag** option is also included, which attaches a route tag to the aggregated external route that was created. The later section in this chapter, "Redistribution into OSPF," discusses route tags in further detail.

When you configure route aggregation on an ABR or an ASBR, OSPF generates a discard route and installs it in the routing table with an administrative distance of 5 (which normally beats anything other than a connected or statically configured route). Figure 4-11 illustrates why OSPF creates and installs this route.

Figure 4-11   *Discard Route in OSPF*

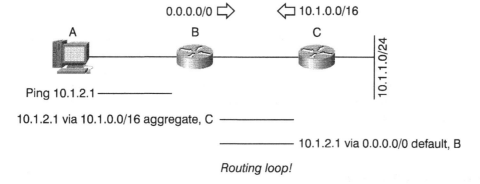

In this network, Router C is connected to 10.1.1.0/24. The network administrator has configured route aggregation on Router C, so it advertises 10.1.0.0/16 toward Router B. Router B is originating a default route, 0.0.0.0/0, toward Router C. What happens if Router C does not build a discard route for the configured summary (aggregate) route?

Assume that Host A transmits a packet toward 10.1.2.1, a destination address that does not exist in the network. The packet is forwarded to the gateway of last resort for the host, Router B. Router B examines its local routing table and discovers that the best route to this destination is through 10.1.0.0/16, toward Router C. Therefore, it forwards the packet.

Router C examines its local tables and finds that it has only the following routes:

- 0.0.0.0/0 via Router B
- 10.1.1.0/24 via connected

The route to 10.1.0.0/16, because it is created locally, would not be installed in the local routing table; rather, it would just be advertised toward Router B through OSPF. Based on this information, the best path to 10.1.2.1 is through the default route, via Router B, so Router C forwards the packet to Router B.

Router B receives the packet, examines its local tables, and forwards the packet back to Router C. How do you prevent this from happening? You do it by creating a discard route at Router C when summarization (aggregation) is configured. This is exactly what Cisco IOS Software does when it creates a route to *null0* and installs it in the local routing table.

If a discard route is created, when Router C receives packets destined to 10.1.2.1, it finds the discard route is the best route, rather than the default route advertised by Router B. Router C will then forward the packet to *null0*, which is the same thing as discarding the packet. This breaks the routing loop.

In some rare cases, the discard route might actually be unwanted, such as when you are using the summarization commands to filter routes rather than to create an aggregate to be advertised into another area. OSPF provides a command, **no discard-route**, to disable the creation of the discard route in these situations.

NOTE   One instance in which the **no discard-route** command might be useful is if an ABR is receiving a default route from within area 0 while generating a default route into an attached area through the **area range** command. In this case, the default route learned from area 0 is removed from the local routing table because the discard route has a lower administrative distance. You can use **no discard-route** in this situation to allow the default route learned from area 0 to be installed in the local routing table.

Filtering Routes in OSPF

There are some situations where suboptimal routing isn't acceptable, so declaring an area as some type of stub area isn't an acceptable alternative. You want to be able to limit the information flooded into these areas in some way, but you do not want to block the flooding of all routing information into the area, as Figure 4-12 illustrates.

In this example, Host A uses some time critical service running on the server attached to Router D. (For instance, this could be a customer account server for a call center, or a Voice over IP [VoIP] gateway of some type.) In other words, it is important for Host A to use the path through Router C when it is available. For traffic that is being forwarded to other destinations, however, it is not important which ABR forwards the traffic out of area 1.

Figure 4-12   *Filtering Summary Routers (Type 3 LSAs)*

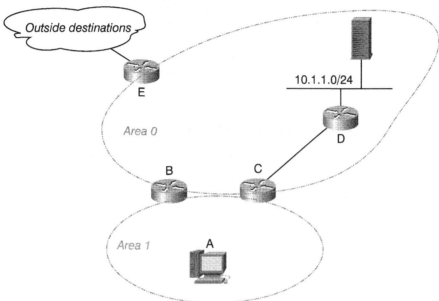

You cannot declare area 1 as any type of stub because of the requirement for optimal routing for at least some destinations: The routers within the area need to know which ABR to use when routing traffic to 10.1.1.0/24. You can, however, filter the LSAs flooded from area 0 into area 1 so information about 10.1.1.0/24 is flooded, while other LSAs are not flooded. To do this, use the **area filter-list command**, as the sample configuration in Example 4-1 shows.

Example 4-1   *Filtering Type 3 Routing Information Into an OSPF Area*

```
!
ip prefix-list permit-optimal permit 10.1.1.0/24
!
router ospf 10
 area 1 filter-list prefix-list permit-optimal in
 ....
```

With this configuration, summary routes (Type 3 LSAs) are flooded into area 1 only if they contain routing information for 10.1.1.0/24. The assumption here is that the network is also configured to provide area 1 with a default route, just like you would with a stub area of some type. The rest of the network remains reachable.

NOTE	Other options are available for filtering routes in OSPF, but they are not covered here. OSPF can filter routes from the local OSPF database, so that only a subset of the local database is installed in the local routing table, using the **distribute-list** command. OSPF can also filter routes as they are being redistributed at an ASBR, and you can filter external routing information at an ABR by using the **area range not-advertise** option.

Deploying OSPF on Specific Topologies

Now that you have a general overview of OSPF deployment, consider some specific topologies that almost every network designer or engineer faces:

- Redistribution into OSPF
- Full mesh topologies
- Hub-and-spoke topologies
- Links that are parallel to an area boundary
- Dial links

Redistribution into OSPF

Although redistribution is not a topology type, per se, it is a common, specific area of OSPF deployment that you need to examine closely. The "Redistribution" section in Chapter 2 covered redistribution extensively, so this section touches on only some OSPF-specific issues.

External Route Metrics

One of the confusing aspects of OSPF external routes is that OSPF can actually assign two types of metrics:

- A Type 1 external metric (OE1)
- A Type 2 external metric (OE2)

The difference between these two metrics is in how the route selection algorithm treats each one and how the total metric is calculated in the route selection algorithm. Figure 4-13 illustrates the difference between these two metric types.

Figure 4-13   *OSPF External Metric Types*

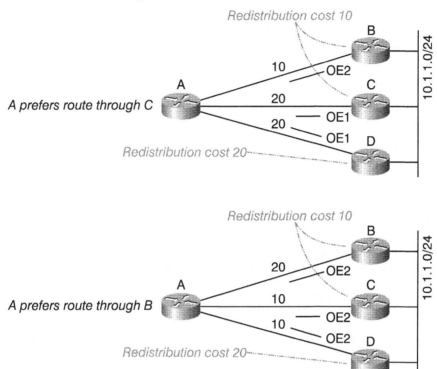

Figure 4-13 illustrates two examples on the same network. Work through each one separately to see why Router A chooses the path indicated.

In the first example, Router A receives three Type 5 external routes that provide reachability information for 10.1.1.0/24:

- An OSPF external route with metric Type 2, a redistributed metric of 10, and a cost to reach the ASBR of 10 through Router B.

- An OSPF external route with metric Type 1, a redistributed metric of 10, and a cost to reach the ASBR of 20 through Router C.

- An OSPF external route with metric Type 1, a redistributed metric of 20, and a cost to reach the ASBR of 20 through Router D.

Router A begins by examining the type of metric contained in each external route. Each contains two Type 1 metrics and one Type 2 metric. Because Type 1 metrics are always preferred over Type 2 metrics, the path through Router B is discarded, leaving the paths through Routers C and D. Router A adds the external metric to the cost to reach the ASBR to come up with a total cost through each ASBR.

In this case, the cost through Router C is 10 + 20, for a total cost of 30. The cost through Router D is 20 + 20, for a total cost of 40. The path with the lower cost is preferred, so Router A chooses the path through Router C as the best path to 10.1.1.0/24, installing this route into the local routing table.

In the second example, all three routes have been switched to Type 2 metrics. Therefore, Router A receives the following:

- An OSPF external route with metric Type 2, a redistributed metric of 10, and a cost to reach the ASBR of 20 through Router B.

- An OSPF external route with metric Type 2, a redistributed metric of 10, and a cost to reach the ASBR of 10 through Router C.

- An OSPF external route with metric Type 2, a redistributed metric of 200, and a cost to reach the ASBR of 10 through Router D.

Router A starts by comparing the metric type of the three routes. It finds that they are all the same, so it must move to the next step in the selection process. Router A then compares the cost to the ASBR on all three routes. It finds the external cost of the route through Routers B and C is 10, while the external cost of the route through Router D is 20. Therefore, it discards the route through Router D, and examines the cost of reaching each of the ASBRs. The cost to reach Router C is 10, while the cost to reach Router B is 20, so Router A will prefer the external route learned through Router C.

If Router A and the three ASBRs were in different areas, how would Router A know the actual cost to each of the ASBRs? By examining the Type 4 LSAs generated by the intervening ABR.

OSPF has two types of external metrics to differentiate between routes injected from another OSPF routing domain and routes injected from some other routing protocol (such as static routes, EIGRP, or IS-IS). If external routes are injected from another OSPF process, the external metric (the metric from the other OSPF process) and the costs to the ASBR are directly comparable and can be added together to reach a total cost to the destination.

If, however, the routes are from a different routing protocol, the other protocol's costs are not going to be directly comparable with OSPF's costs. In this case, OSPF assumes it is always cheaper to route through the OSPF network than through the external network, so it always prefers the route with the lower external cost.

Thus, for Type 1 metrics, OSPF first adds the costs to the ASBR and the external metric together before deciding which path to choose. In contrast, for Type 2 externals, the external metrics are compared only if all the ASBRs are the same distance from the calculating router.

You can use this principle to your advantage when designing redistribution within a network:

- If you would prefer to use the external metrics (the metrics set when redistributing into OSPF) to choose the exit point, regardless of the cost to reach any of the exit points within the OSPF network, use external type 2 metrics.

- If you would prefer to use the most optimal route to the destination, regardless of the exit point, and the redistribution at each ASBR is from the same external protocol, inject the externals with an external Type 1 metric. It is not as important that the routes are redistributed from another OSPF process; it is more crucial for all the routes to be redistributed from a single routing protocol so that all the external metrics are directly comparable.

External Route Selection at ABRs

An ABR that is touching an NSSA might receive two separate types of external routes: Type 5 LSAs and Type 7 LSAs. Each of these might also have the two different metric types discussed in the previous section. If a router has both Type 5 and Type 7 LSAs in its local OSPF database, it does the following:

- Compares all Type 7 and Type 5 LSAs, treating them all as Type 5 LSAs, as described in the previous section.
- If a Type 5 and Type 7 LSA match exactly in metric type, external cost, and internal cost, the Type 5 is always preferred over the Type 7 LSA.

There is no current mechanism for preferring a Type 7 external route to a Type 5 external route if their metric types and metrics match.

Route Selection Between Processes

If you have multiple OSPF processes running on a single router, the steps for selecting the best route between the processes are as follows:

Step 1   **Choose the route from the process that has the lowest administrative distance**—Because all OSPF processes, by default, have the same administrative distance, you need to configure one of the processes with a lower or higher administrative distance manually.

Step 2   **Choose the route that is installed in the table first**—In effect, if an OSPF process attempts to install a route in the local routing table and finds another route with the same administrative distance already installed, it does not install its route.

If you want deterministic installation of routes between two different OSPF processes, make certain you change the administrative distance on one of the two processes so that one process always wins over the other. Currently, you cannot compare the OSPF metrics of routes between two OSPF processes.

Full Mesh Topologies

Full mesh topologies represent a challenge to network scaling primarily because of the rapid increase in possible paths as new nodes are added to the mesh, as Figure 4-14 illustrates.

Figure 4-14 *Node-to-Path Increases in Full Mesh Networks*

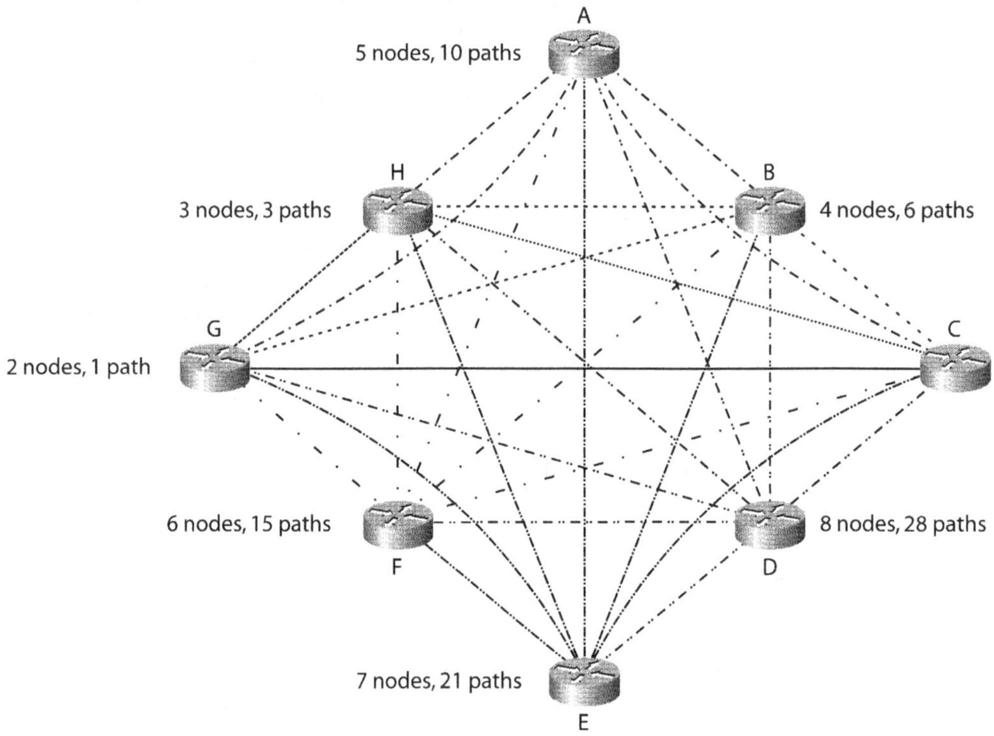

As this network shows, a full mesh that has 8 nodes has 28 possible paths through it. Even placing smaller full mesh networks next to each other in a network can have a dramatic impact on the number of possible paths.

One of the largest impacts of full mesh topologies have on link state protocols is the repitition of flooded LSAs through the network. For instance, in this network, a single change that is flooded through the mesh by one router results in some routers receiving 10 or 20 copies of the link-state update.

How do you reduce the amount of flooding on a full mesh topology? For broadcast networks, you elect a designated router (DR) to reduce the amount of flooding across the network. A full mesh network is similar to a broadcast network, because an update that is flooded by one member of the full mesh topology is received by every other member of that topology, which means it is unnecessary for each router to reflood received packets to each of its neighbors. Because no single router can see the full graph of connectivity, however, a DR cannot be elected on the mesh.

Instead, you can manually control flooding across the mesh by choosing one or two routers as the "reflooders" on the mesh and blocking flooding from all other routers. Two Cisco IOS Software commands allow you to configure OSPF flooding:

- **ip ospf database-filter all out** (an interface-level command)
- **neighbor database-filter** (a router-level command)

You can use either of these commands to block flooding in a full mesh topology. Refer to Figure 4-15 to see how you can use these commands.

Figure 4-15   *Reducing Flooding in a Full Mesh Topology*

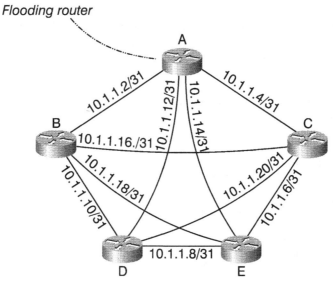

In this network, you want every router in the network to be capable of flooding new information it receives to Router A, and you want Router A to reflood that information throughout the mesh. You will want to make certain at least two flooding paths exist in the mesh when you are designing your mesh blocking. For simplicity in this example, only Router A is used in this network.

The first option is to use the **ip ospf database-filter all out** command. Example 4-2 provides the sample configurations for Router A.

Example 4-2   *Filtering All Flooding from an OSPF Router*

```
!
hostname router-a
!
router ospf 10
 network 10.1.1.0 0.0.0.255 area 0
!
interface serial 0/0
 ip address 10.1.1.2 255.255.255.254
!
```

continues

Example 4-2   *Filtering All Flooding from an OSPF Router (Continued)*

```
interface serial 0/1
 ip address 10.1.1.4 255.255.255.254
!
interface serial 0/2
 ip address 10.1.1.12 255.255.255.254
!
interface serial 0/3
 ip address 10.1.1.14 255.255.255.254
....
```

The configuration for Router A looks like a normal configuration for this type of network. It has an OSPF **network** configuration containing all the serial interfaces and numerous serial interfaces, one for each point-to-point link connecting to adjacent neighbors. Example 4-3 provides the Router B configuration.

Example 4-3   *Filtering All Flooding from an OSPF Router*

```
!
hostname router-b
!
router ospf 10
 network 10.1.1.0 0.0.0.255 area 0
!
interface serial 0/0
 ip address 10.1.1.3 255.255.255.254
!
interface serial 0/1
 ip address 10.1.1.16 255.255.255.254
 ip ospf database-filter all out
!
interface serial 0/2
 ip address 10.1.1.18 255.255.255.254
 ip ospf database-filter all out
!
interface serial 0/3
 ip address 10.1.1.10 255.255.255.254
 ip ospf database-filter all out
....
```

On the link connecting Router B to Router A, the configuration has the normal commands, just an Internet Protocol (IP) address. On the remainder of the serial links, however, **ip ospf database-filter all out** is configured. When B receives a new LSA from an adjacent neighbor, it floods the new LSA to Router A but not to any of its other neighbors on the full mesh.

The second option is to use the router mode configuration **neighbor database-filter** command to block flooding to specific adjacent neighbors from Router B. Although the configuration for Router A is the same, the Router B configuration has changed, as Example 4-4 shows.

Example 4-4   *Filtering All Flooding from an OSPF Router*

```
!
hostname router-b
!
router ospf 10
 network 10.1.1.0 0.0.0.255 area 0
 neighbor 10.1.1.17 database-filter all out
 neighbor 10.1.1.19 database-filter all out
 neighbor 10.1.1.11 database-filter all out
!
interface serial 0/0
 ip address 10.1.1.3 255.255.255.254
!
interface serial 0/1
 ip address 10.1.1.16 255.255.255.254
!
interface serial 0/2
 ip address 10.1.1.18 255.255.255.254
!
interface serial 0/3
 ip address 10.1.1.10 255.255.255.254
....
```

The concept is the same, but the configuration has moved under the router configuration, rather than under the interface configuration.

Hub-and-Spoke Topologies

Hub-and-spoke networks are another common network topology that network designers and administrators face on a regular basis. This section attempts to address two separate issues:

- The options and tradeoffs in handling the links from the hub to the remotes
- Reducing the amount of flooding traffic out to the remotes

Assume the interface connecting Router A to the remote sites, is some form of nonbroadcast multiaccess (NBMA) media, such as Frame Relay or ATM. You can configure the combination of link types and the way that OSPF runs on the links in one of six ways:

- Broadcast
- Point-to-point
- Point-to-multipoint (Broadcast)
- Point-to-multipoint (Nonbroadcast)

Each section that follows covers one combination of logical and OSPF link type.

Treating the NBMA Interface as a Broadcast Interface

The first option is to configure the hub and the spokes as a single broadcast network, as Figure 4-16 shows.

Figure 4-16   *Treating the NBMA as a Broadcast Network*

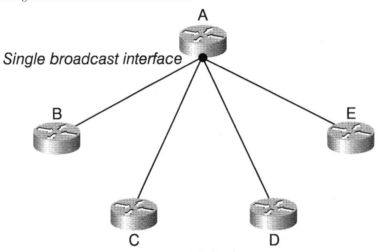

The primary problem to consider when treating the NBMA network as a broadcast network is DR selection. If Router A, for instance, chooses Router B as the DR on the broadcast segment, and Router C chooses Router A, flooding across the NBMA network is broken.

This problem has at least two different solutions:

*   Choose router IDs so that the hub router is always chosen as the DR on the broadcast segment. One way to do this is by carefully choosing the IP addresses on each router, configuring a loopback on each router with an IP address chosen so that the hub router always has the highest loopback IP address. Alternatively, you can configure manual router IDs using the **router-id** command in the OSPF router configuration mode.

*   Configure the remote site routers using the **ip ospf priority** interface-level command so that none of the stubs can ever become the DR.

To specify that the hub router is always chosen as the DR, configuring the OSPF priority on the remote sites is generally simpler than ensuring that the IP addresses are chosen correctly. Configuring the priority provides more information about the intent of the configuration than carefully chosen router IDs.

The main advantage to treating the NBMA network as a single broadcast link is conservation of IP address space. You can use a single IP subnet to number all the routers that are connected to the NBMA network. Doing so can save a good deal of address space if the hub-and-spoke network is large.

NOTE   It might appear that configuring the NBMA as a single broadcast network would also reduce the size of the shortest path first (SPF) tree within the OSPF area, but this is not true. When a DR is elected on a broadcast link, each router that is connected to the broadcast link advertises a connection to the DR. When other routers build their SPF trees, they do not see the broadcast link as a single link, but rather as a single node, the DR, with each router that is connected to the network having a point-to-point link to the DR. Treating the NBMA as a broadcast network results in the same-sized SPF tree as treating the NBMA as a set of point-to-point links.

Example 4-5 provides sample configurations for Routers A and B, using the OSPF priority to force Router A to become the DR.

Example 4-5   *Using the* **ospf priority** *Command to Force the Hub to Be the DR*

```
!
hostname router-a
!
router ospf 10
 network 10.1.1.0 0.0.0.255 area 1
!
interface serial 0/0
 ip address 10.1.1.1 255.255.255.0
 ip ospf network-type broadcast
 ip ospf priority 200
....
```
```
!
hostname router-b
!
router ospf 10
 network 10.1.1.0 0.0.0.255 area 1
!
interface serial 0/0
 ip address 10.1.1.2 255.255.255.0
 ip ospf network-type broadcast
 ip ospf priority 0
```

Setting the **ip ospf priority** to 0 on Router B prevents it from taking part in the DR election process altogether.

NOTE   When using this configuration, the spoke routers will not be able to send traffic to each other. In order to allow traffic to be passed between the spoke sites, you need to make certain the hub router is sending a default route to each of the spoke routers, or configure explicit mapping statements between each spoke's IP address and the hub router's circuit number.

Treating the NBMA Interface as a Set of Point-to-Point Interfaces

Instead of treating the entire NBMA as a single subnet, you can also configure each circuit that is carried on the single NBMA connection as a separate point-to-point link. Using Cisco IOS Software, you can configure a series of point-to-point subinterfaces under the main interface configuration and run OSPF over each of these. Figure 4-17 illustrates, with sample configurations in Example 4-6 following the figure.

Figure 4-17 *OSPF Deployment on an NBMA as Point-to-Points*

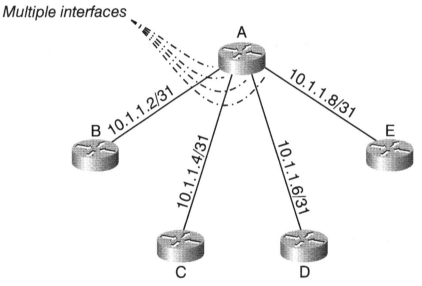

Example 4-6 *Configuring NBMA Interfaces as Logical Point-to-Points*

```
!
hostname router-a
!
router ospf 10
 network 10.1.1.0 0.0.0.255 area 1
!
interface serial 0/0.1 point-to-point
 description to router-b
 ip address 10.1.1.2 255.255.255.254
!
interface serial 0/0.2 point-to-point
 description to router-c
 ip address 10.1.1.4 255.255.255.254
!
interface serial 0/0.3
 description to router-d
 ip address 10.1.1.6 255.255.255.254
....
!
hostname router-b
```

Example 4-6   *Configuring NBMA Interfaces as Logical Point-to-Points (Continued)*

```
!
router ospf 10
 network 10.1.1.0 0.0.0.255 area 1
!
interface s0/0.1 point-to-point
 ip address 10.1.1.3 255.255.255.254
....
```

The main advantage of treating the NBMA as a set of point-to-points is the lessened chance of a misconfiguration bringing down the entire network because of one of the remote site routers being elected DR on a broadcast link. This option requires more configuration because each sub-interface must be created and maintained. It also uses more IP address space because each subinterface that is created requires at least two IP addresses to be assigned. (This is provided that you are using 31-bit prefix lengths. Shorter prefix lengths require more IP addresses to be assigned.)

NOTE   Chapter 7, "High Availability and Fast Convergence," provides different reasons why you would consider treating an NBMA interface as a set of logical point-to-point links. These reasons primarily center on convergence speeds.

Treating an NBMA Interface as a Broadcast Point-to-Multipoint Interface

OSPF also provides a network type that is designed specifically to support NBMA networks: *point-to-multipoint*. The hub router and remote site routers in a point-to-multipoint network treat the network, from an adjacency and SPF tree perspective, as a set of point-to-point links. This means that the following apply:

- Hellos and other OSPF packets are multicast through the NBMA network.

- The hub router advertises each remote site router as a directly connected adjacency, using a host route to identify each adjacent router on the NBMA network. To routers outside the point-to-multipoint network, it's a set of point-to-point links, rather than a single multipoint link.

The main advantages of using the point-to-multipoint network type on an NBMA network are as follows:

- Only one block of IP addresses needs to be assigned to the NBMA network. Point-to-multipoint networks that are deployed on an NBMA network require no more IP addresses than a broadcast or nonbroadcast network across the same NBMA network.

- The configuration is simple.

The primary disadvantage of the point-to-multipoint configuration is the additional routing information that is injected: one host route for each remote site.

Treating an NBMA Interface as a Nonbroadcast Point-to-Multipoint Interface

Configuring the NBMA as a nonbroadcast point-to-multipoint link causes OSPF to not send multicast hello packets across the link. This means you will need to configure each neighbor manually, using the OSPF neighbor configuration command.

This approach has the same advantages and caveats as configuring the NBMA link as a broadcast network, except the additional configuration required to build OSPF adjacencies.

Summary of Interface and OSPF Link-Type Options

Table 4-1 provides a quick overview of the advantages, disadvantages, and attributes of each of the four methods of deploying OSPF across an NBMA network covered in the preceding sections.

Table 4-1   *Overview of the OSPF Deployment Options on NBMA Networks*

	Configuration	**Addressing**
Broadcast	Configure either the router ID or the OSPF priority on each router to force the hub to be elected the DR.	The hub uses a single IP address. All addresses are taken from a single IP address space.
Point-to-Point Subinterfaces	Configure one subinterface per connected remote site router.	The hub uses one subnet per remote site router. The hub router uses one IP address per remote site router.
Point-to-Multipoint Broadcast	Configure interfaces as point-to-multipoint.	The hub uses a single IP address. All addresses are taken from a single IP address space. The hub router advertises a host route to each remote site router through OSPF.
Point-to-Multipoint Nonbroadcast	Configure interfaces as point-to-multipoint. Manually configure each neighbor on the hub router and remote site routers.	The hub uses a single IP address. All addresses are taken from a single IP address space. The hub router advertises a host route to each remote site router through OSPF.

Reducing Flooding to the Spokes

One of the main concerns when deploying OSPF over a hub-and-spoke network is the flooding of routes toward the remote site routers, as illustrated in Figure 4-18.

In this network, Router B floods a routing update about 10.1.2.0/24 to Router A, which then refloods the information back toward Routers C, D, and E. This is fine in normal circumstances, but remote site routers, such as Routers B, C, D, and E, are generally going to be smaller, lower-powered devices, and they are probably connected to Router A through a low-bandwidth link.

These factors indicate the importance of reducing the number of LSAs Router A floods towards these remote site routers.

You can use the same techniques that you used to reduce flooding in a full mesh network to reduce flooding in a hub-and-spoke network. You can block flooding from the hub router, as long as the hub router is an ABR, using either the router-level command **ip ospf database-filter all out** or the interface-level command **neighbor database-filter**.

If you use either of these commands to block flooding toward the remote site routers, you also need to configure a static default route on each of the remote site routers so that they can still reach destinations within the rest of the network. The sample configurations in Example 4-7, from Routers A and B, show how this works using the interface-level command **ip ospf database-filter all out**.

Figure 4-18   *Excessive Flooding Toward Remote Routers in a Hub-and-Spoke Network*

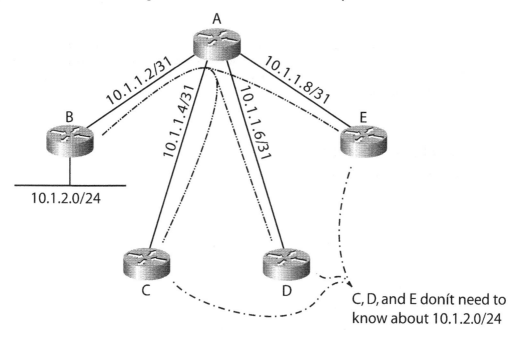

Example 4-7   *Using* **ip ospf database-filter all out** *to Reduce Flooding in a Hub-and-Spoke Network*

```
!
hostname router-a
!
router ospf 10
 network 10.1.1.0 0.0.0.255 area 1
!
interface serial 0/0
```

continues

Example 4-7   *Using **ip ospf database-filter all out** to Reduce Flooding in a Hub-and-Spoke Network (Continued)*

```
 description link to router-b
 ip address 10.1.1.2 255.255.255.254
 ip ospf database-filter all out
....
!
hostname router-b
!
router ospf 10
 network 0.0.0.0 0.0.0.0 area 1
!
interface serial 0/0
 ip address 10.1.1.3 255.255.255.254
!
ip route 0.0.0.0 0.0.0.0 10.1.1.2
....
```

NOTE   You can also originate a default route at the ABR using **default-information originate** instead of using static routes at the remote routers. The command **ip ospf database-filter** all out only filters out learned LSAs, not locally originated ones, so a locally generated default would still be sent to the remote routers.

Links Parallel to Area Boundaries

Figure 4-19 presents a situation that you might encounter. Routers C and D are ABRs, Routers A and B are in area 0, and Routers E and F are in area 1.

What do you do with the link in the middle, between Routers C and D (Link 3)? Should it be in area 0 or area 1? Begin by putting the Link 3 in area 0. It is a direct link between two backbone routers, so it is probably supposed to be in the network backbone.

Assuming that no summarization is configured at the area border, Router C will have two routes to 10.1.2.0/24:

* An inter-area route through the Link Between Routers C and D
* An intra-area route through E, the 512k link in area 1, F, and then D

Because OSPF always prefers intra-area routes over inter-area routes, Router C chooses the path through Routers E, F, and then D rather than the one-hop WAN link through area 0. This is relatively radical suboptimal routing; to fix this, try putting Link 3 in area 1.

However, placing the Link 3 in area 1 presents the same problem—only this time it is for the 10.1.3.0/24 network. Router D prefers the link through B (the 512k link), Router A, and then C, rather than the one-hop path over the WAN link through Router C.

Figure 4-19 *Link in the Middle*

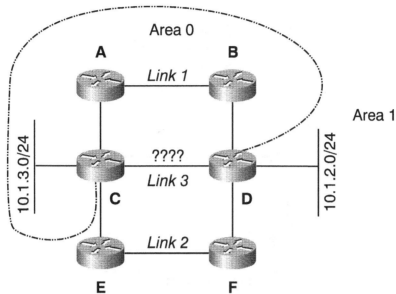

To resolve this, you can go ahead and put the Link 3 in area 0 and then configure some static routes to get around the problem:

- On Router D, a static route for 10.1.3.0/24 via Router C
- On Router C, a static route for 10.1.2.0/24 via Router D

This does not seem like a scalable solution, though, and you are trying to build a network that scales. You need another option.

You could try putting Link 3 in area 1 and then building a virtual link across it so that it is in both area 0 and area 1. However, you should not use a virtual link unless absolutely necessary — and whether it is really necessary is questionable here.

Another option is to create two virtual links at Layer 2 (using 802.1q VLANs, for instance, or by adding an additional frame relay circuit), between Routers C and D. OSPF would then peer across both of these links, once in each area. This is only possible on some network types, though, such as Frame Relay, Ethernet, and some others.

Dial Links

One of the problems you face when using dial backup in OSPF is where the router dials into versus where the area borders are. Figure 4-20 is useful for showing what the problems are so that you can consider some solutions.

Figure 4-20 *Dial Backup in OSPF*

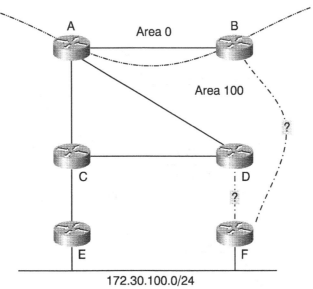

You want Router F to dial up to another router when Router E loses its connection to Router C. You can dial into Router D, A, or B. Which one is best?

The immediate choice is to configure Router F to dial into Router D if the remote segment loses all connectivity through Router E, but this still leaves a single point of failure at Router A. You can remove A as a single point of failure by simply moving the link between Routers A and so it's between Routers D and B. This example assumes moving this link isn't an option.

Dialing into Router A itself is not going to solve the single point of failure problem, so the only other option is to dial into Router B. However, this would mean that two area 100s would appear to be connected to area 0—one through Router A, and the other through Router B. Is this legal?

When an ABR begins building LSAs for area 0, it takes the routing information from each of its other areas and bundles them into summary LSAs (Type 3 LSAs, to be exact). The summary LSAs do not contain area information, so the other routers on the core simply do not know the areas that these destinations are in. The routers know only that to reach these destinations, the next hop is a given ABR.

Therefore, it is legal to have multiple areas with the same area ID attached to the same area 0, and configuring Router F to dial into Router B as a backup is perfectly legal. The only other issue that remains is any possible summarization that might be taking place on Router A, the normal ABR for area 100.

The trick is not to summarize off the dial-in link on Router B. Router B then advertises specific routes to anything behind Router F, and Router A continues to advertise the summaries that it is configured for.

NOTE   In some dial backup situations, you also need to make certain that all the traffic flowing into and out of an area will not flow through the dial link. If the routes that are advertised through the dial backup link are leaked into the rest of the area, the dial backup link might be used for all inter-area traffic. Make certain that you set the metrics for the dial backup link high enough to prevent this from happening.

Point-to-point Broadcast Links

In Data Center and campus networks, using a Gigabit Ethernet link as a point-to-point link is common. It involves tying two routers together through a directly connected fiber or rolled-over copper cable, or connecting two routers on a virtual LAN (VLAN) with no other devices connected. Because OSPF elects a DR on broadcast links, what impact does this have on the SPF tree, and through the SPF tree size, on convergence times in the network? Figure 4-21 illustrates the impact.

Figure 4-21   *Impact of Point-to-Point Broadcast Links*

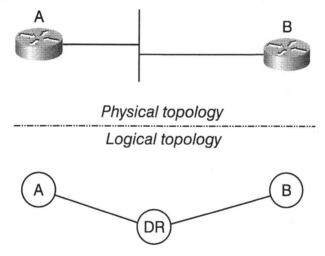

In Figure 4-21, you can see that although the physical topology has only two routers, Routers A and B, connected directly on a point-to-point link, the logical topology has the two routers and a DR node in the center. Routers A and B advertise a link to the DR, and the DR advertises a link back to Routers A and B to complete the connectivity graph over the Ethernet segment.

Each Ethernet segment that is used as a point-to-point link actually adds an extra node to the SPF tree, the DR. This can slow down convergence time because it makes the tree deeper than it really is or needs to be. Beyond the additional work in the SPF calculations, you also have dead time before building an adjacency on a broadcast link, to make certain that you correctly determine the DR on the link.

You can resolve these issues by configuring the Ethernet segment between Routers A and B as a point-to-point link using the interface-level command **ip ospf network-type point-to-point**.

CAUTION   If you configure a link as a point-to-point link using **ip ospf network-type point-to-point**, you should never place devices on the link other than the two routers. The results of doing this might vary with different vendors' equipment, but the results will almost always be bad.

Case Study: OSPF Externals and the Next Hop

One of the more interesting aspects of the OSPF handling of external routes is the forwarding address. Looking at a **show ip ospf database** for an external site reveals the output in Example 4-8.

Example 4-8   *OSPF Database with a Self-Originated Next Hop*

```
router#show ip ospf data extern
        OSPF Router with ID (130.30.4.9) (Process ID 3100)
                AS External Link States
   Routing Bit Set on this LSA
LS Type: AS External Link
   Link State ID: 10.1.1.0 (External Network Number )
   Advertising Router: 130.30.0.193
Network Mask: /24
        Metric Type: 2 (Larger than any link state path)
Forward Address: 0.0.0.0
```

A few fields have been deleted from the preceding output to make it easier to see the fields that are important to the discussion at hand. Three fields are particularly interesting:

- **Routing Bit Set on This LSA** — This means that the route is valid and will be in the forwarding/routing table. The routing/forwarding table is what you see in a **show ip route** command.

- **Advertising Router** — This is the router ID of the router that is advertising this external destination.

- **Forward Address** — This is the address to forward traffic that is destined to this network.

The output in Example 4-8 reveals a forwarding address of 0.0.0.0; this means that forward packets destined to this network are sent to the advertising router. For the routing bit to be set on this LSA, a router LSA must exist for the advertising router in the OSPF database.

However, the forwarding address might be different from the advertising router. Refer to Figure 4-22 for an example.

Here, Routers A and B are running OSPF, and B is learning some routes from other routers through RIP and redistributing them into OSPF. If you look at the external LSA for 172.30.0.0/16 on Router A, you see the output in Example 4-9.

Figure 4-22   *Setting the Forwarding Address in an OSPF External Site*

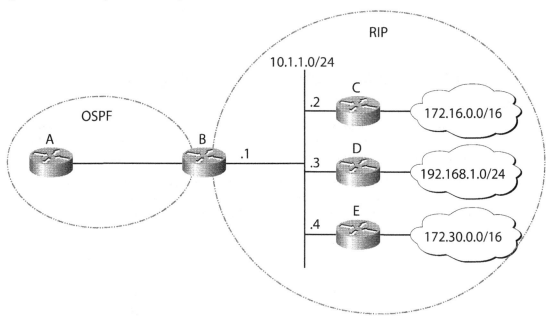

Example 4-9   *OSPF Database with a Third-Party Next Hop*

```
router-a#show ip ospf data extern
        OSPF Router with ID (130.30.4.9) (Process ID 3100)
                AS External Link States
  Routing Bit Set on this LSA
LS Type: AS External Link
  Link State ID: 172.30.0.0 (External Network Number )
  Advertising Router: 10.1.1.1
Network Mask: /16
        Metric Type: 2 (Larger than any link state path)
Forward Address: 10.1.1.2
```

The **Forward Address** field now shows the address of Router C rather than 0.0.0.0. Sometimes you see this, and the **Routing Bit Set on this LSA** field does not appear. This is because the forwarding address must be reachable as an internal OSPF LSA.

For example, if Router B were redistributing the 10.1.1.0/24 network into OSPF in addition to the RIP routes, the next hop, 10.1.1.2, would be an external. OSPF never forwards an external site through an external site. (This is a defense against routing loops.)

Why does OSPF do this? Why not just use the router ID of the redistributing router all the time? The reason is that, in the preceding scenario, Router A might have an alternate path to 10.1.1.0/24 that is much better than the route through Router B.

Case Study: Troubleshooting OSPF Neighbor Adjacencies

One of the various problems you often run into with OSPF is a pair of routers attached to the same network that will not become fully adjacent. If you know the right things to look for, you can quickly deal with this type of problem.

Before troubleshooting neighbors that do not bring up an adjacency, though, you need to make certain they should become fully adjacent. For example, the routers in Figure 4-23 are connected to the same link, but they will never become fully adjacent.

Figure 4-23   *Neighbor Relationships on a Broadcast Network*

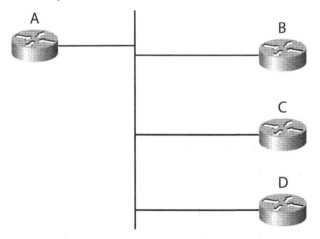

Assume that Router A becomes the DR on this network, and Router B becomes the backup designated router (BDR). Because the DR is responsible for sending Router C any information it learns from Router D, C and D do not need to become fully adjacent.

As a matter of fact, they will not become fully adjacent. Routers C and D will build their neighbor relationship to the two-way state only and will never build a full adjacency.

The routers in Figure 4-24, however, should be building a full OSPF adjacency; they are connected through a point-to-point link, and they are both in area 0.

Figure 4-24   *Two OSPF Routers*

When you look at the **show ip ospf neighbor** output from either router, however, you can see that the adjacency is not being built.

Example 4-10 displays the output from Router A.

Example 4-10 **show ip ospf neighbor** *Output Reveals No Adjacency Built*

```
router-a#show ip ospf neighbor
router-a#
```

The first thing to do when this type of problem occurs is to run **debug ip ospf adjacency** on one of the routers. Example 4-11 displays the debug output from Router A.

Example 4-11 **debug ip ospf adjacency** *Output for Router A*

```
router-a#debug ip ospf adj
OSPF adjacency events debugging is on
router-a#
20:12:35: OSPF: Rcv hello from 172.19.10.1 area 0 from Serial0 172.19.1.2
20:12:35: OSPF: Mismatched hello parameters from 172.19.1.2
20:12:35: Dead R 40 C 80, Hello R 10 C 20
```

This output reveals that you have mismatched Hello parameters. In this case, the Dead and Hello timers are mismatched. The Hello timer on this router (labeled **C** in the debug output) is 20, whereas the Hello timer on the remote router (labeled **R** in the debug output) is 10. Example 4-12 shows the configuration on Router A.

Example 4-12 *Interface Configuration on Router A*

```
!
interface Serial0
 ip address 172.19.1.1 255.255.255.0
 no ip directed-broadcast
ip ospf hello-interval 20
 no ip mroute-cache
!
```

The OSPF Hello interval on this interface has been set to 20. Correcting this should fix the problem. The Hello interval, Dead interval wait time, IP subnet, and link type all have to match for OSPF routers to become fully adjacent.

Other problems, however, are not so easy to find quickly unless you know specifically what you are looking for. Correct the timers, and see if the neighbors come up into FULL state. A few executions of the **show ip ospf neighbor** command reveal the results in Example 4-13.

Example 4-13 **show ip ospf neighbor** *with Corrected Timers*

```
router-a#show ip ospf neighbors
Neighbor ID     Pri   State         Dead Time    Address        Interface
172.19.10.1       1   INIT/  -      00:00:35     172.19.1.2     Serial0
router-a#show ip ospf neighbors
Neighbor ID     Pri   State         Dead Time    Address        Interface
172.19.10.1       1   EXCHANGE/  -    00:00:35      172.19.1.2     Serial0
router-a#show ip ospf neighbors
Neighbor ID     Pri   State         Dead Time    Address        Interface
172.19.10.1       1   INIT/  -      00:00:35     172.19.1.2     Serial0
router-a#show ip ospf neighbors
Neighbor ID     Pri   State         Dead Time    Address        Interface
172.19.10.1       1   EXCHANGE/  -    00:00:35      172.19.1.2     Serial0
```

Even though the mismatched timers have been corrected, the routers still will not become adjacent. They just flip flop between INIT and EXCHANGE modes.

EXCHANGE state means that you are trying to exchange databases with the neighbor, so the logical assumption is that you are getting Hello packets across the link, but not database information.

Why would Hello packets be okay and database packets not be okay? The reason is that Hello packets are small, whereas database packets are large. Prove this theory by pinging with some various-sized packets across the link between the two routers using an extended ping, as demonstrated in Example 4-14.

Example 4-14 *Extended Ping from Router A to B*

```
router-a#ping
Protocol [ip]:
Target IP address: 172.19.1.2
Repeat count [5]: 1
Extended commands [n]: y
Sweep range of sizes [n]: y
Sweep min size [36]: 100
Sweep max size [18024]: 1500
Sweep interval [1]: 100
Type escape sequence to abort.
Sending 15, [100..1500]-byte ICMP Echos to 172.19.1.2, timeout is 2 seconds:
!.............
Success rate is 6 percent (1/15), round-trip min/avg/max = 1/1/1 ms
```

You can see from this that the ping fails with a packet size of 200 bytes, which seems small. Look at the router on the other end of the link and see how the interface is configured. Example 4-15 shows some sample results.

Example 4-15 *Interface Configuration on Router B*

```
interface Serial0
 mtu 100
 ip address 172.19.1.2 255.255.255.0
```

It appears that you have found the problem: The maximum transmission unit (MTU) size is mismatched on the link. One router thinks that the MTU is 100 bytes, and the other end thinks it is 1500 bytes. Because the Hello packets are only 64 bytes, both routers can send and receive them with no problems. However, when it comes time to send and receive maximum-sized database descriptor (DBD) packets, Router B, with an MTU of 100 bytes, drops the 1500-byte packets that Router A generates.

Of course, if the MTU of one end of a link is different from the MTU of the other end of the link, larger packets still fail to cross the link in one direction, regardless of the ability of OSPF to bring up an adjacency. This just shifts the problem from building the adjacency to the more esoteric problem of some applications not working across the link, or File Transfer Protocol (FTP) control sessions working correctly, by data sessions failing.

Review Questions

1 How does OSPF bind the flooding of topology information?

2 What is the rule of thumb to consider when designing around summarization of topology information and summarization of reachability information?

3 What is the general rule of thumb on dealing with complexity in an OSPF network design?

4 What are some of the advantages of placing the ABRs in a three-layer hierarchy at the edge of the network core?

5 What are the disadvantages of placing the ABRs in a three-layer hierarchical network design at the edge of the core?

6 What is the most flexible and generally most successful way to place ABRs in a three-layer hierarchical network?

7 In general, where is the best place to put ABRs in a two-layer hierarchical network? When should you vary from this rule of thumb?

8 What are the types of stub areas, and what routing information do they block at the ABR?

9 When should you use stub areas?

10 Where can you aggregate (summarize) routing information in an OSPF network?

11 What types of routes can you filter in an OSPF network?

12 If two OSPF processes that are running on the same router attempt to inject a route to the same destination into the local routing table, which route is installed?

13 What mechanism can you use to reduce flooding in a full mesh topology?

CHAPTER 5

IS-IS Network Design

The Intermediate System-to-Intermediate System (IS-IS) protocol is typically treated as something of a mystery in the IP networking world. Originally developed by the International Organization for Standardization (ISO) (now called the ITU), IS-IS was designed to route connection-oriented network services (CONS) and connectionless network services (CLNS) packets. Although IS-IS is similar to Open Shortest Path First (OSPF) in theory, it is operationally different enough to confuse network designers who are familiar with OSPF but have not studied IS-IS.

This chapter covers many of the same network designs covered in Chapter 4, "OSPF Network Design," but focuses on how to deploy IS-IS, illustrating some of the differences between the protocols. The chapter begins with deployment on a three-layer and two-layer hierarchy. The chapter then moves into specific topologies and some considerations in scaling IS-IS networks.

NOTE   If you are not familiar with IS-IS, examine Appendix C, "IS-IS Basics of Operation," before reading this chapter. Other good sources of information on the IS-IS protocol are as follows:

- ISO 10589, published by the ITU

- RFC 1195, "Use of OSI IS-IS for Routing in TCP/IP and Dual Environments"

- *IS-IS Deployment in IP Networks*, published by Addison-Wesley, by Russ White and Alvaro Retana

- *Routing TCP/IP*, Volume I, published by Cisco Press, by Jeff Doyle

---

NOTE   You should also read the "Summarization and Aggregation" section of Chapter 4 for general background information on the concepts of summarization and aggregation in a link-state protocol.

Whereas flooding domains are called areas in the OSPF protocol, they are called *routing domains* within the IS-IS protocol, and routers are called *intermediate systems* (*ISs*) within IS-IS. These terms are used throughout this chapter.

In this chapter, the summarization of topology information is referred to as *summarization*, and the summarization of reachability information is referred to as *aggregation*. Although these terms are normally used interchangeably in real network design and maintenance, this chapter makes this distinction just for readability.

Deploying IS-IS on a Three-Layer Hierarchy

IS-IS provides for two levels within the design of the protocol: the level 1 (L1) routing domains, representing the edges of the network; and the level 2 (L2) routing domain, connecting all the L1 domains. IS-IS does not have strict requirements on the placement of the L2 routing domain; the only requirement is that the domain must be contiguous. In other words, only one L2 routing domain can exist within an IS-IS network.

This provides a good bit of flexibility in deploying IS-IS on a three-layer network, as you will see in the following sections.

The Entire Network as a Single Routing Domain

One of the simplest network design solutions is to ignore the hierarchical model and deploy a single IS-IS routing domain across the entire network. This is actually a pretty common solution, especially in smaller networks, in which layering might be important from a traffic flow model, but the route count is low enough for summarization and aggregation not to matter.

The primary question, in this case, is which type of area the network should be built on. Should the entire network be a single L1 domain or a single L1/L2 domain? There is not much to recommend one over the other when considering the actual operation of IS-IS, but one network design reason to use a single L1/L2 domain in this case is *flexibility*.

If the network grows at some point and needs to be split into multiple routing domains, it is easier to add L1 routing domains to an existing network than it is to add an L2 routing domain to the network. You can attach a single L1 router at the edge of the network and push the L1 domain into the network, without impacting routing, if the only domain is an L1/L2 domain, as Figure 5-1 illustrates.

Figure 5-1   *Pushing an L1 Routing Domain into an Existing L2 Domain*

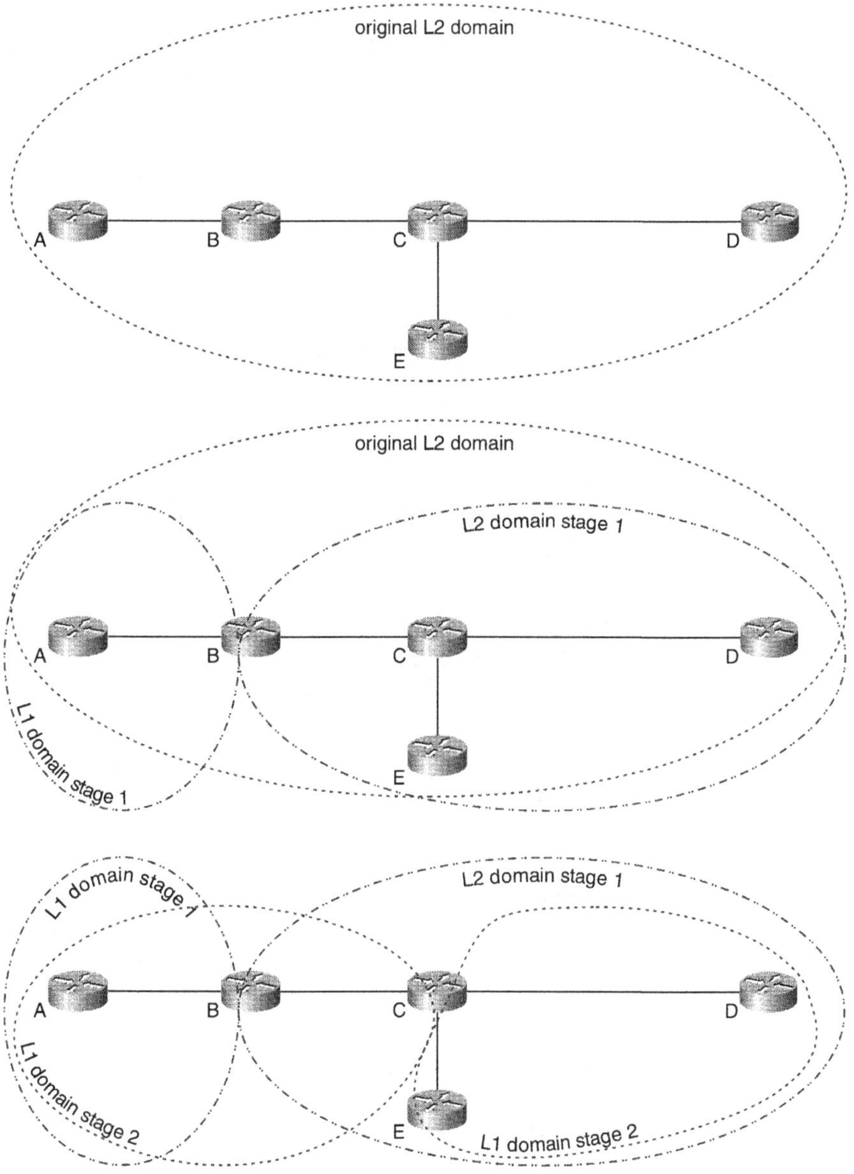

You need to be careful about "cutting off" routers when pushing the L1 domain back, such as Router E in Figure 5-1. When the L1 domain is configured on Router C, Router E needs to remain in the L2 routing domain (as shown in the illustration), be moved into the growing L1 domain, or be placed in a new L1 domain.

Summarization Versus Aggregation: Which Is More Important?

Although summarization of topology information and aggregation of routing information do, in a well-designed network, fall at around the same place, you will sometimes face the decision of placing a flooding domain border where it will optimize the hiding of topology information or optimize the aggregation of address space. In this situation, which should you prefer? Figure 5-2 illustrates the results of a test run by the Cisco Routing Protocols Scaling Team that might provide some answers to this question.

Figure 5-2 *Route Count Versus Router Count*

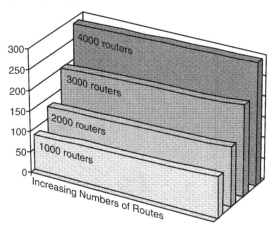

In this test, a moderately sized test bed was configured, and router emulators were used to inject various sizes of topologies and various numbers of routes into the test bed. The routers within the test bed were monitored to determine when IS-IS converged after each topology and set of routes were injected.

From the graph of results, you can see that increasing the number of routes does increase the network convergence time, over a range of about 10 to 15 seconds for each emulated topology. However, increasing the number of nodes in the injected topology—indicated as the number of routers, rather than the number of routes—shows a marked increase in the time it took for the network to converge.

Although you cannot take results from a test using large-scale network emulation as final, the results do seem to bear out what you would expect if you consider the way a link-state protocol works. By adding routers to the test, you are adding nodes into the shortest path first (SPF) tree. Larger SPF trees tend to be more complicated and take longer to compute. By adding routes without adding more routers, however, you are simply adding to the number of leaf nodes on the SPF tree, which takes much less time to insert into the tree. The general rule is to optimize both summarization of topology information and aggregation of routing information where possible, but if you have to optimize to some degree for one or the other, optimize for summarization of topology table information.

Deploying a pure L2 routing domain in IS-IS is not possible, because the L2 routers do not know a path to the edge of the L2 routing domain. The L2 routing information that is contained in IS tables shows only information on how to reach the next hop toward the destination; it does not provide a path to the next hop. Instead, any "L2 domain" that is discussed in this chapter actually refers to an overlapped L1/L2 domain.

The Core as the L2 Domain

One way to deploy IS-IS onto a three-layer hierarchy is to configure the network core as a single L2 routing domain and place the distribution and access layers into various L1 domains, as needed. This design closely mimics an OSPF network with area 0 in the core and the distribution and access layers contained within areas connected to area 0, as Figure 5-3 illustrates.

Figure 5-3   *Pure L2 Core in Three-Layer Hierarchy*

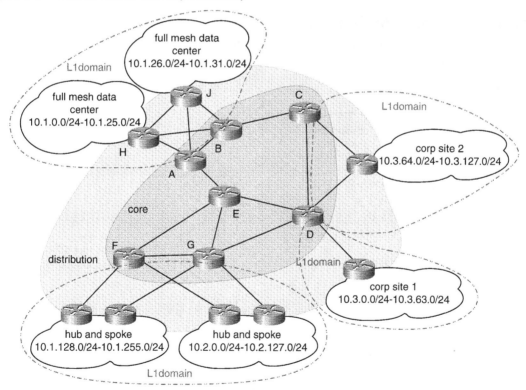

The advantages and disadvantages of constraining the L2 routing domain in the core of the network are familiar, as Table 5-1 illustrates.

Table 5-1 *Constraining the L2 Routing Domain in the Network Core: Advantages and Disadvantages*

Advantages	Disadvantages
The L2 routing domain is contained and probably will not change much, because the core of the network is not subject to many radical changes.	The L1 routing domains have an added design complexity.
Because the L2 routing domain is so limited in size, it should be easy to modify or assign the IP addresses in the network to provide for optimal aggregation.	The distribution layer can become extraneous.
Hiding redundancy within the distribution layer from the L2 routing domain is easy.	The flexibility that IS-IS allows in overlapping L1 and L2 routing domains is not fully taken advantage of.

Merging the Core and Distribution Layers into Level 2

A second option is to make the core and distribution layers into an L2-only routing domain and the various areas within the access layer as L1 routing domains, as Figure 5-4 illustrates.

Figure 5-4 *L1 Access Layer*

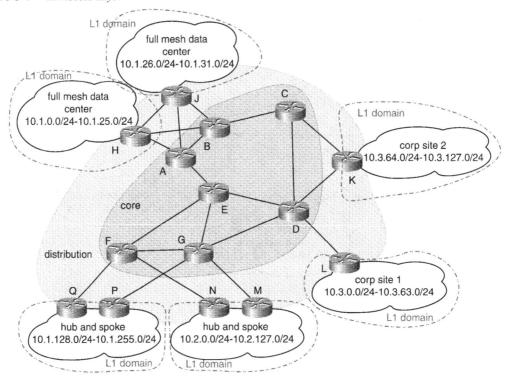

The main advantage with this sort of arrangement is that the L1 routing domains are kept small, which means they can be designed, in some situations, so that all the L1 domains with the same type of topology and requirements can be copied from the same set of configurations.

The disadvantages are as follows:

- The L2 routing domain becomes complex. Not only is the core, with any redundancy within the core, in the L2 routing domain, but the redundant links that connect the core to the user access points are all within the L2 routing domain.

- The flexibility that IS-IS allows in overlapping L1 and L2 routing domains is not fully taken advantage of, which could result in more places where suboptimal routing and other issues occur.

- Because a large amount of redundancy usually exists between the distribution and access layers of the network, in several places, the IS-IS default behavior into the L1 areas (discussed in more detail in the section, "Working with IS-IS Routing Areas," later in this chapter) causes suboptimal routing into the core of the network.

  An example of this in the network illustrated in Figure 5-4 is around the two hub-and-spoke topologies that are connected through Routers F and G. Here you have two possible equal-cost paths presented to Routers Q and P, for instance, although one of the two paths is more optimal for reaching devices that are attached to Corp Site 1.

- Aggregation of routing information might not be as effective if the L1/L2 borders are placed along the edge of the distribution layer or even within the distribution layer.

- The core could become extraneous if the L1/L2 boundary is placed at the outside edge of the distribution layer in all cases. This depends, a great deal, on the design of the distribution layer within the network. If distribution layer routers have several links between them, these links are generally preferred over links through the network core, thus offloading most traffic flowing between various points within the access layer into the distribution layer.

Mixing and Overlapping the Level 1/Level 2 Border

As with OSPF, another option is to take each topological section of the network and consider the L1/L2 boundary within the context of the surrounding network. To this, IS-IS adds the flexibility of overlapping the L1 and L2 routing domains in some cases, rather than forcing the full segregation of area 0 and the outlying areas, as OSPF does. Figure 5-5 illustrates some examples of how you might make these tradeoffs.

Examine each area of the network:

- The two mesh data centers, around Routers A, B, H, and J, are full-mesh topologies, which you would normally attempt to separate into two different flooding domains. However, each full mesh has a small number of routers, as indicated by the small number of routes advertised out of each full mesh (31 in total). Therefore, decreasing complexity within the routing domain is not much of an issue in this case. You can summarize the routes at Routers A and B effectively and keep the redundancy at Routers A, B, H, and J out of the L2 routing domain by placing the L1/L2 boundary at Routers A and B.

- At Routers C, D, and K, you can either include Routers C and D in the routing domain with Corporate Site 2, or you can include Routers C and D in the Level 2 routing domain. The outcome is not much different in either case, as far as the number of routes and the complexity of each routing domain, so leave the L1/L2 border in the distribution layer of the network. This allows summarization to occur in the most natural place within the three-layer hierarchy.

Figure 5-5   *Case-by-Case L1/L2 Domain Border Placement*

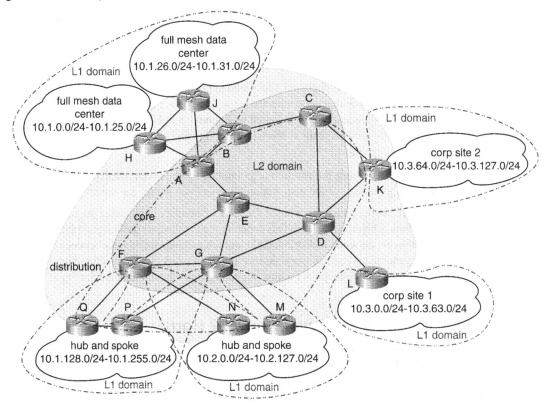

- At Routers D and L, you can either include Router D in the L1 routing domain with Corporate Site 1, or you can place the L1/L2 boundary at Router L so that Router D is entirely in the L2 routing domain. Again, you do not experience much of a tradeoff in terms of routes advertised into the core or the complexity of either the outlying routing domain or the L2 routing domain. For that reason, you might as well leave the L1/L2 boundary positioned on the distribution layer router.

- With OSPF, you have the choice of splitting the two hub and spoke topologies into two different areas, thus splitting up their complexity, or placing them in the same area. Although you still have both of these choices with IS-IS, you also have a third choice: You can overlap the L1 and L2 routing domains to provide more optimal routing, while preserving the split between the two hub and spoke topologies and preserving optimal route aggregation. Here, you place Routers F, G, Q, P, N, and M into the L2 routing domain to provide for optimal routing into and out of the hub and spoke topologies. You place Routers F, G, Q, and P into one L1 routing domain and Routers F, G, N, and M into another L1 routing domain, so that the L1 and L2 routing domains overlap at Routers F and G. You can summarize into the L2 routing domain on each router within both the L1 and L2 routing domains.

Deploying IS-IS on a Two-Layer Hierarchy

As with OSPF, deploying IS-IS on a two-layer hierarchical network is much simpler than deploying IS-IS on a three-layer hierarchical network. Generally, you should place the flooding domain boundaries along the edge of the network core, unless specific situations call for pushing the flooding domain boundary into the aggregation layer or pulling it into the network core. Figure 5-6 illustrates a two-layer hierarchical network, along with proposed flooding domain boundaries.

Figure 5-6   *IS-IS Flooding Domains on a Two-Layer Hierarchical Network*

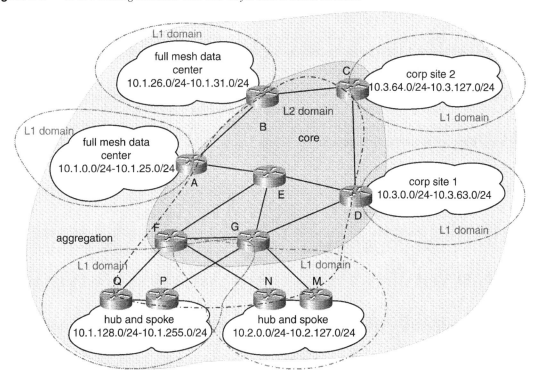

In almost every case, at Routers A, B, C, and D, the L1/L2 border is placed at the edge of the network core. At Routers E and F, however, the decision is more ambiguous. The hub routers in the hub and spoke topologies have been placed in L2 and in their L1 areas, using the capability to overlap the areas to provide optimal routing and topology simplification.

Working with IS-IS Routing Areas

What is the real difference between the L1 and L2 routing domains in IS-IS? Why is it so important to carefully consider where to place the boundary between these two routing domains in an IS-IS network? The following list provides a short overview of each type:

* At the L1/L2 border, routes in the L1 database are added to the L2 link-state packet (LSP), so they appear as leaves off the L2 IS. Topology information from an L1 routing domain is not injected into the L2 routing domain, just reachability information.

* An L1/L2 IS does not inject routing information into an L1 routing domain by default. Instead, any IS that is connected to an L2 routing domain sets the *attached* bit in its L1 LSP, so the intermediate systems within the L1 routing domain know which routers are attached to the L2 routing domain. This acts the same as a default route in IP. In fact, most IS-IS implementations for IP build a local default route pointing to any router with its *attached* bit set.

NOTE   To compare, L1 IS-IS routing domains are similar to OSPF totally not-so-stubby areas (NSSAs).

As an example of how L1 and L2 routing domains look in a real network, examine the IS-IS databases of the three routers that are illustrated in Figure 5-7. Example 5-1 that follows shows the corresponding configuration.

Figure 5-7   *Simple IS-IS Network*

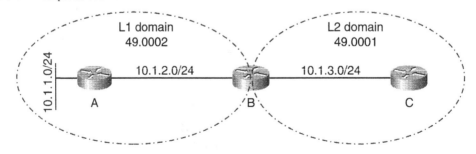

Example 5-1   *Configurations for Intermediate Systems in a Simple IS-IS Network*

```
!
hostname router-a
....
!
interface Ethernet0/0
 ip address 10.1.1.0 255.255.255.0
 ip router isis
!
interface Serial0/2
 ip address 10.1.2.0 255.255.255.0
 ip router isis
!
router isis
 Net 49.0001.1111.1111.1111.00
 is-type level-1
....


!
hostname router-b
....
!
interface Serial0/2
 ip address 10.1.2.0 255.255.255.0
 ip router isis
!
interface Serial0/3
 ip address 10.1.3.0 255.255.255.0
 ip router isis
!
router isis
 net 49.0001.2222.2222.2222.00
....


!
hostname router-c
....
!
interface Serial0/2
 ip address 10.1.3.0 255.255.255.0
 ip router isis
!
router isis
 net 49.0002.3333.3333.3333.00
```

Figures 5-8 illustrates the Router A database.

Figure 5-8 *IS-IS Database Output on Router A*

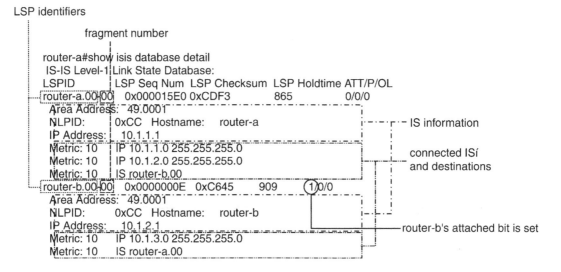

Router A has two L1 LSPs:

* One locally generated (with an LSP ID of **router-a.00-00**)

* One learned from Router B (**router-b.00-00**)

The locally generated LSP of Router A shows 10.1.1.0/24 and 10.1.2.0/24 connected, in addition to the intermediate system **router-b** (which is Router B). The LSP of Router B shows similar information, with 10.1.2.0/24 and 10.1.3.0/24 connected and the intermediate system **router-a** connected.

NOTE   The LSPs of Router A and B might also contain information about the host name of each IS, instead of just their addresses. If they do, their host names are also included in **show isis database**.

When you examine the LSP **router-b.00-00**, you find that the **ATT** bit is set in the right column of indicator flags, which means that this intermediate system is attached to the L2 routing domain.

This causes Router A to build and install a local default route pointing to Router B as the next hop, as shown in the output from the **show ip route** command demonstrated in Example 5-2.

Example 5-2   **show ip route** *from Router A in the Simple IS-IS Network*

```
router-a#show ip route
....
Gateway of last resort is 208.0.12.11 to network 0.0.0.0
....
i*L1 0.0.0.0/0 [115/10] via 208.0.12.11, Serial0/2
```

Router A builds this even though Router B is not explicitly advertising a default route to Router A or into the L1 routing domain. Now look at the Router B IS-IS database in Figure 5-9.

Figure 5-9   *IS-IS Database Output on Router B*

router-b#show isis database detail

IS-IS Level-1 Link State Database:
LSPID   LSP Seq Num LSP Checksum LSP Holdtime ATT/P/OL
2651A.00-00   0x000015E0 0xCDF3   675   0/0/0
   Area Address: 49.0001
   NLPID: 0xCC
   Hostname: router-a   router-b learns about 10.1.1.0/24 from
   IP Address: 10.1.1.1   router-a, adds 10 to the metric (the cost
   Metric: 10   IP 10.1.1.0 255.255.255.0   to router-a), and inserts it in its L2 LSP
   Metric: 10   IP 10.1.2.0 255.255.255.0
   Metric: 10   IS router-b.00
2651B.00-00   0x0000000E 0xC645   722   1/0/0
   ....

IS-IS Level-2 Link State Database:
LSPID   LSP Seq Num LSP Checksum LSP Holdtime ATT/P/OL
router-a.00-00 0x00000002 0x2481   67   0/0/0
   ....
router-c.00-00 0x0000000E 0xBE2F   717   0/0/0
   ....
router-b.00-00 0x0000000E 0xC645   722   1/0/0
   Area Address: 49.0001
   NLPID: 0xCC
   Hostname: router-b
   IP Address: 10.1.2.1
   Metric: 10   IP 10.1.2.0 255.255.255.0   router-a and router-b are
   Metric: 10   IS router-a.00   both connected to
   Metric: 20   IP 10.1.1.0 255.255.255.0   10.1.2.0/24, so both
                                           LSPs show the same metric

Router A, in this network, is maintaining only one IS-IS database, for L1 routing. This is because Router A is configured with the command **is-type level-1** under the **router isis** configuration mode. Because no L2 routing is configured on Router A, the IS-IS process does not maintain L2 routing information.

Router B is maintaining two IS-IS databases: one for the L1 routing domain, and one for the L2 routing domain. In the L1 routing domain, you can see the locally generated LSPs of Router A and B, which are identical to the LSPs shown in the Router A database. Because the Router A and Router B databases are synchronized, this is what you should expect.

The Router B L2 database, however, shows an LSP for Router C, which you will see in Figure 5-10, and a locally generated L2 LSP for Router B. In the locally generated L2 LSP for Router B, you can see two entries for connected IP networks: 10.1.1.0/24 and 10.1.2.0/24. Router B takes the IP reachability information that it learns from Router A, adds the cost to reach Router A, and adds it to its locally generated L2 LSP. In this case, 10.1.1.0/24 is listed in the Router B L2 LSP with a cost of 20.

Why is it that the Router B locally generated L2 LSP does not show 10.1.2.0/24 with a cost of 20? Router B is directly connected to 10.1.2.0/24, and the locally learned route is better than the route to 10.1.2.0/24 learned through Router A. The Router B local copy of its LSP shows the attached bit set, too.

Now look at the IS-IS database on Router C in Example 5-3.

Example 5-3 *IS-IS Database Output on Router C*

```
router-c#show isis database detail

IS-IS Level-2 Link State Database:
LSPID              LSP Seq Num  LSP Checksum  LSP Holdtime ATT/P/OL
router-c.00-00 0x0000000F    0xBC30        887             0/0/0
  Area Address:        49.0002
  NLPID:               0xCC
  Hostname:            router-c
  IP Address:          10.1.3.1
  Metric: 10           IS router-b.00
  Metric: 10           IP 10.1.3.0 255.255.255.0
router-b.00-00 0x0000000E    0xEE0E        857             0/0/0
  Area Address:        49.0001
  NLPID:               0xCC
  Hostname:            router-b
  IP Address:          10.1.2.1
  Metric: 10           IP 10.1.3.0 255.255.255.0
  Metric: 10           IS router-c.00
  Metric: 10           IP 10.1.2.0 255.255.255.0
  Metric: 20           IP 10.1.1.0 255.255.255.0
```

At Router C, the Router B LSP shows a link to 10.1.1.0/24 with a metric of 20. To Router C, it looks like Router B is connected directly to 10.1.1.0/24 (see Example 5-4) .

Example 5-4   *IS-IS Database on Router C in a Simple IS-IS Network*

```
router-c#show ip route
....
Gateway of last resort is not set
i L2 10.1.1.0/24 [115/30] via 10.1.3.2, Serial0/3
....
```

Leaking Routes into an L1 Routing Domain

Normally, an L1 only router sends all traffic that is destined outside the L1 routing domain to the nearest L2 intermediate system, as you have seen by examining the databases of the L1 and L2 intermediate systems in the previous section. Sometimes, however, you might want at least some of the IP reachability information carried in the L2 routing domain to make it down to L1 intermediate systems. Figure 5-10 illustrates one such case.

Figure 5-10   *Solving Suboptimal Routing with Route Leaking*

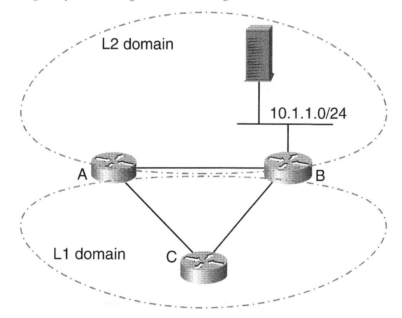

Here, you would like hosts that are connected to Router C to choose the path through Router B to reach the server on 10.1.1.0/24, rather than the path through Router A. Normally, Router C has two default routes—one through Router A and another through Router B—and load shares between the two paths.

How can you provide the more specific information that Router C needs into the L1 routing domain, so that it always chooses the shortest path? You can redistribute 10.1.1.0/24 from the

L2 routing domain into the L1 routing domain at both of the L1/L2 routers. Route leaking is simple to configure. You apply an access list using the **redistribution** command under the **router isis** configuration mode, as demonstrated in Example 5-5.

Example 5-5   *Controlling Redistribution with an Access List*

```
router(config)#access-list 10 permit 10.1.1.0 0.0.0.255
router(config)#router isis
router(config-router)#redistribute isis ip level-2 into level-1 distribute-list 10
```

You can also use an extended access list to permit any route that has a prefix length of 32 bits (any host routes), as demonstrated in Example 5-6.

Example 5-6   *Controlling Redistribution with an Extended Access List*

```
router(config)#access-list 101 ip permit any 255.255.255.255 0.0.0.0
router(config)#access-list 101 ip deny any any
router(config)#router isis
router(config-router)#redistribute isis ip level-2 into level-1 distribute-list 100
```

Aggregating Routes in IS-IS

You can aggregate routes only when they are redistributed into IS-IS or at an L1/L2 border. The command **summary**, under the **router isis** configuration mode, summarizes routes as demonstrated in Example 5-7.

Example 5-7   *Configuring Summarization in IS-IS*

```
router(config-router)#summary 10.1.0.0 255.255.0.0 ?
  level-1    Summarize into level-1 area
  level-1-2  Summarize into both area and sub-domain
  level-2    Summarize into level-2 sub-domain
  <cr>
```

You can summarize from an L1 routing domain into an L2 routing domain, or you can summarize when leaking routes from an L2 routing domain into an L1 routing domain.

Deploying IS-IS on Specific Topologies

This section talks about deploying IS-IS on specific topologies, starting with redistribution and working through full mesh, hub and spoke, and point-to-point broadcast links. It concludes with a discussion of links that are parallel to an L1/L2 boundary.

Redistribution

Redistribution into IS-IS follows the simple and normal pattern of redistribution into all routing protocols in Cisco IOS Software; you use the **redistribution** command in the **router isis** configuration mode. After you have chosen the protocol to redistribute from, you will find a few options for controlling redistribution, as Example 5-8 demonstrates.

Example 5-8   *Configuring Redistribution in IS-IS*

```
router(config-router)#redistribute static ip ?
  level-1        IS-IS level-1 routes only
  level-1-2      IS-IS level-1 and level-2 routes
  level-2        IS-IS level-2 routes only
  metric         Metric for redistributed routes
  metric-type    OSPF/IS-IS exterior metric type for redistributed routes
  route-map      Route map reference
  <cr>
```

NOTE   You need to use **redistribute static ip** when you are redistributing static routes into IS-IS because IS-IS can carry and redistribute both IP and CLNS routes.

You can redistribute routes into an IS-IS L1 routing domain or into an L2 routing domain. You can also set the metric and the metric type—which means that you can redistribute a route into IS-IS as an internal IS-IS route. This might seem a little odd at first, but when you consider that IS-IS was originally designed to carry CLNS routes, and it treats all IP routing information as "external," it makes more sense. The section titled "Metrics," later in this chapter, discusses IS-IS metrics and metric types in further detail.

As with EIGRP and OSPF, you can tag a route when redistributing it into IS-IS, using a route map. You can filter based on the tag when you are redistributing from IS-IS into another protocol. As with all other dynamic protocols, pay close attention to the possibility of routing loops when redistributing between two or more routing protocols at multiple points in your network.

NOTE   To use tags in IS-IS routes, you must configure wide metrics, as discussed later in the section titled "Metrics."

Full Mesh Topologies

As you saw in Chapter 4, full mesh networks pose a challenge for routing protocols that are scaling in a network. Figure 5-11 illustrates.

Figure 5-11   *Node to Path Increases in Full Mesh Networks*

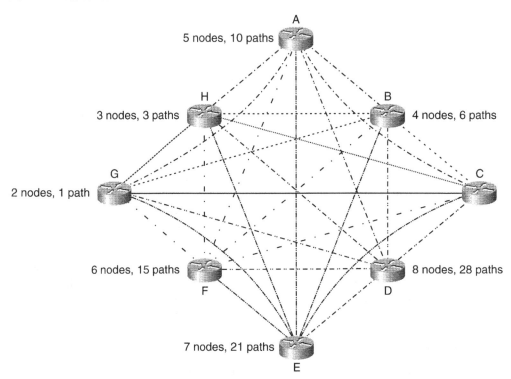

Twenty-eight possible paths will exist through a full mesh network with 8 nodes, and as the number of nodes increases, so will the number of possible paths. IS-IS will flood each LSP learned at the edge of the full mesh 10 or 20 times, up to, possibly, one reflood of the same LSP for each path through the network.

As with a broadcast network, you need to find some way to reduce the amount of flooding across a full mesh network. How do you do that? It is impossible for any router in the network to detect whether a given set of neighbors is connected to a full mesh topology and automatically reduce flooding in some way.

Instead, you can manually control flooding across the mesh by choosing one or two routers to reflood new LSPs that they receive onto the mesh and block flooding from all the other routers. IS-IS allows the manual configuration of a set of intermediate systems to reflood newly learned LSPs on a full mesh network using *mesh groups*.

You can configure a mesh group in Cisco IOS Software in two ways:

- You can place a number of interfaces in the same mesh group. If an LSP is received on an interface that is part of a *mesh group*, the intermediate system will not flood the LSP back out other interfaces in the same mesh group.

- You can mark an interface as *blocked*, which means that the IS will never flood LSPs out of it other than locally originated LSPs. In other words, the locally generated router LSP will be flooded out a blocked interface, but LSPs that are learned through the flooding process will not be flooded out a blocked interface.

Figure 5-12 illustrates this approach.

Figure 5-12   *IS-IS Mesh Groups*

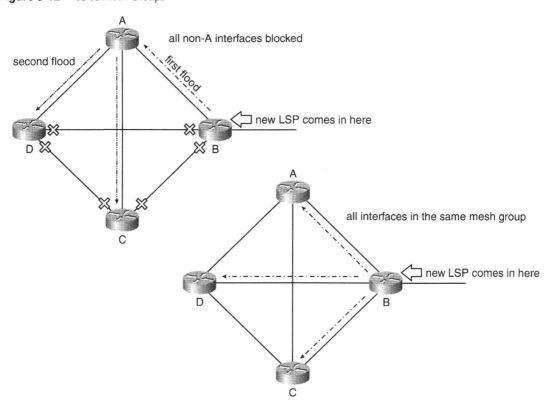

You actually see two cases in this small network: one with all interfaces that are not connected to Router A blocked from flooding completely, and the other with all the interfaces configured in the same mesh group. Consider the blocked flooding option first:

- On Router A, all the interfaces that are connected to Routers B, C, and D are configured with just **ip router isis**, **ip address**, and other required commands to make the links operational. No IS-IS mesh group commands are configured on any of the four interfaces on Router A.

- On Router B, the interface that is connected to Router A is configured as a normal IS-IS interface, with an **ip address**, **ip router isis**, and all commands required to connect the interface. The interfaces that are connected to Routers C and D are configured with an **ip address**, **ip router isis**, and other configurations that are required to make the links operations, but they are also configured with the command **isis mesh-group blocked**.

- The configuration of Router C is similar to that of Router B. The interface that is connected to Router A is configured as a normal routing interface, and the interfaces that are connected to Routers B and D are configured with **isis mesh-group blocked**.

- The configuration for Router D is similar to that of Routers B and C, with the interface that is connected to Router A configured as a normal IS-IS routing interface, and the interface that is connected to Routers B and C configured with **isis mesh-group blocked**.

When Router B receives a new LSP, it floods the new LSP only toward Router A, because the interfaces that are connected to Routers C and D are configured to block flooding. When Router B receives a new LSP, the following sequence of events occurs:

1 Router B floods the LSP over its only unblocked interface, toward Router A.

2 Router A receives the LSP from Router B and floods it over all of its interfaces, because none of them is blocked.

3 Router C receives the LSP from Router A. Except for the interface that connects to Router A, through which Router C received the LSP, all interfaces are blocked for flooding, so Router C does not reflood the LSP.

4 Router D receives the LSP from Router A. Again, all the Router D interfaces are blocked for flooding, except the interface over which it receives this new LSP, so Router D does not reflood it.

Each router that is connected to the full mesh receives only a single copy of the new LSP through the mesh (although each receives other copies through alternate paths in the network). The main concern with configuring a full mesh network in this manner is that a failure at Router A means that a new LSP that is learned at Router B is not flooded to Routers C or D. To prevent this, you can configure two intermediate systems connected to the mesh to reflood newly learned LSPs. This prevents a single router failure from causing the entire mesh to fail, but it also means that each router on the mesh receives two copies of any new LSP that is learned at the edge of the mesh.

The alternate configuration for mesh groups, shown as *all interfaces in the same mesh group* in Figure 5-12, resolves this problem, while continuing to limit flooding through the mesh. For this configuration, the following applies:

- All the interfaces for Router A that connect to Routers B, C, and D are configured with the command **isis mesh-group** *name*, where *name* is the name of the mesh group.

- All the interfaces for Router B that connect to Routers A, C, and D are also configured with **isis mesh-group** *name*, using the same mesh group name, *name*, as configured at Router A.

- The interfaces for Router C that connect to Routers A, B, and D are also configured with **isis mesh-group** *name*.

- The interfaces for Router D that connect to Routers A, B, and C are also configured with **isis mesh-group** *name*.

When Router B receives a new LSP from some intermediate system that is not connected to the mesh network, it compares the name of the mesh group that the LSP is received on (not configured) to the name of the mesh groups that are configured on its other interfaces. Because they do not match, Router B floods the newly received LSP to Routers A, C, and D. When Router A receives this new LSP, it also examines the name of the mesh group that is configured on the interface through which the LSP is received and compares it to the names of the mesh groups on its other interfaces. Because all the interfaces that connect to Routers B, C, and D are configured with the same mesh group, Router A does not flood this newly learned LSP out any of these interfaces.

This solves the problem of a single router failure within a full mesh without introducing additional flooding onto the mesh network. Note that a single router can also be a member of multiple full or partial mesh topologies. Each would have a different name and flood correctly into the topology to ensure the required flooding of routing information through the network.

Hub-and-Spoke Topologies

Hub-and-spoke networks are a challenge when deploying IS-IS, as they are with all link-state protocols. This section discusses two techniques for deploying IS-IS over a point-to-multipoint topology (which is common in hub-and-spoke topologies).

Point-to-Point Links

The easiest and most natural way to deploy IS-IS across a point-to-multipoint topology is to use logical subinterfaces to create point-to-point links across the point-to-multipoint cloud, and then deploy IS-IS across these point-to-point links. For instance, for a Frame Relay network, you can create a logical subinterface for each data-link connection identifier (DLCI), treating each DLCI that is multiplexed onto the single physical interface as a separate logical point-to-point link.

The main disadvantage to deploying IS-IS across a point-to-multipoint network in this way is that it consumes more IP address space. You need a separate subnet for each logical point-to-point circuit that is created using this technique.

NOTE   You can reduce the amount of IP address space wasted by using 31-bit subnet masks on the logical point-to-point links created when you configure the subinterfaces.

Broadcast Interfaces

You can also configure the point-to-multipoint interface as a single broadcast interface, as Figure 5-13 illustrates.

Figure 5-13 *Treating a Point-to-Multipoint Network as a Broadcast Domain*

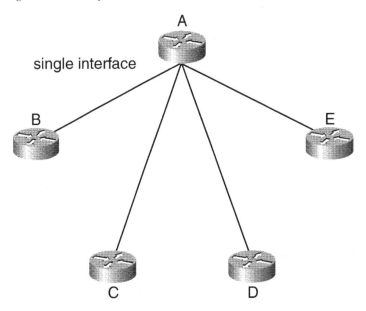

You need to remember, however, that Router C, for instance, cannot see the Router B hellos or other multicast packets. Because the designated intermediate system (DIS) election process is handled through information in the IS hellos (ISHs), and Router C does not receive the ISHs of Router B, what will the impact be?

In this situation, Router C might choose Router A as the DIS, whereas Router A might choose Router B as the DIS. This would cause a major problem with flooding link-state packets (LSPs) through this network. How can you resolve this?

You can set each intermediate system ID (configured using the **net** command under **router isis** configuration mode, in Cisco IOS Software) so that Router A always wins the DIS election process. However, a better practice is to configure the IS-IS DIS priority under the serial interfaces that interconnect these routers, using the **isis priority** command to set the spoke router's priorities to 0. That way, Router A is always selected as DIS.

Point-to-Point Broadcast Links

Any time that you run IS-IS over a broadcast link, the two intermediate systems that are connected to the link elect a DIS to control flooding through the link. Although this is good when numerous intermediate systems are attached to the same broadcast network, it can be bad if only two intermediate systems are attached to the link. Figure 5-14 illustrates.

Figure 5-14   *DIS Election and the Resulting SPF Tree on a Point-to-Point Broadcast Link*

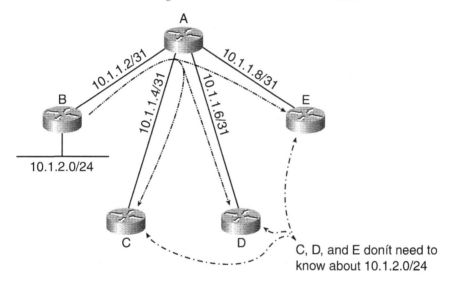

IS-IS elects one of the two intermediate systems that are connected to the link to be a DIS. The DIS advertises a zero-cost link to every router that is connected to the network through a pseudonode LSP, and each router on the network advertises a link to the DIS. In the SPF tree, then, you see an extra hop through the broadcast network. This might not seem like a big deal, but it can increase the time required for SPF to run, slowing down convergence.

On a point-to-point link, it is unnecessary for the two intermediate systems to elect a DIS, because the flooding controls that a DIS provides are unneeded, and the DIS does not require advertising a pseudonode for the network. To prevent IS-IS from electing a DIS in this situation, configure the link as an IS-IS point-to-point link, using the interface level command **isis network point-to-point**.

NOTE   If you configure an NBMA network as a broadcast network using IS-IS, the remote sites cannot communicate with each other. The easiest solution to this problem, if inter-site communication is required, is to map each remote site's IP address to the circuit used to reach the hub router on each remote router.

Links Parallel to Area Boundaries

In many cases, a network design includes links between two L1/L2 intermediate systems, as Figure 5-15 illustrates.

Figure 5-15 *Link Parallel to an L1/L2 Boundary*

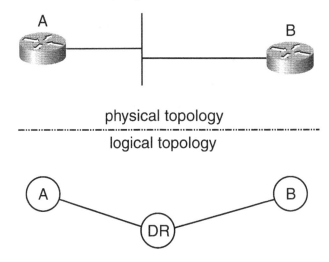

Should you put the link between Routers D and E in the L1 routing domain, or the L2 routing domain? To answer that question, consider the following scenarios:

- If you put the link in the L1 routing domain, Host G always uses the optimal Router D to E link to reach Host H, but Host A always uses the suboptimal path through Routers D, C, and E to reach Host B.

- If you put the link in the L2 routing domain, Host A always uses the optimal link between Routers D and E to reach Host B, but Host G always uses the suboptimal path through Routers D, F, and E to reach Host H.

With IS-IS, this is a simple problem to solve, because a single link can be in the L1 and L2 routing domains at the same time. You simply place the Router D to E link in both routing domains (links are in both L1 and L2 by default), configuring the links as **isis link-type level-1-2**.

Other Considerations in IS-IS Scaling

When you are deploying IS-IS on a large-scale IS-IS network, you also need to consider narrow and wide metrics, LSP flooding reduction, handling LSP corruption, and a number of other issues.

Metrics

When IS-IS was originally designed, the processors that were available for use in intermediate systems tended to be much slower than those available today. Therefore, making the calculation of the SPF tree easier was a prime consideration. One of the various techniques used in IS-IS to simplify the calculation of the SPF tree was to use a single 8-bit field to indicate all the metric information about a specific link.

To do this, you set one bit aside to indicate whether a route was learned internally or through some external source (typically redistributed). You set two bits aside to indicate a class of service, or the type of service that the link supported. In common use, the types of service were never implemented, so IS-IS ended up with the following:

- Internal links limited to a cost between 0 and 63
- External destinations limited to a cost between 64 and 127
- A maximum total path cost of 1023

These numbers leave little room to maneuver in terms of assigning link costs based on link bandwidth or other link characteristics. With the introduction of Multiprotocol Label Switching (MPLS) traffic engineering using IS-IS, the 6-bit metric space was determined to be too small, and a wider metric style was specified.

IS-IS wide metrics are 24 bits wide rather than 6 bits wide. That means interface metrics can now be assigned as high as 16777215, and the total cost of a path through the network can be 4261412864. To configure an IS running Cisco IOS Software to run wide metrics, use the command **metric-style wide** in the **router isis** configuration mode.

Transitioning a running network from narrow metrics to wide metrics is a challenge. If you change some of the intermediate systems within the network, the rest of the routers no longer understand their metrics, and the network fails. You can get around this by using the metric transition mode, configured using the **metric-style transition** command in the **router isis** configuration mode.

The metric transition mode allows an intermediate system to accept both wide and narrow metrics and use them interchangeably. As long as all the interface costs are within the narrow metric range, SPF continues to operate properly, and the network continues to work. After you have configured all the routers in the network to transition mode, you can go back and configure them all into the wide metric mode and then start using the wider range of metrics available.

Although the default link cost on an IS running Cisco IOS Software is 10, you can change the default link costs on all links that are connected to an L1 or an L2 routing domain by using the command **metric** *metric-value* [**level-1** | **level-2**].

Excessive Link-State Flooding

One of the major factors to consider when you are using any link-state protocol is the amount of flooding that occurs. Excessive flooding can cause excessive SPF runs, which eat CPU time and memory on the routers. Of course, you can change the rate at which LSPs are flooded within a network. For more information, see the discussion of high-availability techniques, including fast network convergence, in Chapter 7, "High Availability and Fast Convergence."

Another thing to consider when trying to reduce the flooding rate of LSPs through a network is the link-state aging timer. After a particular LSP ages out, the originating router must reflood it. By default, this occurs every 20 minutes in IS-IS. A full SPF run on every router in the network every 20 minutes with several routes can spell trouble for memory and processor utilization.

Fortunately, you have another option. The aging timers are adjustable in IS-IS (and it is probably a good idea to do so on larger networks). You can set the maximum age for LSPs using the **max-lsp-lifetime** command. You can set the rate at which LSPs are refreshed using the **lsp-refresh-interval** command.

The maximum LSP lifetime must always be greater than the LSP refresh interval; otherwise, IS-IS constantly refreshes its LSPs. In most modern networks, setting the LSP lifetime to the maximum possible and the refresh interval to about half of the maximum is acceptable. If your network experiences much data corruption, it might be better to leave these settings at their defaults.

LSP Corruption

On certain types of links, packet contents can be subject to corruption, but the data link layer error correction fields do not show it. For example, a switch that translates from Token Ring or Fiber Distributed Data Inerface (FDDI) to Ethernet, like the one illustrated in Figure 5-16, could easily corrupt data. However, because the Layer 2 cyclic redundancy check (CRC) must be regenerated when the packet is rebuilt in the new format, the data corruption might go unnoticed.

Figure 5-16   *LSP Corruption*

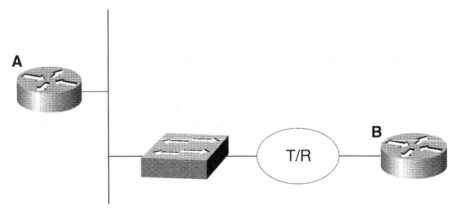

If Router A generates an LSP and multicasts it toward Router B on the Ethernet, the switch, during the translation to Token Ring, can corrupt the packet. When the packet reaches Router B, it passes the Layer 2 checks in the router toward IS-IS for processing.

When the IS-IS process on Router B discovers that the information in the packet is corrupted (by looking at the Layer 3 checksum information), it changes the LSP remaining lifetime field to 0 and refloods the packet to purge the bad information from the network.

Router A sees this reflooding of an LSP it originated, generates a new copy of the LSP, and floods it again to ensure that other routers on the network have current information on its links.

If the switch corrupts the packet again, the entire process repeats itself, possibly causing an LSP reflood storm in the network. The obvious answer to this problem is to fix the switch, but sometimes it is not that easy. While you are fixing the switch, Routers A and B are flooding this LSP back and forth, causing other problems on your network.

Turning off the reflooding part of this problem on Router B is possible by configuring the router to ignore LSPs that have invalid checksums, rather than attempting to flush them from the network. The command to configure this behavior is **ignore-lsp-errors**.

Generally speaking, you do not want to turn off error checking for LSPs, but it might be useful when you are receiving numerous errors, you are tracking these errors through some other means, and you want to return some stability to your network.

Maximum Number of Pseudonodes

When an intermediate system is elected the DIS of a broadcast segment, it advertises a pseudonode LSP, linking the DIS to each of the intermediate systems that is connected to the broadcast network. The network service access point (NSAP) selector space in the system ID of the originating IS distinguishes pseudonode LSPs from normal IS LSPs (see Example 5-9).

Example 5-9   *IS-IS Database Output Showing the Maximum Number of Pseudonodes*

```
router-a#show isis data detail

IS-IS Level-1 Link State Database:
LSPID                  LSP Seq Num  LSP Checksum  LSP Holdtime   ATT/P/OL
router-a.00-00         0x00000136   0xBB58        1189           0/0/0
  Area Address:        49.0001
  NLPID:               0xCC
  Hostname:            router-a
  IP Address:          10.0.12.10
  Metric: 10           IP 10.0.7.0 255.255.255.0
  Metric: 10           IP 10.0.12.0 255.255.255.0
  Metric: 10           IS router-b.01
router-b.00-00         0x00000133   0xC93B        1145           1/0/0
  Area Address:        49.0001
  NLPID:               0xCC
  Hostname:            router-b
  IP Address:          10.0.12.11
  Metric: 10           IP 10.0.13.0 255.255.255.0
  Metric: 10           IP 10.0.12.0 255.255.255.0
  Metric: 10           IS router-b.01
router-b.01-00         0x00000001   0x2630        1180           0/0/0
  Metric: 0            IS router-b.00
  Metric: 0            IS router-a.00
```

In this simple network, two routers are connected through a single Ethernet link, within an L1 routing domain. Router A shows a connection to **router-b.01-00**, and Router B shows a connection to **router-b.01-00**. A third IS, **router-b.01-00**, shows a zero-cost connection to **router-a.00-00** and **router-b.00-00**. Routers A and B do not show each other as connected neighbors.

The third router, **router-b.01-00**, is the pseudonode LSP that is advertised by Router B, which is the elected DIS on the Ethernet link between Routers A and B. You can tell it is a pseudonode because the selector bits—the first two octets after the period in the LSP ID—are set to something other than 00. In this case, Router B has set the selector bits to 1, because this is the first broadcast network that it has been elected DIS on.

The actual range of selector bits available is 0 through 255. However, because the number 00 indicates the intermediate system, an IS has numbers only from 1 through 255 to build pseudonode LSPs. This limits the number of broadcast segments on which an IS can be elected the DIS to 254 links. If an IS is elected DIS on any more links than this, it cannot generate pseudonodes for each of the broadcast networks, and you cannot route through them.

Considering the number of links on which a single IS has been elected DIS and making certain that you do not overflow this 254-link limit, is important. Note that this limit does not imply that an IS can be connected only to 254 links, or even to 254 broadcast links. This limit applies only to the number of links on which the IS can be elected DIS.

NOTE   Several drafts have been written to address this issue, although none of them has actually been implemented by Cisco yet.

Prefix-Driven Routing Table Installation

In many networks, certain servers or other devices (such as voice gateways) are critical and should be reachable before other devices on the network. To accommodate these varying levels of importance among Internet Protocol (IP) destinations, IS-IS running on Cisco IOS Software provides prefix-driven routing table installation.

Three levels of priority exist when this feature is configured:

- **High-priority routes**—Routes that are tagged by the network operator as being important reachable destinations.
- **Medium-priority routes**—All host routes (routes that have a 32-bit prefix length) not marked as a high-priority route.
- **Low-priority routes**—All the other IP destinations that are advertised through IS-IS.

Configuring a prefix-driven routing table installation is simple. It takes advantage of the route tags that IS-IS can carry in a route to designate high-priority routes. On the interface of the IS that connects to a high-priority network resource, enter the configuration as shown in Example 5-10.

Example 5-10   *Configuring Tags in IS-IS*

```
router#configure terminal
router(config)#interface ethernet 0/0
router(config-if)#isis tag 100
```

100 is a tag that the network operator chooses. On all the intermediate systems within the network, enter the configuration as shown in Example 5-11.

Example 5-11   *Configuring Route Installation Priority in IS-IS*

```
router#configure terminal
router(config)#router isis
router(config-rtr)#ip route high-priority 100
```

Use the same tag as when you are configuring the high-priority destinations in interface configuration mode. This configuration results in the IS-IS routes that are marked with the tag specified being given priority when they are installed in the routing table, speeding up convergence for critical resources that are located on those segments.

Hello Padding Suppression

IS-IS normally pads its hellos across a link to the maximum transmission unit (MTU) available to ensure that no mismatch exists in the MTU across the link. (The two intermediate systems do not have a different MTU configured.) This padding is useful, but on some links, it can use excessive bandwidth.

To remove hello padding on links where the padding could take up excessive bandwidth, use the command **no isis hello-padding** in the interface configuration mode. The hellos are still padded until a full adjacency is formed, but after this, the padding is removed, and hellos drop to a small packet size.

Case Study: Troubleshooting IS-IS Neighbor Relationships

In two instances, IS-IS does not form neighbor adjacencies correctly. The first is with misconfigured NSAPs. For example, Router C has just been attached to the network in Figure 5-17, and it is not forming L1 adjacencies with Routers A and B as expected.

Figure 5-17 *IS-IS Neighbors in Different Areas*

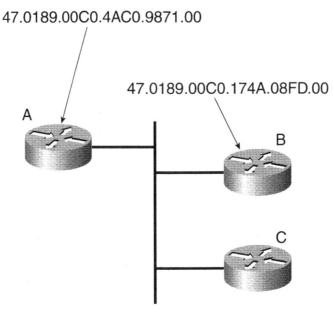

47.0189.00C0.4AC0.9871.00

47.0189.00C0.174A.08FD.00

A

B

C

On Router A, you see the output in Example 5-12.

Example 5-12 *Determining IS Adjacency Types*

```
router-a#show clns neighbor
System Id    SNPA              Interface  State  Holdtime  Type Protocol
B            00C0.174A.08FD    Et0        Up     27        L1   IS-IS
C            00C0.0c76.f096    Et0        Up     26        L2   IS-IS
```

Based on this output, notice that Router A has formed an L1 adjacency with Router B and an L2 adjacency with Router C. This means that C must have been misconfigured with an incorrect NSAP; in other words, the area ID is probably wrong.

Another instance where IS-IS routers do not form a neighbor adjacency is if you are running Integrated IS-IS across a point-to-point link and the IP addresses on the interfaces that the routers are connected through are not on the same subnet. For an example of this, look at Figure 5-18.

Figure 5-18   *IS-IS Neighbors in Different Subnets*

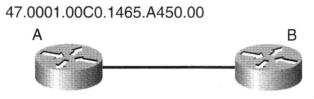

47.0001.00C0.1465.A450.00

A   B

47.0001.00C0.1465.A460.00

When you look at the Router A CLNS neighbors, you see the results in Example 5-13.

Example 5-13   *Determining CLNS Neighbor Types*

```
router-a#show clns neighbor
System Id       Interface   SNPA          State  Holdtime  Type Protocol
00C0.1465.A460 Se0          *HDLC*        Up     297       IS   ES-IS
```

Note that the protocol is *ES-IS*, rather than *IS-IS*; you would expect an IS-IS adjacency between these two neighbors. Because they are ES-IS neighbors, they do not exchange routing tables. Comparing the IP addresses of the interfaces on the two routers reveals what is wrong, as demonstrated in Example 5-14.

Example 5-14   *Determining the IP Address of an Interface*

```
router-a#show ip interface brief
Interface           IP-Address      OK? Method Status          Protocol
....
Serial0             172.19.2.1      YES manual up              up
....
```

Serial 0 on this router is configured as part of the 172.19.2.0/24 subnet. Example 5-15 shows the output of **show cdp neighbor detail**. Cisco Discovery Protocol (CDP) provides information about directly connected devices on the network.

Example 5-15   *Determining the IP Address of the Connected Device*

```
router-a#show cdp neighbor detail
....
Device ID: rp-2501-13a
Entry address(es):
  IP address: 172.19.1.2
  CLNS address: 47.0001.00c0.1465.a460.00
Platform: cisco 2500,  Capabilities: Router
Interface: Serial0,  Port ID (outgoing port): Serial0
```

Serial 0 on the other router is configured as part of the 172.19.1.0/24 subnet. Change the serial 0 interface of subnet A to see if it resolves the problem (see Example 5-16).

Example 5-16 *Reconfiguring the IP Address of the Local Device to Correct Neighbor Adjacency Formation*

```
router-a#config t
Enter configuration commands, one per line.  End with CNTL/Z.
router-a(config)#int s0
router-a(config-if)#ip address 172.19.1.1 255.255.255.0
router-a(config-if)#end
router-a#show clns neighbor
System Id       Interface   SNPA              State  Holdtime  Type Protocol
00C0.1465.A460 Se0          *HDLC*            Up     22        L1L2 IS-IS
```

Now these two routers have correctly formed an IS-IS neighbor relationship, and they can exchange routes. They are forming both an L1 and L2 adjacency; this is the default for Cisco routers that run IS-IS.

Review Questions

1   If you are implementing a single routing domain on a network, should you use a single L1 routing domain or a single completely overlaid L1/L2 routing domain?

2   What types are routes are, by default, sent by an L1/L2 router into an L1 routing domain?

3   How are IP destinations in an L1 routing domain propagated into the L2 routing domain?

4   What mechanism can you use if you want to advertise specific routes contained in the L2 routing domain into an L1 routing domain?

5   What two mechanisms can you use to reduce the impact of a full mesh topology on IS-IS scaling?

6   What are the two possible ways you can treat a point-to-multipoint or hub-and-spoke topology when deploying IS-IS?

7   What two forms of metrics can you use with IS-IS?

8   What is the maximum number of broadcast networks an IS can serve as the DIS on?

PART III

Advanced Network Design

CHAPTER 6

BGP Cores and Network Scalability

Border Gateway Protocol (BGP) is the routing protocol that glues the Internet together. It falls under the Exterior Gateway Protocol (EGP) category—unlike the protocols described in previous chapters, which are Interior Gateway Protocols (IGPs). BGP version 4 is the current version, but throughout this book, it is referred to simply as BGP.

Traditionally, BGP has been used to exchange routing information between different autonomous systems. In the typical configuration, BGP ties Internet service providers (ISPs) to their customers and each other. This chapter does not deal with connections to the Internet or inter-ISP operations. Instead, it presents the proven, robust, and scalable BGP features that allow your network to grow past IGP limitations. The only portion where Internet connectivity is dealt with explicitly is in a series of case studies in the "External Connections" section.

This chapter is not about BGP itself, but how you can use it to scale your network even further. To understand all the concepts covered in this chapter, you need to be familiar with the basic operation of BGP. If you need a quick review, read Appendix D, "Border Gateway Protocol 4 Basics of Operation," before continuing.

As described in Chapters 1 and 2, hierarchy, addressing, summarization, and redundancy are essential components of good network design. Chapters 3, 4, and 5 took this one step further, and described how the techniques used in deploying an IGP is also important. However, there are limits in all network designs, and as your network grows, you will inevitably hit them. The main limitations are the sheer volume of routing information carried in the routing protocol, and the increasing levels of policy required to successfully manage the network. On the other hand, BGP is currently deployed worldwide and carries approximately 155,000 routing entries at the core of the Internet. (This number is growing at the time of this writing. You can track the growth of the Internet by visiting the "CIDR Report" website at http://www.cidr-report.org/.) Some providers have been known to carry closer to 280,000 routes.

Policies are hard to define and enforce with an IGP because of the limited flexibility. Usually, a tag is the only tool available.

In the age of increasingly complex networks (in both architecture and services), BGP offers an extensive suite of knobs to deal with complex policies, such as the following (to name just a few):

- Communities
- AS_PATH filters
- Local preference
- Multiple exit discriminator (MED)

BGP also counters instability by implementing a *route dampening algorithm*. This algorithm is applied when the advertisement of a route is suppressed if it is known to change regularly over time. (All the parameters from the periodicity of the flaps to the type of routes suppressed are configurable.) Although you will follow the structural recommendations given in this book when building networks with the different IGPs studied, BGP is not tied to a set hierarchical model. In fact, the topology can take any form, and the protocol will adapt to it. Look at the Internet, which has no discernible hierarchical structure; it is impossible to pinpoint a core or a distribution layer for the Internet as a whole—and it works.

Neighbors, Routes, and Propagation Rules in BGP

A router using BGP exchanges routing information by forming a neighbor relationship with other routers. BGP routers can establish either internal or external peerings. BGP peers in the same autonomous system (AS) are called iBGP peers, whereas peers in a different AS are called eBGP peers. An AS might have more than one external connection; in that case, it is necessary to have several BGP speakers in the network to maintain routing consistency. Unlike other protocols, the rules of when and if a prefix is advertised to a neighbor depend on the type of neighbor the prefix was learned from. Also, a route is propagated only if it has been selected as the best for a specific destination. (For more details, read Appendix D.) Three combinations are possible:

- **Routes learned from an eBGP peer**—Propagated to all peers
- **Routes learned from an iBGP peer**—Propagated only to eBGP peers
- **Routes originated locally**—Propagated to all peers

Because routes learned from iBGP peers are not sent to other iBGP peers, it is clear that a full logical mesh is needed between them to ensure consistent routing information.

This chapter is a discussion of the use of BGP as a way to scale your network even further. The discussion starts with a description of the implementation in the core of the network (where full routing is required) and expands the concepts to be used in the network as a whole.

Case Study: Troubleshooting BGP Neighbor Relationships

Because BGP is designed as an EGP, rather than an IGP, BGP neighbor relationships are not complex. The primary thing to keep in mind is that all communications between BGP peers are based on Transmission Control Protocol (TCP). Therefore, an IP connection must be in place between the peers before a relationship can be established. Look at the network in Figure 6-1, which has only three routers, to see the problems that are possible.

Figure 6-1   *Simple Network with BGP Peers*

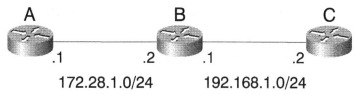

Begin by looking at what Router A would look like with a good, "up and running" eBGP neighbor relationship with Router B. Issuing **show ip bgp neighbor** results in the output in Example 6-1.

Example 6-1   *Displaying the BGP Neighbor Relationship State Between Routers A and B*

```
A#show ip bgp neighbor
BGP neighbor is 172.28.1.2,  remote AS 109, external link
....
  BGP version 4, remote router ID 10.1.1.1
  BGP state = Established, table version = 1, up for 00:00:33
....
Connections established 2; dropped 1
  Last reset 00:01:01, due to : User reset request
  No. of prefix received 0
Connection state is ESTAB, I/O status: 1, unread input bytes: 0
Local host: 172.28.1.1, Local port: 11001
Foreign host: 172.28.1.2, Foreign port: 179
....
SRTT: 710 ms, RTTO: 4442 ms, RTV: 1511 ms, KRTT: 0 ms
```

One main point in the output tells you that this neighbor relationship is up and running fine—the state is established. Other states of interest are as follows:

- **Idle**—No BGP neighbor relationship exists with this neighbor.
- **Connect**—BGP is waiting for TCP to establish a connection.
- **Active**—BGP is trying to connect to a peer by starting a TCP connection.
- **OpenSent**—BGP has established a TCP connection, sent an OPEN message, and is now waiting for an OPEN message from its peer.

- **OpenConfirm**—At this point, the OPEN message has been received and verified; BGP is now waiting for a KeepAlive (or a Notification) message.

- **Established**—BGP can exchange routing information at this point.

The next few sections examine some common BGP neighbor relationship problems. Keep in mind that, as with all networking-related troubleshooting, the best procedure is to start troubleshooting by looking at the basics first. Break down the problem into small parts.

No IP Connectivity

Neighbors cycling between the Idle, Connect, and Active states generally do not have an IP path between them. You cannot do much here except try to figure out why the IP connectivity is poor. Generally, you can use pings and trace routes to find problems at this level. (The specific techniques and procedures to find and correct problems at this level are outside the scope of this book.) A show ip bgp neighbor might result in the output in Example 6-2.

Example 6-2 *Using* **show ip bgp neighbor** *to Determine the State of the Connection Between BGP Neighbors*

```
A#show ip bgp neighbor
BGP neighbor is 172.28.1.2,  remote AS 109, external link
 Index 1, Offset 0, Mask 0x2
  BGP version 4, remote router ID 0.0.0.0
  BGP state = Active, table version = 0
  Last read 00:00:17, hold time is 180, keepalive interval is 60 seconds
  Minimum time between advertisement runs is 30 seconds
  Received 3 messages, 0 notifications, 0 in queue
  Sent 3 messages, 0 notifications, 0 in queue
  Connections established 1; dropped 1
  Last reset 00:00:19, due to : User reset request
  No. of prefix received 0
  No active TCP connection
```

A couple of items should be highlighted from the preceding output:

- **The "BGP state"**—In this case, it indicates "Active." This state was chosen as an example (over Connect or Idle) because it is the most confusing one. "Active" does not indicate that the connection is working; it indicates that the router is actively attempting to establish a connection.

- **The last line in the display**—"No active TCP connection" is a clear indication of what is going on.

eBGP Multihop

eBGP is designed to run only between directly connected neighbors, such as between Routers A and B in Figure 6-1. When attempting to configure Routers A and C as eBGP neighbors, Router A shows the result in Example 6-3.

Example 6-3   *Using* **show ip bgp neighbor** *to Determine the Location of an eBGP Neighbor*

```
A#show ip bgp neighbor
BGP neighbor is 192.168.1.2,  remote AS 109, external link
 Index 1, Offset 0, Mask 0x2
  BGP version 4, remote router ID 0.0.0.0
  BGP state = Idle, table version = 0
  Last read 00:00:18, hold time is 180, keepalive interval is 60 seconds
  Minimum time between advertisement runs is 30 seconds
  Received 0 messages, 0 notifications, 0 in queue
  Sent 0 messages, 0 notifications, 0 in queue
  Prefix advertised 0, suppressed 0, withdrawn 0
  Connections established 0; dropped 0
  Last reset never
  0 accepted prefixes consume 0 bytes
  0 history paths consume 0 bytes
  External BGP neighbor not directly connected.
  No active TCP connection
```

At the bottom of this output, you see the line "No active TCP connection," indicating there is no IP connectivity between this router and its BGP peer. eBGP normally sets the time to live (TTL) in all packets to 1, so when Router A sends a packet to Router C, Router B will drop it (and Router B will also drop Router C's packets to Router A). How can you tell BGP to set the TTL to something other than 1? By using the command **ebgp-multihop**, as Example 6-4 shows.

Example 6-4   *Using* **show ip bgp neighbor** *to Determine the Location of a Multihop eBGP Neighbor*

```
A#conf t
Enter configuration commands, one per line. End with CNTL/Z.
A(config)#router bgp 1
A(config-router)#neighbor 192.168.1.2 ebgp-multihop 2
A#show ip bgp neighbor
BGP neighbor is 192.168.1.2,  remote AS 109, external link
 ....
  BGP state = Established, table version = 93, up for 00:00:19
 ....
  External BGP neighbor may be up to 2 hops away.
Connection state is ESTAB, I/O status: 1, unread input bytes: 0
Local host: 172.28.1.1, Local port: 179
Foreign host: 192.168.1.2, Foreign port: 11008
```

Note that the output of **show ip bgp neighbor** now states the external neighbor might be up to 2 hops away. The default value (if no number is indicated) is 255, but recommended practice is that you configure the actual hop count between the 2 peers to avoid having the sessions take an unexpected path. For directly connected routers that peer using their loopback interface, you should use a hop count of 2.

Other BGP Neighbor Problems

A BGP speaker will not build a neighbor relationship with another BGP speaker if the neighbor's actual AS is not the same as the AS configured in the **neighbor** command. For instance, two routers with the configurations in Example 6-5 will never build a neighbor relationship.

Example 6-5   *Misconfigured AS Numbers Prevent BGP Neighbor Relationships*

```
hostname routerA
!
router bgp 109
 neighbor <B> remote-as 109
hostname routerB
!
router bgp 1
 neighbor <A> remote-as 109
```

The local autonomous system number (ASN) is configured when enabling BGP using the **router bgp** command. The ASN is exchanged in the OPEN message when the BGP session is being negotiated. If the configured **remote-as** is not received in the neighbor's OPEN message, a message (as shown in Example 6-6) can be seen using **debug ip bgp**.

Example 6-6   *Debugging Incorrect ASN Configurations*

```
*Dec 31 12:01:47: BGP: 140.1.10.42 rcv message type 1, length (excl. header) 26
*Dec 31 12:01:47: BGP: 140.1.10.42 rcv OPEN, version 4, holdtime 180 seconds
…

*Dec 31 12:01:47: BGP: 140.1.10.42 bad OPEN, remote AS is 1, expected 109
*Dec 31 12:01:47: BGP: 140.1.10.42 went from OpenSent to Closing
27w2d: %BGP-3-NOTIFICATION: sent to neighbor 140.1.10.42 2/2 (peer in wrong AS) 2 bytes
0001 FFFF FFFF FFFF FFFF FFFF FFFF FFFF FFFF 002D 0104 0001 00B4 8C01 0A31 1002 0601
0400 0100 0102 0280 0002 0202 00
*Dec 31 12:01:47: BGP: 140.1.10.42 send message type 3, length (incl. header) 23
*Dec 31 12:01:47: BGP: 140.1.10.42 local error close after sending NOTIFICATION
*Dec 31 12:01:48: BGP: 140.1.10.42 went from Closing to Idle
*Dec 31 12:01:48: BGP: 140.1.10.42 closing
```

When this error is detected, the BGP session is closed.

Also, you can set the hello and hold intervals for a BGP router, as done in Example 6-7.

Example 6-7   *Setting the Hello and Hold Intervals for BGP Routers*

```
router(config-router)#neighbor 10.1.1.1 timers ?
  <1-4294967295>  Keepalive interval
router(config-router)#neighbor 10.1.1.1 timers 100 ?
  <1-4294967295>  Holdtime
router(config-router)#neighbor 10.1.1.1 timers 100 100 ?
  <cr>
```

The Keepalive interval indicates the time between successive Keepalive messages, used to maintain the session established in the absence of Updates. The Holdtime indicates the time that a router will wait without receiving an Update or Keepalive and before declaring a neighbor down. The default values are 60 sec and 180 sec for the Keepalive and Holdtime intervals, respectively.

Changing the timers might result in faster detection of a failure—three minutes is a long time! Nonetheless, changing the timers to lower values also increases the number of packets that need processing, especially important in routers with numerous neighbors. In general, lower layer mechanisms such as Layer 2 signaling or protocol-independent Keepalives should be used for faster neighbor down detection. The Keepalive and Hold timers are not negotiated between two BGP speakers; rather, each BGP speaker advertises its Hold time. Each BGP speaker compares its locally configured Hold time with the Hold time it receives from its peer, and chooses the lower of these two values. For instance, if a BGP speaker has been configured with a Hold time of 15 seconds, and connects to a peer with a configured Hold time of 10 seconds, both of the routers will use 10 seconds as their Hold time.

The Keepalive timer is always set to one third of the Hold time; if the Hold time is 15 seconds, the Keepalive time will automoatically be set to 5 seconds. The Hold timer can be set to any value greater than 3 seconds.

You can easily become confused when working with connected peers configured with different Hold time settings. Rather than relying on the BGP configuration to determine the Hold time, rely on the output of **show ip bgp neighbors**, as illustrated in Example 6-8.

Example 6-8 *Displaying the Keepalive and Holdtime Intervals for BGP Routers*

```
router#show ip bgp neighbor
BGP neighbor is 192.168.1.2,  remote AS 109, external link
…
Last read 00:00:18, Holdtime is 180, keepalive interval is 60 seconds
…
```

Logging Neighbor Changes

Although many things can go wrong with BGP neighbor relationships, it is useful to log changes in the states of neighbors anyway so that you can tell what happened after any type of event occurs. The configuration for logging neighbor changes is simple, as Example 6-9 demonstrates.

Example 6-9 *Configuring the Logging of Neighbor Changes*

```
router#conf t
Enter configuration commands, one per line. End with CNTL/Z.
router(config)#router bgp 109
router(config-router)#bgp log-neighbor-changes
```

BGP in the Core

The core is the first place in your network where scaling issues will become apparent. This is because the core tends to combine the largest number of routes with the largest amount of traffic, taxing the routers to their limit. Using BGP in the core allows the routes in the core to separated into two parts: routes within the core and routes external to the core.

The iBGP mesh carries the routes external to the core, while the IGP continues to carry just the routes within the core (providing connectivity between the BGP speakers within the core itself). In Figure 6-2, you can see the clear distinction between these two types of routes. iBGP would be used to carry information about the outlying areas of the network, while the IGP would continue to carry reachability information for connections between the routers within the core itself.

Figure 6-2   *Network Core*

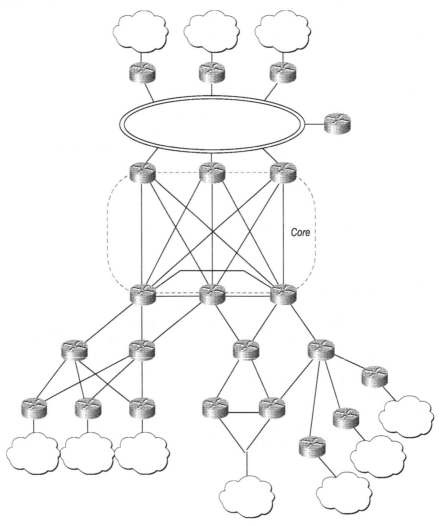

The simplest BGP core is a simple full iBGP mesh. With this type of implementation, you redistribute routes learned from your IGP into BGP at the edge of the core, and then remove the redistributed routing information at the core edge. There are three options for removing routing information once it has been redistributed into the BGP core.

First, you could set iBGPs administrative distance lower than your IGPs, so the iBGP routes are preferred over the IGP routes. This effectively filters the IGP routing information from the core. Second, you could configure a set of explicit route filters at the edge of the core. Finally, you could use a completely different IGP (or a different instance of the same IGP) in the core than the rest of the network. For details on synchronization, see Appendix D.

This approach provides an instant scalable core. In terms of migration, you should overlay BGP on the IGP that is currently in use. After you have redistributed the routes into BGP and verified its consistency (in other words, you have confirmed that all the routes are present in the BGP table), you can start filtering the IGP information at the border. Changing the administrative distance of iBGP to favor its routes over those of IGP is a safe approach prior to filtering.

BGP was not designed as an IGP; its main objective is to carry external routes—routes learned from other ASs or routing domains. BGP cannot detect routing loops within an AS; it can detect loops only in eBGP routes. Because of this, you should not redistribute iBGP routes (routes originated in the local AS) into your IGP. In other words, you cannot pass on the BGP routes to the distribution layer. This leaves you with a single choice—to carry a default pointing back only to the core. If your distribution layer needs at least partial routing information from the core, you need to have an eBGP connection. Another advantage of using eBGP to glue your network together is the added flexibility (in filtering and decision making) that BGP provides.

Case Study: Sample Migration

Consider the network core in Figure 6-2. The first task is to overlay BGP on the existing network without other changes taking place. The configuration is simple and can be standardized for ease of deployment. For this discussion, Open Shortest Path First (OSPF) is the assumed IGP. However, the process is similar for any IGP. Example 6-10 shows the basic configuration, which includes the definition of neighbors and the redistribution of routes from OSPF.

Example 6-10 *Basic Core Router Configuration*

```
router bgp 109
 no synchronization
 redistribute ospf 1 route-map routes-to-core
 neighbor x.x.x.x remote-as 109
 no auto-summary
!
route-map routes-to-core permit 10
 set metric-type internal
```

Note that synchronization and auto-summary are turned off. This last action allows BGP to carry the routing information with the same granularity as the IGP does (not only the classful networks). The MED is set using the **set metric-type internal** command with the purpose of being able to choose the best exit point (shortest IGP distance) in case of multiple options and to obtain metric changes dynamically. Remember: One **neighbor** statement is required for each of the other routers in the core.

As discussed in Chapter 4, "OSPF Network Design," the ABRs might or might not be located at the edge of the core. From the BGP migration point of view, the only advantage of not redistributing at the area border routers (ABRs) but doing it at other routers in area 0 is that they already carry summaries (from the other areas). The configuration in Example 6-9 assumes that the ABRs are not the redistribution points.

If the core edge routers are ABRs, summarization takes place at these routers. The summarized routes, however, are not present in the routing table at the ABRs. Keep in mind that the redistributed routes are the ones present in the routing table. You might need to manually create the summaries and then redistribute them. The sample configuration changes to something similar to Example 6-11.

Example 6-11   *Configuration for Redistributing Locally Summarized Routes*

```
router bgp 109
 no synchronization
 neighbor x.x.x.x remote-as 109
 redistribute static route-map routes-to-core
 no auto-summary
!
router ospf 109
 area 0 range y.y.y.y y.y.y.y
 area 0 range t.t.t.t t.t.t.t
!
ip route y.y.y.y y.y.y.y null0
ip route t.t.t.t t.t.t.t null0
!
route-map routes-to-core permit 10
 set metric 20
```

In this configuration, there is no redistribution from OSPF into BGP. Instead, static routes are configured to match the OSPF summaries, and these static routes are redistributed into BGP.

An advantage of this method is that the routes are "nailed" to the null0 interface (which means they never flap and never go down), ensuring stability in the core regardless of the state of any of the areas. One major difference is the use of the metric. In this case, you can set the metric either with a route map or on each route at the time that they are defined. The disadvantage is the fact that the metrics do not change dynamically.

To verify the consistency of the information in the BGP table, you must compare the data in the routing table (learned via OSPF, in this case) with the data in the BGP table. The output in Example 6-12 demonstrates what you should see (for network 20.1.1.0/24, in this case).

Example 6-12 *Consistency Check*

```
rtrC#show ip route 20.1.1.0
Routing entry for 20.1.1.0/24
  Known via "ospf 109", distance 110, metric 65, type intra area
  Redistributing via ospf 109
  Last update from 140.10.50.6 on Serial0, 00:00:28 ago
  Routing Descriptor Blocks:
  * 140.10.50.6, from 20.1.1.1, 00:00:28 ago, via Serial0
      Route metric is 65, traffic share count is 1

rtrC#show ip bgp 20.1.1.0
BGP routing table entry for 20.1.1.0/24, version 47
Paths: (1 available, best #1)
  Local
    140.10.50.6 from 140.10.50.6 (20.1.1.1)
      Origin incomplete, metric 20, localpref 100, valid, internal, best
```

The main data point to look at is the "direction" of the routes. You want to make sure that the next hops match in both protocols to guarantee that the traffic will follow the same patterns as before the migration.

If these two tables are not uniform, you need to revisit your redistribution points and check your filters (if any). Because LSA filtering can be tricky (at best), changing the administrative distance for the iBGP routes is explored next. To achieve the change, use the following command sequence to set the administrative distance for internal, external, and local BGP routes to 20:

```
router bgp 109
  distance bgp 20 20 20
```

In Cisco routers, the default administrative distance for OSPF routes is 110, and the lowest value is preferred. To verify the effectiveness of the change, look at the routes again, as demonstrated in Example 6-13.

Example 6-13 *BGP Routes with Lower Administrative Distance*

```
rtrC#show ip route 20.1.1.0
Routing entry for 20.1.1.0/24
  Known via "bgp 109", distance 20, metric 20, type internal
  Last update from 140.10.50.6 00:00:09 ago
  Routing Descriptor Blocks:
  * 140.10.50.6, from 140.10.50.6, 00:00:09 ago
      Route metric is 20, traffic share count is 1
      AS Hops 0

rtrC#show ip bgp 20.1.1.0
BGP routing table entry for 20.1.1.0/24, version 47
Paths: (1 available, best #1)
  Local
    140.10.50.6 from 140.10.50.6 (20.1.1.1)
      Origin incomplete, metric 20, localpref 100, valid, internal, best
```

Now the BGP route is the one in the routing table. At this point, the routers in the core have both the BGP and OSPF routes. The final step is to filter the IGP routes from the core. Each IGP offers different tools to achieve the filtering. Please refer to the appropriate chapter in the book, depending on the IGP(s) you are running in your network.

Scaling Beyond the Core

As your network grows toward becoming an international juggernaut, you might find that taking the load off the core routers is not always enough. In that case, it is time to extend the use of BGP to the rest of the network. In general, you can take three different approaches:

- You can divide your network into separate routing domains (connect them using eBGP).
- You can use confederations.
- You can use route reflectors.

iBGP requires a full internal mesh to ensure routing consistency. This internal mesh grows larger as BGP extends throughout the network and, of course, as the network grows. The last two approaches present a scalable way to reduce the number of neighbors while maintaining consistency. Dividing your network into separate autonomous systems and reducing the number of internal neighbors is covered first.

The first two approaches are similar. In fact, both require that you follow these three "easy" steps:

Step 1 Divide the network into multiple regions/areas.

Step 2 Select and configure an IGP for each region/area.

Step 3 Connect each region using BGP.

The "divide and conquer" option that you choose depends on a combination of the topology (resulting from the division) and the external connectivity. The following "rule of thumb" is offered to aid in the decision:

1 Is your network connected to the Internet or are you planning to connect it?

   If no, connect the pieces using eBGP.

   If yes, go to the next step.

2 Did the division result in a two-level hierarchy with a core AS and all the others connecting to it? (See Figure 6-3.)

   If no, use confederations.

   If yes, go to the next step.

3 Where are the connections to the Internet?

   If at least one is not in the core AS, use confederations.

The next couple of pages examine the general case, concentrating on using eBGP connections to tie the pieces together. The section titled "Confederations," later in this chapter, covers the operation of a network using confederations.

Dividing the Network into Pieces

Depending on the topology (both logical and physical) of your network, the division might take place along geographical boundaries, departmental lines, or the hierarchical structure. Figure 6-3 shows a proposed partition of the sample network.

Figure 6-3   *Divided into Regions*

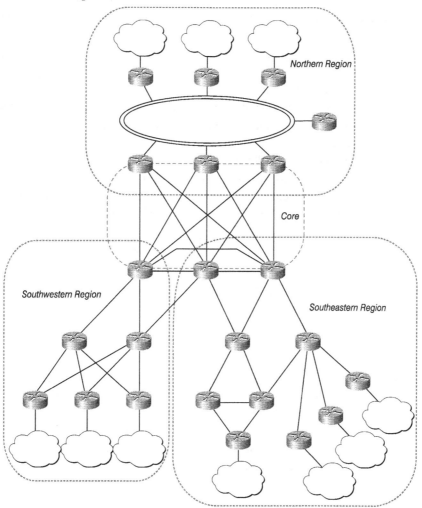

Two factors make this network easy to divide up: the distribution to core connection is very consistent and all summarization is taking place at the distribution to core edge. The most straightforward way to partition this network is along the already existing hierarchical lines (in some networks, other partitioning schemes might be just as or more reasonable). In this case, the local BGP process in the distribution router originates the summarized routes. An eBGP connection carries the routes into the core, allowing for detailed control regarding which routes make it through and what their attributes are. The core routers should be configured in a full iBGP mesh.

At this point, you have managed to split the network into several independent units. From the BGP point of view, the core has a full iBGP mesh and eBGP connections to all the other subnetworks. The subnetworks need to have only a few *BGP speakers*, which are the routers that connect to the core. However, you should consider creating an iBGP mesh inside any of these subnetworks in these situations:

- **Most of the routes from the core are needed** — In this case, you have the same scalability issues that you encountered in the core before. In general, this need might be in conjunction with the next one (transit), but it can also be associated with multiple connections to the core and the desire to select the best path for each destination.

- **The need exists to provide transit to reach other subnetworks** — Clearly, the number of routes increases considerably and needs to be transported to the core. This scenario occurs only on networks that result in more than one layer of hierarchy or that lack a clear core AS.

Until now, you have been dealing with a straight hierarchical network that has a core network and all the other pieces connected to it. BGP, however, allows the flexibility to connect the subnetworks any way you want. BGP takes care of finding the best path to any destination for you.

Connections to the Internet or other networks should take place at the core, and private ASNs should be removed where you attach to the outside world. Distinguishing the regional eBGP connections from the "real" external ones is important.

When multiple connections to the Internet exist, they should be located in the core region. If this is not possible, you must use confederations.

Regional IGPs

After dividing the network into regions, you will have created several "independent" networks. You can design each one to have its own core, distribution layer, access layer, addressing scheme, and internal redundancy. In addition, each region can use its own IGP.

The decision whether to use different IGPs is up to you. Link-state protocols can be tricky in the implementation of filters. If anything, you might end up using different instances of the same protocol in the different regions.

BGP Network Growing Pains

Even BGP can experience some growing pains as the core or the regions grow. Keep in mind that a full iBGP mesh is required. Most likely, the core will have a pervasive BGP configuration (which means that all the routers run BGP). Some of the issues that you need to keep in mind with many neighbors include the following:

- BGP update generation
- Loss of information because of aggregation
- Scaling BGP policies
- Scaling IBGP mesh
- Route flaps

BGP Update Generation Issues

BGP sends only incremental updates. If the network is stable, why is update generation a problem? In general, a few changes (even in a large network) are not an issue. However, consider the work to be done and how to improve it. You need to form one update for every peer. In other words, each time a prefix changes, the router needs to generate the same amount of updates as neighbors that it has. In routers that have a high number of neighbors (even those that experience sporadic changes), this process represents unnecessary work—the router is sending the same update to all its neighbors. You can trim this overhead in the following two ways:

- Reduce the number of updates generated
- Reduce the number of neighbors

Reducing the Number of Updates Generated

To reduce the number of updates generated, you do not have to reduce the number of neighbors. The number of updates can be decreased with the use of peer groups.

A *peer group* is a set of BGP neighbors that shares the same outbound policy, but its inbound policies might be different. You can configure your router to filter out routes sent to some of the departments in the company (the routes to reach the payroll servers, for instance). In general, iBGP peers receive the same updates all the time, making them ideal for arrangement in a peer group. The main advantage, besides ease of configuration, is the fact that the updates are generated only once per peer group. Example 6-14 shows a peer group made up of iBGP peers (and called "internal-neighbors.")

Example 6-14   *BGP Routes with Lower Administrative Distance*

```
router bgp 109
 no synchronization
 bgp log-neighbor-changes
 neighbor peer-group peer-group
```

Example 6-14 *BGP Routes with Lower Administrative Distance (Continued)*

```
 neighbor internal-neighbor peer-group
 neighbor internal-neighbor remote-as 109
 neighbor internal-neighbor route-map in-filter in
 neighbor 1.1.1.1 peer-group internal-neighbor
 neighbor 2.2.2.2 peer-group internal-neighbor
 neighbor 3.3.3.3 peer-group internal-neighbor
 neighbor 4.4.4.4 peer-group internal-neighbor
 neighbor 5.5.5.5 peer-group internal-neighbor
no auto-summary
```

Reducing Neighbor Count

At first glance, the reduction of the number of neighbors does not seem to be possible. After all, you already know that a full iBGP mesh is required for proper operation of the protocol. As far as eBGP peers are concerned, if external information is needed, they have to be there. You can use two methods, however, to achieve a reduction in the number of neighbors—iBGP neighbors, that is:

- Confederations
- Route reflectors

The next two sections cover these methods in greater detail.

Confederations

In short, using confederations to reduce the number of neighbors consists of breaking up the AS into smaller units by following the same procedure outlined in the "Dividing the Network into Pieces" section. The basic difference is that confederations make the network (of smaller pieces) look like one AS to the eBGP peers.

The AS is divided into pieces, and each piece is its own AS (using private numbering), complete with iBGP and eBGP peers. The iBGP peers are the other BGP speakers in the same sub-AS, whereas the eBGP peers are the BGP speakers in the other subautonomous systems and outside the main AS. Each router is configured with the new sub-ASN, but it is given information about which other autonomous systems belong to the same confederation. In general, eBGP peers between the subautonomous systems are treated as ordinary eBGP peers with a couple of exceptions: local preference and MED are passed across AS boundaries, and the NEXT_HOP is unchanged. This behavior allows the main AS to function as one to the outside. If you are confused, look at Figure 6-4.

The real ASN is 1; external neighbors see all three of the ASs as one AS. Internally, the network has been divided into three new subautonomous systems. Routers A, B, and C are all eBGP neighbors inside the confederation. Example 6-15 shows the basic configuration at Router A for a confederation. In it, both the **confederation identifier** and the **confederation peers** are explicitly configured—the rest of the configuration does not change.

Figure 6-4   *Confederations*

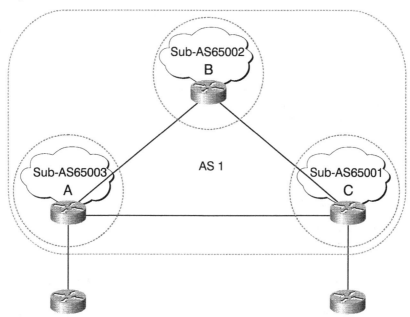

Example 6-15   *Sample Confederation Configuration*

```
router bgp 65003
 no synchronization
 bgp log-neighbor-changes
 bgp confederation identifier 1
 bgp confederation peers 65001 65002
 neighbor b.b.b.b remote-as 65002
 neighbor c.c.c.c remote-as 65001
 no auto-summary
```

The main advantage of using a confederation is it allows you to control the policies within the network, since each confederation AS boundary represents an opportunity to implement policy. If each sub-AS represents a single geographic region, or a single area of administrative control, the sub-AS boundaries provide a convenient place to control the routes and paths within the network core. However, the whole network needs to be migrated to this scheme at about the same time, and leaving one or more routers without a proper confederation configuration can cause routing loops. At all times, each member of a confederation (that is, all the BGP routers in the network) should know what the real ASN is, which subautonomous system it belongs to, and what other subautonomous systems belong to the same confederation. If any of this information is missing, improper information propagation can result.

Route Reflectors

One of the big advantages of route reflectors is that you can stage your migration to them. This means that you can configure one router at a time without disrupting normal operation of the whole network.

In short, route reflectors break the route forwarding rules of iBGP. Route reflectors can readvertise routes learned from one iBGP peer to another iBGP peer. It is important to understand that only the routers configured as route reflectors advertise routes to other iBGP peers. Therefore, only the route reflectors need special configuration. Example 6-16 shows a sample route reflector configuration.

Example 6-16 *Basic Route Reflector Configuration*

```
router bgp 109
 no synchronization
 bgp log-neighbor-changes
 neighbor 1.1.1.1 remote-as 109
 neighbor 1.1.1.1 route-reflector-client
no auto-summary
```

Because route reflectors might be deployed throughout the network at any given time, you can study their implementation in parts of the network illustrated in Figure 6-2. The core maintains a full mesh configuration as long as all the routers at its edge are route reflectors. Some parts of the network might have a two-tier route reflection structure. In general, the best way to place route reflectors in the network is to follow the physical topology. A router that is configured as a route reflector categorizes its iBGP neighbors as clients and nonclients (see Figure 6-5). Clients are routers that depend on the route reflector to receive internal routing information; clients do not need special configuration. In fact, all they need is an iBGP session to the route reflector. A route reflector and its clients are collectively known as a cluster.

Figure 6-5 shows two separate clusters; each one is covered here. Router C is a route reflector that has four clients (Router I, Router G, Router E, and Router F). If both Router I and Router G have external connections, the prefixes are forwarded as follows:

1 Routers I and G receive an external route. (Assume it is for the same prefix.)

2 Both routers announce this prefix to their iBGP neighbor—Router C is their only iBGP peer.

3 Router C compares the routes and selects one best path.

4 Because it is a route reflector, Router C propagates its best path to all its other clients and nonclients. (Router A is the only nonclient peering with Router C, in this case.)

Figure 6-5   *Two-Tier Route Reflector Mesh*

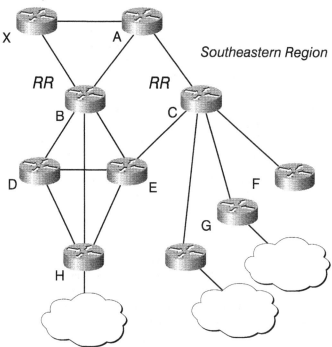

Note that in the case of Router C, the clients do not have iBGP sessions between them. Router B is a route reflector that has three fully meshed clients. The full mesh at the client level yields two different results:

- The route reflector does not have to reflect the information between clients.

- The route reflector is no longer a single point of failure in the cluster. The next section talks about route reflector redundancy.

Although you might be thinking that a fully meshed configuration defeats the purpose of having a route reflector, it is not true. Keep in mind that the objective is to reduce the number of iBGP peers. The clients have a full mesh, but they do not have to peer with the rest of the network. If Router H has an external connection, the prefixes are forwarded as follows:

1 Router H receives an external route, and it propagates it to all of its iBGP peers (Router D, Router E, and Router B).

2 Routers D and E do not do anything more. They follow the rules.

3 Router B propagates the path information (if it is the best path) to its nonclients (Router A and Router X).

As a side note, if Router B were to reflect the best path back to its clients, the clients would receive redundant information. The issue here is not the redundant information that the clients would receive but the processing that the route reflector requires. In other words, it is recommended to have a cluster with a full mesh of clients if clients are present in a significant number or if the physical topology dictates this to be so. The number of clients needed to consider using a full mesh between them depends heavily on the type of router being used as a route reflector and any other functions it might be performing. In other words, to determine the ideal point for your network, monitor the performance and utilization of the route reflectors at the times it needs to send updates to the clients. Your comfort level dictates when to mesh the clients, divide the load between reflectors, or simply dedicate a router just for the route reflector function. The case study "Route Reflectors as Route Servers" talks more about the last option.

Route Reflector Redundancy   As you might have noticed, a route reflector might become a single point of failure. In many cases, this situation is unavoidable because of the physical topology of the network.

You can achieve route reflector redundancy in a couple of ways.

The "classical" case is when the route reflectors are put in the same cluster. Each cluster has a cluster ID (usually the router ID of the route reflector). You need to configure all the reflectors to have the same cluster ID using the **bgp cluster-id** command. The limitation (but also where the additional redundancy is present) is that all the clients need to have iBGP sessions with both reflectors. The route reflectors should be iBGP peers of each other; if a prefix has already been forwarded by one of the reflectors, the others do not forward it. (This is where the cluster ID comes into play.)

The "modern" approach is to have only one route reflector per cluster. In this case, not all the clients need to connect to all the route reflectors (only the ones that need/want the redundancy). Refer to Figure 6-5; Router E is a client of two different route reflectors.

Route Reflector Deployment   What is the best way to deploy route reflectors? Where should you place the reflectors? Before answering these questions, refer to Figure 6-5. A third cluster could have been defined with Router A as the route reflector and Routers B and C as clients, creating a two-level, route reflector architecture.

Keeping in mind the initial objective of using BGP to help scale the network, you would deploy a route reflector architecture in two layers with a full mesh core. Referring to Figure 6-2, you should configure the routers at the network core in a full iBGP mesh. The routers that border with the distribution layer act as an upper layer of route reflectors. A lower layer can be put at the border between the distribution and access layers. These second level route reflectors are clients of the first layer ones.

A rule of thumb to comply with is to follow the physical topology. In other words, define the iBGP peering (between clients, reflectors, or normal internal peers) to match the physical connectivity of the network. This provides simplicity to the network and does not present a false sense of redundancy. Following the physical topology ensures that the forwarding of the traffic is in the intended direction. Note that the clients receive information only from the route reflector—losing visibility of other nodes in the network. Although forwarding loops might be hard to come by (forwarding in an unexpected direction is the most likely result), the only way you can guarantee that the traffic will be delivered to the next hop you chose is if the clients forward the traffic directly to the route reflector. The only way to guarantee it is to have the routers physically connected. Note that each topology is different, and in most cases, it is not until you experience multiple link failures that you find out the whether the route reflectors were placed correctly. Avoid such issues by placing them right from the start.

Figure 6-6 shows another part of the network where you can use route reflectors. In this case, Routers A and B are configured as route reflectors, and Routers C, D, and E are clients of both; note the dual connections. Both the physical topology and the logical BGP connectivity clearly indicate that the packets between clients go through one of the reflectors. The IGP metrics determine which reflector the packets go through.

Figure 6-6   *Dual Connections into Reflectors*

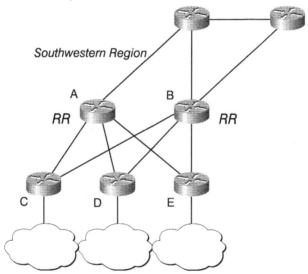

Case Study: Route Reflectors as Route Servers

Sometimes route reflectors are confused with route servers (and vice versa). Route servers are generally used at Internet exchange points. The objective is for routers to peer only with the route server (not all the other routers in the exchange) and obtain all the routing information from it. The route server has the capability of propagating information in a transparent fashion—as if the advertisements were received directly from the router originating it.

Route reflectors also try to reduce the number of peers needed in an iBGP cloud, whereas the route server is typically used with eBGP neighbors. The route server processes no traffic, but the route reflectors do. In fact, route reflectors are usually placed at traffic aggregation points. It is clear that route reflectors and route servers satisfy different needs in the network.

Figure 6-7 illustrates a place in the network where you can use a route reflector as a route server.

Figure 6-7 *Route Server*

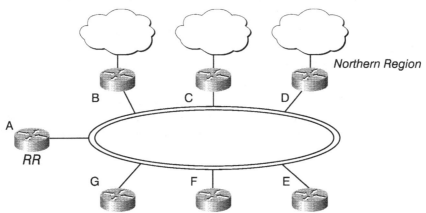

Router A is the route reflector, and it peers with all the other routers on this shared media. The other routers do not peer among themselves. Note that the route reflector is a "router on a stick." In other words, it has only one interface. (This is not necessary, but it makes the example clearer.) All the routes reflected have a next hop that is reachable through one of the other routers so that Router A does not process the data packets. Keep in mind that the route reflector does not change the attributes in the prefixes.

To illustrate this, assume that an external route is learned through Router B. The route is propagated through Router A (the route reflector) to Router E (and all the other clients). Example 6-17 shows what the prefix looks like from Router E.

Example 6-17 *Reflected Route*

```
E#show ip bgp 30.0.0.0
BGP routing table entry for 30.0.0.0/8, version 7
Paths: (1 available, best #1)
  200
    200.200.200.2 from 10.105.1.71 (200.200.200.1)
      Origin IGP, metric 0, localpref 100, valid, internal, best
      Originator : 200.200.200.1, Cluster list: 140.10.245.1

E#show ip route 200.200.200.2
Routing entry for 200.200.200.0/24, Hash 196
  Known via "isis", distance 115, metric 20, type level-1
  Redistributing via isis
  Last update from 10.105.1.76 on Ethernet0, 00:04:25 ago
  Routing Descriptor Blocks:
  * 10.105.1.76, from 200.200.200.1, via Ethernet0
      Route metric is 20, traffic share count is 1
```

Note that the prefix was learned from the route reflector (10.105.1.71), but the next hop is reachable via Router B (10.105.1.76). In this case, the traffic that is destined for 30.0.0.0/8 is forwarded directly to Router B from Router E without going through the route reflector.

External Connections

This section discusses external connections from your network. The best way to explain external connections is with a few case studies.

Case Study: Dual-Homed Connections to the Internet

Because it is common to see networks dual-homed to the Internet through two service providers, one of the questions people ask is how to load share between these multiple connections. This equation has two sides:

- Inbound traffic
- Outbound traffic

Because asymmetric routing is common throughout the Internet, you need to deal with the two traffic flows separately. Along with these two issues, the effects of the use of default routing versus receiving partial/full routing from the providers also is explored in this case study. The last section in this case study deals with the danger of becoming a transit AS.

For the discussion that follows, use Figure 6-8 as a network to work with.

Load Sharing on the Outbound Side

Keep in mind that BGP chooses only one best path for each destination. Therefore, load sharing has to be done manually by changing the configuration of the router. For the outbound case, three variations should be explored depending on the number of routes learned from the eBGP peers:

- No routes received; that is, use a default.
- Full routing received.
- Only partial routes received.

Figure 6-8 *Dual-Homed to the Internet*

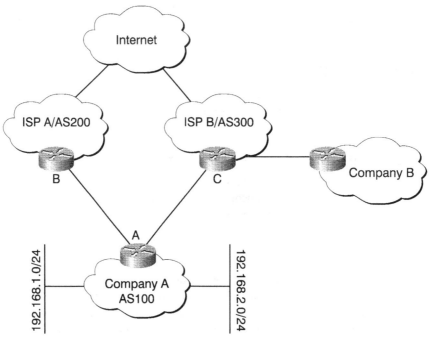

The decisions made change for each case. This is the problem being addressed:

> How do I load share my outgoing traffic between different providers given that each destination has only one best path?

All the answers cannot be offered in this short case study, but hopefully you will realize the importance of examining each situation separately. This problem has no easy and straightforward solution.

Using Default Routes Out

The most obvious, easiest solution is to use static default routes outbound toward both providers and let the router worry about balancing between the two service providers. Of course, when you use this solution, the outbound router might choose to send traffic destined for a network in Company B through ISP A.

This means that the traffic to Company B actually passes through the entire Internet core to reach its final destination rather than passing just the network of ISP B; this is slightly suboptimal routing.

Accepting Full Tables

Another solution is to accept the full Internet routing table from both ISPs and choose the best route based on the BGP attributes for each prefix. This clearly works for destinations like Company B because the router attached to Company A chooses the shortest AS path by selecting the path through ISP B rather than the longer path through ISP A.

While this book doesn't delve into how to select your ISP, or other similar topics, it is important to note one interesting problem you should be aware of.

If you are peering with the same ISP in two different places, or two Tier 1 ISPs with similar distributions of customers, your routers will receive two sets of very similar routes. In these cases, a large number of the routes may be identical all the way down through the BGP selection process until they reach the router ID step, as described Appendix D, or the following page on Cisco.com: http://www.cisco.com/en/US/tech/tk365/technologies_tech_note09186a0080094431.shtml.

Generally, you will peer with two different ISPs, probably one at Tier 1 or 2, and the other at Tier 2 or 3, so this won't be a problem. However if this does happen, you should use route-maps or other filtering techniques, combined with Local Preference or other BGP policy capabilities, to break up the monolith of best paths pointing towards one ISP.

Accepting a Partial Table

One final way of controlling the traffic outbound from your network is to accept only those routes from each provider that are directly attached to them and use a default route to reach the rest of the network in the Internet. In other words, Router A accepts only routes announced from ISP A that belong to it and its customers.

The trick, in this case, is to effectively filter out the routes that do not belong to your provider or their customers. You can achieve the same result in two ways:

- **The easy way**—Ask your providers to advertise to you only their routes and their customer routes. Any provider should be glad to comply.

  A variation involves asking your provider to set a community on its routes and its customer routes. All you have to do is filter out all the routes that do not have the agreed-upon community marking.

  Your choice, along with the use of local preference, guarantees the shortest path to the destinations received.

- **The not-so-easy way**—Set up a filter to accept only routes that have an AS_PATH length of 1 or 2. The value of 1 identifies your provider routes, whereas the value of 2 identifies the customer routes. This might work out well enough, but you leave out any prefix on which the AS_PATH is prepended.

Load Sharing on the Inbound Side

Load sharing on the inbound side is a difficult proposition to start with because you really do not have control over the decisions made by the routers in other autonomous systems. Essentially, you have three choices:

- Prepend entries to your AS path.
- Set your MED outbound.
- Set communities on your outbound advertisements.

The last two options apply only if you are dual-homed to the same provider, as in Figure 6-9.

Figure 6-9   *Dual-Homed to the Same ISP*

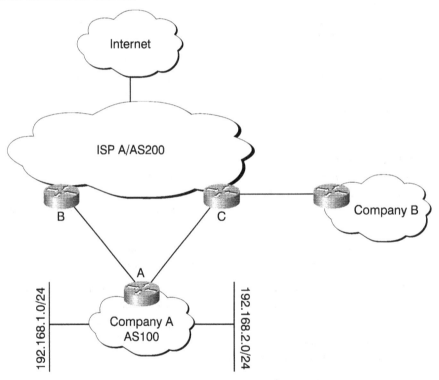

The one thing to remember is that ISPs often aggregate the address space you are advertising through them, and routers always choose the path with the longest prefix length. Before implementing any of these methods, you need to have a discussion with your providers about their aggregation policies. If your providers have a strong aggregation policy, you might not have much control over inbound load, except, perhaps, controlling what you advertise out each link. (See the "Conditional Advertisement" case study.)

Prepending AS Path Entries

Prepending AS path entries is usually fairly effective in controlling traffic that is inbound to your network. It is also rather simple to configure. If you want the traffic that is destined to 192.168.2.0/ 24 to come through ISP A and the traffic that is destined to 192.168.1.0/24 to pass through ISP B (as depicted previously in Figure 6-8), you can use the configuration in Example 6-18.

Example 6-18 *Using* **as-path-prepend** *to Influence Incoming Traffic*

```
Router C:
router bgp 100
 neighbor <A> remote-as 200
 neighbor <A> route-map add-to-200 out
 !
route-map add-to-200 permit 10
 match ip address 5
 set as-path-prepend 100 100
 !
access-list 5 permit 192.168.1.0 0.0.0.255
Router D:
router bgp 100
 neighbor <B> remote-as 200
 neighbor <B> route-map add-to-200 out
 !
route-map add-to-200 permit 10
 match ip address 5
set as-path-prepend 100 100
 !
access-list 5 permit 192.168.2.0 0.0.0.255
```

Making the AS_PATH length longer for 192.168.1.0/24 when it is advertised to ISP A, and vice versa, achieves the objective.

Setting MED Outbound

The MED is an indication (to your neighbor AS) of which path you prefer for incoming traffic. As mentioned previously, you should use the MED only when dual-homed to the same AS (as in Figure 6-9).

The value that you should use for the MED is the metric of your IGP to reach the advertised destination. In other words, you will be indicating the internal topology of your network so that the provider can make an informed decision. The configuration is straightforward, as Example 6-19 demonstrates.

Example 6-19 *Using MED Values to Indicate the Preferred Path for Incoming Traffic*

```
Router C:
router bgp 100
 neighbor <A> remote-as 200
 neighbor <B> route-map set-MED out
 !
```

Example 6-19 *Using MED Values to Indicate the Preferred Path for Incoming Traffic (Continued)*

```
route-map set-MED permit 10
 set metric-type interval
```
```
Router D:
neighbor <B> remote-as 200
 neighbor <B> route-map set-MED out
!
route-map set-MED permit 10
 set metric-type internal
```

Setting Communities

If you refer to Appendix D, you see that the decision algorithm does not compare the MED until after it looks into the local preference and the AS_PATH (among others). This means that the MED value that was set up in the last section might be overridden by those other attributes. It would be nice to be able to change the local preference value of your routing information as seen by your provider. The only downside is that you do not have access to change the configuration of your provider routers.

Do not despair, though. You can make an arrangement with your ISP to set a given community string on your routes, which causes the ISP to set its local preference so that you can control which destinations use a given inbound link. Just call them.

Being a Transit AS

So far, you have learned the issues involving load sharing inbound and outbound traffic across the two service provider links. Consider the situation in which you are running iBGP between routers within your AS, as illustrated in Figure 6-10.

Figure 6-10 *Transit AS*

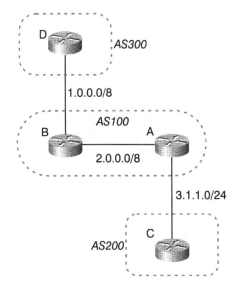

Assuming that Company A is accepting at least a partial routing table from the ISPs that it is connected to, a possible danger is that either ISP will select the path through Company A as its best path to reach networks in other autonomous systems. In fact, AS100 could become a transit network for traffic between its two provider networks. This situation is not desirable mainly because of the burden that AS100 would have to carry because of the potential high traffic load.

You can do a few things to prevent this from happening. First, you can use a default route and not accept BGP advertisements from the two ISPs. Although this solves the problem, it directly undermines any work aimed at providing outbound load balancing.

The easiest way to accept advertisements and prevent transit traffic is by configuring an AS path filter so that you only advertise routes that originate in the local AS. For Routers C and D in this network, this looks like the configuration in Example 6-20.

Example 6-20   *AS Path Filter to Only Advertise Routes Originating in the Local AS*

```
Router C:
router bgp 100
 neighbor <A> remote-as 200
 neighbor <A> filter-list 1 out
ip as-path access-list 1 permit ^$
Router D:
router bgp 100
 neighbor <C> remote-as 300
 neighbor <C> filter-list 1 out
ip as-path access-list 1 permit ^$
```

This configuration allows only routes that originate in the local AS to be advertised to the eBGP peers. One thing that looks odd about this configuration is the **as-path access-list**. Why is the AS_PATH empty?

The AS_PATH attribute is changed only as a route is advertised to an eBGP neighbor. In the Cisco implementation, this occurs after you apply any corresponding filters. (After all, why would you go through the chore of prepending information on routes that might be filtered out?)

Case Study: Conditional Advertisement

Conditionally advertising some routes to upstream neighbors is often useful—particularly if you are trying to control which link is crossed by traffic destined to a particular network. (Refer to "Case Study: Dual-Homed Connections to the Internet" for an example.)

BGP has the capability to conditionally advertise routes; look at Figure 6-11 and work through the example that follows.

Figure 6-11 *Conditional Advertisement*

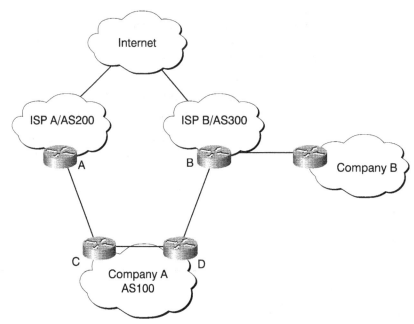

In this case, you want to advertise 172.28.23.0/24 to Router B as long as that link is up, but if it fails, you want to advertise this route to Router A from Router C.

Here, you build a normal eBGP neighbor relationship between Routers B and D and a normal iBGP neighbor relationship between Routers C and D. The only magic is on Router C. Look at the Router C configuration in Example 6-21.

Example 6-21 *Conditional Advertisement Configuration*

```
C#show running-config
Building configuration...
....
!
router ospf 100
 network 0.0.0.0 255.255.255.255 area 0
!
router bgp 100
 network 172.28.23.0 mask 255.255.255.0
 neighbor 10.1.1.1 remote-as 200
 neighbor 10.1.1.1 distribute-list 20 out
 neighbor 10.1.1.1 advertise-map to-advertise non-exist-map if-not-exist
 neighbor 10.1.2.2 remote-as 100
!
access-list 10 permit 172.28.23.0 0.0.0.255
access-list 20 deny   10.1.3.0 0.0.0.255
```

Example 6-21   *Conditional Advertisement Configuration (Continued)*

```
access-list 20 permit any
access-list 30 permit 10.1.3.0 0.0.0.255
....
route-map if-not-exist permit 10
 match ip address 30
!
route-map if-not-exist deny 20
 match ip address 20
!
route-map to-advertise permit 10
 match ip address 10
!
```

The magic is in the **neighbor 10.1.1.1 advertise-map to-advertise non-exist-map if-not-exist**
configuration statement. This tells BGP to advertise those networks permitted by the route map
to-advertise if the networks matched by route map **if-not-exist** are not in the BGP table. In
other words, although the **if-not-exist** route map is satisfied (the routes are present in the BGP
table), no advertisements (matching the **to-advertise** route map) are sent to Router A. You can,
of course, use any name you want in your route maps.

To see if it works, you need to shut down the link from Router B to Router D and see if Router
A picks up the 172.28.23.0/24 network in its routing table via Router C (10.1.1.2), as shown in
Example 6-22.

Example 6-22   *Conditional Advertisement at Work*

```
D(config)#int s1
D(config-if)#shut
D(config-if)#
%LINEPROTO-5-UPDOWN: Line protocol on Interface Serial1, changed state to down
%LINK-5-CHANGED: Interface Serial1, changed state to administratively down
A>show ip route
....
172.28.0.0/16 is subnetted, 1 subnets
B       172.28.23.0 [20/60] via 10.1.1.2, 00:00:25
....
```

Case Study: Route Dampening

One thing that causes major problems in truly large-scale networks is a destination that flaps
regularly or goes up and down several times in succession within a short period of time. BGP
allows a network administrator to stop accepting a route from an external neighbor for a certain
period through dampening. Note that dampening works for eBGP routes only.

The configuration for this capability is simple—it is just a single extra configuration command.
Figure 6-12 shows a simple network composed of two eBGP peers to illustrate how dampening
works.

Figure 6-12 *Simple Dampening Example*

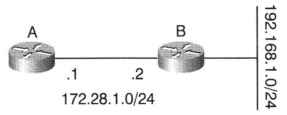

For example, if you want to dampen the routes from Router B in Figure 6-12, configure the following in Router A:

```
router bgp 100
 bgp dampening
```

Assume 192.168.1.0/24 is advertised and withdrawn due to link flaps several times in a row. Router A adds a penalty to the route each time it flaps, which eventually dampens the route. On Router A, this looks like Example 6-23.

Example 6-23 *Monitoring BGP Dampening*

```
A#show ip bgp flap
BGP table version is 7, local router ID is 10.1.1.1
Status codes: s suppressed, d damped, h history, * valid, > best, i - internal
Origin codes: i - IGP, e - EGP, ? - incomplete
  Network          From            Flaps Duration Reuse    Path
 h 192.168.1.0     172.28.1.2        3    00:02:10          100
A#show ip bgp
BGP table version is 7, local router ID is 10.1.1.1
Status codes: s suppressed, d damped, h history, * valid, > best, i - internal
Origin codes: i - IGP, e - EGP, ? - incomplete
   Network          Next Hop          Metric LocPrf Weight Path
 h 192.168.1.0     172.28.1.2             0              0 100 I
```

Note the **h** beside the route in both displays—the route is being marked as a route that is flapping. After a route is dampened, how does it come out of this state? The penalty against the route is halved until it has fallen below the reuse limit. At this point, the route is advertised to BGP neighbors again. You need to be concerned with five attributes of a route when dampening is configured:

- **Penalty**—The penalty that is applied to the route each time it flaps; the default is 1000.
- **Suppress limit**—When the penalty reaches this mark, the route is dampened; the default is 2000.
- **Half-life**—Each time the half-life passes, the penalty that is currently assessed against the route is halved; the default is 15 minutes.

- **Reuse limit**—The penalty must drop below this number for the route to be advertised again; the default is 750.

- **Maximum suppress limit**—The maximum number of half-lives that a route can be suppressed; the default is 4 half-lives.

You can configure these attributes as part of the **bgp dampen** command. To see an example of how this works, look at the penalty that occurs over time for a given route, as shown in Figure 6-13.

Figure 6-13   *Route Dampening Effects*

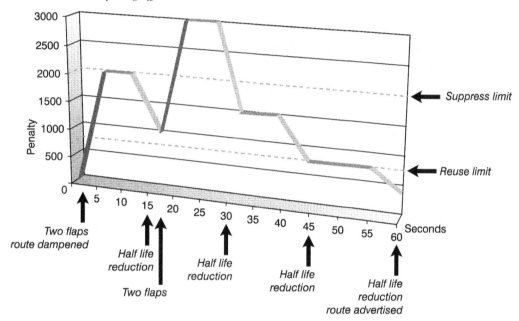

Here, a given route is withdrawn and readvertised by an eBGP router twice in 5 minutes. Each time the route flaps, a penalty of 1000 is applied, for a total of 2000. When the second flap occurs, the route is dampened.

After 15 minutes, the penalty in force against the route decays exponentially to 1000. Immediately after this, the route flaps twice more, raising the total penalty to 3000. 15 minutes later, at the 30-minute mark, the penalty decays to 1500.

At the 45-minute mark, the penalty decays to half its value, to 750, and the route can be reused again.

Review Questions

1   What is an EGP?

2   What prevents iBGP from being an effective IGP?

3   Where do routes that are learned from an eBGP peer propagate?

4   Why is it not a good idea for you to redistribute BGP routes into an IGP?

5   What protocol do all BGP packets ride on top of?

6   If a neighbor relationship between two BGP peers constantly cycles through the Idle, Active, and Connect states, what action should you take?

7   Explain the significance of the next hop in BGP.

8   What possible solutions exist for load sharing outbound traffic to multiple ISPs?

9   All attributes being the same, what breaks a tie in the BGP decision process?

10   What two things can you do to reduce the number of updates generated and sent by a router? Assume that you cannot use filtering.

11   What is the default half-life of a dampened route?

12   How does a route reflector advertise routes it learns from an iBGP peer?

13   What does a confederation of routers appear as outside the confederation area?

14   What is an example of an application of conditional advertisement?

15   Treating the network shown in Figure 4-10 in Chapter 4 as a service provider network (with the access layer connecting to external networks), configure the network to run BGP throughout. What changes would you make to the network? Would you use route reflectors or confederations anywhere?

CHAPTER 7

High Availability and Fast Convergence

As you saw in Chapter 1, "Network Design Goals and Techniques," one of the components of network availability is mean time to repair (MTTR)—how fast the network can react to, and route around, link or device failures. This chapter explores the relationship between high availability and fast convergence technologies in more depth. The chapter begins by analyzing the problems you will face when trying to deploy fast convergence. Then it discusses several techniques that have recently been developed to allow high availability and fast convergence, including these:

- Graceful restart
- Fast down detection
- Exponential backoff
- Speeding up route selection

The chapter concludes with coverage of how to deploy these techniques.

Considerations in Fast Convergence

A network is a complex system of interacting pieces, as anyone who has ever worked with a large-scale network will be glad to tell you. Therefore, when upper-level management hands down requirements for a large network that converges in less than a second, most network engineers just scratch their heads and wonder what those management people are thinking. After all, just about everyone in the network engineering business knows that, generally speaking, scale and speed are contradictory goals. The faster a network converges, the less stable it is likely to be. Fast reactions to changes in the network topology tend to create positive feedback loops, which result in a network that simply will not converge.

Subsecond convergence really is possible, though, even in a large scale network, as recent experience shows. How do you go about building a large-scale network able to converge in times traditionally considered impossible (or improbable, at best)? The best approach to this problem is the same approach you use with other seemingly intractable problems: You break the problem into smaller pieces, and solve each piece individually. When you have solved each of the smaller problems, you recombine them, and see what needs to be adjusted to make it all work together properly.

Following are the pieces of a network that you need to be concerned about when considering subsecond (fast) convergence:

- **The physical layer**—How fast can a down link be detected?
- **Routing protocol convergence**—How fast can a routing protocol react to the topology change?
- **Forwarding**—How fast can the forwarding engine on each router in the network adjust to the new paths that the routing protocol calculates?

This chapter focuses on fast convergence and covers fast down detection mechanisms along the way.

Network Meltdowns

Before beginning the work required to produce convergence times under one second, you need to set some realistic expectations. Configuring a routing protocol to converge quickly increases the likelihood of positive feedback loops, and positive feedback loops cause networks to fail to converge. Using the following example, consider how a single problem can produce feedback that causes a failure to cascade through the network. Examine the network illustrated in Figure 7-1 to see how this sort of cascading failure can occur.

Figure 7-1 *Cascading Routing Failures*

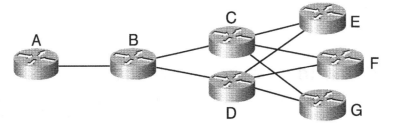

Suppose that the link between Routers D and G flaps. *Flapping* means it cycles between the down and up states slow enough for a routing adjacency to be formed across the link or for the new link to be advertised as part of the topology, but too quickly for the link to be used. In this situation, the adjacency (or neighbor relationship) between Routers D and G forms and tears down as quickly as the routing protocol allows.

Every time the adjacency between Routers D and G changes, the routing information at Routers E, F, and G changes, too. This change in routing information is, in turn, passed on to Router C, which must process it as fast as it can. It is possible for the updates presented to Router C to overcome its capability to process the information, causing Router C to fail or drop its neighbor adjacencies.

At the same time, the constantly changing routing information at Router B causes problems, possibly resulting in its periodically dropping its adjacencies, specifically with Routers C and D. If Routers B, C, and D all consume a large amount of memory and processing power adjusting to apparent topology changes because of changing adjacency states, the flapping link between Routers D and G, which originally caused the problem, can be removed from the network. The routing protocol still does not converge because of the flapping neighbor state between Routers B, C, and D. This is what network engineers consider a classic meltdown in the routing system.

Solving the Meltdown

Typically, when an engineer faces a network in this condition, the first step is to simply remove routing information from the system until the network "settles." This typically involves removing parallel (redundant) links from the routing protocol view of the topology until the routing protocol converges. At this point, the network is examined, routers are reloaded as needed, and the parallel links are brought back up. The network design can then be reviewed in an attempt to prevent a meltdown from occurring again.

Designing Routing Protocols Not to Melt

Routing protocol designers and developers want to move the point at which a routing protocol "melts" as far along the curve of network design as possible. Of course, it is impossible to prevent all network meltdowns through protocol design. Any system has limits where the implementation steps outside the "state machine" and the system simply fails. But how would a routing protocol designer work around this sort of a problem in the protocol? The answer is simple: Slow down.

The main problem here, from a protocol designer point of view, is that Routers D and G are reacting too fast to changes in the topology. If they were to react more slowly, the network would not fall into this positive feedback loop, and the network would not melt. Slowing down is really quite simple. Following are various methods of slowing down:

- Not reporting all interface transitions from the physical layer up to the routing protocol. This is called *debouncing the interface*. Most interface types wait a few milliseconds before reporting a change in the interface state.

- Slow neighbor down timers. The amount of time that a router waits without hearing from a given neighbor before declaring that a neighbor has failed is generally on the order of tens of seconds. The dead timer does not impact down neighbor detection on point-to-point links, because when the interface fails, the neighbor is assumed to be down, but other "slow down" timers exist, too.

- Slow down the distribution of information about topology changes.

- Slow down the time that the routing protocol reacts to information about topology changes.

All four of these methods are typically used in routing protocol design and implementation to provide stability within a routing system. For instance:

- In Intermediate System-to-Intermediate System (IS-IS), a timer regulates how often an intermediate system (router) can originate new routing information and how often a router can run the shortest path first (SPF) algorithm that calculates the best paths through the network.

- In Open Shortest Path First (OSPF), similar timers regulate the rate at which topology information can be transmitted and the frequency at which the shortest path first algorithm can be run.

- In Enhanced Interior Gateway Routing Protocol (EIGRP), the simple rule, "No route may be advertised until it is installed in the local routing table," dampens the speed at which routing information is propagated through the network. Routing information is also paced when being transmitted through the network based on the bandwidth between two routers.

The simplest place to look when trying to decrease convergence time is at these timers. Reduce the time an interface waits before reporting the transition to a down state, reduce the time a router must wait before advertising topology information, and so on. When you look into implementing such changes, however, you remove much of the expected stability in routing systems. The size that you can build a network without melting down decreases below an acceptable threshold, even with modern processors, more memory, and implementation improvements in place.

Another place to attack this problem lies with the frequency, or the rate of change within the network. This is the same concept (speed) from a different angle. How does looking at it from a different angle help you? By allowing you to see it's not the speed at which the network changes causing the positive feedback loop, it is the speed at which these changes are reported. If you could report the changes quickly when they occur slowly, report them more slowly when they occur quickly, or not report some events at all, routing could converge much faster and still provide the expected stability.

Do Not Report Everything You See

It is simple to say that a router should not report all the events of which it is aware, such as link and neighbor failures, but this notion becomes more complicated as you consider the issues involved. What you need to do is sort out which events are important in some sense, and which are not. For instance, if a router loses contact with an adjacent router because the adjacent router restarted for some reason, do not report the resulting change in topology until you are certain the neighbor is not coming back.

The classic questions, however, are these:

- How long do you wait before deciding the problem is real?
- What happens to traffic you would normally forward to that neighbor while you are waiting?
- How do you reconnect in a way that allows the network to continue operating correctly?

Two technologies recently incorporated in routing protocols, Graceful Restart (GR) and Non-Stop Forwarding (NSF), can answer these questions.

Look at the second question first, in relation to the lower layers of the OSI model, Layers 1 and 2. What happens to traffic received by a router while it is restarting? Normally, this traffic is dropped, and any applications that are impacted must retransmit lost data. You can prevent this by taking advantage of the separation between the control plane and the forwarding plane in many modern routers. Figure 7-2 illustrates this division.

Figure 7-2   *Separation of the Control and Data Planes in Routers*

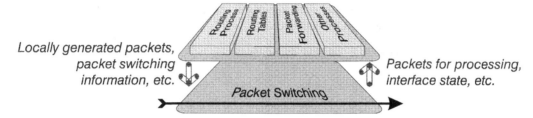

In some routers, such as the Cisco CRS-1, 12000, 7600, and others, the actual switching, or forwarding, of packets is performed by different processors and physical circuitry from the processors that the control plane processes run on (such as routing protocol processes, routing table calculation, and other processes). Because of this, if the control plane fails or restarts for any reason, the data plane can continue forwarding traffic based on the last known good information.

Non-Stop Forwarding

NSF, implemented through Stateful Switchover (SSO) and SSO+ in Cisco products, allows this continuous forwarding to take place, regardless of the state of the control plane. Normally, when the control plane resets, it sends a signal to the data plane that it should clear its tables and reset. With NSF enabled, this signal from the control plane acts as a signal to mark the current data as stale and to begin aging out the information.

After you have gotten this far, you need to be able to bring the control plane back up, resynchronize the routing protocol databases, and rebuild the routing table, all without disturbing the packets that are still being switched by the data plane on the router. This is accomplished through GR.

Graceful Restart

GR, starts by assuming two critical factors:

- The normal hold times are acceptable, within this network environment, for reporting a network event or topology change. If the control plane of a router fails, in other words, the event is not reported until the default hold or dead times normally used by the routing protocol expire, whether or not GR is configured.

- The control plane on the router can reload and begin processing data within the routing protocol hold or dead time.

Figure 7-3 illustrates the basic operation of GR for any routing protocol. The sections that follow go into more detail for each protocol.

Figure 7-3 *Graceful Restart Operation in Routing Protocols*

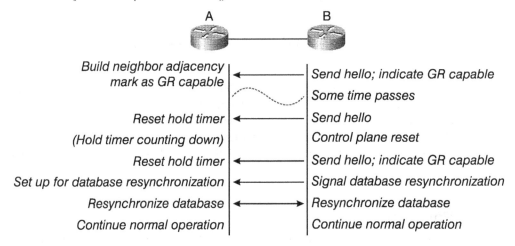

When two routers, Routers A and B in the illustration, begin forming an adjacency (or neighbor relationship, or begin peering, depending on which routing protocol is being run between them), they exchange some form of signaling noting that they are capable of understanding GR signaling and are responding to it correctly.

This signaling does not imply that the router is capable of restarting gracefully or forwarding traffic through a local failure; only that it can support a neighboring router performing a GR. For instance, the Cisco 7200 supports only switching modes where the control and data plane are not cleanly separated, so it cannot fully support GR. The Cisco 7200 can, however, support the signaling that is necessary for a neighboring router to restart gracefully.

Assume some time passes, and Router B is transmitting hello packets to Router A normally, on a periodic basis. Each time Router A receives one of these hello (or keepalive) packets, it resets the Router B hold, or dead, timer, indicating that it should wait that amount of time before declaring Router B down if it stops receiving hellos.

At some point after the routing protocol sends a hello packet, the control plane on Router B resets. While the contol plane is down, the EIGRP hold timer on Router A is still counting down. As long as this timer does not expire, EIGRP will not reset the neighbor adjacency, and Router A will continue to forward traffic to Router B. Normally, any traffic forwarded to Router B would be dropped. However, if Router B is NSF capable, its data plane will continue to forward traffic Router B receives, even while its control plane is failed.

If the control plane on Router B does not recover and allow EIGRP to begin building a new neighbor adjacency before the routing protocol hold timer on Router A expires, EIGRP will declare the adjacency down, and begin routing around Router B. For this example, assume the control plane on Router B recovers before the EIGRP hold timer expires on Router A.

When EIGRP on Router A receives this hello, it acts as though the neighbor adjacency has never failed. In other words, although the EIGRP process on Router B does not have any information about the topology of the network, Router A does not report this failure to the rest of the network. Convergence time, for the network, is effectively reduced to 0.

After the control plane on Router B has completed its reset, it signals Router A to begin resynchronizing its EIGRP databases. Router B controls the GR regardless of which mechanism is used. The two routers then use a protocol specific method to resynchronize their databases and begin operating normally, in a stable condition once again.

EIGRP Graceful Restart

Before. examining how EIGRP neighbors can gracefully restart, review how an EIGRP neighbor restart normally occurs, as illustrated in Figure 7-4.

Figure 7-4   *Normal EIGRP Neighbor Restart*

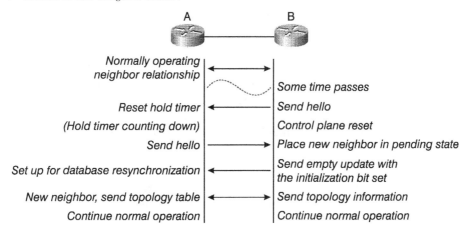

Although Figure 7-4 does not provide all the details on how EIGRP neighbor adjacencies are built (see Chapter 3, "EIGRP Network Design," for more details), it does provide an overview. Assume that Routers A and B have an established neighbor adjacency and are exchanging routing information as it changes. At some point, the Router B control plane resets.

Router A does not immediately detect this change in state (assuming that the A to B link does not indicate a failure during this process). It continues showing Router B as a neighbor, and the hold timer continues to count down. Supose the control plane on Router B recovers before the routing protocol hold timer on Router A expires, so Router A continues to consider Router B a neighbor.

Immediately after the control plane on Router B finishes restarting, it receives a hello from Router A, and adds Router A to its neighbor list. Router B believes it has discovered Router A as a new neighbor for the first time, so it sends Router A an empty update with the initialization bit set. When Router A receives this initialization signal, it examines its local neighbor table and finds a neighbor with the same IP address as the sender.

Router A then removes all the information it has about Router B, including any reachability information it has stored in the local topology table. This then cascades into removing routes from the routing table, declaring some number of routes active and sending queries, removing information from the forwarding tables, and so on. Essentially, Router A acts as though Router B is gone, even though it just rediscovered the existence of Router B.

Routers A and B exchange their topology tables and insert any learned routing information into their local tables. After they do this, they send updates to their other neighbors, detailing newly learned routing information. As you can see from this process, Router A and routers in the network behind Router A do a great deal of work for a temporary, short outage at Router B. Figure 7-5 illustrates how graceful restart resolves this.

The primary differences in the process are in the way Router A reacts to the singals transmitted by Router B during the restart. To start the process, the routing prototol process on Router B sets the restart bit on any hello packets transmitted until it has completed resynchronizing.

If Router B receives a hello from Router A just after it has restarted, Router B responds with an empty update with the initialization and restart bits set. Normally, Router A would respond to an initialization signal by resetting its state about Router B, but the restart bit indicates Router B is still forwarding traffic. Because of the restart bit, Router A will not remove B from its local neighbor table, remove any routes learned from Router B, or transition any routes into active state.

At this point, Routers A and B send each other the routes in their topology tables and send each other an end of RIB (Routing Information Base) marker to signify they have finished. After receiving this end of RIB, Router B stops setting the restart bit in its hellos, and the neighbor relationship continues normally.

GR allows one of the EIGRP neighbors to restart without causing active processing or removal of routing or forwarding information from the nonrestarting router.

Figure 7-5 *EIGRP Graceful Restart*

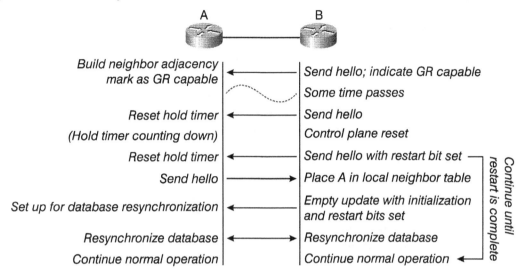

Configuring EIGRP Graceful Restart

EIGRP GR is on by default in Cisco IOS Software Release 12.2(15)T and later. Even for routers that do not support NSF, GR awareness is still turned on so that they can support their neighbors in a graceful restart. You can set the amount of time that EIGRP holds routes that are learned through a restarting neighbor by using the **timers nsf route-hold** *seconds* command in router configuration mode. To verify whether EIGRP is NSF capable and NSF is enabled, use the command **show ip protocols**, as demonstrated in Example 7-1.

Example 7-1 *Verifying That EIGRP Supports NSF*

```
router# show ip protocols
routing Protocol is "eigrp 1000"
....
Redistributing: eigrp 101
EIGRP NSF-aware route hold timer is 240s
....
Distance: internal 90 external 170
```

To enable a router to gracefully restart using EIGRP, if the platform supports NSF, configure **nsf** in the EIGRP router configuration mode as follows:

```
router(config)#router eigrp 100
router(config-rtr)#eigrp nsf
router(config-rtr)#timers nsf ....
```

OSPF Graceful Restart

Two styles of OSPF GR are available, both of which are described in Internet Engineering Task Force (IETF) RFCs and drafts:

- Graceful restart using link local signaling
- Graceful restart using opaque link-state advertisements (LSAs)

To better understand, examine what a normal OSPF restart would look like, and then look at each of these methods to gracefully restart an OSPF adjacency as described in the sections that follow. Figure 7-6 illustrates a normal OSPF restart.

Figure 7-6   *Normal OSPF Restart*

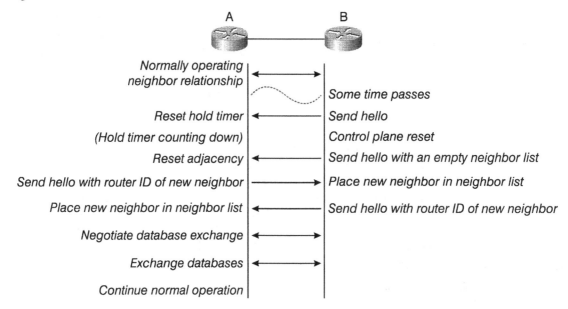

Remember that a router running OSPF always transmits a list of known neighbors in its Hello packets. The receiving routers use this list to ensure that two-way connectivity exists. In other words, Router A wants to make certain that Router B is receiving its hellos before sending Router B topology information.

The first signal that Router B transmits when its control returns begin operating again is a Hello with an empty neighbor list because it no longer has a neighbor state. Router A reacts to this Hello by resetting its adjacency with Router B, including removing the link-state information of Router B and removing any information about paths that are reachable through Router B from its local routing and forwarding tables. In turn, the rest of the routers in the network must converge around this change in the network topology.

OSPF, in general, does not use extensible packet formats; OSPF packets are built using fixed-length fields, rather than Type-Length-Value (TLV) fields, so the addition of a new capability to OSPF requires the creation of a new packet type. The operation of both types of graceful restart outlined in the sections that follow is generally the same, except for the way in which the GR capability is signaled and the way a GR is signaled.

Graceful Restart Using Link Local Signaling

This method of signaling GR, described in the IETF Internet-Draft, "OSPF Restart Signaling," (draft-nguyen-ospf-restart-04.txt), relies on two mechanisms:

- **Link Local Signaling (LLS)**—A mechanism described in the IETF Internet-Draft, "OSPF Link-local Signaling" (draft-nguyen-ospf-lls-02.txt). This draft extends the OSPF Hello packet format to include TLVs, which can then be used to include additional signaling of various types, such as graceful restart capability and a graceful restart.

- **Out of Band Resynchronization**—A mechanism described in the IETF Internet-Draft, "OSPF Out-of-Band LSDB Resynchronization" (draft-nguyen-ospf-oob-resync-04.txt). This draft describes a mechanism through which two OSPF routers can resynchronize their link-state databases at any point.

Figure 7-7 illustrates the restart process using these two mechanisms.

Figure 7-7   *OSPF GR Using Link Local Signaling*

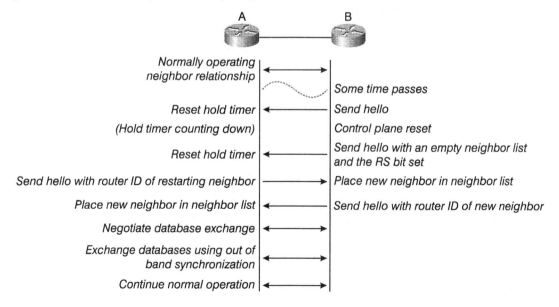

NOTE   LLS is not just used during a graceful restart; it is running all the time between these two adjacent routers. LLS can be used for other extensions to OSPF, such as for extensions to support Mobile Ad Hoc Networks (MANET).

After Router B restarts, it transmits its Hellos with the reset (RS) bit set. The RS bit is defined in the extended options within LLS, until its dead timer has passed. This ensures that every router formerly adjacent with the restarting router either times out or receives a Hello with the RS bit set. Router A resets the OSPF dead timer for Router B when it receives this hello, moves Router B to the two-way state in its neighbor state table, and transmits a hello with the RS bit set. When Router B receives a hello from Router A with the RS bit set, it knows Router A will support its graceful restart.

After this signaling is complete, Routers A and B negotiate a database exchange. This negotiation is identical to a normal database exchange that takes place when two routers initially form an OSPF adjacency, including the exchange of database descriptor blocks and other information. The primary difference is that the packets exchanged have the Restarting (R) bit set and include an LLS extended options block with the LSDB Resynchronization (LR) bit set.

After this resynchronization is complete, Router A moves Router B back into the full state and recomputes the shortest path tree, routing table, and forwarding tables as needed.

Graceful Restart Using Opaque LSAs

This method of graceful restart between OSPF neighbors, described in RFC 3623, "Graceful OSPF Restart," depends on link local opaque LSAs. Opaque LSAs are described in RFC 2370, "The OSPF Opaque LSA Option." Figure 7-8 illustrates how this method of GR works.

Figure 7-8   *OSPF Graceful Restart Using Opaque LSAs*

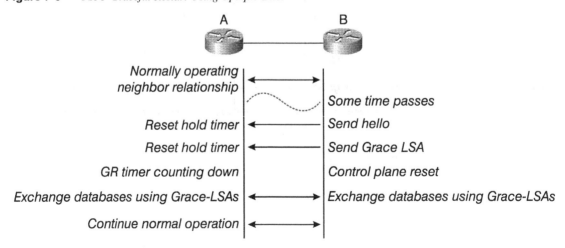

Before restarting, Router B transmits a signal, called a Grace-LSA, indicating that it is about to restart. This is a link local opaque LSA notifying every adjacent router that Router B is about to restart, so they should prepare their local neighbor tables accordingly.

After Router B has restarted, it transmits normal Hellos, along with a Grace-LSA, to indicate that it has restarted. Router B relearns its adjacent neighbors in this stage and then begins exchanging its database with those neighbors using Grace-LSAs.

RFC 3623 states that this procedure can be used for unplanned outages, but it is impossible to determine whether all previously adjacent neighbors have received the initial Grace-LSA, which must be transmitted before Hellos are transmitted by the restarting router. If any component of the database changes between the time Router B restarts and when Routers A and B resynchronize their databases, moving back to the full state, the specifications state the adjacency must be torn down and restarted as if a new adjacency were forming.

NOTE   RFC 3623 is, within the text of the RFC, designed to provide a graceful restart during a planned outage, such as when a router is reloaded to change to another version of the OSPF software or to clean up a problem.

Configuring OSPF Graceful Restart

Cisco IOS Software Release 12.2(15)T and later support the LLS method of OSPF GS. Graceful restart awareness is on by default. The three commands you can use to configure OSPF GR are as follows:

- **capability lls**—Enables and disables the OSPF capability to use the link local signaling extensions to support restarting adjacent neighbors; this is configured from the router configuration mode. LLS is enabled by default.

- **nsf**—Enables the router capability to restart gracefully if the router supports NSF. This is configured under the router configuration mode and is not enabled by default.

- **ip ospf resynch-timeout seconds**—Sets the amount of time that OSPF will wait after out of band synchronization has started to bring the neighbor into full state. If the neighbor is not in full state by the number of seconds configured, the adjacency is torn down and restarted. The resynchronization timeout is configured in the interface configuration mode and defaults to the longer of 40 seconds or the OSPF dead interval.

To determine whether OSPF GR is enabled on a router, examine the output of **show ip ospf neighbor detail**, as demonstrated in Example 7-2.

Example 7-2   *Verifying OSPF GR Operation on a Router*

```
Router#show ip ospf neighbor detail
Neighbor 192.170.1.1, interface address 192.170.1.1
    In the area 0 via interface GigabitEthernet1/0/0
    Neighbor priority is 1, State is FULL, 6 state changes
```

Example 7-2   *Verifying OSPF GR Operation on a Router (Continued)*

```
   DR is 192.170.1.1 BDR is 192.170.1.2
   Options is 0x42
   LLS Options is 0x1 (LR), last OOB-Resync 00:03:08 ago
   Dead timer due in 00:00:36
   Neighbor is up for 00:09:46
  Index 1/1, retransmission queue length 0, number of retransmission 1
   First 0x0(0)/0x0(0) Next 0x0(0)/0x0(0)
   Last retransmission scan length is 1, maximum is 1
   Last retransmission scan time is 0 msec, maximum is 0 msec
```

Note the addition of a new line of information, the LLS Options. In the parentheses on this line, you can see that the only bit set is the LR bit, and a timer indicates the last time that an out of band resynchronization of the database occurred.

Cisco is also implementing the opaque LSA method of gracefully restarting an OSPF adjacency in a future Cisco IOS Software release.

IS-IS Graceful Restart

The normal restart procedure for IS-IS is similar to that for OSPF, as illustrated in Figure 7-9.

Figure 7-9   *Normal Restart in IS-IS*

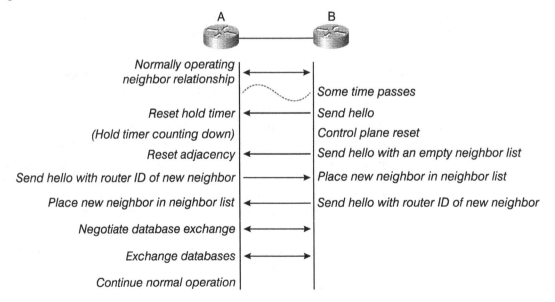

When the control plane on Router B restarts, the first hello IS-IS transmits will contain an empty list of known neighbors. When Router A receives this hello, it will reset its adjacency with Router B, flush the Router LSA Router B originated, and recalculates the shortest path tree to all reachable destinations.

The next hello Router A transmits contains Router B's address, which indicates Router A has received a hello from Router B. Router B then includes Router A's address in its hellos, and the two routers exchange complete sequence number PDUs (CSNPs) and databases. Between the first exchange of hello packets and the first SPF run including Router B on Router A, the network routes around Router B. IS-IS supports two styles of GR:

- Using signaling based on the IETF Internet-Draft, "Restart signaling for IS-IS," (draft-ietf-isis-restart-05.txt).

- A Cisco proprietary mechanism that relies on saving state across the restart to re-establish the IS-IS adjacency.

IS-IS Signaled Graceful Restart (IETF)

IS-IS graceful restart uses extensions to the hello packet format to allow IS-IS router neighbors to continue to route through it while it is restarting. Figure 7-10 illustrates this process.

When Router B restarts, it still sends a hello with an empty neighbor list, but it also includes a new TLV, the Restart TLV, which contains three bits:

- **RS**—The restart request. This bit is set when an intermediate system is restarting and would like its adjacent neighbors to support it through a graceful restart.

- **RA**—The restart acknowledgement. This bit is set when an intermediate system has received a request for graceful restart support from an adjacent neighbor and it supports the graceful restart.

- **SA**—The suppress adjacency indicator. If this bit is set, the restarting intermediate system requests support for a graceful restart but wants its adjacent neighbors to suppress advertisement of their connection to the restarting intermediate system until its databases have been fully synchronized. This bit is typically used by an intermediate system that supports graceful restart but cannot support nonstop forwarding during the restart process.

In this first hello, the RS bit, restart request, is set. It notifies Router A that Router B has restarted and wants to perform a graceful restart instead of resetting the adjacency. Router A responds by including Router B's address in its next hello and by including the Restart TLV with the RA bit set.

Figure 7-10 *IS-IS Graceful Restart Process*

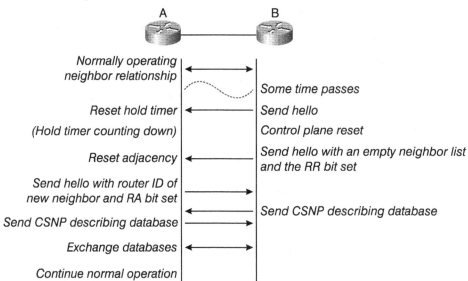

After Router B receives the hello from Router A, it begins sending CSNPs describing its database to Router A. At the same time, Router A also sends CSNPs describing its database to Router B. After the routers exchange these, they compare the information in the CSNPs to their local link-state databases and determine which link-state packet (LSP) to request from the other router.

After the two routers have synchronized their databases, the Restart TLV is removed from the hello packets, and the adjacency proceeds normally.

Configuring IS-IS Graceful Restart

Graceful restart awareness, which allows a router to support an adjacent router gracefully restarting, is on by default on all routers that run releases of Cisco IOS Software later than Release 12.2(15)T. To configure the local router to restart gracefully, if it is an NSF-capable platform, configure **nsf** under the IS-IS router configuration mode, as follows:

```
router(config)#router isis
router(config-rtr)#nsf
```

The **nsf** command has options that allow the configuration of IS-IS GR in the Cisco or IETF modes. The IETF mode uses the hello signaling described previously to gracefully restart, whereas the Cisco mechanism adds no new signaling to the IS-IS protocol.

To determine whether IS-IS GR is working correctly and to examine statistics about the last restart, execute the command **show is-is nsf**, as demonstrated in Example 7-3.

Example 7-3   *Verifying IS-IS GR Operation on a Router*

```
router#show isis nsf
NSF is ENABLED, mode 'cisco'
RP is ACTIVE, standby ready, bulk sync complete
NSF interval timer expired (NSF restart enabled)
Checkpointing enabled, no errors
Local state:ACTIVE, Peer state:STANDBY HOT, Mode:SSO
```

BGP Graceful Restart

The Border Gateway Protocol (BGP) support of graceful restart is documented in the IETF Internet-Draft, "Graceful Restart Mechanism for BGP" (draft-ietf-idr-restart-08.txt). Because BGP uses TCP as its transport mechanism, and BGP peering sessions are unicast, the BGP GR mechanism is different, in several ways, from the GR mechanisms examined so far. Figure 7-11 illustrates a normal BGP restart.

Figure 7-11   *Normal BGP Restart*

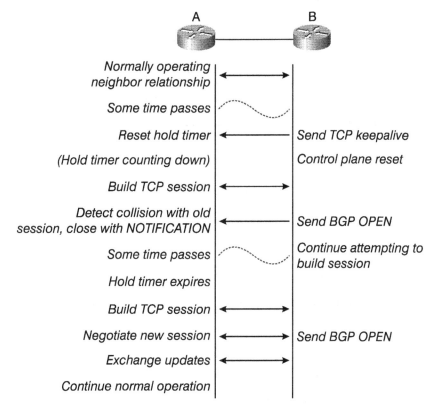

Routers A and B start with a normal BGP peering relationship. When the control plane on Router B resets, it comes back up with no prior knowledge of any previous TCP or BGP sessions. Router B initializes a new TCP and BGP sessions to Router A, and sends a BGP OPEN message over this new session.

Router A examines the router ID of the originating router, and determines it is a peer for which it already has a session. Router A will respond with a BGP NOTIFICATION indicating a session between these peers already exists. Router B will continue trying to open a session with Router A until the dead timer from the old session times out.

After the dead timer from the old session has timed out, Routers A and B will build a new session using the normal BGP session processing. A BGP timer takes at least the length of the hold timer to complete, and considering the amount of time required to negotiate the session, exchange routes, and perform other actions, it could take a good bit longer.

Figure 7-12 illustrates a BGP GR.

Figure 7-12 *A BGP Graceful Restart*

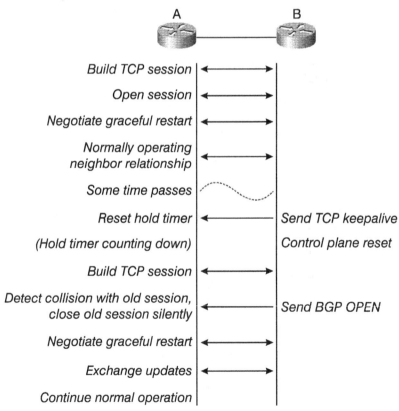

In the initial session negotiation, the BGP peers exchange a GR capability, indicating that both BGP speakers are capable of supporting GR. When the session restarts, Routers A and B build a new TCP session, and Router B sends a BGP OPEN to Router A with the GR capability indicated.

The GR capability in BGP includes a per-address family indicator, such as unicast IPv4, IP-VPN, and others, so that Router B can inform Router A which address families it still has forwarding information for. This is useful in routers that hardware switch some types of traffic and not others, for instance.

Router A detects this new BGP session as a collision with the existing (pre-restart) session. However, rather than closing the new session with a BGP NOTIFICATION, Router A silently closes the old connection and marks all the routing information that it receives from this peer as stale. When the two BGP speakers have finished negotiating the new session, they exchange updates, remove information marked as stale, and continue operating normally.

Configuring BGP Graceful Restart

Three commands control BGP graceful restart in Cisco IOS Software after Release 12.2(15)T:

- **bgp graceful-restart**—In the BGP router configuration mode, enables BGP graceful restart.

- **bgp graceful-restart restart-time seconds**—In the BGP router configuration mode, configures how long BGP allows a restart to continue before declaring the restart unsuccessful and resetting the BGP session.

- **bgp graceful-restart stalepath-time seconds**—In the BGP router configuration mode, configures how long BGP holds paths marked stale before deleting them.

To determine whether GR is running on a Cisco IOS router, execute **show ip bgp neighbors**, as demonstrated in Example 7-4.

Example 7-4 *Verifying BGP GR Operation on a Router*

```
router#show ip bgp neighbors x.x.x.x
BGP neighbor is 192.168.2.2, remote AS YY, external link
BGP version 4, remote router ID 192.168.2.2
BGP state = Established, up for 00:01:18
Last read 00:00:17, hold time is 180, keepalive interval is 60 seconds
Neighbor capabilities:
Route refresh:advertised and received(new)
Address family IPv4 Unicast:advertised and received
Address famiiy IPv4 Multicast:advertised and received
Graceful Restart Capabilty:advertised and received
Remote Restart timer is 120 seconds
Address families preserved by peer:
IPv4 Unicast, IPv4 Multicast
Received 1539 messages, 0 notifications, 0 in queue
Sent 1544 messages, 0 notifications, 0 in queue
Default minimum time between advertisement runs is 30 seconds
```

Fast Down Detection

Rather than not reporting network events through NSF and GR, you can attempt to route around changes in the network topology as quickly as possible. Before you can route around a failed link or device, however, you need to detect its failure. Detecting failure is a major concern in the highly available network.

You can detect a neighbor or link failure in two ways:

* Polling through fast hellos or other packets, transmitted at Layer 2 or Layer 3
* Event-driven notification through monitoring some link property, such as the link carrier

The sections that follow cover these two options.

Detecting a Link or Adjacency Failure Using Polling

One common method to detect a link or adjacency failure is polling, or periodically sending hello packets to the adjacent device and expecting a periodic hello packet in return. The two determining factors in the speed at which polling can discover a failed link or device are as follows:

* The rate at which hello packets are transmitted
* The number of hello packets missed before declaring a link or adjacency as failed

Most protocols wait for three missed hello packets before declaring a neighbor down, or failed. Normally, for Layer 2 links and routing protocols, the hello interval is measured in seconds. For instance:

* EIGRP running over a point-to-point link sends one hello every 5 seconds and declares a neighbor down if no hellos are heard for 15 seconds.
* EIGRP running over a lower-speed point-to-multipoint link sends one hello every 60 seconds and declares a neighbor down if no hellos are received in 180 seconds.
* OSPF normally sends a Hello every 10 seconds and declares a neighbor down if no hellos are heard for 40 seconds. (The default is four Hello packets, not three.)
* Frame Relay LMI messages, the equivalent of a hello, are transmitted every 10 seconds. If an LMI is not received in 30 seconds, the circuit is assumed to have failed.
* HDLC keepalive messages are transmitted every 10 seconds. If a keepalive message is not received within 30 seconds, the circuit is assumed to have failed.

How Fast Does Polling Detect a Down Neighbor?

Suppose that a certain protocol transmits a keepalive or hello packet every 10 seconds and declares a neighbor down after not hearing hello packets for 30 seconds. Actually, this is the maximum amount of time it takes for a neighbor failure to be detected, rather than the average amount of time, as Figure 7-13 illustrates.

Figure 7-13   *Dead Interval Versus Polling Interval*

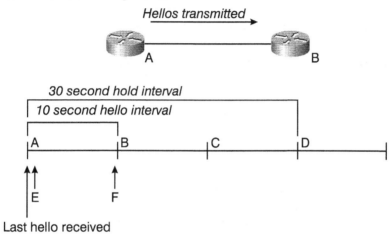

Assume that Router A transmits a hello at time A. When Router B receives this hello, it resets its local dead timer. If the link between Routers A and B fails just a few milliseconds after Router A transmits the hello at time A, the link is down for 29 seconds and some number of milliseconds when the dead timer for Router B expires, and Router B detects the link failure. If the link fails at time F, just a few milliseconds before Router A would have transmitted the next hello (resetting the Router B dead timer again), the link is only down for 25 seconds and some number of milliseconds when the Router B dead timer expires, and Router B detects the link failure. Statistically, this arrangement detects a failed link in 27.5 seconds, on average, rather than 30 seconds. Engineers, however, always count on the worst case instead of the best, so the general assumption is that the link failure occurs at the worst possible time, at time E rather than F.

You can use faster times than the defaults in most protocols. For example:

- OSPF can transmit a Hello every 330 milliseconds and set the dead interval to 1 second in Cisco IOS Software Release 12.0(23)S, 12.2(15)T, and 12.2(18)S. To configure 330-millisecond hellos in OSPF, use the command **ip ospf dead-interval minimal hello-**

multiplier *multiplier* under the interface configuration. The hello interval is always set to 330 milliseconds when this command is configured, and the dead timer is set to 300 milliseconds times the multiplier that is configured.

- IS-IS can transmit a hello every 330 milliseconds and set the dead interval to 1 second using the interface level command **isis hello-interval minimal** [**level-1** | **level-2**]. If you want to change the default dead interval multiplier, use the interface-level command **isis hello-multiplier** *multiplier* [**level-1** | **level-2**]; the hello multiplier is set to 3 by default.

- EIGRP can transmit a hello every second and set the dead interval to 3 seconds, using the interface level command **ip hello-interval eigrp** [*autonomous system*] [*seconds*] and **ip hold-time eigrp** [*autonomous system*] [*seconds*].

Fast hellos have the same problems as any other polling system, however, you must use them cautiously in most environments. Consider a simple case of a single router in a hub-and-spoke configuration with 500 remote neighbors on a single interface and 10 neighbors connected upstream, each on a separate interface—510 neighbors total. Assume that you configure this router to transmit a hello toward each adjacency neighbor every 330 milliseconds. Therefore, the router must transmit as follows:

11 interfaces * 3 hellos per second = 33 hellos per second

This seems to be manageable from the perspective of the router. However, you have to remember that for every hello the router transmits, it receives a hello from each of its adjacent neighbors. That means the router receives the following:

510 neighbors * 3 hellos per second = 1530 hellos per second

In total, then, the router is either transmitting or receiving 1566 hellos per second, which is one hello about every .0006 seconds, or every .6 milliseconds. Timers on this order are hard for computer systems to manage. It is likely that some hello is going to pass through unnoticed. If each of the remote sites is on a separate interface (such as a Frame Relay subinterface), the problem worsens; the router must now send or receive 3060 hellos per second.

Further complicating large-scale deployment of fast hellos are issues such as these:

- Packet drops because of clogged queues, which can be a problem in almost any environment that has highly variable amounts of traffic

- Authentication of routing data because encryption algorithms do not typically run at these sorts of speeds

Although fast hellos are a good solution in some cases, especially over small numbers of point-to-point links, they can run into scaling problems if you try to deploy them in larger scale environments.

One possible way to reduce the processing requirements involved with fast hellos is to implement those hellos in hardware, specifically on line cards, rather than in processes that run on the main processor of the router. Although this takes the load off the processor, it also presents its own set of complications. For instance, suppose that such a hardware-driven system can send a routing protocol hello every 10 milliseconds and keep track of hellos received at that rate from any number of neighbors. If the hardware transmits a hello for a failed process it makes the router appear functional to its neighbors, but is really not. The only way to prevent the hardware from sending hellos for failed processes is to have the hardware poll the process before it sends each hello, which brings you right back to the speed at which the process can handle hellos. Receiving hellos and maintaining neighbor state is much the same. If the process cannot handle notifications as quickly as the hardware can issue them, you are back to the same bottlenecks as before. In all systems, polling is always limited by such factors; event-driven notifications are always more scalable when they are available.

Bidirectional Forwarding Detection

Bidirectional Forwarding Detection (BFD) is a form of fast hello at Layer 2.5. The concept is that by using a single fast hello to detect the presence of an adjacent neighbor, you can avoid the scaling problems associated with each protocol on a router that sends a separate hello packet in every polling interval. Over time, BFD will probably migrate to hardware-supported fast hellos instead of software-supported fast hellos. This solution does reduce the overhead that is associated with several protocols sending fast hellos on a single router.

Note, however, that the scaling properties of any polling system are still retained with BFD; considerations for running fast hellos in hardware were noted earlier. You can find the latest version of BFD in the IETF Internet-Draft "Bidirectional Forwarding Detection" (draft-katz-ward-bfd-01.txt).

Detecting a Link or Adjacency Failure Using Event-Driven Link Failure Notification

If fast polling runs into scaling issues, what other options do you have for quickly determining when an adjacent neighbor or link fails? You could rely on lower-layer devices to monitor the link status and notify the routing protocol when the link fails. Rather than periodically polling, you could then rely on event-driven notification of link failures.

Event-driven link failure notification often covers the case of adjacent neighbor failure. Generally, if a router fails, the links that are connected to that router also fail. For instance, if a router that is connected to an HDLC link fails, the HDLC link itself loses carrier, causing the link to fail.

The sections that follow examine the link failure mechanisms that are offered in several media types and considers the steps you can take to provide fast notification.

SONET

SONET is probably the best known of the fast convergence technologies available; it not only allows the fast detection of down links and devices, but it also provides for link protection, which allows traffic to quickly be switched to a backup fiber link if the primary path fails. This section focuses on the timers that are associated with notification of hard and calculated failures to higher layer protocols. SONET has four types of alarms, as shown in Figure 7-14.

Figure 7-14   *SONET Errors*

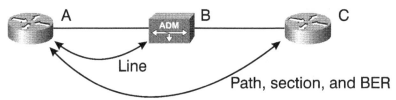

An error that occurs between Router A and the add/drop multiplexer (ADM) is considered a line error, whereas an error between Routers A and B, the two endpoints of the SONET circuit, is considered a path error. A third type of error, the bit error rate error (or BER), is also calculated along the entire path and relates to the percentage of frames arriving with errors in them. You can configure the time between any of these errors occurring and SONET reporting the error up to the interface level in the router, as follows:

- The amount of time between a line error occurring and SONET reporting the error to upper-layer protocols can be configured using the interface-level command **pos delay triggers line** *milliseconds*, with a default of 100 milliseconds.

- The amount of time between a path error occurring and SONET reporting the error to upper-layer protocols can be configured using the interface-level command **pos delay triggers path** *milliseconds*. Path error reporting is not on by default.

- The rate at which errors must occur before SONET reports the line down to upper-layer protocols can be configured using the interface-level command **pos threshold b3-tca** *rate*, if you have path triggers enabled. If you do not have path triggers enabled, you set the BER level at which the link is considered down using the **pos threshold sf** command.

Consider three different networks using SONET links, illustrated in Figure 7-15, and see how these errors work in various environments.

Network A has a pair of routers connected through an automatic protection switching (APS)-protected SONET link. If one of the two fibers fails, the SONET ADMs switch to the other circuit automatically in less than 60 milliseconds. Because the line trigger reporting time is 100 milliseconds by default, Routers A and B do not see an error from this switchover. If it is important to route around this error, you should reduce the line trigger delay to something less than the average time required for an APS switchover to occur.

Figure 7-15   *SONET Errors in Three Different Network Configurations*

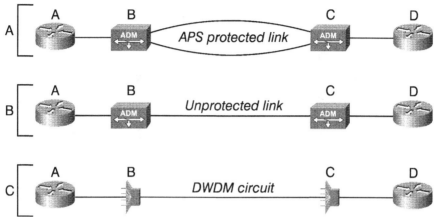

Network B has a pair of routers connected through an unprotected SONET link, with a pair of ADMs along the link. Depending on the number of ADMs along the link, the routers might or might not receive a line trigger when a link between two of the ADMs along the path fails. If you want the routers to receive Layer 2 notification when the SONET link fails, you need to configure path failure monitoring on the two routers.

Network C has a pair of routers connected through an unprotected SONET link across a dense wavelength division multiplexing (DWDM) network. DWDM networks do not participate in SONET signaling, so path failures are not reported to the two routers when a link fails; you must rely on link failures.

Frame Relay

Frame Relay is a popular choice for WAN links; it provides a good deal of bandwidth, with burst capabilities, for a modest price. Frame Relay is especially popular for hub-and-spoke configurations, in which many remote sites are connected to a single router (or a pair of routers) at central locations, or hubs. From a router perspective, a Frame Relay circuit is a point-to-point link; in reality, however, it is a switched circuit, as Figure 7-16 shows.

In this small network, Router A is connected to a Frame Relay switch, B, which then connects into a network of Frame Relay switches, finally connecting to Routers E and H. Two dotted lines represent two virtual circuits running through the Frame Relay network, one between Routers A and E, and the other between Routers A and H.

Figure 7-16 *Frame Relay Network*

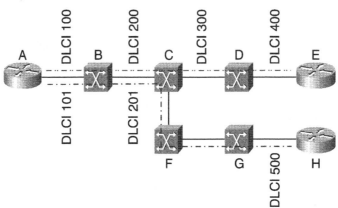

Router A identifies each of these circuits through a data-link connection identifier (DLCI). Router A periodically sends Switch B a Local Management Interface (LMI) packet containing the two DLCI numbers, 100 and 101, for the two active circuits. These LMI packets act as a polling mechanism between the switch and the router. Switch B responds to these polls with an LMI packet indicating the current status of the circuits. Switches B and C might use another set of DLCI numbers to identify these same circuits—in this case, DLCI 200 and 201. Switch B is configured to take all the packets that arrive on DLCI 100 and switch them to DLCI 200; likewise, it takes all the packets that arrive on DLCI 200 and switches them to DLCI 100.

From this illustration, you can see that Frame Relay networks are not end-to-end connections. The Layer 2 status of the network between Router E and Switch D has no impact on the Layer 2 status of the network between Router A and Switch B. If the link between Router E and Switch D fails, Router A and Switch B continue exchanging LMI. Router A thinks the circuit is operational, and it continues forwarding traffic along this path. Thus, Router A only discovers a Frame Relay circuit failure through the loss of Layer 3 routing protocol hellos.

Frame Relay, however, has a solution for this problem—*A-bit signaling*. The A bit, a single bit in the LMI, is set if the circuit is active end-to-end. If the link between Router E and Switch D fails, Switch D clears the A bit in its LMI toward Switch C, which then, in turn, clears the A bit in its LMI toward Switch B. Switch B then clears the A bit in its LMI for DLCI 100 toward Router A, indicating a circuit failure.

For A-bit signaling to work, the following must be true:

* A-bit signaling must be supported throughout the entire Frame Relay network.
* The router must be configured to treat the circuit as a separate interface. In other words, if both DLCIs 100 and 101 are on the same logical interface at Router A, the failure of one of the two circuits does not cause the interface to fail, and no Layer 3 notification of the circuit failure takes place.

To illustrate this second point, consider two possible configurations at Router A.

The configuration in Example 7-5 uses a point-to-multipoint interface and defines which IP address is reachable through which DLCI.

Example 7-5 *Configuring a Frame Relay Link as a Point-to-Multipoint Type Circuit*

```
interface serial 0
 ip address 10.1.1.1 255.255.255.0
 encapsulation frame-relay
 frame-relay map ip 10.1.1.2 100 broadcast
 frame-relay map ip 10.1.1.3 101 broadcast
```

The configuration in Example 7-6 places each circuit on its own subinterface, treating each circuit as a point-to-point link.

Example 7-6 *Configuring a Frame Relay Link as a Set of Point-to-Point Circuits Using Subinterfaces*

```
interface serial 0
 encapsulation frame-relay
 no ip address
!
interface serial 0.1 point-to-point
 ip address 10.1.1.1 255.255.255.254
 frame-relay interface-dlci 100
!
interface serial 0.2 point-to-point
 ip address 10.1.1.3 255.255.255.254
 frame-relay interface-dlci 101
```

In Example 7-5, if one of the two circuits that is tied to the point-to-multipoint interface fails, the interface itself does not fail. As long as the router receives LMI from the connected Frame Relay switch, the point-to-multipoint interface remains up. Furthermore, as long as the routing protocols believe that a valid path exists through the interface, the router continues forwarding traffic across it.

For faster down detection of Frame Relay circuits, it is generally best to use point-to-point subinterfaces rather than a point-to-multipoint interface with numerous circuits tied to it.

It is also important to make certain that the Frame Relay network supports (and has configured) asynchronous LMI, if you are trying to detect a failed circuit quickly. Frame Relay switches always respond to LMI updates that routers send, but unless they support asynchronous LMI and have it configured, they only report a change in circuit state through periodic LMI packets, rather than generating and transmitting an LMI packet to indicate the circuit status change.

If asynchronous LMI is not supported or configured on the link, the routers that are connected to the Frame Relay circuit only find out about a circuit failure the next time they poll their attached switches for circuit status. With asynchronous LMI, the switches do not wait to tell the routers about the circuit status change.

Another possible method of monitoring the circuit status is end-to-end LMI. Here, Routers A and D can directly exchange LMI over the entire circuit, which acts as fast Layer 2 polling.

Ethernet

Ethernet is the most problematic of the broadcast mediums to detect a device or link failure on. Refer to Figure 7-17 for this section.

Figure 7-17 *Ethernet Failed Node or Link Detection*

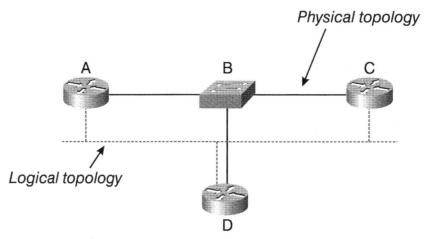

In this small network, Routers A, C, and D are connected through an Ethernet switch, so the physical topology is a series of point-to-point connections to and from the switch. The switch copies frames from one physical connection to another; therefore, the logical topology is a broadcast segment. Routers C and D can receive at the same time any packet that Router A transmits.

If the link between Router C and the switch fails, or Router C itself fails, but not the links between Routers A and B and the switch, how can Router A determine Router C is no longer reachable? In other words, Router A cannot determine, based on the state of its connection with Switch B, whether Routers C and D are reachable across this network.

Most protocols, including routing protocols, count on their periodic hello packets to provide a state indication for each device that is connected to the broadcast network. Detecting down neighbors faster, then, should just be a matter of sending hellos more quickly.

Multiaccess Reachability Protocol

Previous sections demonstrated scaling issues you can encounter with fast hellos, so you really want another mechanism for down neighbor detection, if possible — something that is driven off of Layer 2 events, rather than Layer 3 events. Multiaccess Reachability Protocol (MARP) takes advantage of the point-to-point nature of switched Ethernet networks, along with the intelligence of the switch in the middle, to provide event-driven notification of link or node failure on a switched Ethernet network, as Figure 7-18 illustrates.

Figure 7-18   *MARP Operation*

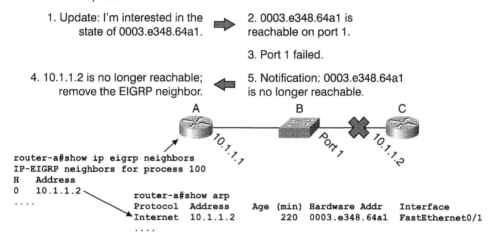

MARP is running on Routers A and C and Switch B in this network. Router A wants to know when Router C fails or is no longer connected to the switched network, because it has formed an EIGRP neighbor relationship with Router C. Router A begins by examining its local Address Resolution Protocol (ARP) cache and determining what the Layer 2 (MAC) address of Router C is. After finding this, Router A periodically multicasts MARP updates onto the network, indicating its interest in the status of Router C.

When Switch B receives these updates, it examines its local switching tables and determines that the Layer 2 address of Router C is reachable through Port 1; therefore, it marks this port. When Port 1 fails, Switch B notes the previous mark and transmits a notification indicating that the Layer 2 address of Router C is no longer reachable. When Router A receives this notification, it examines its local ARP cache. It determines that Router C is no longer reachable and declares its EIGRP neighbor relationship with Router C as failed.

MARP provides a mechanism for devices to notify a switch of their interest in other devices that are connected to the switch. It also provides a mechanism for the switch to notify devices of loss of connectivity to a given device.

Slowing Down When the Network Speeds Up

So far, this chapter has covered several techniques to speed up detection of failed links or neighbors. However, it is dangerous to react more quickly to link and device failures. Faster reaction times mean a greater likelihood of forming positive feedback loops or overwhelming devices in the network when an event occurs at a high rate of change. You can address this issue by slowing the network reaction when events occur rapidly.

The key to this solution lies in keeping a history of past events in some way and exponentially backing off the reporting of events as they occur more rapidly. Following are two mechanisms that implement these types of solutions to rapid changes in the network:

- Link-state exponential backoff
- IP event dampening

The sections that follow cover each of these mechanisms in more detail.

Figure 7-19 *Exponential Backoff in Link-State Protocols*

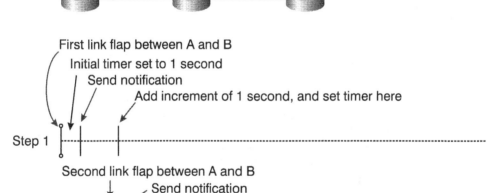

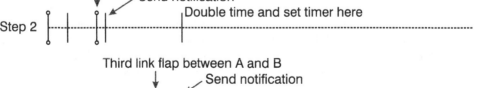

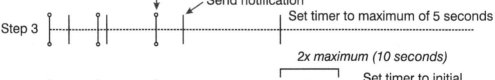

Link-State Exponential Backoff

Refer to Figure 7-19 to examine how exponential backoff works in the reporting of link-state changes in both IS-IS and OSPF.

Work with link flaps between Routers A and B. Three times (not timers) are associated with exponential backoff:

- The initial time
- The incremental time
- The maximum time

The examples that follow explain each of these in context. The update timer is the single timer used in this example; if this timer is running, the router must wait to build and transmit an update. To understand how this works, consider the following:

1   The link between Routers A and B flaps the first time. Router B sets the link-state generation timer to the initial time (1 second) and waits. When the update timer expires, Router B builds a link-state update and transmits it to Router C. The increment time (1 second) is now added to the initial time, and the link-state generation timer is set 2 seconds after the first link-state update is sent.

2   The link between Routers A and B flaps a second time. Router B waits until the link-state generation timer has expired, builds an update, and transmits it to Router C. The last setting of the link-state generation timer (2 seconds) is doubled, to 4 seconds. Because this number is less than the maximum time (5 seconds), the link-state generation timer is set for 4 seconds after the link-state update is transmitted.

3   The link between Routers A and B flaps a third time. Router B waits until the link-state generation timer has expired, builds a link-state update, and transmits it to Router C. The last setting of the link-state generation timer (4 seconds) is doubled to 8 seconds. Because this is greater than the maximum time (5 seconds), the link-state generation timer is set to expire 5 seconds after the link-state update is transmitted.

4   A network operator notices the flapping link and corrects the problem, so the link remains stable. After the link has remained stable for twice the maximum time (10 seconds), Router C resets the link-state generation timer. The next event causes the link-state generation timer to begin at the initial time (1 second) again.

You can apply exponential backoffs to two different timers in link-state protocols:

- The link-state generation timer, the case just examined
- The SPF timer, which determines how often a router runs the SPF algorithm in response to changes in the network

Configuring OSPF Exponential Backoff for LSA Generation

OSPF exponential backoff for LSA generation is called *LSA throttling* and was released in Cisco IOS Software Release 12.0(25)S, 12.3(2)T, and 12.2(18)S. Two new configuration commands are related to this capability:

- **timers throttle lsa all** [*start-interval*] [*hold-interval*] [*max-interval*]—The start-interval is the initial time, the hold-interval is the increment, and the max-interval is the maximum time. This command is available within the OSPF router configuration mode.

- **timers lsa arrival** [*milliseconds*]—This is the rate at which a router accepts LSAs with the same LSA-ID.

The **show ip ospf timers rate-limit** command provides information about the state of LSAs currently being throttled, as Example 7-7 demonstrates.

Example 7-7 *Determining the State of LSAs Being Throttled*

```
Router#show ip ospf timers rate-limit
LSAID: 10.1.1.1    Type: 1   Adv Rtr: 10.100.40.1 Due in: 00:00:00.019
LSAID: 192.168.4.1  Type: 3   Adv Rtr: 10.100.40.1 Due in: 00:00:00.005
```

The **show ip ospf** command includes additional information about the settings of the various throttle timers, as Example 7-8 demonstrates.

Example 7-8 *Displaying Information About Throttle Timer Settings*

```
router#show ip ospf
Routing Process "ospf 4" with ID 10.10.24.4
 ....
 Initial LSA throttle delay 100 msecs
 Minimum hold time for LSA throttle 10000 msecs
 Maximum wait time for LSA throttle 45000 msecs
 Minimum LSA arrival 1000 msecs
```

Configuring OSPF Exponential Backoff for Running SPF

OSPF exponential backoff for SPF is implemented as OSPF SPF throttling, a feature found in Cisco IOS Software Release 12.2(14)S, 12.0(23)S, 12.2(15)T, and later. A single configuration command is added in the OSPF router configuration mode:

```
timers throttle spf spf-start spf-hold spf-max-wait
```

- *spf-start* is the initial SPF schedule delay in milliseconds.
- *spf-hold* is the minimum hold time between two consecutive SPF calculations.
- *spf-max-wait* is the maximum wait time between two consecutive SPF calculations.

Configuring this command adds more information to the output produced by executing **show ip ospf**, as Example 7-9 shows.

Example 7-9   **show ip ospf** *Output After Configuring OSPF Exponential Backoff for Running SPF*

```
router#show ip ospf
Routing Process "ospf 1" with ID 10.1.1.1 and Domain ID 0.0.0.0
 ....
 Initial SPF schedule delay 5 msecs
 Minimum hold time between two consecutive SPFs 1000 msecs
 Maximum wait time between two consecutive SPFs 90000 msecs
```

Configuring IS-IS Exponential Backoff

IS-IS also implements exponential backoff as throttling in Cisco IOS Software Release 12.2 and later. Three new commands are used to configure LSP generation, SPF run, and PRC throttling:

```
lsp-gen-interval [level-1 | level-2] lsp-max-wait [lsp-initial-wait lsp-second-wait]
    spf-interval [level-1 | level-2] spf-max-wait [spf-initial-wait spf-second-wait]
    prc-interval prc-max-wait [prc-initial-wait prc-second-wait]
```

In each case, the *initial-wait* is the initial SPF schedule delay in milliseconds, the *second-wait* is the minimum hold time between two consecutive SPF calculations, and the *max-wait* is the maximum wait time between two consecutive SPF calculations.

NOTE   Both OSPF and IS-IS use a partial route calculation (PRC) when only the leaf nodes on the tree are changed. For instance, if an external OSPF route or a single IP subnet in IS-IS changes, the actual tree is not changed, just one of the destinations that is hanging off the tree. In these cases, a partial route calculation is run instead of a full or incremental SPF.

IP Event Dampening

Dampening is also an exponential backoff mechanism similar to the exponential backoff algorithm. The primary difference is that dampening is applied to events that have a Boolean component: a route that is either advertised or withdrawn, an interface that is either up or down, and so on. Exponential backoff deals with events in general, whereas dampening adds value based on the type of event and the frequency at which the event occurs. Refer to Figure 7-20 for this discussion on dampening.

Figure 7-20 *Dampening*

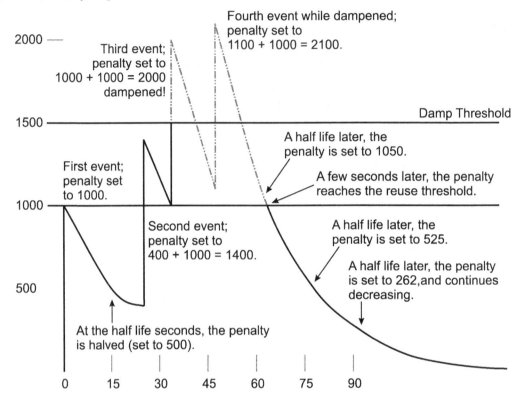

In dampening, the desirability of reporting an event is set using the penalty; the higher the penalty applied to a given item, such as a route or an interface, the less desirable it is to advertise changes in the state of that item. Dampening always leaves the item in the "off," or "down," state, when it stops reporting state changes; this is called the *dampened state*. A penalty is normally added when transitioning from "down" to "up."

Figure 7-20 starts at time 0, with a penalty of 0. When the first event occurs, a penalty of 1000 is added, making the total penalty 1000. As time passes without another event occurring, the penalty is decreased, based on the half-life. Each time the half-life—in this case 15 seconds— passes, the current penalty is halved; therefore, after 15 seconds, the half-life is set to 500.

A few seconds later, while the penalty is still decreasing, the second event occurs: 1000 is added to the current penalty, making the total penalty 1400. Again, as time passes, the penalty decays exponentially, reaching 1000 before the third event occurs. When the third event occurs, 1000 is again added to the total penalty. It reaches 2000, which is above the damp threshold; therefore, future events are dampened by leaving the interface or route in the down state.

Again, as time passes, the penalty is cut in half for each passing half-life, reaching 1100 before the fourth event occurs. When the fourth event occurs, 1000 is again added, making the penalty 2100 and leaving you in the dampened state until the penalty can be reduced again. Over time, the penalty finally drops to 1000 (at around 60 seconds in the example), which is the reuse threshold. At this point, state changes in the item being tracked are once again reported as they occur, unless the penalty reaches the dampen threshold in the future.

Dampening reacts to events by ignoring reporting events if they occur too frequently; exponential backoff reacts to events by reporting each event that occurs but slowing down the reporting of events as they occur more frequently.

Configuring IP Event Dampening

IP event dampening is available in Cisco IOS Software Releases 12.2(11)S, 12.0(22)S, and later. A single new configuration command is added with this feature under the interface configuration mode:

```
dampening[half-life-period reuse-threshold] [suppress-threshold max-suppress-
    time [restart-penalty]]
```

If the single keyword **dampening** is configured in interface configuration mode, IP Event Dampening is enabled with the following default values:

- *half-life-period*: 15 seconds
- *reuse-threshold*: 1000
- *suppress-threshold*: 2000
- *max-suppress-time*: 60 seconds
- *restart-penalty*: 2000

The interface is allowed to change states freely at Layer 2 regardless of the interface state (dampened or in use); an interface that continues to change state rapidly continues to accumulate penalties and continues to be marked as down to the IP subsystem, including the routing protocols.

NOTE   Generally, the parameters that are set for dampening a specific interface depend on the type of interface and the history of the link that the interface is attached to. For instance, if an interface has a long history of flapping, you might want to configure event dampening so that the interface is shut rather quickly. If an interface tends to be more stable, however, you might want to configure event dampening so that the interface has to flap two or three times before it is taken out of service.

Calculating the Route Faster

Another area where you can decrease the convergence speed of a network is in route calculation. How long does it take to calculate the best path to a destination in the network after you have detected and reported an event? The sections that follow consider tuning feasible successors in EIGRP, link-state partial SPF, and link-state incremental SPF.

EIGRP Feasible Successors

EIGRP calculates not only the best path to each reachable destination, but also feasible successors, which are known as loop-free routes to the same destination.

In Example 7-10, the route to 172.17.1.0/24 through 172.17.3.1 has a reported distance of 2167296, whereas the route through 172.18.8.4 has a total, or feasible, distance of 2172416.

Example 7-10 *Feasible Successors in EIGRP*

```
router#show ip eigrp topo 172.17.1.0
IP-EIGRP (AS 100): Topology entry for 172.17.1.0/24
  State is Passive, Query origin flag is 1, 1 Successor(s), FD is 2172416
  Routing Descriptor Blocks:
  172.17.2.1 (Serial0/0), from 172.18.8.4, Send flag is 0x0
      Composite metric is (2172416/18944), Route is Internal
      ....
  172.17.1.0 (Serial0/3), from 172.17.3.1, Send flag is 0x0
      Composite metric is (2684416/2167296), Route is Internal
```

Because the reported distance through 172.17.3.1 is less than the feasible distance through 172.18.8.4, the route through 172.17.3.1 must be loop free. It is a feasible successor.

How can you use this concept to your advantage for faster convergence? Figure 7-21 illustrates the difference between convergence with feasible successors and convergence without them.

The results in Figure 7-21 are from a lab test, rather than a real-world network. Controlled environment testing does not account for all the variables in a real, live network, so use caution when taking any information from the test besides what the test was designed to show: the impact of feasible successors on EIGRP convergence.

Router A, in this illustration, is injecting a variable number of routes toward Router B, as shown along the bottom of the chart. Router B then advertises these routes to Routers C and D, which in turn advertises them to Router E. The links between Routers B, C, and D are adjusted so that Router C is always the best path at Router E, and Router D is either a feasible successor, or not. The amount of time required for Router E to switch from the path through Router C to the path through Router D is measured, and the results, in milliseconds, are shown along the left side of the chart.

Figure 7-21   *EIGRP Convergence Times with Feasible Successors*

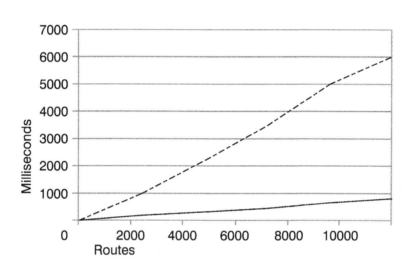

Examining the extremes of the chart, Router E can switch paths for 10,000 routes in less than 1 second if Router D is always a feasible successor. If the metrics are adjusted so that Router D is not a feasible successor, Router E takes about 7 seconds to switch over from the path through Router C to the path through Router D. Whether a path is a feasible successor makes a huge difference in the speed at which EIGRP can switch paths and in the network convergence time.

This makes sense if you consider how EIGRP determines that a nonfeasible successor is loop free: the active process. It always takes time to query neighbors and to receive replies, which slows down network convergence.

You can apply this knowledge to network design by considering not only the best path to each destination from a given area in the network, but also where the feasible successors are and how to tweak the metrics so that you have a feasible successor where possible. Figure 7-22 illustrates one such possible situation.

Figure 7-22   *Considering Feasible Successor Placement*

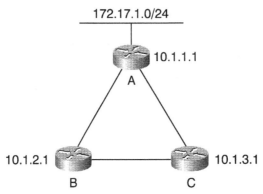

Assume that the Router A to B link and the Router A to C link are equal cost. Example 7-11 shows what the EIGRP topology table looks like at Router B.

Example 7-11   *EIGRP Topology Table at Router B*

```
router-b#show ip eigrp topo 172.17.1.0
IP-EIGRP (AS 100): Topology entry for 172.17.1.0/24
  State is Passive, Query origin flag is 1, 1 Successor(s), FD is 2172416
  Routing Descriptor Blocks:
  10.1.1.1 (Serial0/0), from 10.1.1.1, Send flag is 0x0
     Composite metric is (2172416/18944), Route is Internal
     ....
  10.3.3.1 (Serial0/3), from 10.1.3.1, Send flag is 0x0
     Composite metric is (2684416/2172416), Route is Internal
```

Router B sees two routes to 172.17.1.0/24: one through Router A, and the other through Router C. The feasible distance through Router A is equal to the reported distance through Router C, so the route through Router C is not considered a feasible successor. If the Router A to B link or the Router A to C link fails, at least one query is required to reconverge.

Modifying the metrics on the Router A to C link by decreasing the delay slightly produces the results in Example 7-12.

Example 7-12   *Modifying the Delay to Create an EIGRP-Feasible Successor*

```
router-b#show ip eigrp topo 172.17.1.0
IP-EIGRP (AS 100): Topology entry for 172.17.1.0/24
  State is Passive, Query origin flag is 1, 1 Successor(s), FD is 2172416
  Routing Descriptor Blocks:
  10.1.1.1 (Serial0/0), from 10.1.1.1, Send flag is 0x0
     Composite metric is (2172416/18944), Route is Internal
     ....
  10.1.3.1 (Serial0/3), from 10.1.3.1, Send flag is 0x0
     Composite metric is (2684416/2167296), Route is Internal
```

The reported distance through Router C is now lower than the feasible distance through Router A, so the path through Router C is considered a feasible successor. If the Router A to Router B link fails at this point, Router B converges immediately; 172.17.1.0/24 is not placed in the active state. The key is to set the delay on the Router A to C link so that Routers B and C still prefer their direct connections to Router A.

Configuring the metrics so that Router B considers Router C a feasible successor and Router C considers Router B a feasible successor is impossible. Regardless of how you change the metrics, a link failure on one of the two sides always causes the route to be moved into the active state, with a query/reply process required to prove that the alternate route is loop free.

Link-State Partial SPF

If you examine the directed graph built using SPF, you find three types of objects along that graph, as Figure 7-23 illustrates:

- Edges
- Nodes
- Leaves

Figure 7-23 *Partial SPF*

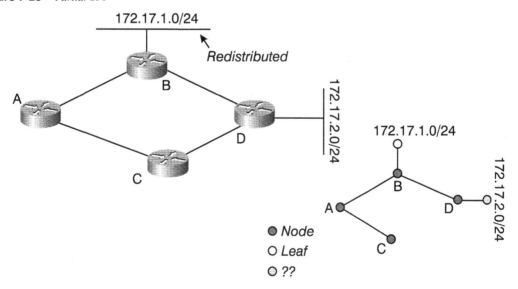

In Figure 7-23, nodes are darkly colored, leaves are white, and edges are represented as lines:

- A, B, C, and D are all treated as nodes in either OSPF or IS-IS.
- The links between the routers are treated as edges.

- The 172.17.1.0/24 network, connected to B, is considered a leaf in IS-IS, because IS-IS treats all IP subnets as leaves off the SPF tree.
- The 172.17.1.0/24 network, connected to B, is treated as a leaf in OSPF, because it is redistributed into the routing protocol, rather than being learned through a network statement. (It is an external, rather than internal, route.)
- The 172.17.2.0/24 network, connected to D, is considered a leaf in IS-IS, because IS-IS treats all IP subnets as leaves off the SPF tree.
- The 172.17.2.0/24 network is treated as a node in OSPF, because it is brought into OSPF through a network statement.

The distinction between a node and a leaf in the SPF matters to a network engineer because changes in leaves in the SPF tree do not cause a complete recalculation of the SPF tree. For instance, if the link from Router B to 172.17.1.0/24 fails, it is simply removed from the SPF tree. The parts of the tree that contain the nodes A, B, C, and D are not impacted by this change. Removing and adding leaf nodes without recalculating the entire SPF tree is called Partial SPF and is a feature of almost every implementation of OSPF and IS-IS, including the implementation in Cisco IOS Software.

The practical implication for a network designer is that externals in OSPF are not always bad. In some situations, redistributing numerous routes that change on a regular basis might make more sense than bringing the routes into OSPF through a network statement, especially if the routes can be summarized or filtered at an area border router (ABR), rather than being passed into the OSPF backbone.

Link-State Incremental SPF

Incremental SPF takes the concept of a partial SPF one step further. If a specific piece of the SPF tree changes, rather than recalculating the entire tree, you can recompute just a section of the tree. Figure 7-24 provides an example of how this works.

Figure 7-24   *Incremental SPF*

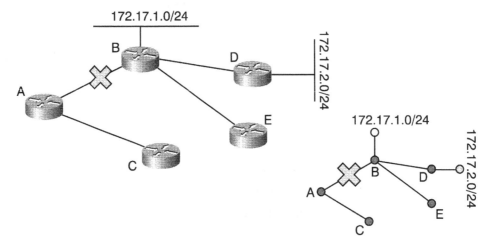

In this network, Router A reaches Routers B, D, and E, 172.17.1.0/24, and 172.17.2.0/24, all through Router B. If the link to Router B fails, and no alternate path exists to Router B, it is unnecessary to recalculate the entire SPF tree to remove the branch behind Router B from the tree. Instead, SPF can safely remove the branch behind Router B and adjust the routing table accordingly, without further calculations. You can run SPF incrementally over the tree, instead of recalculating all the paths through the tree. To implement incremental SPF, you need to keep several additional pieces of information in the SPF tree, including a parent and neighbor list for each node in the tree. What is the impact on the time it takes to run SPF in a real network when incremental SPF is deployed? Figure 7-25 provides some test results in this area.

Figure 7-25   *Changes in SPF Run Times with Incremental SPF*

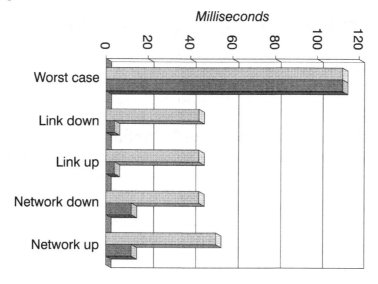

Working from the top down, the first results in the chart show the time required to run SPF (the darker bars) and incremental SPF (the lighter bars) in the worst-case situation—where some change occurred close to the calculating router, which caused a full tree recalculation. The run times are the same, which makes sense, because an incremental SPF should never take more time than a full SPF.

The second set of bars shows the difference in the time required to run SPF when a link fails at some point in the network; the time required to run an incremental SPF is much less than the time required to run a full SPF. The remaining bars show the differential between an incremental SPF and a full SPF in other network change situations. Overall, experience has shown that incremental SPF deployment can reduce SPF run times in a large-scale network by as much as 80 percent.

The farther away that a change is from the router that is running SPF, the more impact SPF has on the SPF run time.

Incremental SPF for IS-IS is implemented in Cisco IOS Software Releases 12.0(24)S, 12.3(2)T, and 12.2(18)S. To enable incremental SPF in IS-IS, execute the following command in the router configuration mode:

```
incremental-spf [level-1 | level-2 | level-1-2] [seconds]
```

The seconds parameter tells the IS-IS process how long to wait after the command is executed before starting to use incremental SPF; the default is 120 seconds.

Incremental SPF for OSPF is implemented in Cisco IOS Software Releases 12.0(24)S, 12.3(2)T, and 12.2(18)S. To enable incremental SPF in OSPF, enter the command ispf in OSPF router configuration mode.

Deploying GR and Fast Convergence Technologies

Up to this point, the chapter has covered the difficulty of fast convergence, the fast polling and event-driven mechanisms for fast convergence, graceful restart, and routing protocol modifications and considerations for fast convergence. With all of this as background, how do you actually deploy these technologies and techniques to provide a fast, stable network?

Graceful Restart Versus Fast Down Detection

Examining all these techniques, only fast down detection and GR appear to be at odds with each other. GR requires a router to be able to restart and signal its adjacent neighbors in a time less than dead time, whereas fast down detection attempts to reduce the amount of time required to detect a failed adjacent peer to the minimum possible. At some point, you are not going to be able to quickly detect a down neighbor and still be able to deploy GR. You need to determine where that point is and how it impacts the deployment of these two technologies.

How Fast Can GR Work?

To determine just how fast a router that is running NSF with stateful switchover (SSO) can switch to the backup route processor and begin rebuilding its routing protocol adjacencies, a series of tests were performed measuring the time from the switchover being initiated to the router transmitting its first hello.

Note that the results in Table 7-1 are from lab tests; as always, lab testing does not replicate a real network, with varying levels of traffic, different modes of failure, and unexpected events. Do not take lab-tested results as a guarantee of any result in the real world.

Table 5-1   *Graceful Restart Lab Tests from Various Platforms*

	OSPF	IS-IS Signaled	IS-IS Cisco
Cisco 7500	< 8 seconds	< 6 seconds	< 6 seconds
Cisco 12000	< 3 seconds	< 3 seconds	< 3 seconds
Cisco 10000	< 3 seconds	< 3 seconds	< 3 seconds

Given the numbers in Table 7-1, what is the minimum practical number of seconds you can set the hold timer and expect graceful restart to operate correctly? Two factors exist beyond the amount of time required to transmit the first hello.

First, consider that the adjacent router hold timer might have been close to expiring when the restart occurred, so you need to add about half the hold time to the amount of time the restarting router needs to restart before transmitting the first hello. Because changing the hold timer to accommodate the time required to restart the router, the hold time must also be increased, which in turn requires a change in the restart timer... To prevent this endless loop, increase the hold time by half of the restart time, rather than the full amount of the restart time.

Second, you should probably provide the safeguard of at least one dropped packet after the restarting router starts. Traffic conditions at just this point might be hard to judge, so it is best to be at least reasonably safe in this area. To find this number, take the restart time, add the time from the consideration in the preceding paragraph, and divide this number by three.

Assume that EIGRP requires similar amounts of time from system restart to generation of the first hello, although you do not have testing on this protocol to prove this assumption. Given this time frame from system restart to the generation of the first hello, the minimum hello and hold timers that you can reasonably expect to work, while preserving the capability to gracefully restart on a Cisco 7500, are as follows:

- 8 seconds outside restart time
- 4 seconds for the timer hold timer of the peer to run
- 3 seconds for one dropped hello at the restart

This makes a hold timer of 15 seconds, with a hello timer of 5 seconds. Lab testing shows that hold times as low as 3 seconds with hello intervals as low as 1 second successfully work on a Cisco 10000 or 12000, but these are in a lab environment and are not recommended as absolute values to go by in the real world. Using the same sort of logic described, the minimum realistic timers appear to be a 6- to 8-second hold timer and a 2-second hello interval.

Balancing Between GR and Fast Down Detection

Determining where to use GR and fast down detection depend mostly on two factors:

- **The type of link across which the adjacency is formed**—If the link supports fast down detection through some event-driven mechanism, GR is not likely to work well with this. Layer 2 quickly detects a down link and reports it to the routing protocol, which causes an immediate neighbor down.

- **The availability of other links through which to route traffic if the link fails**—If the traffic that is crossing this link cannot be routed through an alternate path, GR is the primary means of high availability. This is also true when it would take some time for a backup link to be brought up, such as a dial backup link.

Between these two considerations, most successful deployments of GR are along the network edge or in Data Centers that have many broadcast segments, such as Ethernet.

Deploying Graceful Restart with BGP and an Interior Gateway Protocol (IGP)

You should take several issues into consideration when deploying GR, including how GR reacts when interacting with non-GR capable routers and how interior gateway protocols and BGP interact if neither of them is capable of or configured for graceful restart. Figure 7-26 illustrates a small network with some GR routers connected to a single non-GR router.

Figure 7-26 *Mixing Graceful Restart and Non-Graceful Restart Routers*

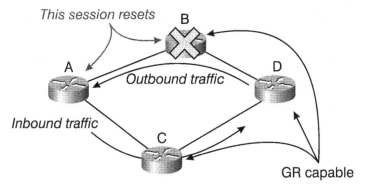

Here, Routers B, C, and D are all configured for graceful restart, but Router A is not. The preferred path from Router A to D and from Router D to A is through Router B, rather than Router C. If the control plane in Router B restarts, its adjacency with Router A fails, causing Router A to choose the path through Router C as the new best path. However, Router D does not drop its adjacency with Router B, so it continues to forward traffic along the C-B-A path. This might result in simple asymmetric routing, or, if unicast reverse path forwarding is configured on Router A, traffic from Router C might be dropped. It is best if all the routers that surround a router configured for GR are capable of supporting GR signaling.

Figure 7-27 illustrates what happens if you have IGP and BGP running over the same set of routers, with one of the protocols configured for graceful restart, and the other one not.

As Figure 7-27 shows, Routers A, B, C, and D are all running GR for their IGP, but not for BGP. Router D is learning 10.1.2.0/24 through BGP from two peers—Routers B and C—with a next hop of 10.1.1.1. Router D is learning about this next hop through two neighbors—Routers B and C—and choosing Router B as the best path to 10.1.1.1. If the control plane in Router B restarts, the BGP sessions reset, causing Router B to lose all its BGP tables and all the forwarding information based on those tables. However, Routers A and D do not reset their IGP adjacencies with Router B.

Figure 7-27 *IGP and BGP with Different Graceful Restart Configurations*

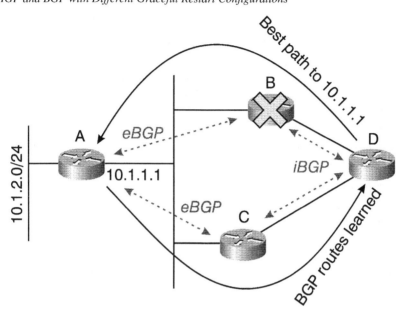

This means that Router D continues to learn about 10.1.2.0/24 through its BGP peering session with Router C, and it continues to believe that the next hop, 10.1.1.1, is reachable through Router B, even while Router B is restarting. However, when the BGP session between Routers A and B resets, Router B loses its route to 10.1.2.0/24. When Router D forwards traffic to Router B that is destined for a host within 10.1.2.0/24, Router B drops the traffic because it does not have a route to 10.1.2.0/24.

To resolve this, if BGP and IGP are both running on the same set of routers, either both of them should be configured for GR, or neither of them should be. Deploying GR in any other way can lead to routing black holes, routing loops, and other problems.

Deploying Exponential Backoff for Fast Convergence

Your primary consideration when deciding how to deploy exponential backoff in a real network is how to set the timers—determining good settings for the initial time, the increment, and the maximum time. Although the setting of these timers depends on your specific network, this section provides a general idea of how to set them here. Timers come in two types:

- Timers for SPF runs
- Timers for link-state update generation

The sections that follow cover both timers.

Setting SPF Exponential Backoff Timers

Begin by setting the initial time to 1 millisecond. Generally, you want the network to react quickly to single events; setting this timer low provides that quick reaction time.

To set the increment properly, you need to know how fast your network normally floods a routing change and runs SPF today. Because you cannot actually measure these numbers without some complicated testing, the best thing to do is to examine the logs provided by IS-IS or OSPF to determine how long it normally takes to run SPF on several routers in your network. Normally, SPF runs take about 50 milliseconds, but this figure can vary considerably.

For OSPF, you can use the command **show ip ospf stat** to examine several SPFs that have been calculated on a router, as Example 7-13 demonstrates.

Example 7-13 *Determining the SPF Calculation Time for OSPF*

```
router#show ip ospf stat
  Area 0: SPF algorithm executed 1 times


  SPF calculation time
Delta T    Intra D-Intra Summ    D-Summ  Ext     D-Ext   Total   Reason
7w0d   0         4876  0       0       0       0       4876    R,
7w0d   0         4968  0       0       0       0       4968    R,
```

The **Delta T** column shows how much time lapsed between each SPF run shown, and each column shows how much time was taken running SPF on a particular type of route. The **Total** column shows the total SPF run time in milliseconds.

For IS-IS, you can use the command **show isis spf-log** to determine the amount of time that each SPF on a router has taken, as Example 7-14 demonstrates.

Example 7-14 *Determining the SPF Calculation Time for IS-IS*

```
router#show isis spf-log
                  Level 1 SPF log
  When    Duration  Nodes  Count     Last trigger LSP    Triggers
00:15:46   3124     40     1            milles.00-00  TLVCODE
00:15:24   3216     41     5            milles.00-00  TLVCODE NEWLSP
00:15:19   3096     41     1            deurze.00-00  TLVCODE
00:14:54   3004     41     2            milles.00-00  ATTACHFLAG LSPHEADER
00:14:49   3384     41     1            milles.00-01  TLVCODE
00:14:23   2932     41     3            milles.00-00  TLVCODE
```

The **Duration** column is the amount of time, in milliseconds, that each SPF run has taken.

After you have set these two times, you need to consider the maximum time you want between SPF runs. If the average SPF run in your network is below 100 milliseconds, a setting of 1 second is pretty safe for this timer; if it is higher, you should set the maximum to this:

(1000/(<average SPF time> * 20)) * 1000

This should keep SPF from consuming more than about 20 percent of your processor utilization and provide the fastest convergence possible within your network.

Review Questions

1 What are the three primary concerns when considering fast convergence in a network?

2 What is a network meltdown, and what is the basic reason behind most network meltdowns?

3 What are the primary techniques that routing protocol designers and implementers use to prevent network meltdowns?

4 What technologies, when combined, allow a network to route through a problem, rather than around it?

5 What time constraints does a router have when it restarts under GR?

6 What are the two types of OSPF GR, and what is the difference between the two?

7 What are the two types of IS-IS GR, and what is the difference between them?

8 What is the fastest hello time available on OSPF and IS-IS? What is the dead interval when the hellos are transmitted this quickly?

9 What is the biggest issue with all fast-polling mechanisms for fast down detection?

10 What is the essential mechanism or principle behind exponential backoff?

11 What is the essential mechanism or principle behind dampening?

12 What part of an SPF tree does a partial SPF recompute?

13 What part of an SPF tree does an incremental SPF recompute?

CHAPTER 8

Routing Protocol Security

Previous chapters covered various aspects of network design, including topics such as hierarchy, summarization, specific topologies, and redundancy. This chapter changes gears and focuses on an area of increasing concern for network designers and administrators: routing protocol security. The chapter begins with a discussion of what routing protocol security is and then examines the sorts of attacks that an attacker might use against a routing system. Next, the chapter covers some protections that are available for improving the security of a routing system. Finally, the chapter concludes with some ideas about how to better protect the validity of the information within a routing system.

Fundamentals of Routing and Security

This section considers some of the fundamental concepts of routing and security so that you can better understand problems and possible solutions later in the chapter. It is important to review exactly what a *routing protocol* is, what a *routing system* is, and review some fundamental security concepts before you begin looking at attacks and defenses.

Understanding What a Routing System Is

Before you learn what a routing system is, consider something more familiar: a routing protocol. While examining what a routing protocol actually does, you can fill in the pieces around the routing protocol, finding, in the end, what a routing system does.

A routing protocol consists of two parts:

- A mechanism through which information about reachable destinations is transmitted between routers within the network.

- An algorithm that determines a loop-free path to each reachable destination within the network.

These two pieces break down into several mechanisms and requirements. For instance, you can periodically transmit routing information, or you can send it reliably only when it changes. If you attempt to reduce network overhead by sending routing data reliably, only when it changes, you need to build neighbor relationships between adjacent routers.

For the second part, you can determine whether a path is loop-free by finding the lowest-cost path to any given destination.

Routing protocols have so much in common because they address the same two problems in many different ways.

In the the definition of what a routing protocol is, one piece, the destination, is not a part of the routing protocol itself. Reachable destinations are carried by the routing protocol; they are not part of the routing protocol itself, but rather a part of the routing system. What other components are part of a routing system?

A routing system, then, is composed of several things:

- A routing protocol.
- The reachability information carried within the routing protocol.
- The set of policies expressed through the routing protocol. Generally, policies in routing systems attempt to force specific traffic to cross specific paths. For instance, one policy might be to load share the available traffic between two possible paths through the network. This can be expressed in a routing protocol by including two possible shortest paths in the routing information passed through the network or through some other means.
- The routers, or rather the network devices that exchange routing information, run the algorithms specified by the routing protocols, and actually forward traffic between the source and the destination.

The rest of this chapter considers the routing system as a whole, rather than considering a specific routing protocol. Some areas of investigation are outside the scope of this book, however. For instance, this chapter includes a discussion on protecting routers as hosts, but it covers only some smaller parts of the entire problem.

Thoughts on Authorization and Authentication

One of the major problems that security geeks face when trying to understand routing security is their lack of routing knowledge. Likewise, one of the major problems that routing geeks face when trying to understand routing security is their lack of security knowledge. It is hard to focus on more than one thing at a time when you can be easily overwhelmed trying to keep up with one technical area.

NOTE   This lack of cross knowledge is dangerous. It is one of the main reasons for the effort put into requirements documents in routing and security. The actual document that explains the requirements for securing a specific system might not be extremely useful, but the process of building the document is.

This short section is a contribution to the dialogue; the assumption is that you already know about routing at this point, so a good place to begin is an explanation of security concepts.

Defining Authentication and Authorization

Authentication and authorization, although commonly interchanged, are not the same. Authentication proves that someone, or something, is who he claims to be. Generally, authentication is a two-part process, using something you have and something you know. For instance, you take your debit card (something you have), and place it in an automated teller. The teller then asks for your pin number (something you know) to authenticate who you are. At this point, you are not authorized to do anything. The machine simply verifies who you are, with some degree of reasonable assurance.

Authorization, on the other hand, is the ability (or permission) to take some action. When you request a cash withdrawal, the teller machine contacts your bank and checks to make certain you are authorized to withdraw money from the account. The teller machine does not assume that you are allowed to withdraw money from an account simply because you have proven who you are; it checks your authorization in a separate process.

Having authorization without authentication is possible. For instance, when you walk into a store to buy something using cash, no one authenticates who you are. The cash might be authenticated, but this process focuses on the cash, rather than the person spending it.

Transiting Authentication and Authorization

Authentication and authorization, to some degree, can be transited. If your mother points someone out to you in a crowd as a childhood friend, you are likely to believe the person if she later walks up to you and starts talking about some school you both attended. You might later disbelieve this person, based on other evidence, but you will begin the relationship with a fundamental level of trust.

Why? Because someone you trust, your mother, told you who this person was. This is a basic form of transitive trust in authentication. This type of transitive trust is also seen in a *web of trust system*, where you might trust that a specific key belongs to a person because someone else you trust told you the key belongs to that person. Transitive authentication has limits, generally in the number of levels through which the trust can be transited, as Figure 8-1 illustrates.

Figure 8-1 *Authentication and Transitive Trust*

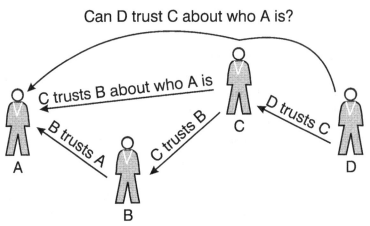

This illustration shows four people. B has some prior relationship with A, so when C asks about A, B can authenticate who A is. When D asks C who A is, can D trust the answer that C gives? It is up to D to decide if it can trust who A is based on the authentication of C. In most systems, this trust depends on several factors, including these:

- The strength of the bonds within the system. For instance, if all of these people are known to work for the same company and share a common interest in giving correct information, the trust bond is probably relatively high, and D has good reason to trust the identity of A from C.

- The relationship between C and D. If the relationship between D and C is strong, it is likely that C is only going to provide good information to D. If C does not consider its relationship to D important, C has no specific reason to provide good information, and the trust level of D is diminished.

- The relationship between A and B. If the relationship between A and B is strong, to the point of "publicly knowable," C has less incentive to lie to D. For instance, if A and B happen to be in a business partnership, D can verify the information for C from other sources, and C has less of a reason to lie about who A is.

Authorization can also be transited in most security systems; Figure 8-2 illustrates.

In this example, a *vice president* grants authority to a *lab manager* to control lab access. This *lab manager*, in turn, authorizes a *lab administrator* to specify which members of a specific team are allowed to use the lab, and under what policies. Authorization originates from the *vice president*, transits the *lab manager*, and finally resides in the *lab administrator*. In addition, a backdoor authorization chain passes from the *vice president* to the *team manager* and finally to the *lab administrator*.

Figure 8-2 *Simple Authorization Chain*

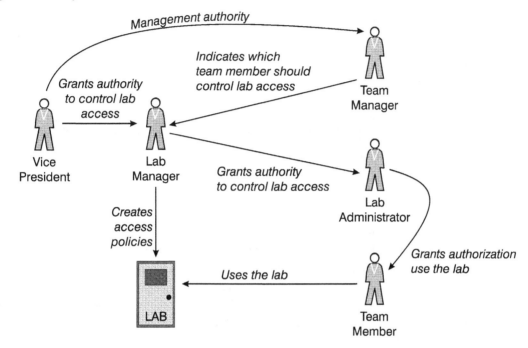

This example also illustrates two other important points in authorization schemes, especially those relying on transitive authorization of some type:

- The ability to *allow* some action does not necessarily mean the ability to *disallow* it. For instance, in this example, the *lab administrator* can allow the *team member* to use the lab, but the *lab administrator* cannot prevent the *team member* from using the lab. This might sound odd, but the *team member* could just as easily go *around* the *lab administrator* and gain access through the *lab manager* authorized by the *vice president*, or even have the *vice president* authorize his use of the lab directly. This issue is pervasive in routing systems; you need to be careful not to take the ability to authorize something as the ability not to authorize, or to prohibit it.

- When authorization is transited, the transitor often does not lose the authorization to do something, but rather just shares it with someone else. In this example, the *lab manager* does not lose the authorization to allow specific individuals to use the lab, but rather just transits the authority to the *lab administrator*. The ability of the *team member* to go around the *lab administrator* and gain access from some other place is based on the *lab manager* not "giving up" his ability to authorize something, but rather sharing a rather specific piece of his authorization. You will also encounter this in routing systems, so it is something you need to pay close attention to.

Figure 8-3 illustrates another problem in transitive authorization and authentication.

Figure 8-3   *Transitive Authorization Versus Authentication*

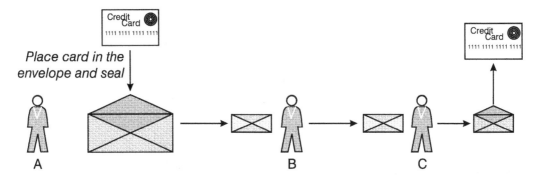

A has taken a credit card he is authorized to use, placed it in an envelope, and sealed it. He passes this envelope to B, who then passes it to C. Assuming that no "dirty tricks," occur along the way, C can examine the envelope's flap to verify the credit card has been transmitted correctly, without alteration, because the envelope is still sealed.

What does the correct transmission of the credit card say about the ability of C to use it to purchase something? Precisely nothing. The point of this example is that you should never take authentication as authorization; correct transmission does not imply authorization to use the information transmitted. This is, again, something you are going to see when examining security in routing systems.

Transiting Authorization in a Routing System

Consider the following two examples of transiting authorization within the context of a routing system, with the goal of trying to understand exactly what you can secure within routing. Refer to the small network illustrated in Figure 8-4 to superimpose the examples given in Figures 8-2 and 8-3 in a routed network.

Figure 8-4   *Transitive Authorization in a Routing System*

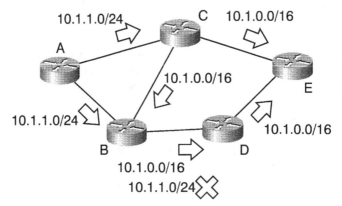

Here, Router A is advertising a route, 10.1.1.0/24, to Routers B and C. Router A has marked the route in some way to prevent Router B from readvertising 10.1.1.0/24 to Router D. For instance, Router A could advertise 10.1.1.0/24 with a metric just shy of the maximum metric available. When Router B receives this advertisement, it increments the metric, making it the maximum, which means that the destination is now unreachable, and Router B does not readvertise 10.1.1.0/24 to Router D.

Because the advertisement for 10.1.1.0/24 is being blocked between Routers B and D, Router A assumes that it should not receive traffic that is destined to any host within 10.1.1.0/24, originating from Router D or beyond, from Router B. However, this expectation can be upset in two possible ways.

First, consider how routing actually works. You can reasonably expect any routes a router receives to be placed in its forwarding table (and thus used to forward traffic). You might, also, reverse this assumption, and expect a router not to have any routing information about destinations which are somehow blocked through the routing protocol. What upsets this second assumption is a simple factor: Routers can receive routing information from several sources.

For instance, in this case, Router E might be manually configured with a static route, pointing traffic destined to 10.1.1.0/24 towards Router D.

This is the same problem illustrated in Figure 8-3. Just because you have received routing information does not mean that you can actually use it, and just because you have advertised (or refused to advertise) routing information does not mean that you can control traffic flow. In reality, packet forwarding occurs on a hop-by-hop basis, with each router basing its forwarding decision on information that is contained in a local table. The routing protocol is not the only source of information used to build forwarding tables on routers, and the path of a specific routing update might have nothing to do with the path of a specific packet being forwarded through the network.

To see the second way that the expectation of A can be upset, examine the 10.1.0.0/16 aggregate route advertised by several routers in Figure 8-4. Router C advertised this aggregate route to Routers B and E, and Router B advertised 10.1.0.0/16 to Router E. At this point, Router E now has two routes to 10.1.0.0/16, both of which contain the 10.1.1.0/24 address space. If, for any reason, 10.1.1.0/24 is blocked between Routers C and E, the 10.1.0.0/16 route is the only routing information that Router E would have about addresses within 10.1.1.0/24. Router E could choose either route, because both are perfectly valid destinations that are reachable through valid paths in the network.

This is directly analogous to the lab manager illustration from Figure 8-2. In this case, Router C (the *lab manager*) is advertising a superset of the destinations that Router A (the *lab administrator*) is advertising. 10.1.1.0/24 is contained within 10.1.0.0/16, in much the same way that the *lab administrator* authorization to allow access to the lab is contained within the *lab manager* authorization to the lab. As long as Router C (the *lab manager*) can advertise a superset of the Router A address space, Router A (the *lab administrator*) has little or no power over the Router D authorization to advertise the 10.1.1.0/24 address space.

From these two examples, you can infer two important points about security in routing systems:

- You cannot infer the path that a packet will take through a network by examining routing protocol updates within the network.

- Authorization to readvertise a specific set of addresses or a specific prefix cannot be transited in a routing system.

These two points have considerable impact when you examine possible solutions to routing system security, specifically in the area of what you can secure.

NOTE   These two examples and the concepts contained in them are drawn from examples given in the (White 2004, Considerations in Validating the Path in Routing Protocols) Internet Engineering Task Force (IETF) Internet-Draft, "Considerations in Validating the Path in Routing Protocols."

Trust and Security

Regardless of how many security mechanisms you set up and how you model the trust in a security system, the entire system still rests on the shoulders of people. Social engineering continues to be the most exploitable security system attack as long as humans have anything to do with security.

This is not to say that you should simply try to take humans out of security; just be realistic about how secure you can actually make a system, and weigh the tradeoffs of more or better security against the cost of providing it. At some point, the cost of a break-in, where proper reaction minimizes possible damage, will be less than the cost of an additional signature or an additional lock.

Another aspect of security systems that you need to be aware of is their brittleness. In his book, Beyond Fear, Bruce Schneier describes the brittleness of a security system as the way in which the security system reacts when it is compromised. This is similar to a diamond, which might be hard on the outside, but, if struck in the right place, shatters into many smaller pieces. Consider the brittleness of a security system. Humans reduce the brittleness of a security system while increasing the chances of social engineering being an effective attack.

How do humans reduce the brittleness of a security system? Brittleness occurs because of predictable reactions. When a diamond is struck at the right angle with the right force, every molecule within the diamond structure reacts in the same way, breaking its bonds with neighbors. Because all the molecules react in the same way, the diamond shatters—diamonds are hard, but brittle. Security systems are similar; if every component in the security system reacts in a specific way to specific threats or events, an attacker can, over time, guess what components will act in specific ways and tailor the attack to take advantage of known reactions. Humans, however, put an element of uncertainty into the system, making it less brittle.

NOTE   Bruce Shneier's book, *Beyond Fear* (Copernicus Books, 2003), is a good starting point to understanding security systems.

You need to be familiar with some specific attacks against a routing system so that you can understand the range of defenses at your disposal.

Over the past several years, security has become a large part of the job of every network manager, with concerns about securing data on the wire (through mechanisms such as IP Security, or IPSec), securing the connection between remote users and the local network (secure sockets and VPNs), security of critical systems within the network (access to databases and other critical information), and others. The routing system is another area that network designers and managers should consider when trying to batten down the hatches.

When you consider the security of any system, first think about the types of attacks that the system is vulnerable to. If someone were to break into the routing system, what kind of damage might they want to do? Being creative in this area pays off because the answers are not as straightforward as they might seem.

After you have considered types of attacks, you will learn some of the more common mechanisms that are available for attacking a routing system and practices you can put in place in your network to protect the routing system. Then you will discover some future directions in routing protocol security.

Determining the Reasons for an Attack on the Routing System

Before this chapter examines how to attack a routing system, it is useful to consider why an attacker would want to compromise the routing system. Discovering why someone would want to attack a specific system often reveals important and unimportant areas to consider when building a defense. An attacker might want to attack a routing system for three primary reasons:

- Disrupting routing to deny service to some particular host, server, or class of devices within the network. This might include injecting false routing information to form a routing loop within the network, which, in turn, causes a link to become overloaded with traffic and fail.

- Misrouting traffic through or to an observation point. For instance, an attacker might modify routing so that data traffic that normally flows over an encrypted link is passed through a covert monitor instead. That enables the traffic to be gathered and analyzed before it is encrypted.

- Injecting false routing information as the basis for another attack. For instance, an attacker might inject false routing information to defeat reverse path forwarding checks and allow traffic that normally would not be accepted at a network edge to be accepted. (This might include spam or a denial of service attack against a specific server.)

Generally, all attacks against routing systems come down to one of these three reasons.

Types of Attacks Against Routing Systems

This section discusses specific classes of attacks that any given routing system is vulnerable to. This list is not exhaustive, but security is always a game of give and take. As defenders close one hole, attackers hunt for new ones. When attackers exploit a new hole, defenders attempt to close it somehow. Unlike physical systems, logical systems do not have a clean "perimeter" that you can guard with virtual attack dogs. This means that the borders, attacks, and defenses are in constant flux.

Disrupting Peering

As discussed in the beginning of the chapter, all modern routing protocols use neighbor adjacencies to reliably transmit routing information through the network. If an attacker can disrupt these peering relationships, he can prevent the routing protocol from functioning properly and cause the network to fail in its ability to forward traffic correctly. Some of the possible attacks to disrupt peering include the following:

- **Packet, port, or buffer flooding**—With these attacks, the attacker attempts to disrupt the capability of one or more routers to transmit or receive routing protocol packets that are necessary for reliable transmission between two neighbors. These types of attacks include simple packet and port flooding attacks, whether they are distributed or not.

- **Transport-level attacks**—Transport-level attacks focus on the semantics of the protocol transport, attempting to destroy peering relationships or prevent the creation of peering relationships by injecting packets, causing the protocol transport to reset or otherwise fail.

- **Protocol-level attacks**—Here, the semantics of the protocol are attacked.

The next four sections discuss specific examples of transport- and protocol-level attacks.

Transport-Level Attacks Against OSPF and IS-IS

Although Open Shortest Path First (OSPF) and Intermediate System-to-Intermediate System (IS-IS) use different transport mechanisms, the processes that they use to discover and maintain neighbor relationships are similar enough to address their vulnerabilities in this area at the same time. OSPF uses an IP-based transport mechanism to discover neighbors, maintain neighbor relationships, and reliably transport routing information between neighbors. IS-IS uses similar transport mechanisms but does not transmit packets over IP; instead, it transports over a separate Layer 2 packet type that is reserved for it, as Figure 8-5 illustrates.

In both OSPF and IS-IS, a neighbor relationship is built only when a router has received its identifier in the hello packet of a neighboring router. Figure 8-6 illustrates the process of forming a neighbor relationship in OSPF and IS-IS.

Figure 8-5 *OSPF Data Transport Versus IS-IS Data Transport*

Ethernet, HDLC, Frame Relay, etc.

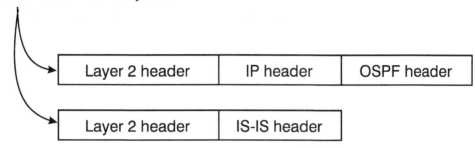

Figure 8-6 *Adjacency Formation in OSPF and IS-IS*

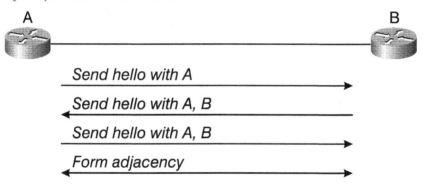

In this illustration, you see the following:

1 Router A transmits a hello with its local identifier in the hello packet.

2 Router B receives this hello. In its next hello, Router B places its local identifier in one section of the hello and the Router A identifier in another section of the hello, indicating neighbors it has heard from on this interface.

3 Router A receives this hello. In its next hello, Router A places its local identifier in one section of the hello and the Router B identifier in another section of the hello, indicating neighbors it has heard from on this interface.

4 When both routers have received hellos with their own local identifier included in them, the neighbor adjacency begins forming.

The reason for this process is simple: It prevents routers from forming an adjacency over a unidirectional link. The neighbor adjacency between two routers is assumed to be valid only as long as the local identifiers of both routers are in the hello packets that are received from the adjacent router.

Although this technique works quite well for preventing neighbor adjacencies along unidirectional links, it also leaves OSPF and IS-IS open to a simple transport-level attack. For an attacker to disrupt the peering relationship between two routers, it can simply send a hello, apparently sourced from one of the two routers, with an empty "heard from" list of neighbors. If an attacker sends a packet to Router A, apparently sourced from Router B, with an empty "heard from" neighbor list, Router A assumes the adjacency with Router B is no longer valid and flushes any routing information it had previously learned from B .

NOTE   Theoretically, this type of attack can be launched against an OSPF router from off segment or from a device that is not connected to the same network as the two OSPF routers that are being attacked. Because the OSPF transport is based on IP and routers forward IP packets in the normal course of operations, OSPF Hello packets target an adjacency that is many hops away. IS-IS does not use IP as a transport, and routers do not forward IS-IS packets as a part of normal operation, so an attacker must theoretically be connected to the same segment as the intended victim to perpetrate this attack against a router that is running IS-IS.

Transport-Level Attacks Against EIGRP

EIGRP uses a slightly different mechanism to prevent neighbor relationships from forming across unidirectional links, so it is not vulnerable to the attacks described in the last section. However, EIGRP is still vulnerable to transport level attacks. There are two mechanisms in EIGRP to tear down a neighbor relationship, and either of these can be used by an attacker to maliciously tear down neighbor relationships:

- A router can transmit a hello packet with all the K values set to 255. K values indicate the weights that each metric (bandwidth, delay, reliability, and so on) should be given in calculating the total metric of each path. These values are sent in each hello to ensure that each router within the network is using the same metric weights, which, in turn, ensures that every router in the network is making consistent routing decisions. All the K values set to 255 is an error condition that is used in EIGRP to indicate that the neighbor adjacency is about to fail, so the receiver should tear down the relationship instead of waiting on another signal (such as a hold interval timeout).

- A router can transmit an empty update with the initialization bit set. This normally indicates readiness to receive routing information from a new neighbor, but it also resets the neighbor state, resulting in a complete teardown of the neighbor relationship.

As with OSPF, because EIGRP uses IP as its transport, an attacker can, in theory, transmit either of these two packets onto a network, connecting multiple EIGRP routers many hops away in the network, allowing the attacker to disrupt peering almost at will anyplace in the network.

Transport-Level Attacks Against Border Gateway Protocol (BGP)

Because BGP is the primary protocol that interconnects not only the Internet but also many other large-scale internetworks, many researchers and operators have scrutinized it in terms of peering security and the ability to disrupt a BGP peering session. Because BGP is based on Transmission Control Protocol (TCP), it is vulnerable to any known TCP attack or vulnerability.

Figure 8-7 illustrates one possible attack against a TCP session.

Figure 8-7   *Inserting a TCP Reset to Tear Down a BGP Session*

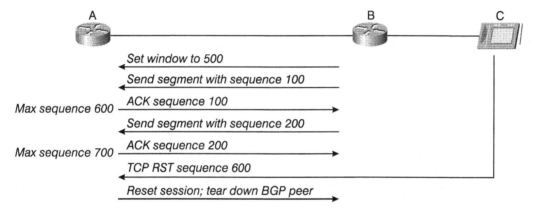

In this network, Routers A and B have a normally operating BGP session. The attacker, Host C, needs to know five things to disrupt the TCP session between Routers A and B and disrupt routing in the network:

- **The source address of the TCP session**—The attacker can discover the Router B IP address in several ways, including examining the next hop addresses that are contained in publicly available routing tables and tracing packet paths through the network.

- **The destination address of the TCP session**—The attacker can discover the Router A IP address through the same mechanisms that he or she uses to discover the IP address of Router B.

- **The source port number**—This is either going to be 179 or some port number above 1023. Generally, the attacker can guess the port number.

- **The destination port number**—This is, again, either going to be 179 or some port number above 1023. The attacker can guess this number by iterating through the available port number space.

- **A sequence number that the intended victim will accept**—Each TCP packet includes a sequence number used for reliable transmission and an assurance that certain data is reassembled in the correct order when it is received. TCP is designed with a range of acceptable sequence numbers. The difference between the lowest expected sequence number and the highest expected sequence number is called the *window*. As long as the attacker can guess a number within this window of possible sequence numbers, the packet is accepted and processed by the intended victim.

Assuming that the attacker knows the source and destination IP addresses for the TCP session, how long will it take to guess the correct source port, destination port, and sequence number? According to Tony Watson's research (*Slipping in the Window: TCP Reset Attacks*, Watson, 2004), this is not difficult to do. A typical attacker should be able to guess these parameters in about 1.7 seconds while generating about 64,000 guesses per second. This means that TCP is vulnerable to this sort of attack.

NOTE   See also *Cisco Security Advisory: TCP Vulnerabilities in Multiple IOS-Based Cisco Products*, published in 2004, for further information on this attack and the mitigations available against the attack in current Cisco IOS Software images.

Protocol-Layer Attacks

Protocol attacks take advantage of protocol semantics above the transport layer, attempting to tear down a peering session or otherwise disrupt routing by taking advantage of specific mechanisms and state changes within a protocol state machine. One example of this is falsely sending a BGP NOTIFICATION message to a BGP speaker, causing the speaker to reset its peering session with a current BGP peer.

Sean Convery and Matthew Franz performed some tests attempting to tear down a BGP session by injecting false information into an existing BGP session. They reported their results at the Black Hat Conference in 2002 (Convery 2002). Based on a set of 1200 tests, using a test tool to generate malformed messages of various types, they discovered only seven possible poor reactions in widely deployed BGP implementations. Each of these seven poor reactions was a defect in the implementations, rather than something traceable to the BGP specification.

Generally, protocol attacks are more difficult than transport-layer attacks because the attacker needs to know more about the routing protocol he is attacking. An attacker who is trying to tear down a BGP peering session can attack TCP more simply than attacking the BGP peer finite state machine. This is true, in part, because attacks against the protocol require a full understanding of the protocol and possibly implementation details that are not available to the general public. The transport layer of most router implementations, however, is better documented and tends to involve simpler state machines and simpler mechanisms to direct attacks against. Further, attacking the protocol generally requires full knowledge of the transport layer that the protocol runs on.

Falsifying Routing Information

Rather than attempting to disrupt the adjacency or peering relationship between two routers, an attacker might decide to inject false routing information so that he can misroute traffic through an observation point and cause a routing loop; Figure 8-8 illustrates.

Figure 8-8   *Modifying Routing Information to Facilitate an Attack*

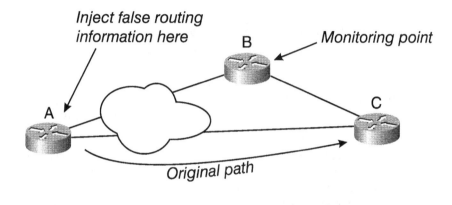

Redirecting traffic through a monitoring point

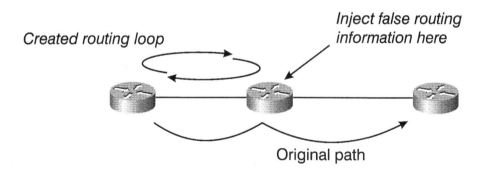

Redirecting traffic into a routing loop

Although this type of attack can be devastating, it is almost impossible to accomplish without either gaining control of one of the routers already connected to the network, or injecting routing information from an unauthorized device connected to the network.

Any attempt to alter routing information between two routers or to inject false routing information through spoofing one end of an established adjacency between two routers is difficult. The real neighbors attempt to correct any perceived errors that are induced in the process.

It is much easier to inject false information by connecting a new router to the network or to break into an existing router. Doing so involves masquerading as a legitimate member of the routing domain or compromising a legitimate member of the routing domain.

Disrupting Routing Domain Stability

Another form of information that is carried within a routing protocol—something that is not obvious by examining the protocol standards or specifications—is the pace or routing information flowing through the network, or the rate at which routing updates are received. If a network is unstable, routing updates are passed through the system quickly, which, in turn, can cause routers to consume a lot of processing power and memory trying to keep up.

Routing protocols have always slowed down the pace of routing updates by injecting wait timers after receiving information about an event but before acting on it. When a router interface is disconnected, it might wait half a second or so before reporting the interface state change to the routing protocol, and the routing protocol might wait before reporting the change to its neighboring routers. A router that is receiving an update describing a change in the network topology might wait before acting on the information by recalculating the topology of the network.

These wait times are not always fixed. In some cases, however, a routing protocol can use an exponential timer, increasing each time a network event is reported. If network events are being reported quickly, the timer slows down to some maximum value over time, which causes the routing protocol to slow down its reaction time as the pace of events in the network speeds up. By slowing down timers when network events speed up, the routing protocol can handle small numbers of changes quickly and still maintain network stability when the network is rapidly changing.

NOTE   Examples of variable wait times based on the speed of network change include OSPF and IS-IS exponential backoff, discussed in Chapter 7, "High Availability and Fast Convergence," and BGP route dampening, discussed in Chapter 6, "BGP Cores and Network Scalability."

An attacker can take advantage of the capability of the routing protocol to dynamically adjust to the pace of network changes by injecting and withdrawing routing information fast enough to keep the network in a slow state all the time. This adversely impacts the convergence time of the network and affects the reliability of the applications that are running on the network. Figure 8-9 illustrates one example.

Figure 8-9 *Slowing Down Network Convergence Through False Injection*

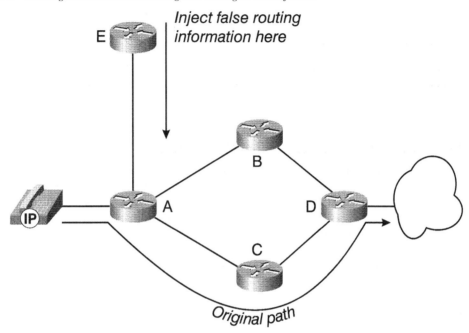

In this network, traffic normally flows from the IP phone through Routers A, C, and D, to the cloud. The alternate path designed into the network passes through Router B, rather than Router C. The timers on the routing protocol are configured so that a failure at Router C causes no more than 100 milliseconds of downtime on the path.

The attacker compromises Router E (or simply attaches to the network and connects Router E) and injects a constant flow of false routing information into the Router A routing table. To maintain network stability, Router A slows down the rate at which it adapts to new routing information, so that it takes 2 or 3 seconds to converge. If the attacker can force a network failure at Router C or is patient enough to wait for a legitimate failure at Router C, the IP phone connectivity is lost for some period of time while the network converges around the failure.

Although this type of attack might appear to be difficult, it does not take much continuous routing information from Router E to force the Router A timers to slow down. One routing update about every two or three seconds is probably enough to slow down the network convergence.

Protecting Routing Domain Legitimacy

One of the two primary areas of concern you discover when examining possible attacks against a routing system is the legitimacy of the routing domain. To protect the legitimacy of the routing domain, you begin by making it as hard as possible to compromise routers within the system. If an attacker can break into a single router, he has an opening through which he can perform any number of attacks to make the network unusable.

Beyond this, if a network engineer plugs a new router into the network, how do the other routers know that the new router is legitimate and actually belongs to the network? You need to consider some of the ways you can protect routers from denial-of-service (DoS) attacks.

Protecting Routers from Being Compromised

The first course of action when securing a network is to prevent the routers and switches that are connected to the network from being compromised. This section provides an overview of techniques you can use to secure a router, but it does not cover every possible mechanism or go into a great deal of detail. You can apply any technique that hardens or prevents a host from being compromised to prevent routers from compromise. In fact, if you are familiar with network security and fundamental network design, you should be familiar with many of these techniques. Design and security converge in many of these common techniques.

Use Passwords

It might seem obvious to say that you should configure passwords on your routers, but it is common for network administrators to use default passwords or not configure a password at all. In a short survey of cases opened by customers through the Cisco Technical Assistance Center, numerous customers had no passwords set on their routers or only a simple password, such as **cisco** or **c1sc0**.

Two types of passwords exist on routers that are running Cisco IOS Software:

- **A password to access the router itself**—Passwords used to access the router include these:
  - The *virtual terminal*, or Telnet, password is configured under the line vty configuration mode and is required for a user to Telnet to the router. Telnet is not the recommended mechanism for accessing a Cisco router, because passwords are sent over the network in clear text format, along with all the configuration information that is entered on the router.
  - A *secure shell (SSH)* password, which is used to access the router using an SSH client from another device. SSH encrypts all the traffic passing to and from the router and is the preferred method for connecting to a router.

— An *HTML server* password, which is used to access the router using a web browser. This is not a preferred mechanism to access the router, because all passwords and other configuration information are transmitted to and from the router unencrypted across the network.

— A *console* password. Although the console password can prevent casual attackers who have physical access to the router console from gaining access to it, a determined attacker can usually defeat a console password. Console passwords cannot replace solid physical security. This can be a major concern when your equipment is collocated in a service provider space or space rented from another company.

- **A password to access configuration mode on the router**—Two user-independent passwords exist for controlling access to the configuration mode of a router that is running Cisco IOS Software:

    — The *enable* password, which allows access to the enable access, or configuration mode, of the router. This password is not stored in an encrypted format on the router, so anyone who can view the configuration (by accessing the router through Telnet, the console, or some other means) can view the password and use it to reconfigure the router. The enable password is not recommended as a method to control access to the configuration mode of Cisco routers.

    — The *enable secret* password, which is similar in scope and purpose to the enable password but is stored in the router configuration using a latchkey encryption algorithm. This is the password recommended for allowing access to the configuration mode of a Cisco router.

The enable and enable secret passwords can coexist on a router that is running Cisco IOS Software. In other words, someone can look at your configuration, discover the enable password, and bypass the enable secret password using the clear text enable password. Always delete any enable passwords after you have a password configured through enable secret.

Any passwords that are configured on a Cisco router should be strong. They should be hard to guess or hard to find using a dictionary attack (which essentially means using a dictionary of common passwords and testing each one until the attacker finds the correct password).

NOTE   A common trick is to set up four virtual terminal lines, which allows up to four people to Telnet in to the router. Rather than setting all four terminal lines to accept the same password, the network administrator sets the first three to accept the same password and the fourth session to accept a different password. If an attacker guesses the correct password, he can only use three of the four Telnet lines, leaving the fourth open for the network administrator to Telnet in and kick the attacker out after discovering the attack.

Rather than setting passwords for Telnet, SSH, and enable access to a router, you can set the router up to use a RADIUS or TACACS server for authentication and authorization. This allows you to control access to Telnet, SSH, and configuration mode on all the routers in your network from one central server. Using a central TACACS or RADIUS server also enables logging of each user activity on a router so that you can track accounts used for malicious configuration or attacks.

Although tracking the activities of users configuring a router can be good from a security perspective, it can cause the mean time to repair (MTTR) during a major outage to be much greater because users wait on their commands to be logged for each configuration change or **debug** command that they enter in the process of troubleshooting and fixing the problem. A fundamental issue always exists with managing security of a network through devices that are connected to the network—you always need to leave yourself some other access that does not require network connectivity to work well or fast. It is a good idea to have fallback passwords configured and to change them on a regular basis just like your normal user passwords.

NOTE   We were once called into a major network problem involving EIGRP neighbor failures on a large network. Several routers periodically timed out all their EIGRP neighbors at the same time throughout the network because of missed hellos. (The EIGRP hold timer was expiring on all the failing neighbors.) On examining these events, we found that the input queues were full of packets in every case, so the EIGRP hellos were being dropped and the routers were timing out their neighbors. We waited until the problem happened again and gathered some sample packets from the input queues to determine what was flooding the network with enough packets to cause EIGRP hellos to fail to be delivered.

When we analyzed the packets, we found that they were all from the RADIUS server, replying to requests to allow us to run the commands to gather the packets from the router interface input queues. Obviously, these packets were not the reason for EIGRP losing enough hellos to drop neighbor adjacencies, but we had to turn off per-command logging and wait until the network failed again before we could find the real problem. Per-command authentication and logging cost us several days in troubleshooting time in this case.

Filter Access to Routers

Another effective mechanism to protect routers from being attacked is to filter all packets that are destined to the routers so that unauthorized people cannot Telnet, open an SSH session, or open an Hypertext Markup Language (HTML) session to the router. How common are routers with open administrative ports in real networks deployed throughout the world?

In the 2002 study of BGP security by Sean Convery referred to earlier, a simple test attempting to open Telnet, SSH, or Hypertext Transfer Protocol (HTTP) sessions on a random number of routers running BGP on the Internet found that 14.5 percent of all the routers tested were accessible. If possible, your routers should be reachable only through some sort of dialup connection, heavily protected through well-known security mechanisms, or by connecting to the network through some sort of virtual private network, or secure tunnel, and from a restricted set of IP addresses.

NOTE   One way to provide more security for your network is to allow management access to your routers only through an out-of-band management network. You can build a completely separate physical topology that can reach each router in the network and does not have overlapping routing information with the actual network destinations, using a completely separate routing protocol or routing processes. Then you can block all management traffic from any user-accessible connection in the network, providing a great deal of security on the management side of your routers.

One technique you can attempt to use involves filtering access to the router addresses at the edge of the network; however, this is far more complex than it first appears. Use the network illustrated in Figure 8-10 to understand this technique and the problems you might face when trying to use it.

Figure 8-10   *Filtering Packets That Are Destined to Internal Devices at the Edge*

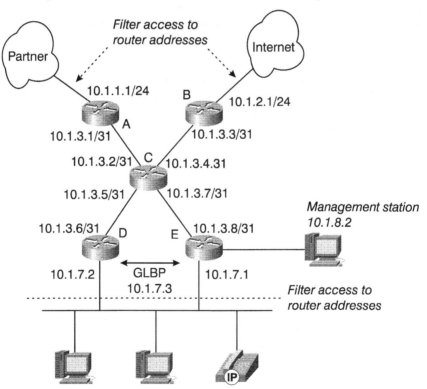

The first inclination when trying to prevent access to the routers from user devices and devices outside the network is to block access to all addresses that end in .1, which are typically routers.

You can immediately see why this would not work in this network, though. Some interfaces use addresses ending in .2 through .8, especially on point-to-point links in the center of the network.

NOTE   These types of filters are usable in some networks, primarily where the network is divided into customers and a provider, and the provider's entire address space, with some exceptions, should be unreachable to the customers. For instance, this sort of filtering might be useful on the edge of the network core, to prevent a compromised distribution layer router from being used to attack a core router.

Can you use another mechanism to filter packets that are destined to the routers? You can manually configure the filters at the edge of the network, but this quickly becomes cumbersome and unmanageable. You can also attempt to filter all packets that have a destination address within the first three addresses of any subnet within the network, but you cannot configure this type of filter (filter packets based on routes in the routing table).

The only other option is to filter these packets on the routers, which is the cleanest, easiest way to configure and manage these filters. Rather than trying to filter based on the destination of the packets as they enter the network, you can filter based on the source of the packets as they enter the routers.

To do this, configure a packet-level filter on the virtual terminal lines (through which an administrator Telnets to the router) or on the other access mechanisms that are configured on the router. The configuration consists of an access list allowing packets sourced from the management station, 10.1.8.2, to be passed through the Telnet session and up to the router processes; packets sourced from any other host are dropped as they are received (see Example 8-1).

Example 8-1   *Using an Access Class to Limit Virtual Terminal Access to a Router*

```
!
access-list 1 permit 10.1.8.2 0.0.0.0
....
line vty 0 4
 access-class 1 in
 password ww
 Login
....
```

Protecting Against Illegitimate Devices Joining the Routing Domain

After you have protected the routers and switches that connect the network, consider preventing an attacker from plugging a router into an open port on the network, forming routing protocol adjacencies with connected devices, and injecting false routing information.

This section discusses two mechanisms that authenticate routing data transmitted between routers: MD5 and IPSec. In all authentication systems, the focus is on authentication and authorization, rather than on protecting data. Protecting routing data from being read on the wire is generally not a concern or focus of security mechanisms in this area.

NOTE   It is assumed that knowledge of a password or a secret configured on the router is a viable form of authentication and authorization. Some argue about this in the security world, because it reduces the normal authentication process of matching something you have and something you know to the simpler process of simply checking something you know.

MD5 Authentication

Message Digest 5 (MD5) is described in RFC 1321, "The MD5 Message-Digest Algorithm" (Rivest, 1992). MD5 signatures are directly embedded in EIGRP, OSPF, and IS-IS packets:

- RFC 2328, "OSPF Version 2," describes an optional cryptographic signature within all OSPF packet formats. One option for filling this field is using an MD5 signature across the contents of the packet, as described in section D.3 (Moy, 1998).

- RFC 3567, "Intermediate System to Intermediate System (IS-IS) Cryptographic Authentication," describes an optional Type-Length-Value (TLV) to add an MD5 signature to IS-IS packets (Li, 2003).

- EIGRP uses a TLV embedded in all EIGRP packets to carry an MD5 signature.

NOTE   You can find information on configuring MD5 for each of the routing protocols at Cisco.com. The easiest way to find this information is to search on the routing protocol, combined with MD5. For instance, to find information on configuring MD5 authentication with MD5, search on "EIGRP MD5."

OSPF version 3 (Coltun, 1999) does not supply authentication within the protocol. In the Abstract of RFC 2740, you find this:

"Authentication has been removed from the OSPF protocol itself, instead relying on IPv6's Authentication Header and Encapsulating Security Payload."

OSPF version 3 counts on signatures provided through IPv6 to validate routing information and prove that a router is a legitimate member of the routing domain.

BGP does not include an option for MD5 authentication information directly in the BGP message formats, either. Instead, BGP relies on MD5 signatures in its transport mechanism, TCP. These signatures are described in RFC 2385, "Protection of BGP Sessions via the TCP MD5 Signature Option," (Heffernan, 1998).

When you use any cryptographic or password-based system, it is important to choose hard-to-break passwords. This notion, discussed previously in relation to passwords used to protect connectivity to routers and passwords to gain access to a router configuration mode, is no different with the secret keys that build the MD5 signatures used in routing protocols. A good reference on choosing good keys for the MD5 algorithm, specifically, is RFC 3562, "Key Management Considerations for the TCP MD5 Signature Option," (Leech, 2003).

Issues with MD5 Peer Authentication

Three issues exist with using MD5 signatures to protect routing protocol peering sessions:

- Changing keys when using MD5 authentication is painful.
- MD5 signatures can be broken, exposing the shared secret key.
- Any type of cryptographic authentication can use large amounts of a router processor under various conditions.

Because MD5 is a shared secret key mechanism, meaning that all the devices using MD5 to sign their packets must share the same secret key, changing the key across several devices requires changing the key on all the devices at the same time. This is a major problem when trying to use MD5 authentication on a large-scale network. The following workarounds make changing the shared secret easier:

- EIGRP and IS-IS allow the use of key chains when configuring MD5 signatures on Cisco IOS Software. Key chains are set up so that signatures built with a given key are accepted during a preset beginning and ending time, and keys are automatically changed at specific times. Although key chains must be configured manually, the ability to manually preconfigure all the devices in a network to change keys at a preset time makes it possible to change your MD5 secret without bringing down the network.

- Most BGP implementations allow an existing peering session to stay up with failing MD5 signatures for the dead interval. This gives you time to change the MD5 secret on both routers in the peering session without losing network connectivity.

No good solutions are available for managing MD5 keys in a large-scale network, however. Some work has been undertaken in the past to remedy this by allowing MD5 keys to be exchanged through one of the various standard key exchange mechanisms, but this work has made no progress for several years.

The primary reason for lack of progress is the second risk identified when using MD5 signatures: Many engineers in the security fields no longer consider MD5 signatures to be cryptographically strong. MD5CRK, http://www.md5crk.com, was a distributed computing project to break the MD5 hash algorithm in a short period of time. The project closed down with the publication of the paper "Collisions for Hash Functions MD4, MD5, HAVAL-128 and RIPEMD," by Xiaoyun Wang, Dengguo Feng, Xuejia Lai, and Hongbo Yu, at Shandong University (2004).

They discovered that collisions could be found in the MD5 algorithm in less than 24 hours, making the MD5 algorithm insecure. Further research has verified this result and shown other ways to find collisions in MD5 hashes. That is why most security professionals are moving away from MD5 hashes and toward more complex and difficult to break hash algorithms.

IPSec

IPSec is standardized in a series of IETF RFCs, a list of which is available on the IPSec working group home page, http://www.ietf.org/html.charters/ipsec-charter.html.

NOTE   You can find additional information about IPSec at

- http://www.vpnc.org/ietf-ipsec/

- http://www.ipsec.dk/

Two basic types of protection are specified in the IPSec standards:

- **Encapsulating Security Payload (ESP)**—ESP encapsulates the entire payload of the IP packet into an encrypted "blob of bits." Nothing is readable out of this blob of bits until it is de-encrypted.

- **Authentication Header (AH)**—AH builds a cryptographic signature based on the contents of the original packet header (IP addresses, options, and so on), rather than the entire packet. This is lighter weight, because it does not require the cryptographic algorithm to be run over the entire packet; however, it also does not cover the packet contents.

Two modes of operation are specified within IPSec:

- **Transport**—The IPSec header is placed after the packet IP header. That way, only the contents of the packet are covered (or affected) by the encryption process. Note that an authenticated header makes sense only in the transport mode of IPSec.

- **Tunnel**—The entire original IP packet is encapsulated, or tunneled, within another IP packet. The original packet is placed in the tunnel packet as an encrypted payload. Using tunnel mode, the original destination, port numbers, and other information are not visible.

Figure 8-11 illustrates the possible combinations of protection and transport with IPSec.

From this short description, you know that the type of protection you want is somewhere between these two. You want a signature to protect the entire packet, not just the header, but you do not want the packet to be encrypted, just signed. IPSec allows this type of protection by using *NULL encryption* with ESP. This means that the ESP signature over the entire packet will be generated, but the packet will not be encrypted (although it is still encapsulated inside a tunnel).

Figure 8-11 *Transport Versus Tunnel Mode in IPSec*

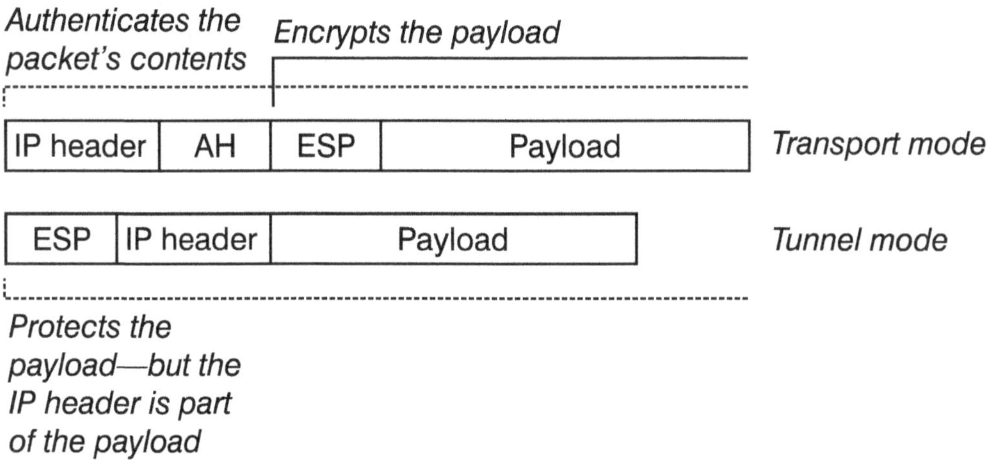

The problem with IPSec, from a routing protocol perspective, is twofold:

- IPSec requires a sizeable amount of overhead in terms of tunneling packets. A router must build a packet and then encapsulate it within another IP header before sending it. The receiving router must remove the "outer" IP header (if IPSec is running in tunnel mode) in the decryption process to retrieve and process the actual data that is transmitted in the packet.

- IPSec is designed for point-to-point communications. Using IPSec for multicast traffic is difficult to configure and maintain.

These two problems push IPSec toward usefulness for only one routing protocol, BGP. Because BGP builds peering sessions over point-to-point TCP sessions, the IPSec design works well with BGP sessions, particularly eBGP. Some work is progressing to make IPSec perform well in multicast environments, but the requirement to tunnel routing protocol packets to gain a signature over the entire contents of the packet might require too much processing for the speed of data flows and processing time needs of routing protocols.

Protecting Routers from Denial-of-Service Attacks

Denial of service (DoS) attacks, in common usage, are attacks that attempt to make a device unreachable by flooding the device with difficult-to-process packets. The general idea is that the attacker can exhaust one of the various resources (memory, processing time, buffer space, and so on) of the victim so that the victim cannot receive and process packets. This in turn makes the device unavailable for its normal operations.

DoS attacks tend to be effective in part because they are so hard to defend against. For instance, adding encryption to a link does not really protect a device from a DoS attack. In fact, adding encryption generally makes a DoS easier to execute, because the intended victims require more processing time and memory for each packet received. The sections that follow cover two possible but imperfect defenses against DOS attacks:

- Edge filters
- The Generalized TTL Security Mechanism (GTSM)

Edge Filters

The first line of defense against a DoS attack is good filtering at the edges of your network. Although filtering based on the IP addresses of specific routers within your network might not work well, you can filter based on the types of traffic that are allowed into the network.

By default, your network should not allow Interior Gateway Protocol (IGP) traffic at any edge, including user attachment points. You should not be using an IGP to connect to an outside network under normal circumstances (see the section, "Use an Exterior Gateway Protocol for all Extranet Connections," later in this chapter), so IGP packets do not need to pass through any edge or along any connection to an untrusted device.

You can use two mechanisms to filter IGP traffic at the edge of your network:

- By destination IP address
- By protocol type

For instance, you can filter all OSPF traffic based on the OSPF IP addresses, 224.0.0.5 and 224.0.0.6, or you can filter OSPF traffic at the edge of your network by filtering OSPF type IP packets. Filtering traffic by type rather than destination address is more effective, because you can direct these packets at unicast or directed broadcast addresses and at the "correct" multicast address for the protocol.

The Generalized TTL Security Mechanism

The Generalized TTL Security Mechanism (GTSM) was originally conceived as a mechanism to prevent DoS attacks against eBGP peers, especially along the "customer facing edge" of an Internet service provider network. Because of this, GTSM was originally called the *BGP TTL Security Hack (BTSH)*, but it has been generalized for use in many other situations, including with other routing protocols, Network Time Protocol, and so on. Figure 8-12 illustrates how GTSM works.

Figure 8-12 *Generalized TTL Security Mechanism*

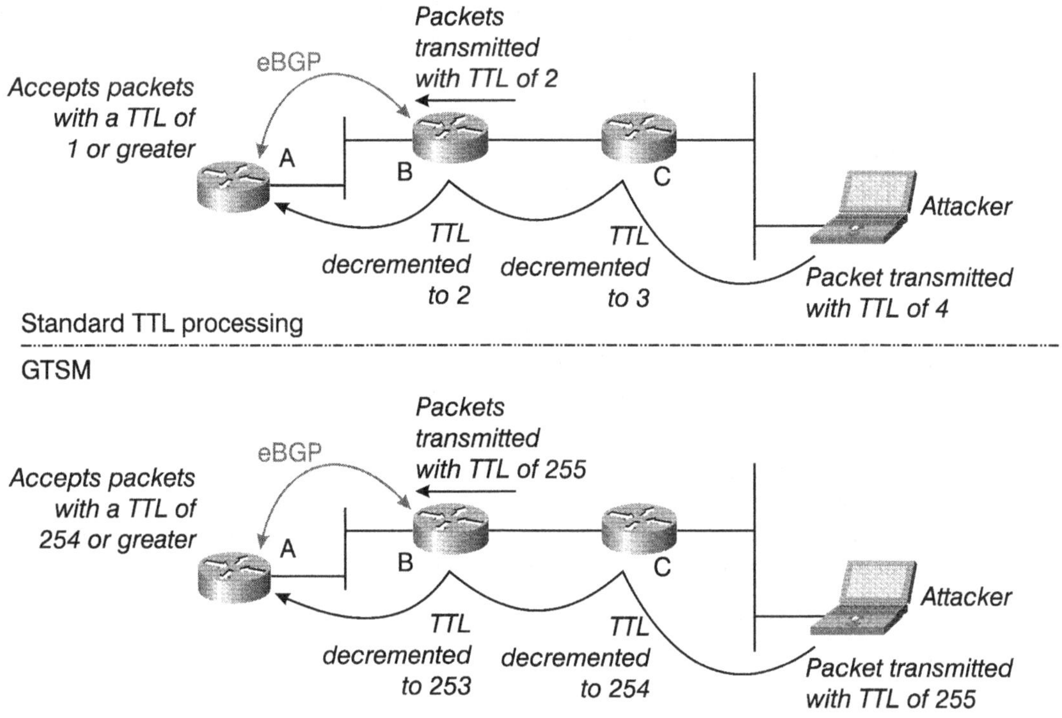

In this network, Routers A and B are running eBGP, and an attacker who would like to disrupt the eBGP peering session is attached to Router C. In normal IP processing, Router A generates IP packets for the eBGP peering session with a TTL of 2, meaning that the packet cannot travel through more than two routers before being discarded.

NOTE   The Time to Live (TTL) mechanism was originally conceived as a way to limit the damage possible from packets being caught in a forwarding loop.

Router A, after receiving packets, checks to make certain that the TTL is at least 1, and then it processes them. An attacker can generate packets with a TTL of 4 in this network and be assured that Router A will receive and process them. That is because the TTL of the attacker's packets is still more than 1 when the packets reach Router A.

GTSM shifts the numbers used in the TTL number space to the other end. Router A is now configured to accept packets of only a certain type—in this case BGP packets—if they have a

TTL greater than 254. Router B generates its BGP packets with a TTL of 255 so that when they reach Router A, they still have a TTL high enough for Router A to accept and process them.

However, the attacker cannot generate a packet with a high enough TTL so that Router A will accept and process its packets. The attacker cannot generate a packet with a TTL higher than 255, and Router C always decrements the TTL on IP packets that it forwards; therefore, the attacker cannot attack Router A directly. Any attacker who attempts to attack Router A through BGP must be connected to Router A.

If the BGP session passes through multiple hops, Router A can set its minimum TTL to a number lower than 254. Doing so allows attackers within the "TTL scope" to attack, too, but GTSM can still limit the range from which an attacker can operate.

GTSM is described in RFC 3682, "The Generalized TTL Security Mechanism" (Gill, 2004). Cisco has applied GTSM to BGP and is planning to apply it to EIGRP, OSPF, and Network Time Protocol (NTP). Other IETF Internet-Drafts have been written applying GTSM to the Label Distribution Protocol (LDP) used in Multiprotocol Label Switching (MPLS) and other protocols.

To configure GTSM for BGP peering sessions on Cisco IOS Software, use the following command in BGP configuration mode:

```
neighbor neighbor-address ttl-security hops hop-count
```

Protecting Routing Information

Beyond protecting peering relationships, you should attempt to protect the information that is carried within the routing system. This section covers three areas:

- Connections to business partners
- Connections to the Internet
- Connections to hosts and servers within the network

Extranet Connections

Prime points at which an attacker can inject false routing information into your network are at extranet connections. These are places where your network connects to networks outside your administrative control, primarily for business-to-business transactions or information sharing. Examples of these types of connections include connections to outside services, such as an outside financial company providing payroll or other financial services, a supplier where the connection is used for automatic reorders, and other systems and customers to whom you provide services. These types of connections tend to be prime points for false routing information to be injected because they represent trusted relationships, generally using an interior gateway protocol to exchange routing information.

In fact, such connections can be the source of many internal routing problems, regardless of whether they are intentional. Figure 8-13 illustrates two such possible situations.

Figure 8-13 *Possible Impacts of Exchanging Routing Information with Outside Networks*

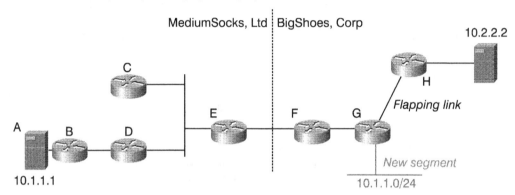

MediumSocks, Ltd., has an inventory-sharing arrangement with BigShoes Corp. To facilitate this agreement, the two companies have set up an extranet connection between their networks, shown here between Routers E and F. MediumSocks has a server, 10.1.1.1, that has long been used for internal purposes and is not reachable to hosts in the BigShoes network. BigShoes does not know that MediumSocks is using the 10.1.1.0/24 range of addresses, and BigShoes sets up a new segment, 10.1.1.0/24, attached to Router G. When this segment is advertised into BigShoes' routing protocol, it is also advertised into MediumSocks' network, becoming the preferred path, at Router C, to 10.1.1.0/24. This cuts off internal access to the 10.1.1.1 server from behind Router C in the MediumSocks network. Although you can resolve this problem by using simple route filtering at the Router E to F border between the two companies, it is not always simple to find this sort of problem or to remember to configure filtering at the edge when a new subnet is added so that the problem does not occur again in the future.

Another problem with sharing routing information in this way is the impact that changes in one network have on the other network. For instance, suppose that the server MediumSocks hosts actually interact with is 10.2.2.2, behind Router H. The Router G to H link becomes unstable, flapping constantly; each time it flaps, the MediumSocks network must converge to account for this change in network topology.

Both of these cases demonstrate the impact of simple misconfigurations, miscoordination, or failing links, which are normal events. However, you can also use these sorts of events as attacks against the network routing system. Thus, you should use techniques to prevent these types of network events in another network from causing damage to your network. The sections that follow cover techniques to protect your network from attacks or to keep routing information from other routing domains from causing problems in your network.

Use an Exterior Gateway Protocol for All Extranet Connections

The cardinal rule for all connections to extranets is never to use an IGP to dynamically exchange routing information with an outside routing domain. Always use Exterior Gateway Protocols (EGPs) or static routes, rather than dynamically exchanging routing information through an IGP. Because many network administrators find it unacceptable to use static routes, primarily because of redundancy and resiliency reasons, this discussion focuses on using an EGP, BGP, to exchange routing information with an outside routing domain.

Using BGP to exchange just a handful of routes might seem overly protective, but consider these facts:

- BGP is designed to handle the rapid changes that are involved in dealing with routing information outside the control of the local network administrator.

- A great deal of research has gone into security for the BGP protocol because it is such a widely used EGP. EGPs operate between routing domains, which means they operate between mutually defensive parties. In contrast, IGPs operate within a single, trusted, administrative domain.

- Because BGP is an EGP, administrators can build and act on policies, rather than just on reachability information.

Based on these facts, you should use BGP when exchanging routing information with any routing domain that is outside your administrative control, if static routes will not suffice.

NOTE   In the case of the provider edge/customer edge (PE/CE), the service provider does not accept external routing information into its IGP. Instead, this information is redistributed into BGP in a specific way so that the routes can be redistributed back into the IGP of the customer without losing the original routing information.

Filter Routes Aggressively at the Extranet Edge

Filtering at the network edge should be based on allowing the minimum necessary, rather than accepting everything except a few selected networks. In other words, filters that are used to limit the routes learned through BGP at the network edge should deny all routes by default, permitting only those that are necessary to reach the hosts and servers needed in each network.

Beyond this basic filtering, make certain that your outside peer does not advertise your routes to other peers again. Although it is impossible to guarantee this, you can mark the routes you advertise to your extranet peer with the NO_EXPORT community, which instructs their routers not to advertise the route to any of their external peers.

NOTE   For the NO_EXPORT community to work, you must configure **neighbor** [*neighbor-address*] **send-community** on every neighbor to which you are sending this advertisement.

Assuming that your outside connections are not designed to allow those outside networks to transit your network to another destination (which is true of most enterprise networks), you should refuse to accept any routes from an extranet peer that does not originate within the extranet and refuse to propagate any route learned from an extranet peer to any other external BGP peers you might have configured. The easiest way to accomplish both of these tasks is to use AS Path filters on every eBGP peering session in your network. Effectively, you want to filter any routes you receive that have an AS Path length greater than 1 (or any AS Path that contains more than one autonomous system), and you want to prevent your edge routers from advertising any routes that do not originate within your autonomous system (any route that has an AS Path length of greater than 1) .

Dampen Prefixes Aggressively at the Extranet Edge

Route dampening is designed to prevent constant changes in a single prefix learned from an eBGP peer from destabilizing the local routing system. This can specifically address concerns about constantly changing routing information, impacting the stability and convergence times of local routing.

The route dampening parameters given in most examples are not aggressive enough for most extranet connections, however. You will probably want to dampen routes you have learned from an extranet much more quickly than routes you have learned from an Internet Service Provider (ISP) for two reasons:

- The AS Path of routes learned from an extranet peer should only be 1. That means convergence times should be quick, and little of the characteristic churn normally involved in large internetwork convergence should be present.
- The routing information learned from an extranet peer is typically redistributed back into an IGP to facilitate reachability from the interior of your network to the extranet destinations (unless you are running BGP on all routers along the path to networks requiring reachability to the destinations in the extranet) .

BGP route flap dampening has five parameters:

```
bgp dampening half-life-period reuse-threshold suppress-threshold maximum-
    suppress-time restart-penalty
```

It is important to consider how many times a route should flap before dampening it, and how long you want it to be dampened before you allow it to be reinstalled in the routing table. You probably want the route to be suppressed rapidly, but you also want it to be advertised again in a fairly short period of time after it stops flapping. You also want to omit it from the table for as long as it is flapping.

Limiting Route Count at the Extranet Edge

Extranet connections tend to have a limited scope. There exists a set of well-defined routes that are accepted, so it is relatively easy to know, with some margin of error, how many routes you should be receiving over an extranet connection. One other filter you can implement on your network edge to prevent an outside network from flooding your network with extraneous network information, possibly overloading your network, is to limit the number of routes that your routers can learn through BGP from the extranet.

Generally, you should set the maximum number of prefixes accepted to a low number. For example, if you would normally expect the number of prefixes received across the BGP session with an extranet to be less than 20, you set the maximum number of prefixes allowed to 30. Doing so permits some change in the partner network and provides some protection for your network.

Connections to the Internet

Connections to the Internet are often treated in the same way that connections to extranets are treated; however, you must consider several differences between the two, including these:

- Route filtering
- Protecting the local network from becoming a transit
- Different parameters in route dampening

Some of these issues are not directly related to security, so they are touched on here only to give a complete picture of BGP use when connecting to an ISP.

For more information on general recommendations when connecting to an ISP, see RFC 3013, "Recommended Internet Service Provider Security Services and Procedures," (Killalea, 2000).

Route Filtering

Route filtering is important for network security when you are connecting to the Internet through a service provider, but generally it is a different type of filtering from what is applied to extranet connections. Rather than denying all routes by default and permitting only a limited number of routes, you want to permit most routes, denying only specific routes. The routes you want to deny are these:

- Internal routes, or anything that you advertise out toward the service provider, should be filtered so that you cannot relearn those destinations from the service provider.
- Private address space, defined in RFC 1918, "Address Allocation for Private Internets," (Rekhter, 1996).
- Other addresses that are not used, or otherwise should not be accepted, called *bogons*. For more information on bogons, see The Team Cymru Bogon Reference Page at http://www.cymru.com/Bogons/.

Protecting Against Transit

If a network is connected to two ISPs, it is possible for the two ISPs to see the network as a transit network, capable of passing traffic between the two ISPs; Figure 8-14 illustrates.

Figure 8-14   *Two Service Providers Transiting Traffic Through an Enterprise Customer*

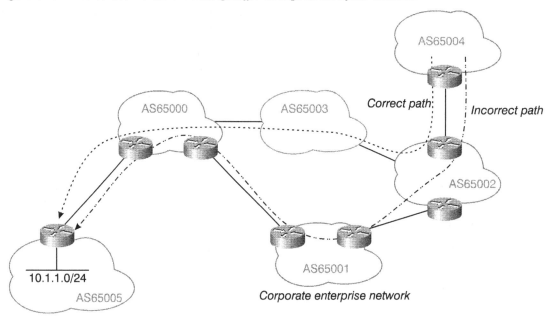

Traffic that is sourced from inside AS65004 and destined to 10.1.1.0/24 should travel to AS65002, a service provider, and then through AS65003, another service provider, to AS65000, and finally to AS65005. However, it is possible for traffic to flow from AS65004 to AS65002, and then through AS65001 to AS65000 to AS65005, using the corporate network of AS65001 as a transit between AS65002 and AS65000. It is important for the routers at the edge of AS65001 to be configured to prevent routing information learned from AS65000 from being advertised to AS65002, and to prevent routing information learned from AS65002 from being advertised to AS65000. Otherwise, AS65001 could become a transit for this (or any other) traffic.

The simplest method that AS65001 can use to prevent becoming a transit between AS65000 and AS65002 is to configure route filters on its edges (peering sessions) with the two service providers. On the BGP peering sessions at its edges, the network administrator of AS65001 can implement the configuration in Example 8-2.

Example 8-2   *AS Path Filters to Prevent Transit*

```
!
ip as-path access-list 1 permit ^$
!
route-map prevent-transit permit 10
 match as-path 1
!
router BGP 650001
 neighbor x.x.x.x route-map prevent-transit out
 ....
```

This short **as-path access-list** only permits routes that have an empty AS Path to be advertised to the eBGP peers along the edge of AS65001. This effectively permits only routes that originate within AS65001 to be advertised outside the autonomous system.

Route Dampening

The primary difference when using route dampening on a connection to an Internet service provider versus using route flap dampening on a connection to a partner is the aggressiveness of the dampening parameters. For more information on the recommended route dampening parameters when connecting to an ISP, see *RIPE Routing-WG Recommendations for Coordinated Route-flap Damping Parameters (ripe-229)*, located at http://www.ripe.net/ripe/docs/ripe-229.html.

Future Directions in Routing Protocol Security

Routing protocol security is an area of intense research, with many new ideas being considered and new systems designed. This section covers two specific mechanisms currently under development:

- 802.1x
- Secure Origin BGP (soBGP)

Protecting Against Illegitimate Devices Joining the Routing Domain

The earlier section, "Protecting Routers from Denial-of-Service Attacks," discussed manually configured filters to prevent an unauthorized server or host connected to the user segments of the network from sending routing information. Manually filtering based on packet type along the network edge shares the problems that all manually configured filtering mechanisms share; however, the filters are only as good as the humans who configure and maintain them. Figure 8-15 shows how 802.1x works.

Figure 8-15 *802.1x Operation*

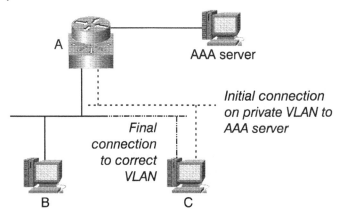

When Host C first connects, Router A, shown here in a Layer 3 switch, places it on a *private VLAN*, which allows the host to communicate only with Router A and no other devices on the network. Router A sends an authentication/authorization request to the AAA server, and the AAA server returns a challenge to Router A. This challenge is passed on to the connecting host, which replies, and the reply is forwarded to the AAA server.

The AAA server reply contains the correct VLAN to place the newly connected host in; Router A configures the port that the host is connecting to in the proper VLAN based on this information.

New extensions are being considered for the 802.1x mechanism to allow the AAA server to pass a set of filters back to the requesting router. This will allow the router to automatically filter out all traffic that the host should not be sending, such as routing protocol packets. This sort of mechanism will tie the ability to send routing protocol packets onto the network to the AAA records set up by the network administrator, rather than to the port.

Secure Origin BGP (soBGP)

Following are two goals to address when considering security in terms of BGP:

- **Is the autonomous system that originates the destination (prefix) authorized to advertise it?**—In other words, if a router receives an advertisement for the 10.1.1.0/24 network originating in AS65500, can you verify that AS65500 is supposed to be advertising 10.1.1.0/24?

- **Does the autonomous system that is advertising the destination actually have a path to the destination?**—In other words, if a router is receiving an advertisement from a BGP peer in AS65501 for 10.1.1.0/24, can you verify that AS65501 actually has a path to the autonomous system originating at 10.1.1.0/24?

This section describes soBGP as a security system providing a deployable, robust mechanism for meeting these two goals.

Begin at the Beginning: Who Are You?

The first step in securing anything is authentication; each participant must have some way of knowing who the other participants are and what information they will be using to sign or encrypt their data. This is a classic problem in cryptography, called *key distribution*. You must have a way to receive keys to sign or encrypt data and then to validate that the keys received actually belong to the participant you believe they belong to.

This problem is addressed in soBGP using an *EntityCert*, which ties an autonomous system number to a public key (or a set of public keys) corresponding to a private key that the autonomous system will be using to sign various other certificates. An EntityCert is defined in soBGP as an X.509v3 certificate, similar to those used by Transport Layer Security (TLS) and IPSec. The main problem you face when accepting an EntityCert is knowing whether the key that is carried within the certificate is actually the key of the advertising autonomous system.

soBGP resolves this uncertainty by requiring a third party to sign the EntityCert, validating that this autonomous system actually belongs with this key. Then you can use a small number of "root keys" distributed out of band to validate a set of advertised EntityCerts. These are used in turn to build up the database of known good autonomous system/key pairs in the system, allowing even more EntityCerts to be validated. Thus, EntityCerts can form a web of trust, built on the public keys of a small number of well-known entities, such as top-level backbone service providers, key authentication service providers (such as VeriSign), and others, as Figure 8-16 illustrates.

Figure 8-16   *Web of Trust*

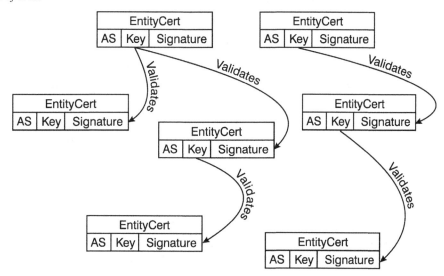

<table>
<tr><td>NOTE</td><td>Although any third party can sign an EntityCert, the receiver has to trust the signer. It is much like your mother telling you to trust the local baker. You are likely to put more faith in your mom's recommendation than someone you just met off the street.</td></tr>
</table>

The key that each autonomous system distributes in its EntityCert is actually the public half of a private/public key pair. An autonomous system keeps its private key entirely private, holding it on one highly secure device in its network (which is not even required to be online), and generates signatures for other certificates as needed. Only the public key of an autonomous system is ever exposed in this way, so no special protection mechanisms (for example, tamper-resistant hardware) are required at any border to prevent private keys from being compromised.

The First Goal: Are You Authorized?

You have distributed a public key per autonomous system, so you can now build a certificate providing authorization for an autonomous system to advertise a specific block of addresses. This authorization is provided through an *Authorization Certificate*, or *AuthCert*. An AuthCert ties an autonomous system to a block of addresses that the autonomous system can advertise, as Figure 8-17 illustrates.

Starting at the top of the illustration, some autonomous system (AS) has authorized AS65000 to advertise prefixes within the block 10.0.0.0/8. The AuthCert is signed using the authorizing AS key. To delegate some part of this block of address space to another autonomous system, AS65001, AS65000 builds an AuthCert tying 10.1.0.0/16 to AS65001. AS65001, in turn, suballocates a smaller part of this address space to AS65002 by building an AuthCert tying AS65002 to 10.1.1.0/24.

Any device that is receiving these three AuthCerts can check them by doing the following:

- Looking up the public key of the authorizer and verifying the signature on the AuthCert
- Making certain the authorizer is permitted to advertise the address space from which it has suballocated this block of address space

The device then builds a local table of address blocks and corresponding autonomous systems authorized to advertise prefixes within those address blocks. You can check received updates against this database to verify the originating autonomous system authorization to advertise a prefix.

Blocks of address space are used here, rather than individual prefixes; an AuthCert can authorize an autonomous system to advertise any number of prefixes within a block of addresses. This reduces the number of certificates within the system, thereby reducing overall cryptographic processing requirements. If a specific AS desires per-prefix authorization, it can build individual AuthCerts for each allocated prefix, rather than for blocks of address space.

Figure 8-17   *Authorization Example*

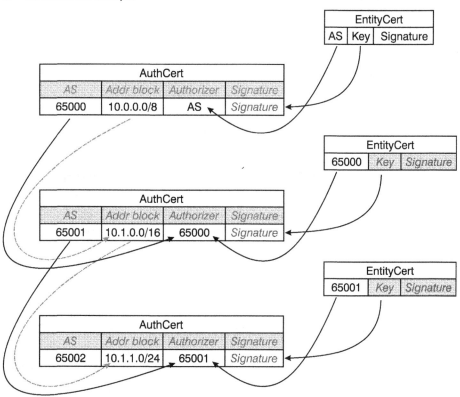

AuthCerts are not advertised as independent certificates within soBGP; instead, they are wrapped in a *PrefixPolicyCert*. PrefixPolicyCerts contain an AuthCert, a set of policies the originator would like to apply to prefixes advertised within this block of addresses, and a signature generated using the authorized private key of the autonomous system. PrefixPolicyCerts can include the longest prefix length allowed within the address block, a list of autonomous systems that might not be or must be in the AS Path of routes to destinations within the address block, or other policies.

In reality, the per-prefix policies that are available to the originator are limitless; the main problem is enforcing those policies when other autonomous systems receive them.

The Second Goal: Do You Really Have a Path?

Thesecond goal is to be able to verify that the advertiser of a given route actually has a path to the destination. This goal is met in soBGP by building a topology map of the entire path of the internetwork. Each autonomous system that is attached to the internetwork builds an

ASPolicyCert, which contains, primarily, a list of its peers, and is signed using the private key of the originator. Using this list of transit peers, you can build a map of the internetwork topology, as Figure 8-18 illustrates.

Figure 8-18 *Connectivity Graph Example*

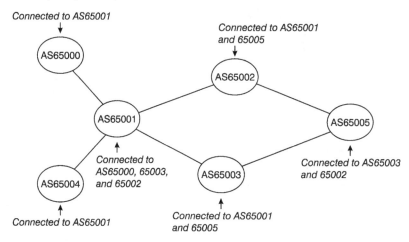

If AS65005 receives an update from AS65002, claiming it can reach a destination in AS65000 through the path {65002, 65001, 65000}, it can do the following:

- Check to make certain that AS65002 claims to be connected to AS65001 in its ASPolicyCert, and AS65001 claims to be connected to AS65002 in its ASPolicyCert.
- Check to make certain that AS65001 claims to be connected to AS65000 in its ASPolicyCert, and AS65000 claims to be connected to AS65001 in its ASPolicyCert.

If, for instance, AS65002 claims a path to a destination inside AS65000 through the path {65002, 65000}, AS65002 would be able to discover the path was invalid, because AS65000 does not claim to be connected to AS65002. This simple two-way connectivity check along a graph can be mixed with various policy statements—stating a specific peer is not a transit, is not advertising certain peers, and so on—to provide a much wider range of policies than AS Path-based methods.

NOTE   For more information on soBGP, please see the following IETF Internet-Drafts:

- Architecture and Deployment Considerations for Secure Origin BGP (soBGP), draft-white-sobgparchitecture-00

- Extensions to BGP Transport soBGP Certificates, draft-ng-sobgp-bgpextensions-00

- Secure Origin BGP (soBGP) Certificates, draft-weis-sobgp-certificates-02.txt

All these drafts are works in progress, rather than accepted, or deployed, solutions. Several articles in various industry publications are available on this topic, too.

Review Questions

1 What is authentication?

2 How is authorization different from authentication?

3 What two things are normally used to prove authentication?

4 What three things determine the strength of transited authentication?

5 Is it possible, in a routing system, to authorize someone to readvertise a prefix you are advertising to him?

6 Why are humans an important part of any security system?

7 What are the primary attacks available against a routing system?

8 What is the primary line of defense available to protect the legitimacy of a routing system?

9 Why is it that packet filters that block access to router addresses from outside the routing domain do not work well in most networks?

10 What is your primary line of defense against DoS attacks on routers?

11 What is the difference between a device that is running GTSM and one that is not running GTSM in terms of the TTL check for packets received?

12 What routing protocol should you use when connecting to outside networks?

13 What steps can you take to protect your routing information at the network edge?

References

Cisco 50960 (2004). "Cisco Security Advisory: TCP Vulnerabilities in Multiple IOS-Based Cisco Products." Downloaded from http://www.cisco.com/warp/public/707/cisco-sa-20040420-tcp-ios.shtml. August 2004.

Convery, Sean and Matthew Franz (2002). "BGP Vulnerability Testing: Separating Fact from FUD v1.1." Downloaded from http://www.blackhat.com/presentations/bh-usa-03/bh-us-03-convery-franz-v3.pdf. August 2004.

Coulton, R., D. Ferguson, and J. Moy. RFC 2740, "OSPF Version 3." 1999.

Gill, V., J. Heasley, and D. Meyer. RFC 3682, "The Generalized TTL Security Mechanism (GTSM)." 2004.

Heffernan, A. RFC 2385, "Protection of BGP Sessions via the TCP MD5 Signature Option." 1998.

Killalea, T. RFC 3013, "Recommended Internet Service Provider Security Services and Procedures." 2000.

Leech, M. RFC 3562, "Key Management Considerations for the TCP MD5 Signature Option." 2003.

Li, T. and R. Atkison. RFC 3567, "Intermediate System to Intermediate System (IS-IS) Cryptographic Authentication." 2003.

Moy, J. RFC 2328, "OSPF Version 2." 1998.

Rekhter, Y., B. Moskowitz, D. Karrenberg, G.J. de Groot, and E. Lear. RFC 1918, "Address Allocation for Private Internets." 1996.

Rivest, R. RFC 1321, "The MD5 Message-Digest Algorithm." 2002.

Schneier, Bruce. *Beyond Fear.* New York: Copernicus Books, 2003.

Wang, X., D. Feng, X. Lai, and H. Yu (2004). "Collisions for Hash Functions MD4, MD5, HAVAL-128, and RIPEMD." Downloaded from http://eprint.iacr.org/2004/199.pdf, August 2004.

Watson, Paul (Tony) (2004). "Slipping in the Window: TCP Reset Attacks." Downloaded from http://www.osvdb.org/reference/SlippingInTheWindow_v1.0.doc, August 2004. Other references include http://osvdb.org/displayvuln.php?osvdb_id=4030.

White, R., B. Akyol, and N. Feamster (2004). "Considerations in Validating the Path in Routing Protocols," draft-white-pathconsiderations-02.txt.

White, R (2004). "SAFE: Best Practices for Securing Routing Protocols." Downloaded from http://www.cisco.com/en/US/netsol/ns340/ns394/ns171/ns128/networking_solutions_white_paper09186a008020b51d.shtml, August 2004.

White, R. (2003). "Securing BGP Through Secure Origin BGP." *The Internet Protocol Journal*, September 2003. Downloaded from http://www.cisco.com/en/US/about/ac123/ac147/ac174/ac236/about_cisco_ipj_archive_article09186a00801c5a9b.html, August 2004.

CHAPTER 9

Virtual Private Networks

Virtual private networks (VPNs) of all types are a growing area of network design and deployment. VPNs are used for a wide variety of tasks, from connecting remote users to the corporate network to interconnecting corporate sites. Using VPNs to interconnect sites, building a network on top of a service provider infrastructure, is the focus of this chapter.

NOTE   This chapter does not cover carrying VPN information through routing protocols, such as how Open Shortest Path First (OSPF) and Intermediate System-to-Intermediate System (IS-IS) interact with Multiprotocol Label Switching (MPLS) to create MPLS/traffic engineering (TE).

The chapter begins with a look at three options for routing over an MPLS VPN and then delves into IPSec and general routing encapsulation (GRE) tunnels and some of the implications of routing over these types of tunnels in a network. The chapter concludes with a look at the Next Hop Resolution Protocol (NHRP) and the interaction between NHRP and GRE tunnels.

MPLS

MPLS originated with the Cisco mechanism of *tag switching*, which involved switching IP packets over ATM networks. MPLS has grown beyond ATM networks and is now used in purely routed networks as a way for service providers to transport customer traffic with overlapping addresses across their network. This chapter does not cover much on the service provider side of MPLS; rather, it focuses on the design and deployment issues for a customer who is using one of the various MPLS offerings from a service provider.

NOTE   For more information on the service provider, or Border Gateway Protocol (BGP), side of MPLS deployments, refer to these resources:

- *MPLS and VPN Architectures*, by Ivan Pepelnjak and Jim Guichard (Cisco Press, 2002)

- *Traffic Engineering with MPLS*, by Eric Osborne and Ajay Simha (Cisco Press, 2002)

- *Practical BGP*, by Danny McPherson, Srihari Sangli, and Russ White (Addison-Wesley Professional, 2004)

This section begins with a review of some MPLS basics and then covers three styles, or modes, of routing through an MPLS tunnel network:

- Overlay
- Peer-to-peer
- BGP/MPLS

MPLS Basics

MPLS was originally conceived as a mechanism to improve switching speed. In fact, if you look through the MPLS chapter of *Advanced IP Network Design* (Retana 1999), you would find that this was the primary reason given for using MPLS in the core of a network. Since 1999, though, much has happened in the routing and switching worlds. Two primary events have happened:

- IP switching has caught up to, or kept pace with, switching based on a flow label. Through the use of specialized application-specific integrated circuits (ASICs), routers have been able to catch up to, and in some cases, surpass, the speed at which switches operate. In fact, the entire concept of a "Layer 3 switch" is based on a router being able to forward packets as fast as a switch.

- A market in VPNs has grown where none existed before. In the "bad old days" of network design, the only way to interconnect two geographically separated locations was through some sort of private line, or perhaps a Frame Relay circuit. Today, service providers allow customers to build VPNs across the service provider infrastructure, giving enterprises a way to build long-distance circuits without paying the cost of installing and maintaining a dedicated line.

Another reason that service providers prefer to use VPNs to build interconnections between their customer sites is that traffic injected at one end of a VPN always follows the same path through the network. In other words, VPNs switch traffic along a deterministic path, whereas IP packets can be switched along one of several paths through a network. This determinism makes it easier to engineer the flow of traffic across a large-scale network.

Figure 9-1 provides an illustration of a network as the basis for the discussion that follows on how an MPLS network works.

Figure 9-1   *Simple Network Illustrating Switching by Tags*

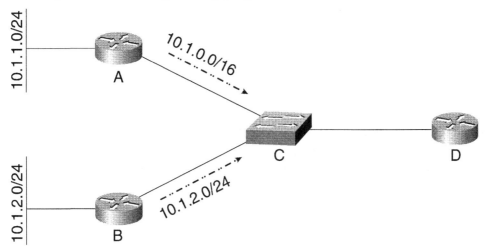

Because Router A is advertising a summary and Router B is a component within that summary, Router C has two entries in its routing table:

- 10.1.0.0/16 via A
- 10.1.2.0/24 via B

These two entries are passed to Router D, so it will also have two entries in its table:

- 10.1.0.0/16 via C
- 10.1.2.0/24 via C

If Router D receives a packet that is destined to 10.1.2.1, it first finds two matches for this destination. It must compare the prefix length of these two matches to determine the best path.

Instead of using the IP address to switch the packet, these routers could assign labels to represent each hop along the path and then switch based on these labels.

For instance, assume the following to be true:

- Router A assigns the label 100 to the destination 10.1.0.0/16, which it is advertising to Router C.
- Router B assigns the label 200 to the destination 10.1.1.0/24, which it is advertising to Router C.
- Router C assigns the label 300 to 10.1.0.0/16 and advertises this upstream to Router D.
- Router C assigns the label 400 to 10.2.0.0/16 and advertises this along to Router D.

When Router D receives a packet that is destined to 10.1.2.1, it notes that this route corresponds to 10.1.0.0/16, which is labeled 400. Therefore, Router D marks the packet with the label 400 and forwards it to Router C. Instead of looking at the destination address and choosing the next hop based on the longest prefix match from the IP routing table, Router C looks up the label, 400, and sees that this belongs 10.1.0.0/16, which is labeled 100. Router C swaps the labels and passes along the packet.

Router B, when it receives the packet, sees from the label (200) that this packet is destined to a directly attached subnet, strips the label off the packet, and forwards it normally.

Overlay Routing over MPLS VPNs

The simplest way to use MPLS VPNs is to treat them as simple point-to-point links or tunnels, running an Interior Gateway Protocol (IGP) directly over them. Figure 9-2 illustrates this type of network.

Figure 9-2   *Overlaying Routing onto an MPLS VPN*

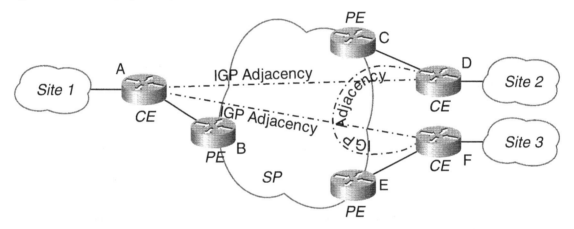

This network shows two types of routers:

- **Provider edge (PE) routers**—The last routers owned and maintained by the service provider, these are also the demarcation point between the customer network and the service provider network. The MPLS tunnels through the service provider network are terminated on the PE routers. In Figure 9-2, Routers B, C, and E are PE routers.

- **Customer edge (CE) routers**—The last routers owned and maintained by the customer. In Figure 9-2, Routers A, D, and E are CE routers.

When you overlay routing on top of an MPLS VPN, CE routers form direct neighbor relationships (or adjacencies) with other CE routers that are connected to the MPLS network.

If the MPLS network is set up as a set of hub-and-spoke tunnels, the spoke CEs peer only with the hub CE, and the hub CE peers with all the spoke CEs. This configuration has the same advantages and disadvantages as a hub-and-spoke network over a Frame Relay cloud or other media. This setup reduces the number of neighbor adjacencies configured and built, but it also forces traffic between the spoke sites to pass through the hub site.

If the MPLS network is set up as a full or partial mesh of tunnels, the CEs peer with every other CE that is connected to the MPLS cloud. This allows communication between each site directly, but it can require many neighbor adjacencies to be built and maintained if the number of sites is high.

When you overlay routing over the MPLS tunnels, it looks just like routing over any Layer 2 circuit technology.

Peer-to-Peer (Redistributed) Routing over MPLS VPNs

Instead of building IGP adjacencies through the MPLS cloud, you can redistribute customer routes into BGP at the CE or PE router, carry them through the service provider network, and then redistribute them back into the customer IGP, as Figure 9-3 illustrates.

Figure 9-3   *Peer-to-Peer Routing Through an MPLS VPN*

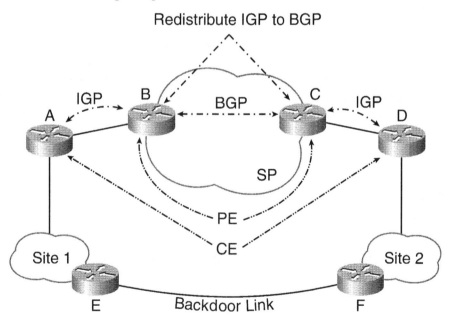

Here, the customer is passing its routes to the PE through an IGP, and the PE is redistributing between the IGP and BGP. Each CE router now peers only with a single PE, rather than with all the other CEs, through the MPLS VPN. This makes the MPLS VPNs more scalable than a full or partial mesh of point-to-point or point-to-multipoint links and routing adjacencies.

The peer-to-peer solution for carrying customer routes across the MPLS VPN does have some major problems, however:

- Redistribution loops are a real danger if more than one redistribution point exists between BGP and the customer IGP at any given customer site. Routes can be redistributed from BGP into the customer IGP, pass through the customer site, and then be redistributed back into BGP, possibly causing a routing loop. To resolve this, you need to employ filtering or route tags at any point where IGP-to-BGP redistribution is configured.

- Backdoor links cause major problems in this situation. Assume that a route is injected into the network shown at Site 1 and carried as an internal route through the backdoor link into Site 2. This route is also redistributed into BGP at Router B. From Router B, the route is carried through BGP to Router C and then redistributed back into the customer IGP at Router D. If you examine the local IGP tables on Router F, you find an internal route learned from Router E and an external route learned from Router D. The internal route is always chosen over the external route, and the backdoor link is always preferred over the MPLS VPN link, which probably is not what the network designer intended. To get around this, you can force all the routes to be external or use some other technique to force the path over the MPLS VPN to be used.

- Overlapping customer routes cannot be supported in the service provider network. If two customers redistribute the same route into the service provider BGP at separate PEs, one of the two routes is always chosen over the other one, causing reachability failure for one of the two customers. BGP can choose and propagate only one route to any given destination through a network (except in some special cases, such as load sharing).

BGP/MPLS VPNs were designed to resolve the scaling problems of overlaying an IGP on top of an MPLS VPN cloud and the problems associated with redistributing routes into BGP, through the service provider network. The section that follows examines how BGP/MPLS VPNs work.

BGP/MPLS VPNs

BGP/MPLS VPNs are similar to the peer-to-peer redistribution model of passing routes through a service provider network, with two critical differences:

- Each customer route is carried through BGP separately, so no two customer routes are mixed up.

- Routes that are redistributed into BGP have additional information tagged onto them, so they can be retrieved from BGP without losing the route information carried within the customer IGP.

Figure 9-4 illustrates the process of carrying a route through a service provider network using a BGP/MPLS VPN.

Figure 9-4   *Carrying Routes Through a BGP/MPLS VPN*

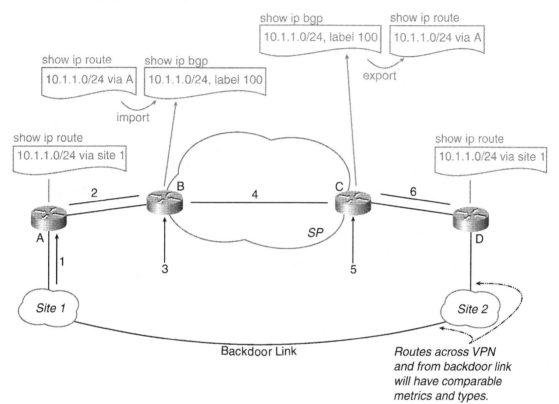

The following list documents the transactions that occur, beginning with a route originating within Site 1 and passed to Router A through some IGP, and following it through the service provider network to Site 2.

1   The route originates with a router within Site 1.

2   Router A, the CE, distributes the route through an IGP to Router B.

3   Router B, the PE, accepts the route and places it in a VPN routing/forwarding (VRF) table.

The route is imported from the VRF into BGP on Router B. In this process, the route is marked with a route target, a route distinguisher, and a set of communities indicating the IGP cost and other information (such as whether the route was an internal or an external route).

4   The route is carried through BGP to Router C. The route is not installed in any of the routing tables of the intermediate router. The assumption is that an MPLS VPN tunnel exists between Routers B and C to carry the traffic between the two PEs, so it is unnecessary to forward traffic to the destination in the routing update.

5   Router C, a PE, learns the route through BGP and inserts the route in its local BGP table. Based on the route target and the route distinguisher, the route is installed in a VRF on Router C.

The IGP process on Router C examines the routes that are installed in the VRF and determines which ones have the additional BGP communities carrying additional IGP information. For any routes that are installed in the VRF for which BGP has this additional information, the IGP exports the route into the local IGP tables.

6   The routes that are redistributed from BGP into the customer IGP at the PE are then advertised through the IGP to Router D, the CE at Site 2.

The customer routes are carried from Site 1 to Site 2, through the import/export process, without losing the IGP-specific information that is required to build the local routing tables at each site correctly. You can compare routes that are learned through the backdoor link between the two sites directly to the routes that are learned through the MPLS VPN. That way, you can set the metrics across the two paths so that they are both used correctly.

To understand how this works better, consider how a packet that is sourced someplace in Site 1 is forwarded by each router in the path to Site 2; Figure 9-5 illustrates.

Figure 9-5   *Forwarding Through a BGP/MPLS VPN*

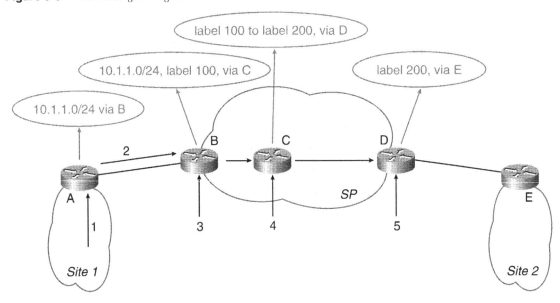

The next steps follow the forwarding of a packet through this network:

1 The packet originates within Site 1 and is forwarded to Router A.

2 Router A examines the destination IP address, 10.1.1.1, looks up the correct routing table entry, and finds that the next hop is Router B.

3 Router B determines which VRF to use based on the interface that the packet is received on and looks up the entry in this VRF, resulting in a next hop and a label. Router B pushes the label, 100, on the MPLS label stack and forwards the packet to Router C.

4 Router C examines its local forwarding table based on the MPLS label. Router C discovers that the packet needs to be relabeled as 200 and forwarded to Router D. Router C removes (pops) the first MPLS label, 100, and replaces it with (pushes) a new label, 200. It then forwards the packet to Router D.

5 Router D examines its local tables and finds that the MPLS label 200 maps it to the VRF that is associated with Site 2. This VRF has routing information for packets that are destined for 10.1.1.1. Router D removes (pops) the MPLS label, looks up 10.1.1.1 in the correct VRF, and finds that the next hop is Router E.

From examining how an MPLS/BGP VPN works, you can understand the advantages that it has to offer:

- Each CE needs to build a peering relationship only with the PE that it is attached to, rather than to every other CE in the network.

- Information that is carried in the IGP, such as metrics, internal or external route origination, and other information, is preserved through the MPLS VPN. This allows routers to directly compare routes learned through an MPLS/BGP VPN to routes learned through other paths in the network.

Now that you understand how BGP/MPLS VPNs work in general, the sections that follow examine how they are actually implemented in Enhanced Interior Gateway Routing Protocol (EIGRP) and OSPF.

EIGRP

EIGRP supports BGP/MPLS VPNs through the EIGRP PE/CE feature, which is available in Cisco IOS Software Release 12.2(15)T and later, and the backdoor support described in this section is available in Cisco IOS Software versions 12.3(8)T and later. Figure 9-6 illustrates basic EIGRP PE/CE support.

Figure 9-6 *EIGRP PE/CE Support*

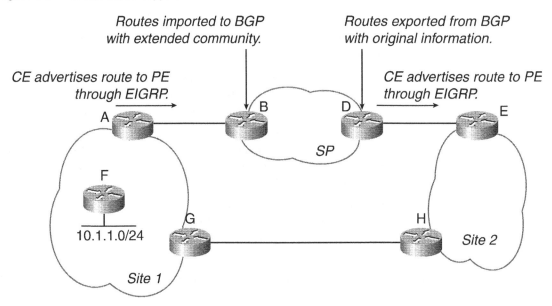

Router F advertises 10.1.1.0/24 into Site 1 through EIGRP, so both Routers A and G receive it. Router G distributes the route through Router H into Site 2. Router A, the CE, receives 10.1.1.0/24 through EIGRP and advertises it to Router B.

Router B imports the route into BGP, attaching a route target and route distinguisher indicating the correct MPLS/VPN. That way, Router C will receive the route and install it in the correct local VRF for forwarding from Site 2. When Router B imports 10.1.1.0/24 into BGP, it also attaches BGP extended communities 0x8800 through 0x8805, containing the following information:

- Bandwidth
- Delay
- Reliability
- Load
- Maximum transmission unit (MTU)
- External information, including the originating router identifier, tags, and other information

The BGP route, with this extended community, is passed through the service provider BGP to Router D. Router D examines the route target and route distinguisher and installs the route in the correct VRF for Site 2. EIGRP notes that 10.1.1.0/24 is newly installed and examines the BGP table to discover that the extended community 0x8800 is present. EIGRP takes the information in the BGP extended community and translates it back into the correct information in the EIGRP route in the local topology table. 10.1.1.0/24 is then advertised to Router E with the correct EIGRP information.

Although no EIGRP neighbor relationship is formed across the service provider network, the EIGRP routing information is passed through the service provider network intact. The MPLS/VPN link is seen as a zero-cost link to EIGRP within Sites 1 and 2.

EIGRP queries are not sent through the service provider network. If Router B receives a query, it examines its local topology table for routes that match the query. If its local topology table has no routes that match the query, Router B replies that the route is unreachable instead of attempting to build a query through the service provider network.

The configuration on the PE router in Example 9-1 show how you can configure basic EIGRP MPLS/VPN PE/CE support.

Example 9-1 *Configuring Basic EIGRP MPLS/VPN PE/CE Support*

```
ip vrf RED
 rd 100:1
 route-target both 100:1
 exit
interface FastEthernet 0/0
 ip vrf forwarding RED
 ip address address mask
 end
....
router bgp as-number
 no synchronization
 neighbor address remote-as as-number
 address-family vpnv4
 neighbor address remote-as as-number
 neighbor address send-community extended
 exit-address-family
 address-family ipv4 vrf RED
 redistribute eigrp eigrp-as-number
 no synchronization
 exit-address-family
....
router eigrp eigrp-as-number
 address-family ipv4 vrf RED
 network address inverse-mask
 redistribute bgp as-number metric....
 autonomous-system as-number
 exit-address-family
```

A Routing Loop Through the Backdoor Connection

Figure 9-7 illustrates what happens if the connection to 10.1.1.0/24 fails.

Figure 9-7 *EIGRP MPLS/VPN Backdoor Link Routing Loop*

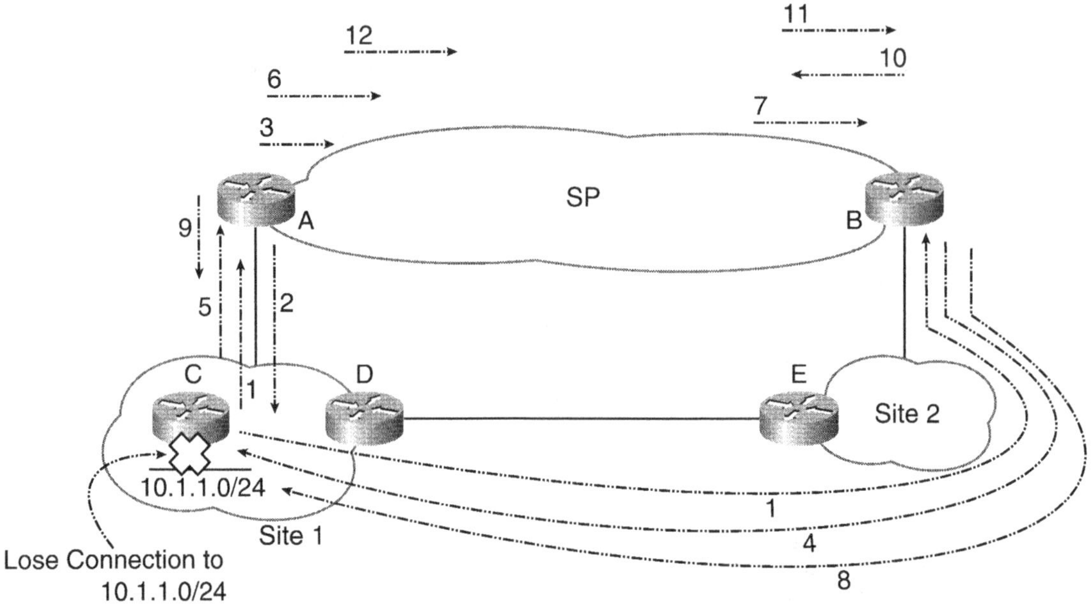

Examine what happens when Router C loses its connection to 10.1.1.0/24:

1 Router C sends an EIGRP query, looking for another route to this network. The query reaches Routers A and B. The query that reaches Router B does so through Routers D and E.

2 Router A replies, indicating that the destination is not reachable (with a metric of infinity) because it is the edge of the EIGRP routing domain.

3 Router A updates its local BGP table and generates a withdraw across the service provider network, indicating that it has lost connectivity to 10.1.1.0/24.

4 Router B replies, indicating that 10.1.1.0/24 is reachable because the route is being learned through BGP and is still installed in its local tables.

5 Router C receives the reply originating at Router B, which indicates that the route is still reachable through another path (across the backdoor link). Router B installs this path in its local tables and sends an EIGRP update to Router A.

6 Now Router A has a valid path to 10.1.1.0/24, through Site 1, so it sends a BGP update through the service provider network toward Router B.

7 Router B receives the initial withdraw from A and removes the BGP route from its local tables.

8 Router B removes the route from its EIGRP tables and generates an EIGRP query into Site 2, looking for another path toward 10.1.1.0/24.

9 The query reaches Router A, which realizes that the query is coming through its path to reach 10.1.1.0/24. Router A replies that the route is not reachable and updates its local tables.

10 The BGP update from Router A reaches B, so B installs this route in its local tables. Router B now sends an EIGRP update indicating that 10.1.1.0/24 is reachable.

11 Router A adjusts its local BGP table based on removing 10.1.1.0/24 from its local EIGRP table and sends a BGP withdraw toward Router B. You are now at Step 1 again in this network.

A complicated routing loop forms in the network when Router C loses its connection to 10.1.1.0/24, based on timing differences between BGP updates, BGP withdraws, EIGRP updates, EIGRP queries, and EIGRP replies. It is a lot like a tongue twister, except that it is an EIGRP mind twister!

The loop persists until the 10.1.1.0/24 route that is being withdrawn and readvertised reaches either the maximum hop count (100 hops in EIGRP) or the maximum EIGRP metric.

By configuring the following, you can set the maximum number of hops allowed in EIGRP to reduce the amount of time that this loop exists:

```
router eigrp autonomous-system
 address-family ipv4 vrf vpn-color
 metric maximum-hops maximum-hop-count
```

If you are going to use this technique, set the maximum number of hops to the diameter of the network. That way, routing loops will not last more than one pass through the steps described earlier. A better practice, however, is to use the EIGRP Site of Origin (SoO) feature to block the routing loop from occurring.

EIGRP SoO

To prevent the routing loop from forming, EIGRP developers created an SoO attribute for EIGRP routes. The EIGRP SoO indicates which site in a BGP/MPLS network a route originated from so that the route can be filtered, preventing the routing loop described in the preceding section. You can deploy EIGRP SoO at the PEs and the backdoor link between the two sites, or only at the PEs. Figure 9-8 illustrates deploying EIGRP SoO at the PEs and the backdoor link between the two sites.

Figure 9-8 *Deploying EIGRP SoO at the PEs and the Backdoor Link*

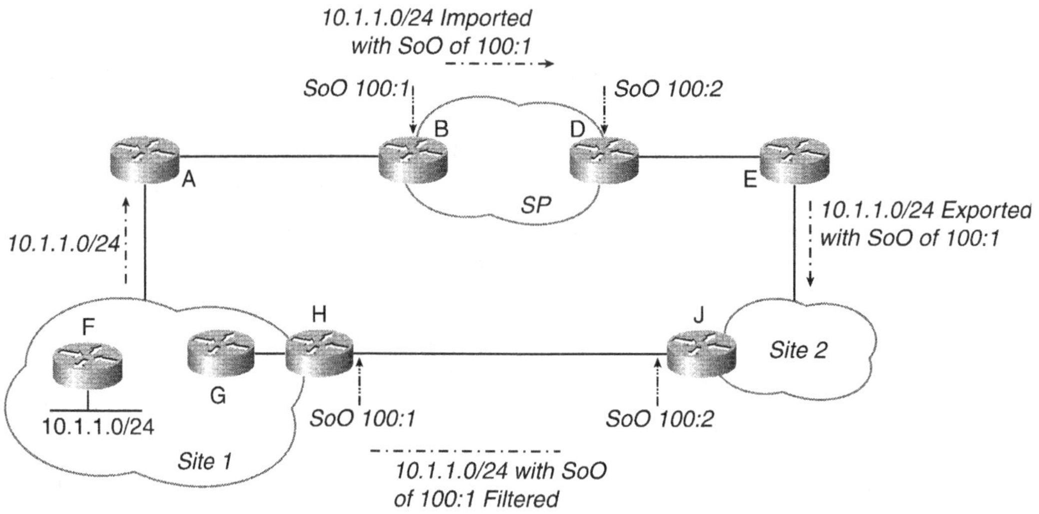

Follow the path of an update about one specific route, 10.1.1.0/24, through the network to see how marking the route with an SoO prevents the routing loop described in the preceding section.

1 10.1.1.0/24 originates at Router F and is advertised through EIGRP to Router A and then to Router B, the PE.

2 As Router B imports the route from EIGRP into BGP, it adds an EIGRP SoO to the route, 100:1.

3 The route is then passed through the service provider network to Router D, where it is exported from BGP into BGP. The SoO that Router B adds is retained. That way, when Router J receives the route for 10.1.1.0/24, it is still marked with an SoO of 100:1.

4 Router J advertises 10.1.1.0/24 to H, which is also configured to mark routes that are advertised toward Router H with the same SoO, 100:1.

5 When 10.1.1.0/24, marked with an SoO of 100:1, is received by Router H, it is ignored because the route originated in the site occupied by Router H.

This prevents the routing loop described in the previous section at Step 4, because the reply indicating reachability through the other PE router would be stopped at Router H.

If the link between Router G and the remainder of Site 1 fails, Router H still rejects the route to 10.1.1.0/24 that is advertised through the backdoor link (between Routers H and J). Any users who are attached to Router G can no longer reach that destination. A link failure causing a single site to fracture into two pieces, then, causes the piece that is connected to the backdoor link to lose connectivity.

Figure 9-9 illustrates an alternate solution to preventing routing loops through backdoor links.

Figure 9-9   *EIGRP SoO Implemented at the PEs Only*

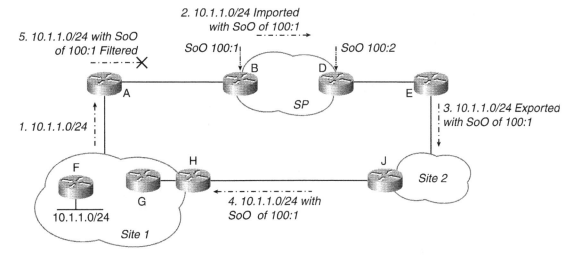

In this network, only the PEs are marking routes with an SoO and filtering routes based on the SoO that is carried within a route:

1 Here, 10.1.1.0/24 is advertised by Router F toward Router A, which then advertises the route to Router B.

2 Router B imports the route into BGP, attaching an SoO of 100:1. Router B advertises it through the service provider network to Router D.

3 Router D exports 10.1.1.0/24 to EIGRP, leaving the SoO attached, and advertises it to Router E.

4 The route is then advertised through EIGRP to a point in the network in which the route originated by Router F is the best path, rather than the route learned from Router D through the BGP/MPLS VPN.

5 If the route learned through the backdoor link is the best path all the way to Router B, it is filtered on Router B because of the SoO. This prevents the routing loop discussed in the previous section at Step 5. The update transmitted through the network would have an SoO of 100:1 and would be filtered by Router A.

Deploying EIGRP SoO at the PEs only permits the routing loop to stay in the network longer, but it also prevents the routing loop from becoming semi-permanent. The best deployment for your network depends on the length of time you want to tolerate the routing loop versus the loss of connectivity if one of the sites fragments.

Example 9-2 demonstrates how to configure a router running EIGRP to mark routes with an SoO.

Example 9-2 *Configuring an EIGRP Router to Mark Routes with an SoO*

```
interface e0/0
  ip vrf sitemap SoO
route-map SoO permit 10
  set extcommunity SoO 1:1
```

EIGRP and the BGP Cost Community

In Cisco IOS Software Release 12.3(8)T, 12.0(27)S, and later, EIGRP also supports using the custom decision process capability of BGP to prefer the best EIGRP route within a BGP/MPLS VPN, as Figure 9-10 illustrates.

Figure 9-10 *EIGRP Support for BGP Custom Decision Process*

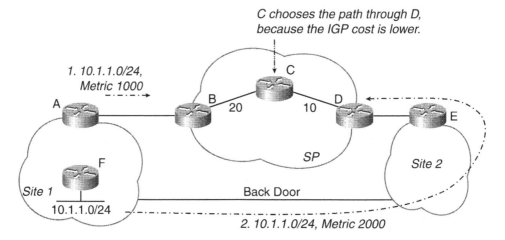

1 Router F originates 10.1.1.0/24 into Site 1, which is then advertised to Router B, the PE, with an EIGRP composite metric of 1000. (The EIGRP composite metric is derived from the bandwidth, delay, and other metrics carried by EIGRP. See Appendix A, "Enhanced Interior Gateway Routing Protocol for IP Basics of Operation," for further details.)

2 10.1.1.0/24 is also advertised through the backdoor link between the two sites. It reaches Router D, another PE, with an EIGRP composite metric of 2000.

Both of these routes are imported into BGP and carried through the service provider network to Router C.

How does Router C know which path to 10.1.1.0/24 is the best path? Because the EIGRP metrics are hidden in communities that BGP does not take into account when determining the best path, BGP has to rely on its standard best path algorithm to decide.

When all other factors (AS path length, local preference, multiple exit discriminator, and so on) are equal, the path that has the closest next hop, or the lowest IGP metric to the next hop, is chosen. In this case, the path through Router D, the PE for Site 2, is chosen, because the IGP cost to Router D is lower than the cost to Router B. Because Router D can reach 10.1.1.0/24 only through the backdoor link, however, this is not the optimal path.

To resolve this, EIGRP supports the BGP custom decision process, as outlined in the IETF draft *draft-retana-bgp-custom-decision-00.txt*.

NOTE   For further information on this feature, see http://www.cisco.com/en/US/products/sw/iosswrel/ps5207/products_feature_guide09186a00801a7f74.html, or search for "BGP Cost Community" at Cisco.com.

To enable Router C to make the best routing decision, EIGRP injects the route metric as a cost community with an insertion point before the local preference. This allows Router C to decide which BGP path is best based on the site with the lowest cost to reach the destination.

OSPF

OSPF operation over a BGP/MPLS VPN is similar to the way that EIGRP operates, using BGP communities to carry OSPF routing information through the BGP network of the service provider. Figure 9-11 illustrates.

Figure 9-11   *OSPF Sham Links*

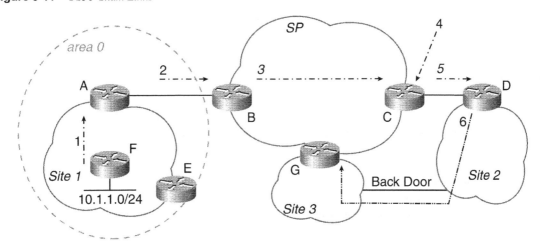

In this network, the following occurs:

1 Router F originates 10.1.1.0/24 as an OSPF Type 1 route into area 0, in Site 1.

2 The route is advertised through OSPF to Router A, the CE, which then creates a Type 3 summary because Router A is the Area Border Router (ABR). This Type 3 route is advertised to Router B, the PE, and imported into BGP.

3 The OSPF route information is encoded in extended BGP communities. The route is marked with the correct route target and route distinguisher and advertised through the service provider network.

4 When Router C receives the BGP update for 10.1.1.0/24, it installs it in the correct VRF for Site 2 and then exports the correct information into the local OSPF database.

5 Before the OSPF Type 3 route is advertised to Router D, the *down bit* is set on the route. The down bit indicates that the route has been advertised from a PE to a CE. It is set on Type 3, 5, and 7 routes advertised from a PE to a CE.

6 10.1.1.0/24 is advertised across the backdoor link and reaches Router G with the down bit set. Router G rejects the route, preventing loops from forming across the BGP/MPLS VPN and the backdoor link, just as the EIGRP SoO does.

If the 10.1.1.0/24 route works its way across the backdoor link and back to Router A, it is rejected at Router A because the down bit is set.

NOTE   OSPF sham links are described in the IETF draft *OSPF as the PE/CE Protocol in BGP/MPLS IP VPNs*, draft-ietf-l3vpn-ospf-2547-01.txt. The use of the down bit in OSPF BGP/MPLS VPNs is described in the IETF draft *Using an LSA Options Bit to Prevent Looping in BGP/ MPLS IP VPNs*, draft-ietf-ospf-2547-dnbit-04.txt.

IPSec

IPSec is designed primarily as a security protocol for encrypting IP traffic between two devices. RFC 2411 provides an overview of the various documents that define IPSec and their interrelationship. IPSec builds point-to-point tunnels rather than point-to-multipoint, and the encryption on the tunnel means that the routers in the tunnel path cannot read the actual destination of the packet, just the tunnel endpoint. These two factors combine to make point-to-point tunnels the only deployment option for IPSec VPNs (without using multipoint GRE tunnels, discussed in the next section). IPSec tunnels can, however, be built between devices other than routers, making them useful in various situations. Figure 9-12 illustrates.

Figure 9-12   *IPSec Tunnels*

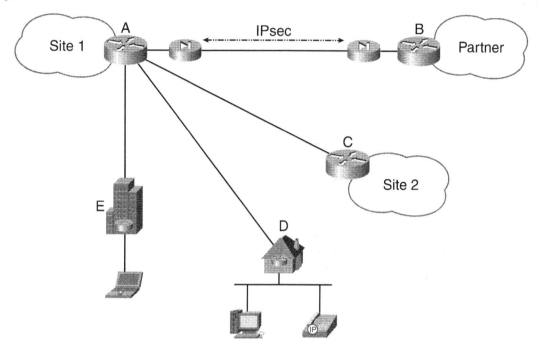

In this illustration, Router A is the hub of an IPSec hub-and-spoke network that is being used for multiple applications:

- It routes over an IPSec tunnel that is built between the two firewalls to provide connectivity to a partner. In this case, the IPSec tunnel can be built between the firewalls or across the firewalls, between Routers A and B.

- It terminates an IPSec tunnel built between Site 1 and Site 2, over which routing is running. Here, it is used as a method to connect multiple sites within the network across a service provider network.

- It terminates an IPSec tunnel built from the home network, D, and the corporate network. The IPSec tunnel, in this case, does not have routing running across it. It terminates at the router within the house network.

- It terminates an IPSec tunnel originating at a laptop connected to some outside network, providing an alternative to remote dialup.

The routing that is required to connect multiple sites using an IGP or provide reachability to a partner network through BGP is overlaid on top of the IPSec tunnels that are built to each site.

GRE

GRE tunnels are simple to configure and easy to maintain, but they do require ample processing power to terminate. This is primarily because of the additional overhead of encapsulating each packet with a new header, including performing any required fragmentation and reassembly because of the additional header. Configuring a GRE tunnel is easy. Just create a tunnel interface, configure the source address, and configure the destination address (see Example 9-3).

Example 9-3 *Configuring a GRE Tunnel*

```
Router#configure terminal
Router(config)#interface tunnel 1
Router(config-if)#ip address 10.1.1.1
Router(config-if)#tunnel source 10.2.1.1
Router(config-if)#tunnel destination 10.3.1.1
```

GRE tunnels, in their basic form, are point-to-point. The service provider through which they are run has no idea about the content of the tunnels or the actual destination address. A VPN that is built through GRE tunnels builds a routing adjacency for each tunnel in the network, which is generally not a scalable solution. The section "Dynamic Multipoint IPSec VPNs," later in the chapter, covers another form of GRE tunnels: multipoint GRE.

NOTE Some line cards are now designed specifically to terminate tunnels of various types, including GRE tunnels. These special-purpose line cards allow numerous tunnels to be terminated on a single router, enabling highly scalable tunnel-based VPNs of various types, including GRE.

NHRP

Rather than trying to build a tunnel from every possible source to every possible destination, NHRP enables you to create a "route server." This server allows the sources and destinations to use the information it provides to build tunnels dynamically, as illustrated in Figure 9-13.

Figure 9-13 *Full Mesh Neighbors*

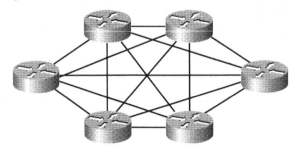

As you know, the full mesh design in Figure 9-13 results in 6(6–1)/2, or 15 paths through the network. Suppose that you want to reduce the paths through the network by making the network a hub and spoke.

The real difficulty with this design (other than the single point of failure) is the amount of traffic that must pass through the hub router. If all of these links are 2.4 Gbps, the hub router would need to switch traffic at 12 Gbps or faster. It must be possible to spread this work out a bit.

If you are using a lower-layer media that supports switched virtual circuits (SVCs), such as ATM (or Frame Relay SVCs), you should be able to take advantage of them to make direct connections between the spoke routers when needed.

Consider these issues:

- How does the router know that a given destination is reachable by some means other than through the hub router?
- How does it know which SVC to use (which number to dial, so to speak) to reach this destination?

This is where NHRP comes in. In NHRP, several routers are configured as route servers. Each router advertises its reachable destinations, along with an SVC to reach those destinations, to this route server.

When a router wants to reach a given destination, it queries the route server to find out about a direct path through the cloud. If a direct path exits, the route server brings up an SVC to the next hop and passes along the traffic. This effectively provides the advantages of a full mesh topology while providing the scalability of a partial mesh topology.

Case Study: NHRP in an ATM Network

In the network shown in Figure 9-14, traffic that is sourced from 172.16.2.0/24 and destined to 172.16.1.0/24 normally flows through Router A, which is at the hub of the switched ATM network. Instead of having all this traffic pass through one router, however, it makes more sense to have Routers B and C set up SVCs to one another when they are needed.

Figure 9-14 *NHRP in an ATM Network*

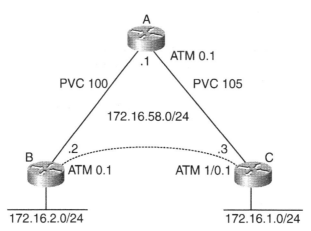

To accomplish this goal, you can run NHRP over the ATM cloud. Example 9-4 shows the configuration for Routers A and B.

Example 9-4 *Sample Configuration for NHRP over an ATM Network*

```
! Router A
interface ATM0
 no ip address
 atm pvc 5 0 5 qssal
 atm pvc 16 0 16 ilmi
!
interface ATM0.1 multipoint
 ip address 172.16.58.1 255.255.255.0
 ip nhrp network-id 1
 ip nhrp interest 101
 ip ospf network point-to-multipoint
 atm esi-address 852852852852.01
 atm pvc 100 0 40 aal5snap inarp 5
 atm pvc 105 0 90 aal5snap inarp 5
!
router ospf 1
 network 0.0.0.0 0.0.0.0 area 0
!
access-list 101 deny ip any any
! Router B

interface Ethernet0
 ip address 172.16.2.1 255.255.255.0
!
interface ATM0
 no ip address
 atm pvc 5 0 5 qsaal
 atm pvc 16 0 16 ilmi
```

Example 9-4   *Sample Configuration for NHRP over an ATM Network (Continued)*

```
!
interface ATM0.1 multipoint
 ip address 172.16.58.2 255.255.255.0
 ip nhrp network-id 1
 ip nhrp interest 101
 ip route-cache same-interface
 ip ospf netowrk point-to-multipoint
 atm esi-address 145145145145.01
 atm pvc 100 0 40 aal5snap inarp 5
!
router ospf 1
 network 0.0.0.0 0.0.0.0 area 0
!
access-list 101 permit ip any any
```

Router C is identical to Router B except for IP addresses and ATM information. To understand how this works, walk through a Telnet session from a host on the 172.16.2.0/24 network to a host on the 172.16.2.0/24 network:

1 Router C sends its traffic for the 172.16.2.0/24 network toward Router A because it has a route for that network in that direction through OSPF.

2 Router A notices that this destination is reachable through an interface on Router C, which is in the same NHRP group that Router B is in.

3 Router A sends the Router C connect information (its ATM address) to Router B. It also sends the ATM address for Router B to Router C.

4 Routers B and C open an SVC to each other, and traffic between the 172.16.1.0/24 and the 172.16.2.0/24 networks flows along this path.

Example 9-5 shows the ARP cache on Router B before the Telnet session between the hosts takes place.

Example 9-5   *Router B ARP Cache Before Telnet Session*

```
Router-B#show arp
Protocol  Address      Age(min)  Hardware Addr    Type  Interface
....
Internet 172.16.58.1 3           VCD#0100         ATM   ATM0.1
```

As Example 9-6 shows, after the Telnet session, Router B builds an ARP cache entry for this destination over the newly established SVC between Router B and Router C.

Example 9-6   *Router B ARP Cache After Establishing an SVC Between Routers B and C*

```
Router-B#show arp
Protocol  Address      Age(min)  Hardware Addr    Type  Interface
....
Internet 172.16.58.1 71          VCD#0100         ATM   ATM0.1
Internet 172.16.2.1  1           VCD#0060         ATM   ATM0.1
```

Dynamic Multipoint IPSec VPNs

The preceding sections covered IPSec and GRE tunnels, in addition to NHRP. The problems with using a tunneling technology to build a large-scale network through a service provider network are as follows:

- Building and maintaining the tunnels—If the network is designed as anything other than a simple hub and spoke, the correct set of tunnels to allow traffic to pass between the right set of sites can be difficult to build and almost impossible to maintain.

- Tunnels are all point-to-point—This increases the load on your IGP and makes configuring and maintaining the IGP much more difficult.

Combining these technologies with a new form of GRE tunnel, the *multipoint GRE*, can solve many of these problems, as Figure 9-15 illustrates.

Figure 9-15 *Dynamic Multipoint GRE Tunnels*

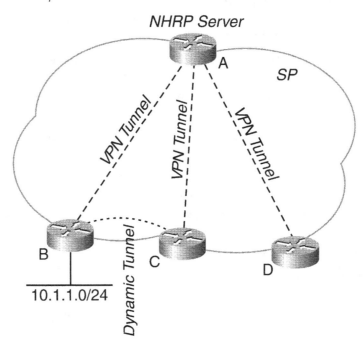

The network designer would like to build a set of tunnels as shown in Figure 9-15 but wants the routers to be able to build a partial mesh based on real-time traffic flows. For instance, if Router C has traffic that is destined to 10.1.1.0/24, that traffic does not need to pass through Router A. Instead, the traffic should flow directly to Router B.

Figure 9-15 is similar to the network in Figure 9-14, but instead of being built over an ATM network, it is built using a set of GRE tunnels encrypted using IPSec. Just as you can build an ATM SVC between Router C and Router B as needed, you can also build a tunnel dynamically between these two routers. At Router C, the main thing you need to know is the actual next hop to build the dynamic tunnel to, which is precisely the piece that NHRP is designed to provide. The following steps detail how this works:

1 Router A is configured with a multipoint GRE tunnel, IPSec encrypted, to each of the remote sites. Router A becomes the hub of a standard hub-and-spoke network, using a multipoint GRE tunnel, and can communicate directly with any site.

2 Router A is also configured as an NHRP server. This means it can receive, store, and answer queries about reachable destinations within the network.

3 Routers B, C, and D are configured with a GRE tunnel, IPSec encrypted, to Router A; furthermore, they are configured as NHRP remotes. Each remote site router advertises the destinations that are reachable through that site toward Router A.

4 Routers B, C, and D are also configured to run an IGP through these tunnels so that they can learn routes from any router they have built a tunnel to. At the beginning, they only learn routes that are reachable through Router A.

5 Router C receives a packet that is destined to 10.1.1.1. At this point, it only has routes to destinations behind Router A, the hub of the network, from the IGP that is configured through the tunnels. Because Router C does not have a route to 10.1.1.1, it queries the NHRP server for information on how to reach this destination.

6 Router A examines its NHRP tables and determines that 10.1.1.1 is reachable through Router B. It sends this information along with the correct next hop to reach Router B through the service provider network.

7 Router C, on receiving this information, dynamically builds a tunnel through the service provider network and exchanges routes with Router A.

8 Router C now has a route to 10.1.1.0/24, through which it can forward traffic for 10.1.1.1.

This combination of technologies allows a mesh of tunnels to be built dynamically through a service provider network, connecting sites as they need to be connected, without the configuration overhead of manually building the mesh of tunnels. Example 9-7 shows the configuration for Routers A, B, and C. (The Router B configuration, which is not shown, is identical to that of Router C.)

Example 9-7 *Configuring Dynamic Multipoint IPSec VPNs*

```
!
hostname router-a
!
crypto ipsec profile vpnprof
  set transform-set trans2
  !
```

Example 9-7 *Configuring Dynamic Multipoint IPSec VPNs (Continued)*

```
interface Tunnel0
 bandwidth 1000
 ip address 10.2.1.1 255.255.255.0
 ip mtu 1436
 ip nhrp authentication test
 ip nhrp map multicast dynamic
 ip nhrp network-id 100000
 ip nhrp holdtime 600
 no ip split-horizon eigrp 1
 delay 1000
 tunnel source Ethernet0
 tunnel mode gre multipoint
 tunnel key 100000
 tunnel protection ipsec profile vpnprof
 !
interface Ethernet0
 ip address 192.168.100.1 255.255.255.0
!
hostname router-c
!
crypto map vpnmap1 10 IPSec-isakmp
 set peer 192.168.100.1
 set transform-set trans2
 match address 101
 !
 interface Tunnel0
 bandwidth 1000
 ip address 10.2.1.2 255.255.255.0
 ip mtu 1436
 ip nhrp authentication test
 ip nhrp map 10.2.1.2 192.168.100.1
 ip nhrp network-id 100000
 ip nhrp holdtime 300
 ip nhrp nhs 10.2.1.1
 delay 1000
 tunnel source Ethernet0
 tunnel destination 192.168.100.1
 tunnel key 100000
 crypto map vpnmap1
 !
 . . .
 !
access-list 101 permit gre host 192.168.100.2 host 192.168.100.1
 !
```

Review Questions

1 What was the original intent of MPLS?

2 What is the major use of MPLS today? Why has it changed?

3 What are the three primary methods to route across an MPLS VPN through a service provider network?

4 What is the primary drawback of overlaying routing information on top of an MPLS VPN?

5 What is the primary drawback in the peer-to-peer model of building a network on top of MPLS VPNs?

6 How does a BGP/MPLS VPN carry IGP routing information through BGP?

7 How does EIGRP prevent backdoor routing loops when it is configured to run across a BGP/MPLS VPN?

8 How does OSPF prevent routing loops through backdoor connections when it is running across a BGP/MPLS VPN?

References

Pepelnjak, I. and J. Guichard. *MPLS and VPN Architectures*. Indianapolis: Cisco Press, 2002.

Osborne, E. and A. Simha. *Traffic Engineering with MPLS*. Indianapolis: Cisco Press, 2002.

McPherson, D., Sangli, S., and R. White. *Practical BGP*. New York: Addison-Wesley, 2004.

Retana, R., Slice, D., and R. White. *Advanced IP Network Design*. Indianapolis: Cisco Press, 1999.

PART IV

Appendixes

A

EIGRP for IP Basics of Operation

Enhanced Interior Gateway Routing Protocol (EIGRP) is an advanced distance vector protocol that offers many advantages:

- **Minimal use of network resources in normal operation**—EIGRP only transmits small hello packets during normal operation to maintain neighbor relationships; it has no periodic routing updates (flooding of the routing table to neighbors).

- **Restricted use of network resources when reacting to network topology changes**—EIGRP only transmits information about what has changed and restricts (paces) the rate at which it sends packets so that it will not overwhelm a link.

- **Rapid convergence**—EIGRP converges quickly during topology changes, primarily because it computes all loop-free paths available to a given destination, rather than just the lowest-cost path (explained in more detail in the next section, "The Diffusing Update Algorithm (DUAL)").

- **Scalability**—EIGRP can scale into large networks because no periodic updates are used and a minimal use of network resources during convergence exists.

A major revision of the protocol occurred in Cisco IOS Software Release 10.3(11), 11.0(8), and 11.1(3). The recommended practice is to run software implementing the later revision of EIGRP to promote stability and interoperability.

Cisco IOS Software Release 12.0(7)T introduced the stub feature, and IOS Software Release 12.1(5)T added Stuck in Active (SIA) enhancements. The stub feature was by far the most significant change to occur in the protocol to improve scalability, and the SIA enhancements dramatically improved the stability of EIGRP. Both features are extremely valuable capabilities and will be explained in further detail later in this appendix.

EIGRP is based on the Diffusing Update Algorithm (DUAL) to find the best loop-free paths through a network.

DUAL

Typical distance vector protocols, such as Routing Information Protocol (RIP), use the distance (metric—in most cases, the hop count) to a destination network to determine the best path and save the vector (next hop) for only the best path. If the best path becomes unusable, the router waits until the next set of updates from each of its neighbors to find a new path (or rediscover an old path that was previously discarded).

Waiting for periodic updates to discover alternate paths to a destination slows convergence time dramatically. For example, if the network in Figure A-1 is running Routing Information Protocol (RIP), Router B would choose the path to 10.1.4.0/24 by examining the hop count through each available path. Because the path through Router C will be two hops, and the path through Router A will be three hops, Router B would choose the path through Router A and discard the alternate path it learned through Router C.

Figure A-1   *A Simple Network*

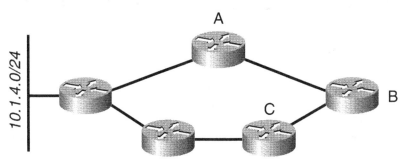

If Router A's path to 10.1.4.0/24 fails, Router B will continue believing that the best route to this destination is through Router A until it has not heard about 10.1.4.0/24 from Router A for three update periods (90 seconds in RIP). After Router B has timed the route through Router A, it must still wait for Router C to readvertise the route, which occurs every 30 seconds in RIP. Not including holddown time, it could take between 90 and 120 seconds for Router B to switch from the path through Router A to the path through Router C to reach 10.1.4.0/24.

Rather than discarding information about alternate paths, EIGRP builds a topology table from each of the neighboring routers' advertisements and converges by either looking for an alternate route in the topology table or querying the neighboring routers that are running EIGRP if it knows of no other route.

EIGRP, then, must provide the following:

- Some means of building and maintaining neighbor relationships. Because EIGRP does not periodically readvertise routes, it relies on neighbor relationships to determine if the routes through a given neighbor are still usable.

- A way of determining if a given path that is advertised by a neighbor contains a loop. EIGRP must be capable of determining if forwarding traffic along a route would cause the packets to loop, so a list of valid alternate routes is available.

- A method of querying neighbors to find previously unknown paths. Split horizon and other circumstances can cause a router not to advertise all the destinations it can reach. Because EIGRP does not rely on periodic updates, routers must be capable of querying neighbors to find alternate hidden routes.

Neighbor Relationships

EIGRP conserves network bandwidth by using nonperiodic, incremental updates. This means that changes to the network topology are transmitted between routers as needed. After a neighbor relationship has been established, full routing updates are not sent, and no periodic updates occur.

The basic problem with nonperiodic updates is determining when a path through a neighboring router is no longer available. You cannot time out routes, expecting a new routing table from neighboring routers every so often.

To this end, EIGRP relies on neighbor relationships. If the neighbor that a router has learned a path through is reachable, the path is assumed to be valid. Because neighbor relationships are so important to the operation of the protocol, they warrant further discussion. Returning to Figure A-1, examine the neighbor relationship between Router A and Router B. Assume that Router B is powered up and running. When Router A is powered on, it begins sending hello packets out each of its interfaces. When Router B receives Router A's first hello (only one simple situation is pertinent to the discussion here), Router B sends a hello packet with the initialization bit set. Router A receives this hello packet with the initialization bit set and begins transmitting its full routing table to Router B.

After Router A and Router B have finished exchanging their routing tables, they maintain this neighbor relationship with periodic hello packets. How often are hello packets transmitted?

Determining how often to send hello packets is a matter of balancing between fast convergence and minimal network utilization. On higher speed and point-to-point links, it is generally safe to transmit hello packets rather frequently; on lower bandwidth multipoint links, however, bandwidth conservation becomes more important.

Specifically, hellos are sent every 5 seconds on the following:

- Broadcast media, such as Ethernet, Token Ring, and Fiber Distributed Data Interface (FDDI)
- Point-to-point serial links, such as PPP or High-Level Data Link Control (HDLC) leased circuits, Frame Relay point-to-point subinterfaces, and ATM point-to-point subinterfaces
- High bandwidth multipoint circuits, such as ISDN PRI and Frame Relay multipoint circuits greater than T1 (as configured using the interface **bandwidth** command)

Hellos are sent every 60 seconds on multipoint circuits with T1 bandwidth or slower, such as Frame Relay multipoint interfaces, ATM multipoint interfaces, ATM switched virtual circuits, and ISDN BRIs.

The rate at which hello packets are sent is called the hello interval. You can adjust it per interface using the **ip eigrp hello-interval** command. The amount of time that a router considers a neighbor up without receiving a hello or some other EIGRP packet is called the hold time. The hold time is typically three times the hello interval; therefore, the hold times are 15 seconds for a 5-second hello interval and 180 seconds for a 60-second hello interval by default. You can adjust the hold time with the **ip eigrp hold-time** interface command. If you change the hello interval, the hold time is not automatically adjusted to account for this change; you must manually adjust the hold time to reflect the configured hello interval.

The possibility exists for two routers to become EIGRP neighbors even though the hello and hold timers do not match, because the hold time is included in hello packets. A router keeps a neighbor up as long as it receives EIGRP packets from that neighbor within the hold time that is advertised in the hello packet of the neighbor.

Although no direct way exists to determine the hello and hold intervals, executing the **show ip eigrp neighbor** command several times in a row can provide you with a good idea of what the hello interval and hold timers are for a neighboring router. (**show ip eigrp neighbor** cannot be used to determine the hello and hold timers on this router.) Consider the results in Example A-1.

Example A-1 *Determining Hello Interval and Hold Timers with the* **show ip eigrp neighbor** *Command*

```
router#show ip eigrp neighbor
IP-EIGRP neighbors for process 1
H   Address     Interface   Hold Uptime    SRTT   RTO   Q  Seq
                                 (sec)   (ms) Cnt Num
1   10.1.1.2    Et1           13 12:00:53   12    300   0  620
0   10.1.2.2    S0           174 12:00:56   17    200   0  645

router#show ip eigrp neighbor
IP-EIGRP neighbors for process 1
H   Address     Interface   Hold Uptime    SRTT   RTO   Q  Seq
                                 (sec)   (ms) Cnt Num
1   10.1.1.2    Et1           12 12:00:55   12    300   0  620
0   10.1.2.2    S0           173 12:00:57   17    200   0  645

router#show ip eigrp neighbor
IP-EIGRP neighbors for process 1
H   Address     Interface   Hold Uptime    SRTT   RTO   Q  Seq
                                 (sec)   (ms) Cnt Num
1   10.1.1.2    Et1           11 12:00:56   12    300   0  620
0   10.1.2.2    S0           172 12:00:58   17    200   0  645
```

The Hold column never gets above the hold time and should never get below the hold time minus the hello interval (unless, of course, you are losing hello packets). If the Hold column usually ranges between 10 and 15 seconds, the hello interval is 5 seconds and the hold time is 15 seconds. If the Hold column usually has a wider range—between 120 and 180 seconds—the hello interval is 60 seconds and the hold time is 180 seconds. If the numbers do not seem to fit one of the default timer settings, check the interfaces on this router and the neighbor because the timers have probably been configured manually.

The possibility exists for a link that is passing traffic in one direction to result in only a "half relationship" between two neighbors. Both routers would report retransmission limit exceeded errors at the console, and one router would have high Q Counts and an SRTT of zero in **show ip eigrp neighbor.** (The **Q** Count column indicates how many packets are waiting to be sent to this neighbor. The SRTT indicates the normal wait time after sending this neighbor a packet before receiving a reply.)

Metrics

Before this appendix discusses the way that EIGRP implements DUAL, you need to understand the metrics used. EIGRP uses the minimum bandwidth and the total delay to compute metrics. You can use other metrics by adjusting the "k" values, but that is not recommended. Adjusting the "k" values is complex; it is possible to create routing loops when trying to use these other metrics.

The formula that EIGRP uses to compute the metric from the minimum bandwidth and the total delay (or the sum of the delays on the path) is as follows:

$$\left[\frac{10^7}{min(bandwidth)} + \Sigma\ delays \right] *256$$

Refer to Figure A-2 to examine how this works in a simple network.

Figure A-2   *EIGRP Metrics*

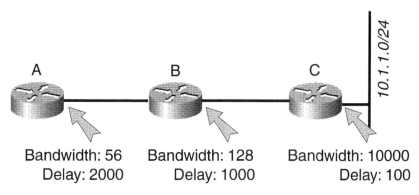

When Router C advertises 10.1.1.0/24, it sets the bandwidth to 10000 and the delay to 100. When Router B receives the advertisement, it compares the bandwidth in the advertisement (10000) to the bandwidth of the interface from which it received the advertisement (128) and uses the lower of the two, in this case 128. Router B then adds the delay configured on the interface it received the advertisement through to the delay in the advertisement, so the total delay is 1100. When Router A receives the advertisement from Router B, it performs the same procedure, reducing the minimum bandwidth to 56 and adding 2000 to the delay, for a total delay of 3100.

At B, the total metric to 10.1.1.0/24 would be as follows:

$$\left[\frac{10^7}{128} + 1100 \right] *256 = 20281600$$

At A, the total metric to 10.1.1.0/24 would be this:

$$\left[\frac{10^7}{56} + 3100 \right] *256 = 46507776$$

In case you were wondering, infinity is 4,294,967,296, which is 2^{32}. You will probably get a different answer on some of these if you use a calculator to check them. That is because routers do not do floating-point math, so they truncate the decimal places at each division.

Loop-Free Routes

To understand how EIGRP determines whether a path is valid (loop free), look at Figure A-3, which is a simple geometric figure. Each of the lines is assigned a length of 1 for simplicity. (You will see this again using real metrics later in this appendix.)

Figure A-3   *Model for Valid Route Discovery*

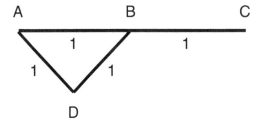

Because the length of each of these line segments is 1, the following total distances would be true:

- B→C = 1
- A→B→C = 2
- D→B→C = 2
- A→D→B→C = 3
- D→A→B→C = 3
- B→A→D→B→C = 4
- B→D→A→B→C = 4

If Router A were to somehow advertise to Router B that it had a path to Router C through Router D, the total distance it would advertise would be 3. This is greater than Router B's best path to Router C, which is 1. In fact, it is mathematically impossible for Router A ever to advertise a better route to Router C than Router B's best path because it would always include the distance between Router B and Router C.

Given this, it is relatively simple for Router B to determine if the path to Router C that Router A is advertising has already passed through Router B (is looped, or invalid). Simply compare the total distance that Router A is advertising with the best path currently known. If the path that Router A is advertising is longer (has a higher total distance) than the best path currently known, it is possible that the path is a loop, and it should not be used.

With this in mind, use Figure A-4 as an example and see how this works with real metrics.

Figure A-4   *EIGRP Loop Detection*

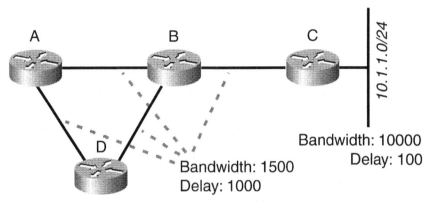

Router B receives three advertisements for 10.1.1.0/24:

- Through Router A with a metric of 2500096
- Through Router C with a metric of 281600
- Through Router D with a metric of 2500096

Normally, Router B would only receive one of these advertisements (through Router C) because of split horizon. Split horizon is turned off in this example to explain how EIGRP finds invalid routes based only on the metrics.

Router B adds the metric through the interface from which it receives the advertisements and now has the following paths:

- Through Router A with a metric of 2756096
- Through Router C with a metric of 1988096
- Through Router D with a metric of 2756096

Now Router B chooses the best path (lowest metric) to 10.1.1.0/24, which is through Router C, and uses this as a *measuring stick*. Because the distances advertised both by Router A and Router D (before Router B adds in the metrics through its interfaces) are higher than the best path (after Router B adds in its interface metrics), neither of these paths is valid.

Remember from the previous example in Figure A-3 that it is mathematically impossible for the metric through Router A or Router D to be lower than the total distance to the destination if the path contains a loop (passes through Router B more than once).

To put this in EIGRP terms, the following applies:

- The distance to the destination advertised by the neighbor is the *reported distance*.
- The best metric available to the network is the *feasible distance*.

- The neighbor with the best metric to a destination is the *successor.*
- Any neighbors whose reported distances are less than the feasible distance are *feasible successors*. (They are advertising a loop-free route.)

This model is conservative. It sometimes decides that a route is a possible loop when it really is not.

Clearing the Topology Table and Querying Neighbors

After EIGRP has built a topology table and decided which paths are not looped, it needs some way to adjust to changes in that topology table. Because EIGRP uses nonperiodic updates, it does not time routes out of its table; the route must be removed by new information from a neighbor or through tearing down a neighbor relationship.

When a router loses its connection to a destination, it first examines its topology table to determine if it has a feasible successor for that destination. If it does, it does the following:

- Removes the old route.
- Replaces the old successor with the new one.
- Recomputes the topology table for that destination. (Changing the feasible distance might produce a new set of feasible successors.)
- Updates any neighbors on the change in its path.

If, however, a router loses its route to a destination and it has no other loop-free routes to that destination, it queries each of its neighbors to see if any of them has another path. This might seem unnecessary at first glance, but it really serves three purposes:

- To re-evaluate paths that might have been rejected as looped.
- To learn of paths that might not have been originally advertised because of split horizon rules.
- To inform all neighbors that this router no longer has a path to this network. If the neighbors are relying on this path to reach this destination, they need to find a new path because this one is no longer available.

In Figure A-5, if Router D's interface on 10.1.1.0/24 goes down (later you discover the cable dangling out of the router, of course), Router D immediately marks this destination as unreachable and queries each of its neighbors—Router B and Router C in this case—for a new path to this destination (1).

Both Router B and Router C are using Router D as their successor to this network. They mark the destination as unreachable and query each of their neighbors (2 and 3). Because the link between Router A and Router C is faster than the link between Router A and Router B, Router A is using Router C as its successor to this network, and the query from Router C arrives first. (This is true in theory, anyway. These events can occur in many other sequences, but the end result is the same, so only one possible sequence is followed here.)

Figure A-5   *Query Path Through a Network*

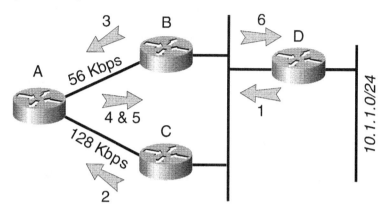

When Router A receives the query from Router C, it examines its topology table and notes that it has a feasible successor for this destination through Router B, and queues a response for Router C. Assume that the query from Router B arrives before that response is sent. Router A now notes that it has no other feasible successors and marks the route as unreachable. Router A then adjusts its response to Router C to make the replied metric unreachable. It also sends a packet to Router B that this path is unreachable (4 and 5).

When these replies arrive at Router B and Router C, they remove the destination from their topology tables and send responses back to Router D that this path is unreachable (6). After Router D has received all the answers (replies) to its queries, it sends updates to Router B and Router C to notify them that 10.1.1.0/24 is no longer reachable. Router B and Router C, in turn, propagate this information to Router A.

SIA

A route could be in the Stuck in Action (SIA) state for many reasons, the most likely of which is a poorly performing link (or a series of borderline links) in the query path. Other possibilities include a router that cannot immediately answer the query (out of memory or high CPU utilization are common) or the network being so large that the queries cannot travel throughout the network in less than three minutes.

When a router queries its neighbors about a route, the route is placed in active mode while awaiting the replies. (The router is actively seeking a path to this destination.) Prior to Cisco IOS Software Release 12.1(5)T, when the SIA enhancements were integrated, if a route remained active for three minutes, it was considered SIA. When a route is SIA, the neighbor that has not answered is reinitialized, effectively clearing the SIA route and clearing all other routes through that neighbor.

The SIA process was significantly changed in Cisco IOS Software Release 12.1(5)T. Figure A-6 illustrates these changes, and the list that follows describes the changes in further detail.

Figure A-6 *Modified SIA Process Integrated into Cisco IOS Software Release 12.1(5)T*

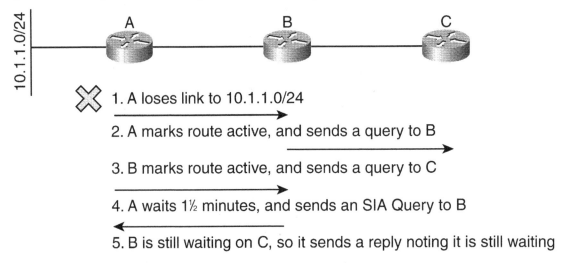

1 Router A loses its connection to 10.1.1.0/24. This could be because of an interface failure, operator intervention, or any number of other causes.

2 Router A examines its topology table and finds it has no other loop-free path to 10.1.1.0/24. Router A marks 10.1.1.0/24 as active and sends a query to its only neighbor, Router B.

3 Router B examines its topology table and finds it has no other loop-free path to 10.1.1.0/24. Router B marks the route as active and sends a query to Router C. The assumption, at this point, is that Router C does not reply to Router B, although it acknowledges receiving the query.

 After three minutes, Router A would normally mark 10.1.1.0/24 as SIA and reset its neighbor relationship with Router B, even though the problem is actually between Router B and Router C.

4 After 1.5 minutes, Router A sends an SIA query. This occurs well before the normal active timer expires (3 minutes), so the route should not be marked as SIA before the SIA query is transmitted.

5 Router B replies to the SIA query, indicating that it is still waiting on one of its neighbors to answer an outstanding query. This allows the neighbor relationship between Router B and Router C to either correct itself or be reset, while maintaining the neighbor relationship between Router A and Router B.

What this changed process does is allow the routers to check the status of the peer more than just once. If the communication problem preventing the reply from occurring is between these routers, it will be discovered. If the communication problem is farther downstream, these routers will retain their neighbor relationship while the query process continues.

Even this process cannot continue forever, however. A router sends the SIA query a maximum of three times. If at the end of one query and three SIA queries (approximately 6 minutes) a reply has still not been received from all the neighbors that the router queried, the route is considered SIA and the steps described in the preceding list occur. The offending neighbor is reinitialized and the SIA route (and all others through that peer) is reset.

Bounding Queries

The stability of a large-scale EIGRP network often depends on the range of a query through the network. If a query must travel from one end of a large network to the other, the odds are high that SIAs will be common. Essentially, the greater the number of routers and links that a query must travel, the greater the likelihood of encountering a poor link or a router that cannot answer immediately, and the greater the likelihood that a route will become SIA.

The three primary ways to bind the range of a query are as follows:

- Summarization
- Stub routers
- Distribution lists

The sections that follow discuss summarization and stub routers.

Summarization

EIGRP routes, external and internal, can be summarized manually or automatically (called *autosummarization*). Manual summarization can be configured at any bit boundary using the following interface-level command:

```
ip summary-address eigrp autonomous system summary address mask
```

With the preceding configuration in place, EIGRP does the following:

- Builds a routing table entry for this summarized network to the interface null0
- Advertises the summary out the interface that it is configured on
- Advertises the components of this summary as unreachable out the interface that it is configured on

The route is marked as a summary in both the routing table and the topology table on the router where the summarization takes place (the router that is generating the summary).

Autosummary occurs when a router is on the boundary of two major networks. A router that is running EIGRP automatically creates a summary for each of the major networks to advertise toward its neighbors in the other major network.

In Figure A-7, Router B would build a route for 10.0.0.0/8 to null0 and advertise it to Router C. (Router B uses an 8-bit mask for this summary because a 10.x.x.x address is a Class A address in classful routing.) Router B would also build a route for 172.16.0.0/16 to null0 and advertise it to Router A. (Again, Router B chooses a 16-bit mask for this summary because a 172.x.x.x address is a Class B address in classful routing.) You can modify this behavior by configuring **no auto-summary** under the router EIGRP process on Router B, so Router B would advertise the subnets rather than the major network summaries.

Figure A-7 *Autosummarization in EIGRP*

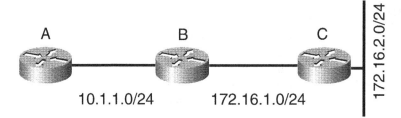

A caveat exists concerning autosummary and external routes in EIGRP: External routes are not autosummarized unless an internal component of the same major network is available. In the network illustrated in Figure A-7, if Router A and Router B are running EIGRP, and Router B and Router C are running RIP or some other protocol, Router B would advertise the 172.16.1.0/24 rather than 172.16.0.0/16 to Router A. If, however, Router C is running RIP toward its Ethernet and EIGRP toward its serial (with both Router A and Router B running EIGRP), Router B would autosummarize. That is because the 172.16.1.0/24 network is an internal route, and it is in the same major network as the external from RIP.

This has some implications for designs that use multiple EIGRP autonomous systems. If the autonomous system borders are on major network boundaries, designs of this type do more harm than good because autosummarization is defeated.

Stub Routing

EIGRP's stub routing feature is one of the most important scalability features added to EIGRP in its history. Prior to the stub feature, it was extremely difficult to remove the access routers from the Query scope of a network. These routers tend to be the smallest, slowest, cheapest routers, with the least memory and horsepower in the entire network. In many enterprise designs, 80 percent of the routers in the network are these low-powered and generally less stable access routers. Prior to the stub feature, every one of these routers might be involved in the Query process.

With the creation of the stub feature, these "weakest link" routers can be removed completely from the Query scope for the vast majority of the network. Using this one feature makes it possible for the Query scope in the network to be reduced by 80 percent—the weakest at 80 percent, at that!

You need to understand the definition of a stub router. In EIGRP terminology, a *stub router* is a router at the edge of the EIGRP network. A stub router connects to one or more local networks and is the pathway from these local networks to the distribution layer and the rest of the network. The stub router might be dual-homed to multiple distribution routers, but its responsibility is to provide connectivity for the local networks to the rest of the network and nowhere else.

Stub routers are never transit routers! Transit routers transport traffic that is sourced from a nonlocal network and destined to a nonlocal network. A transit router is in the *middle* of the path from source to destination rather than being at the *end* of the path, as is a stub router. Why is it so important to recognize the distinction between a stub router and a transit router? The reason is that if you define a router as stub when it really needs to be transit, you will badly break your network.

Normally, stub routers are at the edge of the network, in the access layer of three-layer networks, and the aggregation layer of two-layer networks. This is not always true, but these areas of your network are the best place to start looking when you are considering deploying the EIGRP stub feature.

Now that you know what a stub router is, how does it work? A stub router changes the Query process by taking advantage of the fact that it is known to be at the edge of the network, and nontransit. Because the stub router is at the edge of the network, EIGRP knows that it does not need to send a Query to the stub router looking for an alternative path to reach other locations in the network. The mere fact that you know where the stub router is in the topology of the network means that you can take a shortcut in the Query process and leave the stub router out of it.

How do you know the stub router is at the edge of the network? The network designer, who knows the topology of the network, defines a stub router using the following command syntax:

```
router eigrp 1
 eigrp stub [connected][redistributed][static][summary][receive-only]
```

The options at the end of the **stub** command define the types of local routes that are allowed to be sent, but that is not pertinent to the discussion of how the stub feature helps Query scope. Just realize that you can limit which types of routes are advertised. By default, connected and summary routes are advertised.

When a router is defined as a stub router, it includes information in its hello packets advising the distribution layer routers that it connects to that it is a stub. When the distribution layer router receives the Hello defining the neighbor as a stub router, it notes that in the information it keeps about the neighbor and removes the stub router from the list of neighbors that it should send queries to. It is as simple as that!

By defining as many remote routers as stub as possible (keeping in mind that they must be at the edge of the network), you might be able to reduce your Query scope as much as 80 percent, without impacting reachability or reliability. What a savings!

Using the Metrics

Whenever you are trying to change the path that EIGRP chooses between two routers, the best practice is to change the delay metrics along the path, rather than the bandwidth metrics. The primary reason for this is that the bandwidth configured on the interface affects the operation of EIGRP's reliable transport mechanism.

Using the **bandwidth** statements to influence routing decisions can have unintended consequences because the installation of a new link can unexpectedly override your bandwidth configuration. The delay metrics are cumulative, so their affect is more predictable and manageable in the long run.

Load Balancing

Like all other protocols on a Cisco router, if EIGRP discovers up to size equal-cost paths (by default) to a given destination, it installs all routes in the routing table, and the router load balances (or traffic shares) over them. EIGRP, however, has the capability to install unequal-cost routes in the routing table, and the router shares traffic over them in proportion to their metrics. Use the **variance** command in router configuration mode to allow EIGRP to load balance over paths with unequal metrics.

The variance is a divider. If a route's distance, divided by the variance configured, is less than or equal to the best metric, the route is installed in the routing table. For example, if you have paths with metrics of 100, 200, 300, and 400 in the topology table, and the variance is set to the default value of 1, only the path with a metric of 100 is used.

If you set the variance to 2, both the best path (with a metric of 100) and the path that has a metric of 200 are installed in the routing table. Setting the variance to 3 includes the route that has a metric of 300, and so on. The router load balances over these multiple paths in proportion to their metrics.

OSPF Basics of Operation

Open Shortest Path First (OSPF) is a protocol that was originally standardized in RFC 1131. It was subsequently updated in RFC 1247 in 1991 and then went through several other updates and revisions. The current protocol standard is described in RFC 2328. To fully understand current implementations of OSPF, you need to read the following RFCs:

- RFC 2328, "OSPF Version 2"
- RFC 3101, "The OSPF NSSA Option"
- RFC 1793, "Extending OSPF to Support Demand Circuits"
- RFC 2370, "The OSPF Opaque LSA Option"

Several other useful extensions are available beyond the base OSPF protocol, as described in the following RFCs:

- RFC 3137, "OSPF Stub Router Advertisement"
- RFC 3630, "Traffic Engineering (TE) Extensions to OSPF Version 2"
- RFC 3623, "Graceful OSPF Restart"

OSPF is a *link-state* protocol that has many advantages, among which are low traffic levels during normal operation and rapid convergence.

General Theory of OSPF

In a typical distance vector protocol, each router advertises its table of reachable destinations *(vectors)* and the distances to them *(distance)* on each of its interfaces on a regular basis *(periodic updates)*. OSPF routers advertise the state of their directly connected links to all routers on the network (through *flooding*). Although OSPF uses periodic updates, long periods of time exist between them, reducing network traffic to a minimum. Each router receives these *link-state advertisements* (LSAs) from its neighbors and floods them out each of its other interfaces, making certain that all routers on the network receive all LSAs.

After all routers have received all advertisements, they perform a *shortest path first* (SPF) calculation to find a loop-free path to each destination on the network. OSPF uses *neighbor relationships* to reliably flood LSAs. It enforces hierarchy and restricts flooding domains in a network through *areas*.

Router IDs

Each router that is running OSPF on a network must have a unique identifier—the *router ID*. This router ID is used in combination with an LSA sequence number to detect duplicate LSAs and to prevent a router from accepting an LSA that it originated.

The router ID is chosen from among the IP addresses on a Cisco router; it is either the highest IP address from any operational interface (interface and line protocol both up), or it is the address of the lowest numbered loopback interface. The recommended practice is to use loopback interfaces or the **router-id** command in the router OSPF configuration mode to set the router ID because this provides more stability in the network and makes the router ID more predictable.

LSAs

LSAs are classified by type, each type serving a different purpose:

- **Router Link State (type 1)**—These LSAs contain information about the following:
    - A router's connected (fully adjacent) neighbors
    - Connected stub networks (networks on which this router has no neighbors)
    - IP reachability information for connected point-to-point networks
- **Network Link State (type 2)**—These LSAs are generated by the designated router to advertise connectivity to a broadcast (multiaccess) network and connections to all the routers that are connected to the broadcast network.
- **Summary Network Link State (type 3)**—These LSAs advertise internal networks to routers in other areas *(interarea routes)*. Each intra-area route might represent a single destination or a set of destinations aggregated into one route. Summaries are only generated by area border routers (ABRs).
- **Summary ASBR Link State (type 4)**—These LSAs advertise the location of an autonomous system boundary router. Routers that are trying to reach an external network use these advertisements to determine the best path to the next hop. They are generated by Autonomous System Boundary Routers (ASBRs).
- **External Network Link State (type 5)**—These LSAs redistribute routes from other autonomous systems, generally using a different routing protocol, into OSPF.
- **External Network Link State (type 7)**—These LSAs are similar to type 5 LSAs, but they represent externally reachable destinations within a not-so-stubby area (NSSA).

Figure B-1 illustrates the first five of these LSA types in a small network.

Figure B-1   *Primary LSA Types in an OSPF Network*

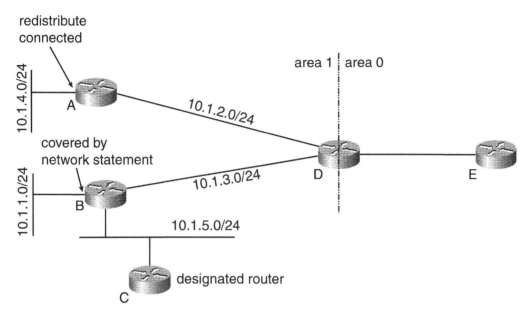

What would each router in this network originate, and why?

- Router A would generate a type 1 LSA with the following:
    - A bit set indicating that it is an ASBR, because it is redistributing.
    - A connection to Router D.
    - A connection to 10.1.2.0/24.
- Router A would generate a type 5 LSA with a connection to 10.1.4.0/24, because it is redistributing that connected interface into OSPF.
- Router B would generate a type 1 LSA with the following:
    - A connection to Router D.
    - A connection to the pseudonode that is advertised in the type 2 LSA of Router C. Router B does not advertise a connection to 10.1.5.0/24 or to Router C, because this is a broadcast network with a designated router.
    - A connection to 10.1.1.0/24.
    - A connection to 10.1.3.0/24.
- Router C would generate a type 1 LSA with connection to the pseudonode that is advertised in its own type 2 LSA. Router C does not advertise a connection to 10.1.5.0/24 or to Router B, because this is a broadcast network with a designated router.

- Router C would generate a type 2 LSA with the following:
  - — A connection to Router C.
  - — A connection to Router B.
  - — A connection to 10.1.5.0/24.
- Router D would generate a type 1 LSA into area 1 with the following:
  - — A connection to Router A.
  - — A connection to Router B.
  - — A connection to 10.1.2.0/24.
  - — A connection to 10.1.3.0/24.
- Router D would generate a type 1 LSA into area 0 with a connection to Router E, and include a connection to the network between Routers D and E.
- Router D would generate a type 4 LSA into area 0, including the cost to reach Router B. This type 4 LSA is generated because Router B is setting a bit in its router LSA (type 1), indicating that it is an ASBR.
- Router D would generate a type 3 LSA including the following:
  - — A connection to 10.1.1.0/24.
  - — A connection to 10.1.2.0/24.
  - — A connection to 10.1.3.0/24.
  - — A connection to 10.1.5.0/24.
- Router D would react with the following:
  - — Reflood Router A's type 5 LSA into area 0.
  - — Not reflood Router B's type 1 LSA into area 0.
  - — Not reflood Router C's type 1 LSA into area 0.
  - — Not reflood Router C's type 2 LSA into area 0.

LSA Age

Each LSA that is flooded to the network has an age parameter *(LSAge)*, which is set by the originating router to 0. When a router receives an LSA from a neighbor, it begins aging it out by adding 1 to the LSAge for each second it holds the LSA in its database. When the LSAge equals *MaxAge*, the router sets the cost to unreachable, floods the LSA, and then removes the LSA from its database. This clears any LSA from the network that is not periodically refreshed.

Because of this aging-out mechanism, OSPF routers must reflood their LSAs periodically to prevent them from being timed out. How often a router floods its LSAs is called the *LSRefreshTime*. The MaxAge is set to 1 hour, and the LSRefreshTime is set to 30 minutes.

Reliable Flooding of LSAs

When a router receives an LSA or the status of one of its directly connected links changes, it marks the database entry and builds a list of neighbors to which this entry needs to be flooded. As the router builds a packet to send (which can contain more than one LSA), it does the following:

- Chooses database entries marked for sending and places them in the packet
- Notes in the database neighbors to which the LSA has been advertised

As acknowledgments are received, neighbors are removed from the *waiting for acknowledgment* list that is associated with the LSA. Every so often, the router checks this list of outstanding acknowledgments to see if some neighbors have not responded; it resends the LSA to those that have not. This interval is configurable on a per-interface basis using the **ip ospf retransmit-interval** command on a Cisco router.

Building Adjacencies

Because adjacencies are vital to the reliable flooding of these LSAs, you should examine how an adjacency is built and discuss some special cases. Figure B-2 shows two routers connected to the same network.

Figure B-2   *Building Adjacencies*

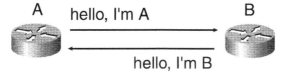

When Routers A and B are first attached to the common serial link, they begin sending *Hello* packets on this network. Next, the routers begin receiving each other's Hello packets. When A and B receive each other's Hellos, they place their new neighbors in an *init* state, as illustrated in Figure B-3.

Figure B-3   *Init State*

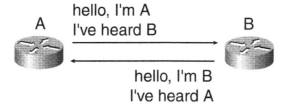

After placing a new neighbor in an init state, a router begins including the router ID of that neighbor in its Hellos. After a router has received a Hello from a neighbor with its router ID enclosed, the router places the neighbor in a *two-way* state. This *two-way* state ensures two-way communication between the routers before exchanging database information. Routers do not enter the two-way state if the link type, Hello time, wait time, or dead time do not match.

After determining that an adjacency should be built (routers remain in a two-way state under some circumstances — see the next section, "Adjacencies on Multiaccess Networks"), the routers begin to negotiate the exchange of their OSPF databases. If a new router on the network were to wait until normal flooding occurred to obtain a complete database, it could take a half an hour to do so. During that time, the router would not be able to reach all areas in the network and could cause routing loops.

This stage is called *exstart*; a master and slave are chosen to synchronize the database exchange based on the router IDs of the two routers. The master controls the exchange of the *database descriptors* (DBDs) between the routers, as illustrated in Figure B-4.

Figure B-4   *Exstart*

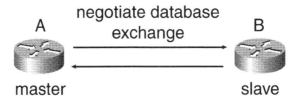

After the routers have negotiated which one will control the DBD exchange, they begin exchanging DBDs, as illustrated in Figure B-5.

Figure B-5   *Exchange*

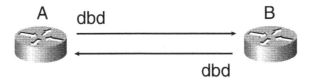

These DBDs do not really contain link-state information. They just describe each router's database. Each DBD contains a list of LSAs and LSA sequence numbers, by which each LSA in a router's database can be uniquely identified. After all the DBDs have been exchanged, each router compares the list of LSAs received through the DBDs against its local database, and requests the set of LSAs required to synchronize its databases.

After the two routers have finished requesting the LSAs required to synchronize their databases, they move their neighbor adjacency into the *full* state.

Adjacencies on Multiaccess Networks

It is not efficient for every router on a multiaccess (broadcast or nonbroadcast multiaccess [NBMA]) network to build full adjacencies with every other router on that network, so OSPF uses the concepts of *designated routers* (*DRs*) and *backup designated routers* (*BDRs*) to reduce the number of adjacencies built and consequently reduce the number of LSAs flooded throughout the area for the common network. Each router on the network builds a full adjacency with the DR and BDR and leaves all other neighbors on that network in the two-way state. The DR is responsible for advertising a link to the network and for flooding LSAs to other routers on the link.

The DR and BDR are elected based on the router priority (configured on a per-interface basis on a Cisco router with **ip ospf priority**) and the router ID.

Assuming that all three of these routers were connected to the same Ethernet segment, as shown in Figure B-6, at the same time (unlikely, but possible if you tried hard enough), each would see each other's Hellos, progress to the two-way state, and begin electing a BDR and a DR for this link.

Figure B-6   *A Multiaccess Network*

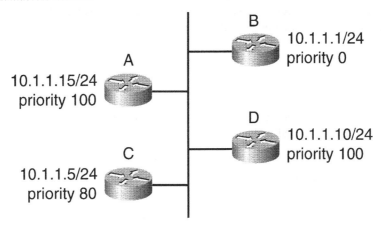

To better understand what transpires, look at this scenario from the perspective of Router A.

Router A will receive three Hellos, one each from Routers B, C, and D. Because B's priority is set to 0 (which means Router B cannot become the DR or the BDR), it keeps its neighbor state with Routers A, C, and D at two-way.

The Hello from Router C indicates that it has a priority of 80 and an ID of 10.1.1.5. The Hello from Router D indicates that it has a priority of 100 and an ID of 10.1.1.10.

Router A first compares the priorities of the other routers with its own; Router D's matches, but Router C's is lower. Because Router C has a lower priority, it is removed from the possibilities.

Because Router D's matches, the router ID is used to determine the BDR, (The BDR is always elected first.) Router A's router ID is higher than router D's, so Router A is chosen as the BDR.

Now Router A determines that the link has no DR, so it promotes the BDR to the position of DR and then elects a new BDR. Router A promotes itself to DR and examines each of its other neighbors in the two-way state to see which should become the BDR. Once again, Router B is not considered because its priority is 0. Router A compares the Hellos from the remaining two neighbors and discovers that Router C has a lower priority than D. Therefore, the new BDR is Router D.

The order in which this occurs is of some importance because the process must be repeatable when the DR is lost. The BDR is promoted, and a new BDR is elected.

Because getting all of these routers to connect to the link at the same moment is too difficult, you need to examine how an OSPF router deals with a new link when a DR and a BDR already exist. Assume that Routers B, C, and D are attached to this Ethernet and have been running for some time. What happens when A is attached?

Without Router A, Router D is the DR, and Router C is the BDR. When Router A is first attached, it sees Router D's Hellos asserting that it is the DR, and it does not attempt to re-elect a new one (even though it would be chosen if a new election were to occur). This prevents unecessary DR election by allowing the router connected to the link the longest become, and stay, the DR.

Areas

OSPF provides for and enforces hierarchical network design through *areas*. Four types of areas are provided for in OSPF:

- An *area*, which is a nontransit flooding domain that is connected to area 0.

- A *totally stubby area*, in which all routers receive a default route only, and any connections to other autonomous systems are not allowed.

- A *stubby area*, into which external routes are not flooded, but internal summaries are.

- A *not-so-stubby area (NSSA)*, which is the same as a stubby area, except that connections to other autonomous systems (external connections) are allowed.

The *backbone area*, which is *area 0* (or 0.0.0.0), is not really considered a different area type, although it is unique from all the other OSPF areas:

- All traffic transits through the backbone area.

- All other areas must touch the backbone area in at least one place.

- Area 0 must be topologically contiguous.

All areas can be identified with a single integer (area 1) or with a four-octet number similar to an IP address (area 1.1.1.1). Routers that border or touch two areas — the backbone and some other area — are known as ABRs, as shown in Figure B-7.

Figure B-7   *ABRs and ASBRs*

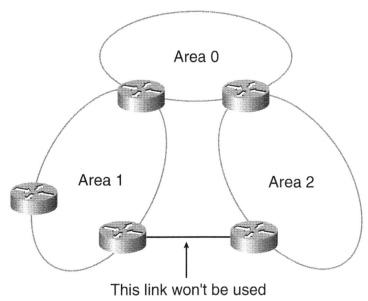

This link won't be used

All traffic between areas (interarea traffic) passes through the backbone; links between areas that do not pass through the backbone area will not be used.

External Route Injection

External routes — routes from other autonomous systems or protocols — are injected into OSPF by ASBRs. External routes are flooded throughout all areas of the OSPF autonomous system without change (this means no summarization).

External routes within OSPF also have a *forwarding address* field, which allows an OSPF router to act as a *route server.*

In Figure B-8, Router B is an ASBR for the OSPF cloud. It is learning routes from Routers A and C through RIP. Router D is not learning these RIP routes, but is advertising an internal OSPF link to the Ethernet segment that connects Routers A, B, C, and D. When Router B advertises routes it has learned from RIP, it puts Router A and C's IP addresses in the *forwarding address* field, so Router E can forward traffic to them directly, rather than through Router B specifically. This means that other routers could choose the route to Router D to get to Routers A or C, even though Router D is not advertising these routes. Router B is acting as a route server in this case for the externally derived BGP routes.

Figure B-8 *External Route Injection*

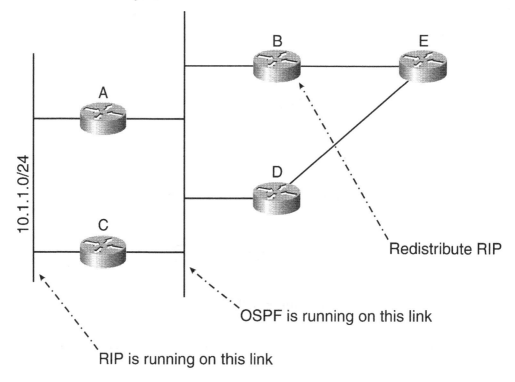

If the forward address field is set to 0.0.0.0, the router that is advertising the external route is where the traffic should be forwarded. If a router wanted to forward traffic to the external network that was advertised, it would look for an ASBR link state to determine how to reach the autonomous system boundary router that was advertising the external route.

Virtual Links

Sometimes the backbone area becomes divided, or an area loses contact with the backbone (generally, when a network outage has occurred). For these situations, the designers of OSPF provided the *virtual link*. The virtual link acts as a tunnel, allowing traffic to traverse to and from the backbone area to pass through another area.

Router A in Figure B-9 has gone down, effectively partitioning area 1 from the rest of the network, making it unreachable. The network administrator could, by configuring a virtual link between Routers B and C across the backup link, make area 1 accessible until Router A is repaired and restored to service.

Figure B-9   *Virtual Links*

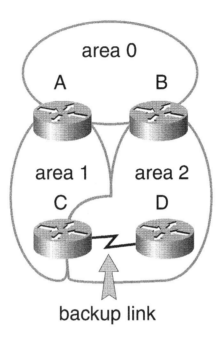

One of the most confusing aspects of configuring virtual links is the mysterious area number included in the command. This is not the area you are trying to reach or repair, but rather the area through which the virtual link passes.

Integrated IS-IS Basics of Operation

Intermediate System-to-Intermediate System (IS-IS) was standardized by the International Telecommunication Union (ITU) in the International Organization for Standardization (ISO) standard 10589 in 1990. IS-IS was originally designed for use with End System-to-Intermediate System (ES-IS) to provide routing information for Connectionless Network Service (CLNS) and other routed protocols that the ITU standardized.

The Internet Engineering Task Force (IETF) has, over the years, added extensions to IS-IS to support IP routing, Multiprotocol Label Switching (MPLS) traffic engineering (TE), and other capabilities, through a series of RFCs, including these:

- **RFC 1195**—"Use of Open System Interconnection (OSI) IS-IS for Routing in TCP/IP and Dual Environments"
- **RFC 2973**—"IS-IS Mesh Groups"
- **RFC 3567**—"Intermediate System-to-Intermediate System (IS-IS) Cryptographic Authentication"
- **RFC 3784**—"Intermediate System-to-Intermediate System (IS-IS) Extensions for Traffic Engineering (TE)"
- **RFC 3847**—"Restart Signaling for Intermediate System-to-Intermediate System (IS-IS)"

NOTE   You can find all Reqeust for Commands (RFCs) online at http://www.ietf.org/rfc/rfcxxxx.txt, where *xxxx* is the number of the RFC. If you do not know the number of the RFC, you can try searching by topic at http://www.rfc-editor.org/cgi-bin/rfcsearch.pl.

Until 2003, the IETF issued only informational RFCs for the IS-IS protocol, which means they are not authoritative for building interoperable implementations of the protocol. This has led to the reissuance of many of these modifications to the protocols by the ITU. The IETF has recently, however, decided to issue *standards track* RFCs for IS-IS. The ITU can refer to these as authoritative definitions of how the protocol works, directly, so the entire community can work together on specifying new extensions to the protocol.

General Theory

IS-IS is a link-state protocol; each router (called an intermediate system, or IS) floods the state of its links to every other IS within a flooding domain. Each IS within the flooding domain then uses Dijkstra's shortest path first (SPF) algorithm to build a tree of shortest paths to each reachable node within the network. After this tree is built (or as it is being built), the IP networks that each node can reach are added as leaf nodes to the tree, to provide reachability information to every destination in the network.

IS-IS allows the network designer to break the network into flooding domains. Level 1 (L1) flooding domains are interconnected through a single, contiguous, level 2 (L2) flooding domain. Two intermediate systems within the same flooding domain build either an L1 and an L2 adjacency or just an L1 adjacency, whereas two intermediate systems within different flooding domains can build only an L2 adjacency. The type of adjacency built depends on each intermediate system's configuration and addresses.

Because routers in link-state protocols rely on all the routers within a given routing area to have information in their databases to preclude routing loops, IS-IS does not generally permit filtering of routing information.

CLNS Addressing

To understand the way IS-IS allows hierarchy, you need to understand a little about CLNS addressing. CLNS identifies nodes on a network (hosts or routers) using network service access points (NSAPs).

The fields typically found in an NSAP are as follows:

- **NSAP Selector (NSEL)**—Identifies the user or service on a particular host, much like a TCP or UDP port number. This is also called the *service identifier.*
- **System ID**—Identifies an individual system or host.
- **Area Address**—Identifies the flooding domain where this device resides.
- **Initial Domain Identifier (IDI)**—Identifies the routing domain that this system is in. This is a variable-length field.
- **Authority Format Identifier (AFI)**—Identifies the authority assigning this address and the format of the address. This is a 1-byte field.

NSAPs can be a maximum of 20 bytes in length and are divided into two major parts:

- **Initial domain part (IDP)**—The IDI and AFI are part of the IDP.
- **Domain specific part (DSP)**—The NSEL, System ID, and Area Address are considered part of the DSP.

For the NSAP 47.0012.00C0.A94B.51C1.00, the fields are as follows:

- **47.00**—AFI and domain.
- **12**—Area address.
- **00C0.A94B.51C1**—System ID. This is always 6 bytes.
- **00**—Service identifier. This is always 1 byte.

You will often see a service identifier of 00, which means *this system*, rather than some upper-level entity on this system. The AFI and IDI are often treated as one piece, rather than as two separate pieces. Continuing with this addressing example, the following applies:

- Anything sent from this host and destined to 47.0012.xxxx.xxxx.xxxx.xx would be within the level 1 flooding domain and would be routed using level 1 routing.
- Anything sent from this host to 47.00xx.xxxx.xxxx.xxxx.xx would be level 2 routed.
- Anything else would need to be routed between domains (interdomain routed).

Whereas IP addresses are assigned to a wire or link, NSAPs are assigned to a host. Therefore, a system (such as a router) that has connections to multiple networks has multiple IP addresses, one for each network it attaches to, but only one NSAP.

Routing

When a group of end systems (hosts) and intermediate systems (routers) with the same area IDs in their NSAPs are connected, they begin forming adjacencies using ES-IS and IS-IS. Hosts rely on the nearest L1 router within their area to forward all traffic for them, unless they are redirected. A router can use ES-IS to tell a host to send its packets for a given destination to another L1 router or to tell a host to send its packets directly to the receiving ES (if they are on the same physical link).

Figure C-1 illustrates the concepts of IP routing in a network that is running IS-IS.

Figure C-1   *IP Routing in an IS-IS Network*

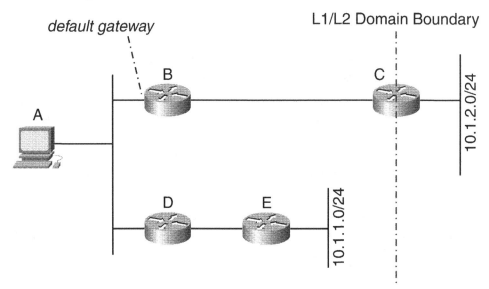

Because IP hosts do not support the ES-IS protocol, an IP host would be directed to the closest IS through its configured default gateway. Intermediate systems that are running in an IP network will use Internet Control Message Protocol (ICMP) redirects to direct a host to use another exit point for specific destinations. For instance, in the network illustrated in Figure C-1, if Host A sends a packet destined to 10.1.1.1 to its default gateway, Router B will send an ICMP redirect to Host A noting it should use Router D to reach this destination.

Intermediate systems send any traffic with a destination outside the area to the nearest level 2 IS. L1 intermediate systems have no routing knowledge outside their local flooding domain beyond the capability to reach the L2 intermediate systems along the edge of the flooding domain. For instance, in the network illustrated in Figure C-1, if Host A sends a packet destined to 10.1.2.1 to Router B, its default gateway, Router B will see it has no route for 10.1.2.1 in its local routing table. It will send the packet to the nearest L1/L2 border router (the nearest *attached* router), Router C. Router C will then forward the packet to the correct destination.

If the packet that is being forwarded is a CLNS or other ISO addresses packet, the L2 routers within the L2 flooding domain forward the packet to the nearest L2 router connected to the L1 domain indicated in the destination address, and the packet is routed through the L1 domain to the correct host.

Metrics

IS-IS has two types of metrics:

- **Narrow metrics**—As specified in the original IS-IS documents, narrow metrics are only 6 bits, with each link (interface) within the network taking a cost between 0 and 63. Path metrics are 10 bits wide, with a total cost for any path in the network between 0 and 1023. These numbers were chosen to restrict the depth of the SPF algorithm, so that routers implementing IS-IS would be able to run SPF and would converge must faster. External metric types are indicated by setting the seventh bit in the metric. That is why some implementations show external metrics as starting at 128, rather than 0.

- **Wide metrics**—These metrics are 24 bits wide. Therefore, a path through the network can have a cost ranging from 0 to 4261412864, whereas a single link or interface can have a cost between 0 and 16777215. Externals are indicated through a bit outside the scope of the metric.

Building Adjacencies

When an IS-IS router is connected to a broadcast (or multiaccess) network, it immediately begins sending IS-IS hellos. When a router is connected to a point-to-point link, it waits until it builds an ES-IS adjacency with the device on the other end before determining whether it should transmit IS-IS hellos. These hellos are always padded to the maximum transmission unit (MTU) size of the link. Therefore, two routers will not build an adjacency over a link with different MTUs configured on either end.

When two IS-IS neighbors first begin bringing up an adjacency, they exchange complete sequence number protocol (CSNP) protocol data units (PDUs) to synchronize their databases. After a pair of routers has become adjacent, partial sequence number PDUs (PSNPs) are used to request and send information about a subset of the link-state database.

To reduce the problems associated with building a full mesh of adjacencies on multiaccess links, such as Ethernet or Token Ring, IS-IS builds pseudonodes. One of the intermediate systems (ISs) is specified as the designated IS (DIS); this router becomes the pseudonode on the network.

All routers that are attached to the multiaccess network build an adjacency with this DIS, rather than with one another. The router with this highest Subnetwork Point of Attachment (SNPA), which is normally the same as the Layer 2 address of the router's interface, is elected the DIS. All the other routers on the link form an adjacency with the DIS, rather than with each other. The router with the highest SNPA is selected. DIS status is pre-emptive, unlike DR status in

OSPF. If a new router with a higher priority is connected to a multiaccess link, it takes over the role of DIS.

The DIS is responsible for generating PSN (PseudoNoDe) link-state packets (LSPs) for all adjacent routers on the multiaccess network. These packets are for reporting the link status of other routers to the multiaccess network. The DIS also broadcasts a packet containing information on every LSP in its database every 10 seconds (configurable) onto the link for which it is the pseudonode; this packet is a complete sequence number PDU (CSNP).

Other routers on the multiaccess network examine these CSNPs to determine whether their database is complete. If it is not complete, the routers request particular LSPs from the DIS using Partial Sequence Number PDUs (PSNPs).

One interesting point to note is that it is possible for different L1 and L2 DISs to coexist on the same multiaccess network. Each level of routing has a separate election process, and the same router might or might not be both L1 and L2 DIS for a given multiaccess link.

LSP Flooding and SPF Recalculation Timers

IS-IS, like OSPF, uses a complex recursive algorithm for calculating the best path to a particular destination, and it ages out LSPs every so often. The intervals at which these events normally occur is configurable on Cisco routers. Chapter 5, "IS-IS Network Design," discusses the importance of adjusting these timers in large IS-IS networks.

Use the **spf-interval** command to adjust the interval at which IS-IS runs SPF. The default interval is 5 seconds. Each LSP advertised also contains a Remaining Lifetime field (also known as the *max-lsp-lifetime*, or *Maxage*) that determines how long the LSP should be kept in memory before it is timed out. As a router times out LSPs in its database, it floods to all other routers that this destination is no longer reachable. Aging out occurs when the Remaining Lifetime field reaches 0.

If an LSP is flooded with a lifetime of 0, the LSP is removed from the databases of the ISs that are attached to the network. This is called *purging* the LSP.

The router that is originating an LSP times the LSP out of its database slightly faster than normal, so it should flood a new copy of the LSP before any other router on the network times it out and marks it as unreachable. Although the default Remaining Lifetime is 20 minutes, the originating IS times out an LSP in 15 minutes. You can use the **max-lsp-lifetime** command to adjust the Remaining Lifetime that a router places in LSPs it generates. You can use the **lsp-refresh-interval** command to adjust the rate at which the originating router times out its own LSPs.

Neighbor Loss and LSP Regeneration

Refer to Figure C-2 to see what happens when Router B reboots for some unknown reason.

Figure C-2   *IS-IS Adjacency*

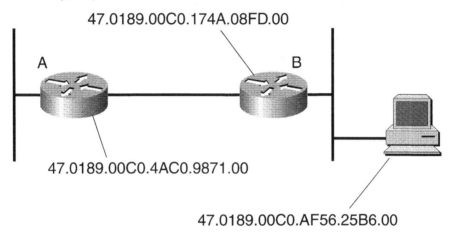

Router A does not, as you might expect, immediately flush the LSPs that Router B has advertised. It waits until the Remaining Lifetime fields for these LSPs reach 0 (they time out), and then floods to the rest of the network that they are unreachable and flushes them from its database. Router A does not flush the LSP that is advertised by Router B for NSAP 47.0189.00C0.AF56.25B6.00 until its Maxage timer reaches 0. When Router B finishes rebooting and rebuilds its adjacency with Router A, it sends this LSP to Router A with a sequence number of 1.

When Router A receives this LSP, it examines its database and finds that it has an existing LSP for this destination with a higher sequence number. Router A then replies to Router B with a copy of this later LSP. Router B, on receiving this later LSP, sets its LSP sequence number for this destination so that it is higher than the copy that Router A replied with.

IP Integration into IS-IS

IP routing is integrated into IS-IS via carrying IP reachability information in LSPs. All Internet Protocol (IP) networks are considered externals, and they always end up as leaf nodes in the shortest path tree when IS-IS runs SPF.

This means that changes in IP reachability alone result in only a partial SPF run (partial route calculation, or PRC). The routers in the tree need to calculate only the parts of the tree in which the leaf node for that destination network resides.

Only L2 routers can summarize IP destinations to shorter masks.

Multiple net Statements

From time to time, you might see a Cisco router configured with multiple **net** statements under router IS-IS. This is a useful technique for merging two domains or transitioning from one addressing scheme to another, but it is not generally recommended.

When you configure two **net** statements, the router combines, or merges, the databases into one database. This means that routing between what might normally be considered domains ends up appearing as simple L2 routing.

Border Gateway Protocol 4 Basics of Operation

Border Gateway Protocol version 4 (BGP-4, or just BGP), is an exterior gateway routing protocol used between routing domains or autonomous systems. BGP is the protocol used between all Internet service providers and in the cores of other large networks.

BGP provides extremely stable routing between autonomous systems even with huge routing tables. It also provides network administrators with a great deal of control over routing decisions.

A Path Vector Protocol

BGP is unique among all the currently used routing protocols because it relies on information about the vector (direction) to a destination and the path to a destination to prevent routing loops. All other commonly used routing protocols, such as Open Shortest Path First (OSPF), Intermediate System-to-Intermediate System (IS-IS), and Enhanced IGRP (EIGRP), rely on metrics or costs combined with some level of topology information to prevent routing loops. To illustrate, look at Figure D-1.

Figure D-1   *Path Vector Example*

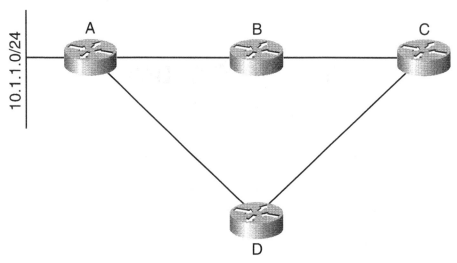

Suppose that Router A originates a route to 10.1.1.0/24 toward Router B. In the information on how to reach this destination, Router A notes that it is the first router in the path. Router B receives this route, adds itself to the path, and advertises the destination to Router C. Router C adds itself to the path and advertises it to Router D.

Therefore, when Router D receives the route to 10.1.1.0/24, it sees the path is through Routers C, B, and A. Router D likewise adds itself to the path and advertises it back to Router A. When Router A receives this advertisement, it sees that it is already in the path to this destination and rejects the route.

This, essentially, is how BGP works—except instead of individual routers marking the route with some information, each *autonomous system (AS)* in the path marks the route. Any router that receives the route can verify whether the path to this destination is a loop by checking the autonomous systems listed in the path to see if the AS they are in is already listed.

Look at Figure D-2 for a more concrete example of how this works.

In this case, Router A originates a route for 10.1.1.0/24 toward Router B, which, in turn, forwards the route to Router C. When it advertises 10.1.1.0/24, Router A adds its local AS number to the AS path attribute of the route.

Router C forwards the route to Router D and adds that AS (AS2) to the AS-path. Router D then forwards the route to Router E.

When Router E receives this route, it examines the AS-path and sees that the AS it is in, AS1, is already in the AS-path. Because of this, Router E assumes that this advertisement represents a loop (it does from an AS level view) and discards the advertisement.

Figure D-2   *AS-Based Path Vector Example*

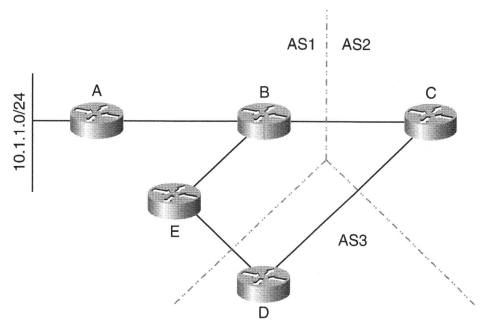

Path Decision

Because BGP does not rely on a metric to determine whether a path is looped, the metrics it does use are more policy based—that is, network administrators can use them to set policies for routers to employ when selecting a path.

BGP advertises only the best route to each of its neighbors (unless BGP multipath is configured, which is covered in Chapter 8, "Routing Protocols Security"). Following are these metrics, listed from most important to least important:

1 Administrative weight

2 Local preference

3 Locally originated routes

4 Shortest AS-path

5 Lowest origin

6 Multiple exit discriminator (MED)

7 Prefer externals

   8 Path through nearest neighbor based on Interior Gateway Protocol (IGP) metric

   9 Path through neighbor with the lowest router ID

The sections that follow discuss some of these metrics.

Administrative Weight

The administrative weight is a locally assigned metric, not carried in BGP itself. Therefore, it impacts only the BGP best path operation on the router where the weight is configured. The administrative weight is not used in many situations within normal BGP deployments.

Local Preference

Local preference is generally set by a route map when a destination network (prefix) is advertised or received from a BGP peer. The local preference is advertised with the prefix throughout the AS.

The local preference sets a preferred exit point for this destination from the AS.

AS Path Length

The path that has the shortest AS-path length is preferred if all factors that have more weight than path length are equal.

MED

The MED, or metric, is generally set using a route map when a prefix is advertised to a neighboring AS. This is carried with the prefix whenever it is advertised, through all autonomous systems. The MED is considered a hint about which entry point into an AS the administrator would like traffic for that destination to use. It is generally checked only if the AS-paths on two routes are not only equal in length, but are identical. In other words, the MEDs of two prefixes learned from different neighboring autonomous systems would not be considered.

Lowest Router ID

If all else is equal, the path through the neighbor with the lowest router ID is preferred. This final metric can become an issue when an AS has two connections to another AS.

<table>
<tr><td>**NOTE**</td><td>For more information on the BGP best path calculation, please see http://www.cisco.com/warp/ public/459/25.shtml.</td></tr>
</table>

Community

From the discussion of BGP's best path algorithm in the preceding section, you can see that BGP is designed to eliminate looped routes. Consider policy as the guiding factor in determining which path to choose among the remaining loop-free paths. A community is another expression of policy within BGP.

A community is a string of numbers that tags a prefix. You can then use this tag for things like the following:

- **Entry point control**—Because the MED, in many cases, is not used in path determination (because the AS path of two routes must be the same for the MED to be compared), a system exists whereby a router that is receiving a prefix with a given community string set sets its local preference.

  See RFC 1998 for more information.

- **Propagating quality of service (QoS) information**—Two BGP peers could make an arrangement so that tagging a prefix with a given community string results in the packets destined to the advertised destination being treated differently.

Communities are set and checked using route maps. (See the section titled "Route Maps," later in this appendix, for more details.)

Operation

Most advanced routing protocols have some system of neighbor discovery (generally a hello protocol) so that routers can discover neighbors and trade routing information reliably. BGP is an exception because it requires the manual configuration of neighbor relationships; it does not discover neighbors automatically. Like other advanced routing protocols, though, BGP requires a reliable transport system to ensure that packets are not lost between peers. BGP uses Transmission Control Protocol (TCP) for reliable transport.

When a router that is running BGP (a BGP speaker) is configured to build a neighbor relationship with another BGP speaker, it first builds a TCP connection over which to transport information. (Port 179 is the well-known port for BGP.) This means that Internet Protocol (IP) connectivity between BGP speakers must exist before you can set up a BGP session between the two routers.

After a neighbor relationship is set up between two routers, the routers trade full routing information (as allowed by any filters that are applied). After this, BGP speakers send only incremental updates to neighbors, advertising or withdrawing prefixes as necessary.

Exterior BGP

BGP peers in two different autonomous systems automatically form an eBGP neighbor relationship. Look at Figure D-3 for an overview of how eBGP works.

Figure D-3   *eBGP Peers*

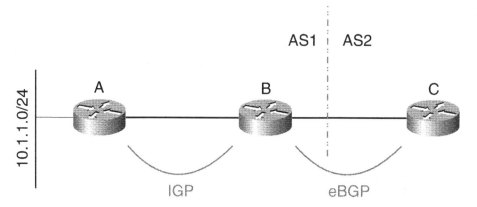

Router A is advertising the 10.1.1.0/24 prefix through some Interior Gateway Protocol (IGP) to Router B, which has an eBGP neighbor relationship with Router C. This route can be injected into BGP by Router B in several ways:

* **Redistribution**—Router B could be redistributing routes from the IGP used between A and B into BGP. This will result in the origin code for the redistributed routes being marked as "incomplete."

* **network statement**—Router B could have a **network** statement configured under **router BGP** that matches 10.1.1.0/24. Unlike many other routing protocols, a **network** statement in BGP does not indicate which interfaces to run BGP on, but rather which prefixes to advertise. If a router has an exact match (including prefix length) in its routing table for a **network** statement under **router bgp,** it will advertise this prefix. Routes that are originated using a **network** statement will be marked with an origin code of IGP.

* **aggregate-address statement**—Router A could be summarizing the 10.1.1.0/24 network into a larger block of IP addresses through an **aggregate-address** statement configured under **router bgp.** Routes that are originated using a **summary-address** statement will be marked with an origin code of IGP.

After Router B has determined it should advertise this prefix to C, it sends an update. The AS path field in this update contains just Router B's AS, because the destination originates within Router B's AS. The next hop for this route is Router B's IP address.

Router B might or might not install this prefix in its routing table, depending on other routes available to this prefix, and so on.

Interior BGP

When a BGP speaker is configured with a neighbor in the same AS, these routers become iBGP peers. To understand iBGP better, look at Figure D-4.

Figure D-4   *iBGP Peers*

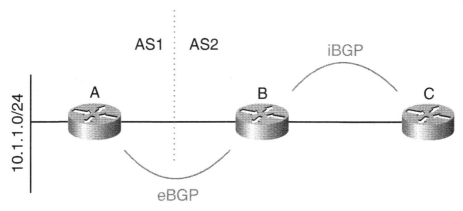

In Figure D-4, Router A is advertising 10.1.1.0/24 as an eBGP route to Router B. Router B, in turn, is advertising this route through iBGP to Router C.

When this prefix is passed to Router C, the next hop is not changed (it remains Router A's IP address), and the AS path is not changed (because the prefix was not advertised across an AS boundary). The AS path not changing explains one of the most severe restrictions of iBGP: iBGP peers cannot advertise a route learned via iBGP to another iBGP neighbor. The network in Figure D-5 adds a few more routers to provide you with a better idea of why iBGP peers must be full mesh.

Figure D-5   *iBGP Peers*

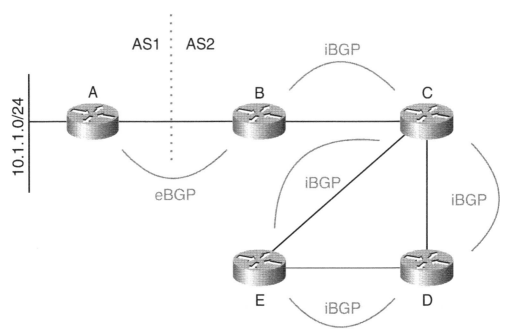

Here, Routers B and C, Routers B and D, and Routers C and D, have iBGP peering relationships, but Routers B and D do not. If iBGP peers could advertise routes learned through iBGP to other iBGP peers, you could follow the chain of events that would occur when 10.1.1.0/24 was advertised from Routers A to B.

Router B would advertise this prefix to Router C, which would in turn advertise it to Router D. Router D would advertise 10.1.1.0/24 to each of its peers, including Router E, which would advertise it to Router C. At this point, Router C has received two iBGP advertisements for 10.1.1.0/24: one through Router B, and one through Router E.

Which path does Router C choose? Because the next hop and AS path are not changed when a prefix is advertised from one iBGP peer to another, Router C has no way of knowing that the path it is learning from Router E is a loop.

To prevent this sort of problem, iBGP peers are not allowed to advertise a route learned through iBGP to another iBGP neighbor. The practical application of this rule results in another: iBGP peers must be fully meshed. There are ways around the full mesh rule in iBGP, but they are covered in Chapter 8, rather than here.

The Next Hop Attribute

As stated previously in the chapter, the next hop attribute in the advertised prefix is not changed between iBGP neighbors. You can set the next hop to another router than the advertising router when eBGP is running across a multiaccess network. For an example, look at Figure D-6.

Figure D-6   *Next Hop on a Multiaccess Network*

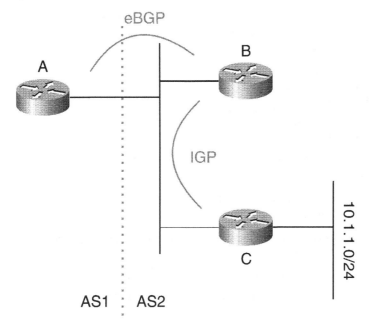

Router C is advertising the 10.1.1.0/24 network to Router B via an IGP, and Router B is in turn advertising this prefix to Router A via eBGP. Because it does not make sense in this situation for the traffic to flow from Router A to B, then over the same Ethernet to Router C, Router B advertises the next hop as Router C.

You can use the **neighbor** *peer-address* **next-hop self** command to alter this behavior. In this network, if Router B were configured with **next-hop self**, Router A would send traffic destined to 10.1.1.0/24 to Router B, which would, in turn, forward the traffic to Router C.

Filtering

Because BGP focuses on administrative control of routing, it is only natural for BGP to have vast filtering capabilities. BGP's vast filtering capabilities is one of the most confusing areas of configuring BGP. BGP allows users to filter or modify routing information using route maps, prefix lists, and distribution lists.

Route Maps

Filtering in BGP on Cisco routers is typically done using route maps, which are constructed as a set of matches and sets within a sequence. The matches specify the conditions that a prefix must match to be considered or to have the **match** statements configured applied to it. The **set** statement determines what is to be done to the prefix after it is determined that the prefix matches.

The sequences represent the order in which **route-map** statements are checked, much like BASIC line numbers represented program execution order. A typical route map would look something like this:

```
route-map filter permit 10
 match something
 set something
route-map filter permit 20
 match something
 set something
```

In the route map named **filter**, the permit sequence 10 will be evaluated before the permit sequence 20.

To give you a better idea of the types of filtering that are possible with a route map, following is a short list of possible matches:

- **ip address**—Matches either the IP address listed or the IP addresses permitted by the listed access list
- **as-path**—Matches the path listed in an AS-path list
- **community-list**—Matches a given community string from a community-list
- **metric**—Matches a given MED value

If the prefix advertised is permitted by the condition in the **match** statement, you can apply a **set**. Some possible **set** statements used to alter the prefix are as follows:

- **set community**—Sets the community string that is associated with the prefix
- **set metric**—Sets the MED that is associated with the prefix
- **set local-preference**—Sets the local preference that is associated with the prefix
- **set weight**—Sets the administrative weight that is associated with the prefix
- **set origin**—Sets the BGP origin code
- **set as-path-prepend**—Prepends extra hops onto the AS-path

These various combinations allow you to filter (or classify) prefixes advertised by a neighbor and then set the prefix's various attributes. The administrator has fine control over what path is chosen through the network.

Prefix Lists

BGP also supports the use of prefix lists for filtering the destinations received from or advertised to a peer. You can configure a prefix list similarly to a route map, with sequence numbers within the given prefix list being used to determine the order of evaluation, or similarly to access lists, with the order of operation being determined by the order of configuration. A simple prefix list example is as follows:

```
!
ip prefix-list prefixlist seq 5 permit 10.1.1.0/24
ip prefix-list prefixlist seq 10 permit 10.1.2.0/24 ge 25
```

In this example, the prefix list **prefixlist** is configured to permit 10.1.1.0/24 specifically, permit all routes within 10.1.2.0/24, regardless of their prefix length, and deny (or don't match) all other routes.

Distribution Lists

You can also control prefixes that are accepted from or advertised to a neighbor using distribution lists. Standard access lists that are used as distribution lists operate as expected, blocking those prefixes that are denied and allowing those prefixes that are permitted.

You can use extended access lists, however, to filter based on the subnet mask and the destination network. The standard form of the extended access list is as follows:

```
access-list number permit | deny protocol source wildcard destination wildcard
```

Further options for dealing with protocol types or port numbers are not listed here, in addition to some keywords. When you use an extended access list as a BGP distribution list, the syntax becomes this:

```
access-list number permit | deny ip network wildcard subnet mask wildcard
```

This allows you to configure a distribution list that filters out all destinations in the 10.0.0.0 network with a prefix length of greater than 24 bits, for example.

```
access-list 101 permit ip 10.0.0.0 0.255.255.255 0.0.0.0 255.255.255.0
```

Synchronization

iBGP synchronization is probably one of the least understood concepts in BGP. To understand why synchronization between the IGP and BGP routing tables is important when deciding if a route should be advertised to an eBGP peer, examine Figure D-7.

Figure D-7 *Synchronization*

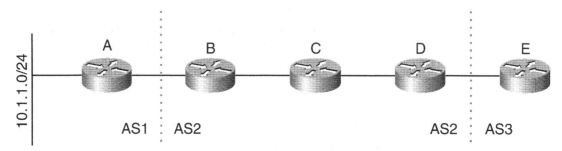

AS2, as pictured in Figure D-7, is a transit AS, which means that it passes traffic between two other autonomous systems. In other words, hosts that are connected to Router E should be able to send traffic across AS2 to destinations in 10.1.1.0/24.

Assume that Routers A and B are eBGP peers, Routers B and D are iBGP peers, and Routers D and E are eBGP peers. Router C, in the middle of AS2, is only running some IGP to Routers B and D.

Router E transmits a packet along its path to 10.1.1.0/24 toward Router D. Router D, in turn, forwards this packet to Router C. When Router C receives this packet, it must have a route to 10.1.1.0/24 to forward it correctly. Because Router C is running only an IGP, the eBGP routes learned from AS1 would need to be redistributed into the IGP running between Routers D and C for C to know how to reach 10.1.1.0/24.

One solution in this situation is to have Router C run iBGP with both Routers B and D rather than redistributing the routes into the IGP.

However, it is common to find situations like this, where the AS in the middle (in this case AS2) is not expected to transit traffic between the two autonomous systems on the outside, but is just trying to gain connectivity to destinations in both of these networks. In this case, it is valid for Router C not to know about any of the routes in these other autonomous systems. (It might lead to suboptimal routing if Router C does not know this, but it is valid.)

If AS2 is not a transit AS, synchronization is not important and can be turned off.

Summarization

BGP can summarize routes that are advertised to peers using the **aggregate-address** command. As an example, assume that you have multiple subnets of the 172.30.0.0/16 network, and you want to advertise this summary if any of these subnets exist. The following configuration advertises the 172.30.0.0/16 prefix and all the subnets for which **network** statements and matching routes are in the routing table:

```
router bgp 1
 neighbor 10.1.1.1 remote-as 2
 network 172.30.1.0 mask 255.255.255.0
 network 172.30.8.0 mask 255.255.255.0
 network 172.30.14.0 mask 255.255.255.0
 network 172.30.25.0 mask 255.255.255.0
 network 172.30.42.0 mask 255.255.255.0
 aggregate-address 172.30.0.0 255.255.0.0
```

To advertise the summary address only, use the **summary-only** keyword on the **aggregate-address** command:

```
aggregate-address 172.30.0.0 255.255.0.0 summary-only
```

When a BGP speaker originates a summary, it usually places only its AS number in the AS-path. This can lead to loops if the prefixes that are being summarized are from several eBGP peers, rather than originating within the AS of the router.

To prevent these loops from occurring, use the **as-set** keyword in the **aggregate-address** command:

```
aggregate-address 172.30.0.0 255.255.0.0 as-set
```

This command tells the router to place all the autonomous systems in the AS-paths from each component in an AS-set and advertise them with the route.

IP Network Design Checklist

As a network engineer, you will often approach a new network or a new piece of a familiar network and find you need some sort of guideline to examine and evaluate the network design. The checklist provided in this appendix is designed to help you ask the right questions, and make certain you do not forget anything critical to your understanding of the network design.

This list is, of course, just a starter list. You could probably add several new entries to it as you examine networks in your everyday work. You might also find that some areas are more important in certain situations than others.

Basic Network Operations Questions

1 What routing protocols are in use in the network?

   Answer: RIP-1, RIP-2, Enhanced Interior Gateway Routing Protocol (EIGRP), Open Shortest Path First (OSPF), Intermediate System-to-Intermediate System (IS-IS), and Border Gateway Protocol (BGP) can all be valid answers to this question. The point is to take an inventory of the protocols in use as a starting point for understanding how this network is designed.

2 How are IP addresses assigned in the network?

   Answer: Are IP addresses assigned based on the order in which people request them, based on geographic locations or organizational (political) boundaries, or based on a security policy of some type? Alternatively, are IP addresses assigned based on the topological location of the device or segment within the network?

3 How many routes, on average, are present in the routing table within each routing domain in the network?

4 What is the ratio of the total number of reachable destinations within the network to the number of routes within an average router's routing table in the network?

   Answer: This question is pointed at finding out how effective summarization of reachability information has been implemented in the network. For instance, if you find that each distribution, access, or aggregation layer routing domain normally has about 500 routes, and you find approximately 2000 routes in the core of the network, you can probably consider aggregation of routing information as one area of investigation to improve the deployment of this network. If, however, you find the ratio of the total number of subnets to the number of routes in any specific router's routing table is high—the number of routes is high compared to the size of the average router's routing table—aggregation is probably fairly effectively deployed in this network.

5 Starting from any edge of the network and working toward any other edge of the network, how many points of summarization or redistribution would you be likely to encounter? What would the result be if you considered these measures for the ten most critical paths through the network?

   Answer: This question attempts to provide some idea of the complexity and depth of the network design. The more points of redistribution you would encounter in a representative path, the more complex the network design is likely to be. Encountering two points of summarization from edge to edge would probably be normal in most network designs. Encountering fewer might indicate aggregation of routing information is a point where some work could be done. Encountering more than two might indicate a large, complex network, which might benefit from some simplification in its design.

6 How would you characterize the use of redundancy in the network?

   Answer: How many parallel links or paths exist between any two points in the network? You want to explore how much redundancy is relied on for resiliency in the network's design, and how likely you are to see failures related to excessive redundancy within the network.

7 Within each routing domain in the network, rate the importance of resilience. Is resilience critical, nice to have, or not important at all? Can you quantify how long of an outage is acceptable within each routing domain, and why?

8 How important is fast convergence within the network? Why?

   Answer: List those applications that might benefit from or require fast convergence times, and why. Also investigate what the critical paths are for these applications, and what impact fast convergence has on the resiliency of the network design.

9 In general, how difficult is the network to troubleshoot?

   Answer: Exploring specific areas where troubleshooting has often proved troublesome in the past can lead to insights about what areas in the network might need some design focus. Also consider areas that do not break often. How hard might they be to troubleshoot if they do break?

10 What is the impact to summarization if specific links or devices fail?

   Answer: Explore how summary metrics would be impacted through network failures, routing black holes, or other problems that might exhibit themselves when you investigate the impact of link and device failure on the aggregation of routing information.

11 What is the typical rate of change of routing information within the network?

Answer: Examine what changes on a regular basis, and why. If particular areas of the network appear to have a high rate of change, it might be useful to examine why those changes occur. How can you dampen those changes or reduce the area across which those changes impact devices?

12 If a device or link fails, how many routers, on average, are impacted, or how many routers must recompute their routing tables?

Answer: This question, when applied across the network, specifically within each routing domain, can provide some insight on how well the network has been divided and what types of techniques might be useful in improving the network's convergence properties.

Topological Layout

1 Can you describe your network in terms of routing domains and how those routing domains are linked?

Answer: Is the network broken into smaller pieces, or it is designed to have no natural "break points," where hierarchy and information aggregation can be used and configured?

It is often helpful to use the information contained just in the routing databases to draw a network diagram, such as the link-state database from IS-IS or OSPF, or to use the EIGRP topology table from each router.

2 Within each routing domain, what is the dominant, or primary, topological construct?

Answer: Each routing domain should have one primary type of topology within the domain. For instance, some areas of the network might be dominated by large hub and spoke topologies, whereas a full or partial mesh might dominate others. Perhaps some areas of the network can simply be classified as a full mess topology.

3 How are the routing domains in the network interconnected? What sort of hierarchy do these interconnections follow, if any?

Answer: Is the network designed around a flat network design, a two-tier hierarchy, or a three-layer hierarchy?

4 Can you point out the two to ten most complex topologies within the network?

Answer: Using this information, you can determine how well the network design separates complex areas of the network from other complex areas of the network. This question works well with a question about the number of routers impacted by a single device or link failure.

Redistribution and Interconnection

1 Is redistribution being used in this network?

Answer: Include redistribution between static routes, connected routes, and dynamic protocols here.

2 If redistribution is configured between dynamic routing protocols, among how many different areas of the network is it configured?

Answer: For instance, are there two primary domains, or areas, within the network, each running a separate instance of routing, and redistribution is configured between the two domains? Do more than two domains exist? How many places does redistribution interconnect various domains within the network?

3 For each pair of routing domains between which redistribution is configured, how many points of redistribution are configured?

Answer: The primary piece of information is the number of mutual points of redistribution between pairs of routing domains within the network.

4 At every point where mutual redistribution between two routing domains running dynamic routing protocols is configured, what sorts of filtering are configured to control the redistributed routes?

Answer: Here, you are trying to determine whether mutual redistribution could be causing routing loops, even if those routing loops have not been noticed in the past. You are also looking for the potential for routing loops.

5 Are multiple routing domains being interconnected through some other mechanism than route redistribution?

Answer: For instance, a large network might have several large routing domains interconnected using BGP in the core, or some other technique.

Security

1 Does the network have a written security policy?

2 What is the security policy concerning devices that are attached to the network?

Answer: Does a device that is connecting to the network need to run or employ specific protocols or techniques? For instance, is some form of Layer 2 authorization employed to prevent unauthorized connections to the network? Does a policy exist about open ports or other ways to prevent unauthorized access to the network?

3 What is the security policy concerning routing within the network?

Answer: Has a specific policy been designed to thwart attacks against the routing system?

4 What mechanisms are in place to react to a security breach or a security incident?

5 Should access be restricted to specific devices in the network? How should this restricted access be achieved?

NOTE   For more information on security as it relates to routing specifically, please see Chapter 8, "Routing Protocol Security."

Answers to Review Questions

Chapter 1

1 What is the first thing you should think about when designing a new network?

   Answer: Think about the purpose of the network. What sorts of traffic will the network carry, and what types of applications will be running on the network?

2 What are the primary goals in any network design?

   Answer: The primary goals are reliability and resilience, manageability, and scalability.

3 How do you define a reliable network?

   Answer: A reliable network delivers almost all accepted traffic to the right destination within a reasonable amount of time.

4 What elements in Layer 3 network design impact the delay and jitter budgets through the network?

   Answer: The topology of the network determines the number of hops and delays across each hop through the network. Routing protocols impact the path that traffic takes through the network, impacting the delay and jitter (traffic engineering). The reliability of the network at Layer 3 impacts the delay and jitter through the network; a constantly converging network has constantly changing delay and jitter.

   Although this book focuses on Layer 3 and routing, specifically, it is important to remember that Layer 2 design has a major impact on network resiliency and reliability.

5 What are the two primary considerations when determining when a network has failed?

   Answer: Are all the applications that are required for the business to run still available? If not, what is the cost of an application being unusable?

6   What elements are important in determining the time required to restore a network to service (or an application running on a network to service) after it has failed?

Answer: The two elements include the amount of time that it takes for the network to detect and recover from a failure, and the amount of time required to troubleshoot and take any actions necessary to correct the failure.

7   What are important day-to-day management tasks in administering a network?

Answer: The two important management tasks are taking a network baseline and documenting the network.

8   What types of documentation are important for network management and troubleshooting?

Answer: The important documentation includes Layer 2 and Layer 3 network diagrams, addressing, and summarization plans.

9   What two methods can you apply to determine where redundancy is needed in a network to increase resiliency?

Answer: You can analyze points of failure (single, double, and so on) and perform statistical analysis.

10   What are the MTBF and MTTR?

Answer: The mean time between failure (MTBF) is the amount of time that a system can be expected to run before it fails. The mean time to repair (MTTR) is the amount of time, on average, required to restore a system to operation after it has failed.

11   What two types of information are typically hidden in networks?

Answer: Topology information and reachability information (or reachability detail) are typically hidden in networks.

Chapter 2

1   What is one of the key concepts required to build a large-scale network?

Answer: One of the key concepts is layering through abstraction. It involves breaking the network into logical vertical layers at the network (IP) level so that you can break the network into zones, giving you edges along which to hide information.

2   What four types of traffic are you concerned with when considering hierarchical network layers? Why is it important to plan interzone and interlayer connectivity carefully in a network?

Answer: The four types of traffic found in a layered network design are interlayer, intralayer, interzone, and intrazone. You must plan interlayer and interzone connectivity carefully to keep the network complexity down. More interlayer connectivity must be planned carefully to control the complexity of the network. As these types of connectivity increase, the network complexity also increases, making it more difficult to plan traffic flow and manage the network.

3   What is the general rule of thumb in communications networks for traffic that is destined to local and remote destinations? Is this rule always true?

Answer: Generally, 80 percent of the traffic is directed to local destinations, whereas 20 percent is directed to remote destinations. This rule is not always true, however. It depends on the most commonly used resources, the speed and cost of high-speed links, and other factors.

4   What is the point of traffic aggregation in a network design?

Answer: Traffic aggregation in a network design takes advantage of the topological locality of traffic and provides edges along which traffic can leave or enter a zone.

5   What is meant by routing policy? What types of policy are included in this concept?

Answer: Routing policy is the controls that are placed on the routing information as it is propagated through the network. Information hiding—both topological and reachability—and traffic engineering are included in routing policy.

6   What are the primary functions of each layer in a two-layer hierarchy?

Answer: The core layer forwards interlayer and interzone traffic, whereas the aggregation layer aggregates traffic, provides user attachment, and controls traffic admittance. Routing policy is implemented along the core/aggregation edge.

7   What are the primary functions of each layer in a three-layer hierarchy?

Answer: The core and distribution layers aggregate traffic and provide interzone traffic forwarding, although the core is the primary high-speed interconnection between the routing zones. The access layer provides user attachment, and the access and distribution layers provide traffic admittance. Route policy is primarily implemented in the distribution layer, although traffic engineering can occur in any layer.

8   What are the primary considerations when deciding how many layers a network should have?

Answer: The primary considerations for determining the number of network layers include network geography (how large of an area the network covers), network topology depth (the number of hops between the edge and the core), network topology design (meshiness and complexity of the network design), and policy implementation.

9   Explain the concept of hiding layers within layers.

Answer: Rather than creating a single set of layers within a network, you can divide a network into multiple administrative domains, each with its own layered structure. Thus, a single aggregation layer zone within a network might actually contain its own core and aggregation layers.

10 What is the best method for assigning IP addresses within a hierarchical network?

Answer: Assigning IP addresses based on the logical topology is the best possible method, although bits can be "stolen" from the IP address space to indicate other information, such as the division or physical location of an address.

11 What are some techniques you can use to work around poor addressing schemes or misplaced addresses?

Answer: To work around poor addressing schemes or misplaced addresses, you could leak more specifics and smaller summary blocks. Essentially, you can use "the longest prefix match always wins" rule to summarize as much as possible, allowing more specific information to leak through to ensure proper routing.

12 Why does a summarization black hole occur, and how can you solve it?

Answer: A summarization black hole occurs when two routers that are advertising the same summary cannot reach the same destinations within those summaries. The simplest way to resolve this problem is to make certain that the two routes share unsummarized routing information across some link between them.

13 What are the alternatives to IGP-to-IGP redistribution?

Answer: The alternatives to IGP-to-IGP redistribution include using static routes to inject routing information at the edge of the network or carrying the external routing information in an external protocol, such as BGP.

14 What two techniques can help you overcome possible permanent routing loops when using multiple points of redistribution?

Answer: You can filter routes based on your knowledge of which routes have originated in which routing domain, or you can automatically tag routes as they leave one routing domain and enter another and then filter them based on these tags.

Chapter 3

1 What are the two basic tools you can use to summarize routes (or hide destination details) in EIGRP?

Answer: The two routes are summarization and distribution lists.

2 How can you tell that a route is a summary when you look at the routing table?

Answer: It is marked as a summary and the next-hop interface is null0.

3 What is the default administrative distance for a summary route? What is the problem with this?

Answer: A local summary route has a default administrative distance of 5 and can displace valid routes that are learned from other routers, and it can cause a router to throw packets away unintentionally.

4 What bounds a query?

Answer: Distribution lists and summarization bound a query, because they limit knowledge of specific destinations.

5 How far beyond one of the possible query bounds does a query travel?

Answer: A query generally travels one hop, or until a router that does not have information about that specific destination receives the query.

6 What is the primary advantage to summarizing between core routers rather than between the distribution layer and core?

Answer: The core routers has enough information to make optimal routing decisions.

7 How is it possible to "black hole" packets when summarizing destinations behind dual-homed remotes into the core?

Answer: Even if one of the distribution routers loses connectivity with one of the remotes, it still advertised a summary covering the destinations that are available at the disconnected host.

8 Why should summarization be configured outbound from the distribution layer routers toward access layer routers at remote sites?

Answer: Summarization should be configured to reduce the amount of traffic on the distribution layer to remote router links and to bound queries at the remote router.

9 What is the most common problem with dual-homed remotes? What options are available to resolve it?

Answer: The most common problem is that remote routers appear to be transit paths to EIGRP. To resolve that problem, you can summarize routes outbound from the distribution layer toward the access layer routers.

10 What methods can you use to break a redistribution routing loop?

Answer: You can use the following methods to break a redistribution routing loop: distribute lists, route maps, prefix lists, setting the administrative distance on routes that are likely to produce loops, and using administrative tags in external routes to mark the routes and block their redistribution.

11 Under what conditions is the administrative distance ignored between EIGRP and IGRP?

Answer: The administrative distance is ignored when an IGRP route and an EIGRP route in the same autonomous system compete for inclusion in the routing table.

12 What options do you have for generating a default route in EIGRP?

Answer: One option is to redistribute a 0.0.0.0/0 default route. Another option is to configure an **ip default-network**, but that is not the preferred method.

13 How can you prevent multiple parallel links within a network from being used as transit paths?

Answer: You can prevent this by not running EIGRP on some paths; you accomplish this by using the **passive-interface** command.

14 What does EIGRP use to pace its packets on a link?

Answer: EIGRP uses the bandwidth that is configured on the interface to pace its packets on a link.

Chapter 4

1 How does OSPF bind the flooding of topology information?

Answer: OSPF binds the flooding of topology information by breaking the network into areas. At the area boundary, an ABR summarizes the routing information, removing the topology information, and advertises just reachability and cost into the adjoining area.

2 What is the rule of thumb to consider when designing around summarization of topology information and summarization of reachability information?

Answer: It is always better to design around the summarization of topology information and then tweak the design as needed to provide optimal reachability summarization. Blocking topology information has a much larger impact on the convergence speed of the network.

3 What is the general rule of thumb on dealing with complexity in an OSPF network design?

Answer: Always separate complexity from complexity where possible.

4 What are some of the advantages of placing the ABRs in a three-layer hierarchy at the edge of the network core?

Answer: Placing the ABRs in a three-layer hierarchy at the edge of the network core contains the size and complexity of area 0, generally providing for better route aggregation. Doing so also facilitates pushing the complexity entailed from adding redundancy in the distribution layer out of area 0.

5 What are the disadvantages of placing the ABRs in a three-layer hierarchical network design at the edge of the core?

Answer: Placing the ABRs in a three-layer hierarchy at the edge of the network core pushes more complexity into the distribution layer, possibly making the distribution layer harder to manage. It can also make the distribution layer extraneous because most of the traffic naturally flows through the core rather than from distribution layer router to distribution layer router.

6   What is the most flexible and generally most successful way to place ABRs in a three-layer hierarchical network?

Answer: The most flexible and successful way to place ABRs in a three-layer hierarchical network is to take each point in the core/distribution layer boundary as a separate case and place the ABR at each location based on careful consideration of the tradeoffs.

7   In general, where is the best place to put ABRs in a two-layer hierarchical network? When should you vary from this rule of thumb?

Answer: In general, you should place ABRs at the core/aggregation layer edge in most two-layer hierarchical network designs. The exceptions occur when specific areas of the topology would be better summarized or complexity would be better split from complexity, which could lead you to place an ABR within the aggregation layer.

8   What are the types of stub areas, and what routing information do they block at the ABR?

Answer: Stub areas block external routing information; totally stubby areas block external and summary routing information. NSSAs block external routing information but allow external information to be originated within the area. Totally NSSAs block external and summary routing information and still allow the injection of external routing information within the area.

9   When should you use stub areas?

Answer: You should use stub areas whenever possible.

10   Where can you aggregate (summarize) routing information in an OSPF network?

Answer: You can aggregate routing information in an OSPF network in an ABR or ASBR.

11   What types of routes can you filter in an OSPF network?

Answer: You can filter Type 3 information at an ABR or external information at an ASBR.

12   If two OSPF processes that are running on the same router attempt to inject a route to the same destination into the local routing table, which route is installed?

Answer: The first route is installed if two OSPF processes that are running on the same router attempt to inject a route to the same destination into the local routing table.

13   What mechanism can you use to reduce flooding in a full mesh topology?

Answer: You can block flooding on several of the routers in the full mesh network and leave just a couple of "designated flooders," using **ip ospf database-filter all out** or **neighbor database-filter**.

Chapter 5

1 If you are implementing a single routing domain on a network, should you use a single L1 routing domain or a single completely overlaid L1/L2 routing domain?

Answer: It is normally recommended that you use a single, fully overlaid L1/L2 routing domain, because it is easier to add L1 areas onto the edge of an L2 network than to try to split an L1 area with a new L2 area.

2 What types are routes are, by default, sent by an L1/L2 router into an L1 routing domain?

Answer: No routes fit this description. The L1/L2 IS normally sets the attached bit, which causes L1-only routers within the routing domain to build an IP default route pointing toward the L1/L2 border. However, no routes are, by default, injected into an L1 routing domain.

3 How are IP destinations in an L1 routing domain propagated into the L2 routing domain?

Answer: They are added to the L2 LSP of the L1/L2 router and given the cost of reaching the destination in the L1 routing domain.

4 What mechanism can you use if you want to advertise specific routes contained in the L2 routing domain into an L1 routing domain?

Answer: You can use route leaking to do this.

5 What two mechanisms can you use to reduce the impact of a full mesh topology on IS-IS scaling?

Answer: You can block all flooding on specific interfaces that are connected to the mesh, or you can place the interfaces that are connected to the mesh in a mesh group. Doing this means that no router re-advertises anything it learned across the mesh back into the mesh.

6 What are the two possible ways you can treat a point-to-multipoint or hub-and-spoke topology when deploying IS-IS?

Answer: You can treat a point-to-multipoint or hub-and-spoke topology as a broadcast network or as a set of logical point-to-point links.

7 What two forms of metrics can you use with IS-IS?

Answer: You can use narrow metrics, which provide a 6-bit metric space, and wide metrics, which provide a 24-bit metric space.

8 What is the maximum number of broadcast networks an IS can serve as the DIS on?

Answer: The maximum number of broadcast networks that an IS can serve as the DIS on is 254.

Chapter 6

1 What is an EGP?

Answer: EGP stands for Exterior Gateway Protocol, which is a protocol designed to carry routing information between autonomous systems. BGP is an EGP.

2 What prevents iBGP from being an effective IGP?

Answer: iBGP cannot determine whether a path within an AS is a loop because the AS path remains the same within the AS. No mechanism can detect intra-AS loops.

3 Where do routes that are learned from an eBGP peer propagate?

Answer: If selected as the best path to all peers, iBGP and eBGP propagate the routes.

4 Why is it not a good idea for you to redistribute BGP routes into an IGP?

Answer: You should not redistribute BGP routes into an IGP because BGP is not an effective IGP, and redistributing iBGP routes into an IGP can cause routing loops. Also, in many cases, BGP carries Internet routes, and that load could be too much for an IGP to handle.

5 What protocol do all BGP packets ride on top of?

Answer: BGP packets ride on top of TCP.

6 If a neighbor relationship between two BGP peers constantly cycles through the Idle, Active, and Connect states, what action should you take?

Answer: If a neighbor relationship between two BGP peers constantly cycles through the Idle, Active, and Connect states, check to make certain IP connectivity is good between them.

7 Explain the significance of the next hop in BGP.

Answer: The next hop in BGP indicates the address of the router in the next AS to which the traffic should be forwarded. In other words, the next hop does not have the traditional meaning of the "next router," but it might indicate a router that is several hops away. The next hop is not changed inside an AS by default, so it should always point to an external peer. This information is significant because there must always be a way (inside the AS) to reach the next hop. The IGP must always provide reachability to the next hop.

8 What possible solutions exist for load sharing outbound traffic to multiple ISPs?

Answer: Possible solutions for load sharing outbound traffic to multiple ISPs include using only default routes out, accepting the full Internet routing table, using local preference or MEDs to prefer one path to another for certain external destinations, and accepting only a partial routing table.

9 All attributes being the same, what breaks a tie in the BGP decision process?

Answer: The router ID of the advertising router breaks a tie in the BGP decision process if all attributes are the same.

10 What two things can you do to reduce the number of updates generated and sent by a router? Assume that you cannot use filtering.

Answer: To reduce the number of updates generated and sent by a router, you can either reduce the number of neighbors or reduce the number of updates required to send the entire routing table using peer groups.

11 What is the default half-life of a dampened route?

Answer: The default half-life of a dampened route is the rate at which the penalty is divided in half. It is 15 minutes in a Cisco router.

12 How does a route reflector advertise routes it learns from an iBGP peer?

Answer: The route reflector reflects routes that are learned by iBGP to other clients (IBGP peers) of the route reflector.

13 What does a confederation of routers appear as outside the confederation area?

Answer: A confederation of routers appears as a single AS outside the confederation area.

14 What is an example of an application of conditional advertisement?

Answer: An example of an application of conditional advertisement is to advertise destinations that are normally sent to one provider through another provider if the connection through the normal provider fails. Back up!

15 Treating the network shown in Figure 4-10 in Chapter 4 as a service provider network (with the access layer connecting to external networks), configure the network to run BGP throughout. What changes would you make to the network? Would you use route reflectors or confederations anywhere?

Answer: This question can be answered different ways. Provide your own answer here.

Chapter 7

1 What are the three primary concerns when considering fast convergence in a network?

Answer: When considering fast convergence in a network, you need to be concerned with how you can detect fast down links and nodes, how fast the routing protocol can converge around changes in the network topology, and how fast you can update the forwarding tables in each device based on the new tables that are calculated by the routing protocols.

2 What is a network meltdown, and what is the basic reason behind most network meltdowns?

Answer: A network meltdown occurs when the routing protocol does not converge, regardless of how much time it has. Most network meltdowns are caused by a rapid succession of events that lead into a positive feedback loop within the routing protocol.

3 What are the primary techniques that routing protocol designers and implementers use to prevent network meltdowns?

Answer: To prevent meltdowns, routing protocol designers and implementers slow down the detection of rapidly occurring events, slow down the propagation of information throughout the network, and slow down the speed at which the routing protocol calculates the tables of best paths through the network.

4 What technologies, when combined, allow a network to route through a problem, rather than around it?

Answer: NSF and GR, when combined, allow a network to route through a problem, rather than around it. NSF allows a router to continue forwarding traffic through a restarting peer, based on the ability to keep forwarding state through the restart. GR allows the routing protocols to resynchronize their tables and rebuild the local routing and forwarding tables, without the network converging around the restarting router.

5 What time constraints does a router have when it restarts under GR?

Answer: A router must restart and begin transmitting routing protocol packets within the dead interval of the routing protocols that are configured on the router.

6 What are the two types of OSPF GR, and what is the difference between the two?

Answer: OSPF can signal a graceful restart using link local signaling or opaque LSAs. Link local signaling uses an extension to the hello and other OSPF packet formats to signal state during a graceful restart, and out of band signaling resynchronizes the two adjacent neighbor databases. Opaque LSAs are used in the alternative method to signal and resynchronize the adjacent neighbor databases.

7 What are the two types of IS-IS GR, and what is the difference between them?

Answer: IS-IS can either gracefully restart by using signaling to recover all the state lost when the router control plane restarts, or it can checkpoint the local tables and simply verify that they are correct after the router has gracefully restarted.

8 What is the fastest hello time available on OSPF and IS-IS? What is the dead interval when the hellos are transmitted this quickly?

Answer: Both OSPF and IS-IS can transmit hellos every 330 milliseconds and use a dead interval of 1 second.

9 What is the biggest issue with all fast-polling mechanisms for fast down detection?

Answer: The scalability of the solution is the biggest issue with fast-polling mechanisms.

10 What is the essential mechanism or principle behind exponential backoff?

Answer: The essential principle of exponential backoff is to slow down when events in the network are being reported more rapidly.

11 What is the essential mechanism or principle behind dampening?

Answer: The essential principle behind dampening is to prevent the reporting of an event if it occurs too frequently.

12 What part of an SPF tree does a partial SPF recompute?

Answer: A partial SPF recomputes just the leaf nodes of an SPF tree, or information that is external to the tree itself.

13 What part of an SPF tree does an incremental SPF recompute?

Answer: An incremental SPF recomputes just the branches of the tree from the point where the change has taken place to the leaves, or the end of the tree.

Chapter 8

1 What is authentication?

Answer: Authentication is proving someone is who he says he is, and nothing more.

2 How is authorization different from authentication?

Answer: Whereas authentication proves who someone is, authorization proves someone is allowed to do certain things.

3 What two things are normally used to prove authentication?

Answer: Authentication is proved by something you have, such as a credit card, and something you know, such as a password, a piece of personal information, or a personal identification code.

4 What three things determine the strength of transited authentication?

Answer: The three things that determine the strength of transited authentication are the strength of the bonds within the system, the relationship between the person making the claim and the person verifying it, and the relationship between the person verifying the claim and the person asking for verification.

5 Is it possible, in a routing system, to authorize someone to readvertise a prefix you are advertising to him?

Answer: This is not possible primarily because you cannot prevent someone from readvertising the address space within the prefix through an aggregate, and you cannot force someone to readvertise the prefix. Authorization is not transitive in a routing system in this way.

6 Why are humans an important part of any security system?

Answer: Humans are an important part of any security system because they are flexible and might react to threats or security breaches in ways that machines cannot be programmed to react. Humans reduce the brittleness of the security system.

7 What are the primary attacks available against a routing system?

Answer: The primary attacks available against a routing system are disrupting peering, falsifying routing information, and disrupting the routing domain stability.

8 What is the primary line of defense available to protect the legitimacy of a routing system?

Answer: The primary line of defense is using proper security measures on individual routers and other devices within the routing system, such as strong passwords to prevent unauthorized people from connecting to a router or gaining configuration control of a router.

9 Why is it that packet filters that block access to router addresses from outside the routing domain do not work well in most networks?

Answer: Packet filters do not work well in these cases because most networks conserve address space in a way that makes it impossible to know which set of destination addresses should be filtered at the network edge.

10 What is your primary line of defense against DoS attacks on routers?

Answer: The primary line of defense against DoS attacks on routers is filters at the edge of the network, blocking traffic based on the type of traffic or the protocol.

11 What is the difference between a device that is running GTSM and one that is not running GTSM in terms of the TTL check for packets received?

Answer: If a device is not running GTSM, it only checks to make certain that the TTL of any received packets is valid, which means more than 1. If a device is running GTSM, it checks for a configured minimum value in the TTL.

12 What routing protocol should you use when connecting to outside networks?

Answer: When connecting to outside networks, you should use BGP, because it is designed for interconnecting networks.

13 What steps can you take to protect your routing information at the network edge?

Answer: To protect your routing information at the network edge, filter routes aggressively, limit the number of routes permitted to be advertised through the edge, and configure route dampening to prevent problems in a connected network from causing problems in your network.

Chapter 9

1 What was the original intent of MPLS?

Answer: The original intent was to provide fast switching through an ATM network core by removing the Layer 3 lookup, using routing protocol control over the switched paths from the edge of the ATM cloud.

2 What is the major use of MPLS today? Why has it changed?

Answer: MPLS is used today primarily to tunnel customer traffic through a service provider network. The primary reasons it has changed are the new market demand for VPNs, which are being used in the place of dial and private line networks, and the increased switching speed of routers, especially through the use of ASICs.

3 What are the three primary methods to route across an MPLS VPN through a service provider network?

Answer: The three primary methods are overlay, peer-to-peer, and BGP/MPLS VPNs. Overlay overlays IGP routing on top of the MPLS VPN tunnels. Peer-to-peer redistributes routes into and out of the service provider BGP cloud. BGP/MPLS VPNs import and export routing information into and out of the service provider BGP cloud.

4 What is the primary drawback of overlaying routing information on top of an MPLS VPN?

Answer: Each site must create a set of MPLS tunnels, one to every other site it needs to communicate to, and then build an IGP adjacency across these tunnels. This method is difficult to deploy and maintain.

5 What is the primary drawback in the peer-to-peer model of building a network on top of MPLS VPNs?

Answer: Redistributing routes into and out of BGP at the service provider edge loses routing information and makes loops across backdoor links possible.

6 How does a BGP/MPLS VPN carry IGP routing information through BGP?

Answer: A BGP/MPLS VPN carries IGP routing information through BGP by attaching extended communities to the BGP routes. When a route is imported from IGP into BGP, the IGP routing information is placed in an extended community. When a route is exported, the IGP routing information is pulled from the extended communities and placed in the IGP routing table.

7 How does EIGRP prevent backdoor routing loops when it is configured to run across a BGP/MPLS VPN?

Answer: EIGRP prevents backdoor routing loops when it is configured to run across a BGP/MPLS VPN by attaching an SoO to the routes as they are imported from EIGRP into BGP.

8 How does OSPF prevent routing loops through backdoor connections when it is running across a BGP/MPLS VPN?

Answer: OSPF prevents routing loops by setting a down bit in routes when they are exported from BGP into OSPF at the provider edge.

Which Routing Protocol?

Among all the thorny questions that network engineers are asked on a regular basis, probably among the hardest is this one:

> My network currently runs Enhanced Interior Gateway Routing Protocol (EIGRP). Would I be better off if I switched to Open Shortest Path First (OSPF)?

You can replace the two protocols mentioned in this sentence with any pair of protocols among the advanced interior gateway protocols (OSPF, Intermediate System-to-Intermediate System [IS-IS] and EIGRP), and you have described a question that routing protocol engineers are asked probably thousands of times a year. Of course, convergence is always faster on the other side of the autonomous system boundary, so to speak, so it is always tempting to jump to another protocol as soon as a problem crops up with the one you are running.

How do you answer this question in real life? You could try the standard, "It depends," but does this really answer the question? The tactic in the Routing Protocols Escalation Team was to ask them questions until they went away, but none of these answers really helps the network operator or designer really answer the question, "How do you decide which protocol is the best?"

Three questions are embedded within this question, really, and it is easier to think about them independently:

- Is one protocol, in absolute terms, "better" than all the other protocols, in all situations?

- If the answer to this first question is "No," does each routing protocol exhibit some set of characteristics that indicate it would fit some situations (specifically, network topologies) better than others?

- After you have laid out the basics, what is the tradeoff in living with what you currently have versus switching to another routing protocol? What factors do you need to consider when doing the cost/benefit analysis involved in switching from one routing protocol to another?

This appendix takes you through each of these three questions. This might be the first and last time that you hear a network engineer actually answer the question, "Which routing protocol should I use?" so get ready for a whirlwind tour through the world of routing.

Is One Protocol "Better" Than the Others?

The first thing you need to do with this sort of question is to qualify it: "What do you mean by better?" Some protocols are easier to configure and manage, others are easier to troubleshoot, some are more flexible, and so on. Which one are you going to look at?

This appendix examines ease of troubleshooting and convergence time. You could choose any number of other measures, including these:

- **Ease of management**—What do the Management Information Bases (MIBs) of the protocol cover? What sorts of **show** commands are available for taking a network baseline?

- **Ease of configuration**—How many commands will the average configuration require in your network configuration? Is it possible to configure several routers in your network with the same configuration?

- **On-the-wire efficiency**—How much bandwidth does the routing protocol take up while in steady state, and how much could it take up, at most, when converging in response to a major network event?

Ease of Troubleshooting

The average uptime (or reliability) of a network is affected by two elements:

- How often does the network fail?
- How long does it take to recover from a failure?

The network design and your choice of equipment (not just the vendor and operating system, but also putting the right piece of equipment into each role and making certain that each device has enough memory, and so on) play heavily into the first element. The design of the network also plays into the second element. The piece often forgotten about when considering the reliability of a network is how long it takes to find and fix, or troubleshoot, the network when it fails.

Ease of management plays a role in the ease of troubleshooting, of course; if it is hard to take a baseline of what the network is supposed to look like, you will not do so on a regular basis, and you will have a dated picture to troubleshoot from. The tools available for troubleshooting are also important. Of course, this is going to vary between the implementations of the protocols; here, implementations in Cisco IOS Software illustrate the concepts. Table G-1 outlines some of the troubleshooting tools that are available in EIGRP, OSPF, and IS-IS, in Cisco IOS Software.

Table G-1 *Cisco IOS Software Troubleshooting Tools for EIGRP, OSPF, and IS-IS*

	EIGRP	OSPF	IS-IS
Debug Neighbors	Neighbor formation state; hello packets.	Neighbor formation state; hello packets.	Packets exchanged during neighbor formation.
Log Neighbor State	Yes.	Yes.	No.
Debug Database Exchange and Packets	Packets exchanged (updates, replies, and so on), with filters per neighbor or for a specific route.	Packets flooded, with filters for specific routing information. Packets retransmitted.	Packets flooded.
Debug Interactions with the Routing Table	Yes.	No.	No.
Debug Route Selection Process	Yes (DUAL[1] FSM[2] events).	Yes (SPF[3] events).	Yes (SPF events).
Show Database	Yes, by specific route and route state.	Yes, by LSA[4] type and advertising router.	Yes, by LSP[5] ID or type of route.
Event Log	Yes; understandable if you comprehend DUAL and its associated terminology.	Yes; only understandable if you have access to the source code.	No.

[1] DUAL = Diffusing Update Algorithm

[2] FSM = finite state machine

[3] SPF = shortest path first

[4] LSA = link-state advertisement

[5] LSP = link-state packet

From this chart, you can see that EIGRP generally provides the most tools for finding a problem in the network quickly, with OSPF running a close second.

Which Protocol Converges Faster?

I was once challenged with the statement, "There is no way that a distance vector protocol can ever converge faster than a link-state protocol!" An hour and a half later, I think the conversation tapered off into, "Well, in some situations, I *suppose* a distance vector protocol *could* converge as fast as a link-state protocol," said without a lot of conviction.

In fact, just about every network engineer can point to reasons why he thinks a specific routing protocol will *always* converge faster than some other protocol, but the reality is that all routing protocols can converge quickly or slowly, depending on a lot of factors strictly related to network design, without even considering the hardware, types of links, and other random factors that play into convergence speed in different ways with each protocol. As a specific example, look at the small network illustrated in Figure G-1 and consider the various options and factors that might play into convergence speed in this network.

Figure G-1   *Simple Network*

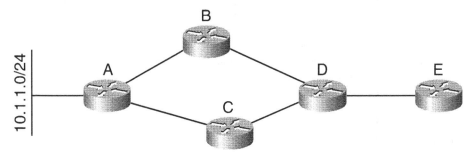

This figure purposefully has no labels showing anything concerning routing protocols configuration or design; instead, this section covers several possible routing configurations and examines how the same protocol could converge more or less quickly even on a network this small through just minor configuration changes.

Start with EIGRP as an example:

- The Router A to C link has a bandwidth of 64 kbps.
- The Router A to B link has a bandwidth of 10 Mbps.
- The Router B to D and Router C to D links have equal bandwidths.

With this information in hand, you can determine that Router D is going to mark the path to 10.1.1.0/24 through Router B as the best path (the *successor* in EIGRP terms). The path through Router C will not be marked as a *feasible successor*, because the differential in the metrics is too great between the two paths. To the EIGRP process running on Router D, the path through Router C cannot be proven based on the metrics advertised by Routers B and C, so the path through Router C will not be installed as a possible backup route.

This means that if the Router B to D link fails, Router D is forced to mark 10.1.1.0/24 as *active* and send a query to Router C. The convergence time is bounded by the amount of time it takes for the following tasks:

- Router D to examine its local topology table and determine that no other known loop-free paths exist.
- Router D to build and transmit a query toward Router C.
- Router C to receive and process the query, including examining its local EIGRP topology table, and find it still has an alternate path.
- Router C to build a reply to the query and transmit it.
- Router D to receive the reply and process it, including route installation time and the time required to change the information in the forwarding tables on the router.

Many factors are contained in these steps; any one of them could take a long time. In the real world, the total time to complete the steps in this network is less than two or three seconds.

Now change the assumptions just slightly and see what the impact is:

- The Router A to C link and A to B links have equal bandwidth.
- The Router B to D link has a bandwidth of 64 kbps.
- The Router B to C link has a bandwidth of 10 Mbps.

As you can tell, the network conditions have been changed only slightly, but the results are altered dramatically. In this case, the path to 10.1.1.0/24 through Router C is chosen as the best path. EIGRP then examines the path through Router B and finds that it is a loop-free path, based on the information embedded in EIGRP metrics. What happens if the Router B to C link fails?

The process has exactly one step: Router D examines its local EIGRP topology table and finds that an alternate loop-free path is available. Router D installs this alternate route in the local routing table and alters the forwarding information as needed. This processing takes on the order of 150 milliseconds or less.

Using the same network, examine the various reactions of OSPF to link failures. Begin with these:

- The Router B to D link has a cost of 20.
- All other links in the network have a cost of 10.
- All routes are internal OSPF routes.

What happens if the Router B to C link fails?

1   Router B and C detect the link failure and wait some period of time, called the link-state advertisement (LSA) generation time. Then they flood modified router LSAs with this information.

2   The remaining routers in the network receive this new LSA and place it in their local link-state databases. The routers wait some period of time, called the shortest path first (SPF) wait time, and then run SPF.

3   In the process of running SPF, or after SPF has finished running (depending on the implementation), OSPF will install new routing information in the routing table.

With the default timers, it could take up to one second (or longer, in some situations) to detect the link failure and then about three and a half seconds to flood the new information. Finally, it could take up to two and a half seconds before the receiving routers will run SPF and install the new routing information. With faster times and various sorts of tuning, you can decrease these numbers to about one second or even in the 300-millisecond range in some specific deployments.

Making Router D an area border router (ABR) dramatically impacts the convergence time from the Router E perspective because Router D has to perform all the preceding steps to start convergence. After Router D has calculated the new correct routing information, it must generate and flood a new summary LSA to Router E, and Router E has to recalculate SPF and install new routes.

Redistributing 10.1.1.0/24 into the network and making the area that contains Routers A, B, C, and D into a not-so-stubby area (NSSA) throws another set of timers into the problem. Router D now has to translate the Type 7 external LSA into an external Type 5 LSA before it can flood the new routing information to Router E.

These conditions do not even include the impact of multiple routes on the convergence process. EIGRP, for instance, can switch from its best path to a known loop-free path for 10,000 routes just about as fast as it can switch 1 route under similar conditions. OSPF performance is adversely impacted by the addition of 10,000 routes into the network, possibly doubling convergence time.

You can see, then, that it is not so simple to say, "EIGRP will always converge faster than OSPF," "IS-IS will always converge faster than EIGRP," or any other combination you can find. Some people say that OSPF always converges faster than EIGRP, for instance, but they are generally considering only intrarea convergence and not the impact of interarea operations, the impact of various timers, the complexity of the SPF tree, and other factors. Some people say that EIGRP always converges faster than any link-state protocol, but that depends on the number of routers involved in the convergence event. The shorter the query path, the faster the network converges.

If you align all the protocol convergence times based on the preceding examination, you generally find the convergence times in this order, from shortest to longest:

   1 EIGRP with feasible successors.

   2 Intrarea OSPF or IS-IS with fast or tuned timers.

   3a EIGRP without feasible successors.

   3b Intrarea OSPF or IS-IS with standard timers.

   3c Interarea OSPF or IS-IS.

The last three are highly variable, in reality. In any particular network, OSPF, IS-IS, and EIGRP without feasible successors might swap positions on the list. The network design, configuration, and a multitude of other factors impact the convergence time more than the routing protocol does. You get the best convergence time out of a routing protocol if you play the network design to the strengths of the protocol.

Which Designs Play to the Strength of Each Protocol?

The natural question, after you have decided that network design plays into the suitability of the protocol (you have seen this to be the case for convergence speed, but the same is also true of any other factor you might consider for a given routing protocol, including management, troubleshooting, configuration, and so on) is this:

What sorts of network designs play into the strengths of any given routing protocol?

This is not an easy question to answer because of the numerous ways to design a network that works. Two- and three-layer network designs, switched cores versus routed cores, switched user access versus routed user access—the design possibilities appear to be endless. To try to put a rope around this problem, the sections that follow examine only a few common topological elements to illustrate how to analyze a specific topology and design and try to determine how a routing protocol will react when running on it.

The specific types of network topologies considered here are as follows:

- Hub-and-spoke designs
- Full mesh designs
- Highly redundant designs

After you consider each of these specific topology elements, you learn the general concepts of hierarchical network design and how each protocol plays against them.

Hub-and-Spoke Topologies

Hub-and-spoke network designs tend to be simple in theory and much harder in implementation. Scaling tends to be the big problem for hub-and-spoke topologies. The primary focus here is the capability of a routing protocol to maintain a multitude of routing neighbors and to converge to massive network events in an acceptable amount of time. Assume, throughout this section, that you are always dealing with dual-homed hub-and-spoke networks, as Figure G-2 illustrates.

Figure G-2   *Dual-Homed Hub-and-Spoke Network*

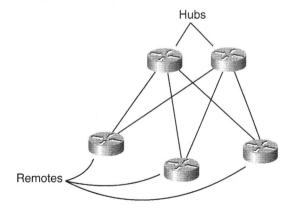

Start by considering the following simple question:

> How many spokes or remote routers does it take to really start stressing any routing protocol that is running over a hub-and-spoke network design?

The answer to this question always depends on various factors, including link speed and stability, router processing speed and packet switching speeds, and other factors. However, general experience shows that a high-speed router (in terms of processing power) with reasonably good design supports at least 100 remote sites with any modern routing protocol.

When considering network designs in which hundreds of remote sites are available, however, you need to use special techniques with each protocol to scale the number of remote sites attached to a single pair of hub routers. Look at each protocol to see what types of problems you might encounter and what types of tools are available to resolve those problems:

- OSPF floods topology information to each router within an area and summaries of reachability information into the area. You can place all the remote site routers into one or more OSPF *stub areas*, which cuts down on the amount of information flooded out to each remote site. Any change on a remote site is still flooded to every other remote site within the same area. For that reason, the design becomes a tradeoff between the number of areas that you want to manage and that the hub routers support and the amount of information that you can flood through the low-speed links connecting the remote stub sites.

- IS-IS also floods information to each router within an area. It does not, by default, flood information from the core of the network (the L2 routing domain) into each area. Again, you still face the tradeoff of how many level 1 routing domains you want to support at the hub routers versus how much information you can flood toward each remote router.

- The primary factor in determining scaling and convergence time in an EIGRP hub-and-spoke network is the number of queries the hub router needs to generate or process when the network changes, and the number of updates the hub router needs to generate toward the remote. Normally, if a hub loses several routes, for instance, it needs to generate queries for each of those routes to each of the remote sites. The remote sites then query the other hub router, which must process and reply to each of the queries. If the number of routes is high, this can be a processor- and memory-intensive task, causing the network to converge slowly, especially if the links between the remote sites and the hub routers are low speed. In this situation, you can summarize routers at the core toward the remote routers and block the routing information transmitted up toward the core routers. You can also cut down on the query range into the hub-and-spoke network dramatically. EIGRP, however, also provides a special operational mode for the remote sites; you can configure the remote sites as *stubs*, which indicates to the hub routers that the remote sites are never used for transiting traffic. If the remote sites are configured as stub routers, the hub router never queries them for lost routes, and the scaling properties change dramatically.

EIGRP, in theory, scales much better in a hub-and-spoke topology—and this is true in real networks, too. You often find EIGRP hub-and-spoke networks that have more than 500 remote sites attached to a pair of hub routers, over low bandwidth links, in the wild. In contrast, you tend to see OSPF and IS-IS hub-and-spoke networks top out at around 200 remote sites, even if higher bandwidth links are involved.

Full Mesh Topologies

Full mesh topologies are a less common design element in networks, but they are worth considering because the scaling properties of a routing protocol in a full mesh design indicate, to some degree, the scaling properties of the same protocol in a partial mesh design. You can think of a full mesh topology as a special case of a partial mesh topology. Again, look at the challenges and tools that are available for each protocol. Use the network illustrated in Figure G-3 throughout this discussion.

Figure G-3   *Full Mesh Network*

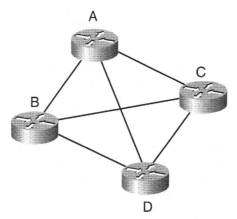

- Each OSPF router sends topology information to each adjacent neighbor within an area (flooding domain). If Router A receives a new link-state advertisement (LSA), Router D receives three copies of this new LSA: one from Router A, one from Router B, and one from Router C. The Cisco IOS Software implementation of OSPF does have an option to control the flooding through a full mesh network, using the **database filter-out** command.

- IS-IS is similar to OSPF; each router sends topology information to each adjacent neighbor. Cisco IOS Software enables you to control flooding through *mesh groups*.

- Each router in an EIGRP network sends each of the routes it is using to forward traffic to each neighbor. In this network, Router D is going to receive three copies of any new routing information that Router A receives, one copy from Router A, one from Router B, and one from Router C. These three copies of the routing information might be the same, but they indicate reachability through three different next hops (or neighbors). Reducing the information propagated through the mesh is difficult, at best. You can filter these routing updates through some paths within the mesh to decrease the amount of information flooded through the mesh, but that also reduces the number of paths usable through the mesh for any specific destination.

OSPF and IS-IS flood extra information through a mesh topology by default, but you can use tools to reduce the amount of flooding in highly meshed topologies. EIGRP sends updates through each router in the mesh, but it is difficult to reduce the number of these updates unless you want to decrease the number of paths that the network actually uses through the mesh.

In the real world, OSPF and IS-IS scale better in highly meshed environments, especially if you implement flooding reduction techniques. This is a matter of scale, of course; networks that have a mesh network of 20 or 30 routers work fine with any of the three routing protocols. However, when the mesh starts surpassing this number of routers, the special techniques that OSPF and IS-IS offer to scale further can make a difference.

Interaction with Hierarchical Designs

Traditional network design is based on layers, either two or three, that abstract the network details into "black boxes" and divide functionality vertically through the network to make management and design easier:

- The two-layer model has *aggregation* and *core layers*, or *areas*, within the network.
- The three-layer model has *access*, *distribution*, and *core layers*.

How do these layered network designs interact with each protocol? Consider each protocol in turn.

OSPF splits flooding domains into areas that are separated by ABRs. Because every router within an area must share the same link-state database to calculate loop-free paths through the network, the only place that route aggregation can be performed is at an ABR. ABRs actually aggregate two types of information:

- Information about the topology of an area that is hidden from other areas at these border edges
- Aggregation of reachability information that can be configured at these border edges

This combination of route aggregation points and flooding domain boundaries in the network implies several things:

- In all three-layer network designs with OSPF, you should place the ABR in the distribution layer of the network.
- In all two-layer network designs with OSPF, you should place the ABR at the aggregation to core layer edge of the network.
- The most aggregation points that you can cross when passing from one edge of the network to the opposite edge of the network is two.

These topological limitations might not be major in smaller networks, but in networks that have thousands of routers, they could impose severe restrictions on the network design. Network designers and operators normally break up OSPF networks at this size into multiple administrative domains, connecting the separate domains through BGP or some other mechanism.

IS-IS is similar to OSPF in its restrictions, except that IS-IS allows the core and outlying flooding domains to overlap. This introduces a degree of flexibility that OSPF does not provide, but you can still only aggregate routing information at the edges where two flooding domain meet, and you cannot build more than two levels of routing into the network.

EIGRP, as a distance vector protocol, does not divide the concepts of topology summarization and routing aggregation; topology beyond one hop away is hidden by the natural operation of the protocol. Figure G-4 illustrates the conceptual difference among EIGRP, OSPF/IS-IS, and RIP in terms of topology information propagated through the network.

Figure G-4   *Topological Awareness in Routing Protocols*

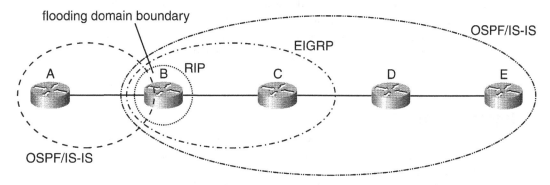

If you examine the scope through which routing information is transmitted (or known) within a network, you find the following:

- The Bellman-Ford algorithm, used by the Routing Information Protocol (RIP) and the Interior Gateway Routing Protocol (IGRP), uses only information about the local cost to reach a given destination. If Router B is running RIP, it considers only the total cost of the path to reach a destination at Router E when deciding on the best (loop-free) path.

- Diffusing Update Algorithm (DUAL), used by EIGRP, considers the local cost to reach a given destination and the cost of each neighbor to reach the same destination when calculating which available paths are loop free. EIGRP uses an awareness of the topology that is one hop away from the calculating router.

- OSPF and IS-IS, which are link-state protocols, do not use information about the metrics of a neighbor; rather, they count on being aware of the entire topology when calculating a loop-free path. At a flooding domain border, OSPF and IS-IS act much like distance vector protocols. Router A does not know about the topology behind Router B; it only knows the cost of Router B to reach destinations that are attached to Router E.

Because topology information is hidden in the natural processing of EIGRP routing updates, EIGRP is not restricted in where it can aggregate routing information within the network. This provides a great deal of flexibility to network designers who are running EIGRP. Multiple layers of aggregation can be configured in the network. This means that moving from one edge of the network to the opposite edge of the network could mean encountering many more than two aggregation points.

The practical result of the EIGRP capability to aggregate routing information anywhere in the network is that many existing large-scale (2000 router and larger) networks run within a single EIGRP process or administrative domain. The feasibility of building networks this large is based on the capability to use route aggregation to divide the network into multiple layers, or sections, each acting fairly independently of the other. Although it is possible to build an OSPF or IS-IS network this large, designing and managing this network is more difficult because of the restrictions that link-state protocols place on aggregation points.

In general, up to some relative size, the protocols are relatively equal in their capability to work with hierarchical network designs. OSPF and IS-IS tend to be less flexible about where route aggregation can be placed in the network, making it more difficult, in some situations, to fit the network design and the protocol design together. EIGRP excels at fitting into hierarchical network design.

Topological Rules of Thumb

After examining these various network topologies and how each routing protocol tends to react, you can see that when a network does not reach the edge of a specific protocol capability on any given topology, any of the routing protocols is fine. If your network has a specific predominant topology type, however, such as large-scale hub-and-spoke or large-scale full mesh topologies, choosing a protocol to fit those topologies makes sense. You can always compromise in complex areas of your network design by making effective and stable topological design areas in which the routing protocol is really stretched to the edge of its capabilities.

What Are the Tradeoffs?

In many networks, the final decision of which routing protocol is "best" comes down to these issues:

- **Convergence speed**—How important is convergence speed? How much flexibility do you have in the design of your network around convergence speeds?

- **Predominant topologies**—Does your network design have one dominant type of topology? Would a full mesh or large-scale hub-and-spoke topology benefit from running one protocol over another?

- **Scaling strategy**—Does your scaling strategy call for dividing the network into multiple pieces, or does it call for a single IGP domain, with the network broken up into pieces through route aggregation and other techniques?

- **Maintenance and management**—Which routing protocol fits the network management style of your day-to-day operations? Which one seems easier to troubleshoot and manage in your environment?

Beyond the technical factors are some nontechnical ones. For instance, if you decide to switch protocols, what is the cost for the long term? You need to consider training costs, the cost of revised procedures, design effort, and possible downtime while you convert the network from one protocol to another.

In some situations, this might not be an issue. For instance, if two networks are being merged because of a corporate merger, and each runs a different protocol, the decision might be more open to consideration. If you are going to need to convert one half of the network or the other, you can more carefully consider the technical considerations and make a decision based on those considerations alone. However, if your network is stable today, you should think twice about switching protocols unless a change in the business environment or some major shift in the way the network is built indicates it is an important move to make to meet the needs of the enterprise.

INDEX

Numerics

802.1x, 343–344

A

A bits, Frame Relay, 286
ABRs (area border routers), BGP, 234
abstraction through layering, 35–36
access layer, routing, 83
    best next hop, 86–87
    dual-homed remotes, 85–86
    single-homed sites, 84
access lists, 204
access-list command, 204
active process, EIGRP, 110–112
Active state, BGP neighbors, 227
add/drop multiplexer (ADM) error, 284
adjacencies
    building, 403–404
    detecing failures, 280–283
    IS-IS, 217, 318
        building, 415–416
    link flaps, 262
    on multiaccess networks, 405
    OSPF, 318
administrative distance
    BGP, 235
    preventing redistribution routing loops,
        131–132
advertisements, BGP, 226
    conditional advertisements, 255
aggregation
    IS-IS, 190
    OSPF, 160–162
    versus summarization, 192
aggregation layer, summarization, 98
aging timer (link state), 214
AH (Authentication Header), 333
algorithms, BGP, 226
analyzing redundancy
    MTBF, 23–24
    MTTR, 24–25
application programming interfaces, 48
areas, 198, 201–202, 406
    boundaries, IS-IS, 212

AS_PATH length, BGP load sharing, 249
as-path access-list command, 343
ASPolicyCerts, BGP, 347
AS (autonomous systems)
    autosummarization, 137
    BGP, 226, 233
    discontiguous, 138
    EIGRP, 136–139
assigning IP addresses, 50–53
ATM (Asynchronous Transfer Mode), NHRP
  case study, 373–375
attached bits (IS-IS), 198
attacks
    BGP, 321
    disrupting peering, 318
        flooding, 318
        protocol-level attacks, 318
        transport-level attacks, 318
    disrupting routing domain stability, 324–325
    DoS, 334–335
        preventing via edge filters, 335
        preventing via GTSM, 335, 337
    EIGRP, 320
    falsifying routing information, 323–324
    IS-IS, 318, 320
    OSPF, 318, 320
    protocol-layer attacks, 322
    TCP resets, 321
AuthCerts, soBGP, 346
authentication, 311
    MD5, 331–333
    RADIUS servers, 328
    soBGP, 345–346
    transiting trust, 311–313
    versus authorization, 313
Authentication Header (AH), 333
authorization, 311
    versus authentication, 313
    RADIUS servers, 328
    soBGP, 346–347
    TACACs servers, 328
    transiting trust, 311–316
autosummarization, 137, 393

H

I

J-K-L

M

Q

P

R

S

T

U-V

W-X-Y-Z